Tony Stead • Linda Hoyt

Explorations *in* Nonfiction Writing

Grade
5

*first*hand

HEINEMANN

DEDICATED TO TEACHERS™

DEDICATED TO TEACHERS™

*first*hand
An imprint of Heinemann
361 Hanover Street
Portsmouth, NH 03801-3912
firsthand.heinemann.com

Offices and agents throughout the world

"Dedicated to Teachers" is a trademark of Greenwood Publishing Group, Inc.

Library of Congress Cataloging-in-Publication Data

CIP data is on file with the Library of Congress

Explorations in Nonfiction Writing, Grade 5
ISBN 10: 0-325-04220-9   ISBN 13: 978-0-325-04220-6 (Lesson Book)
ISBN 10: 0-325-04217-9   ISBN 13: 978-0-325-04217-6 (Guide)
ISBN 10: 0-325-04221-7   ISBN 13: 978-0-325-04221-3 (Mentor Texts)
ISBN 10: 0-325-04447-3   ISBN 13: 978-0-325-04447-7 (Poster Pack)
ISBN 10: 0-325-03786-8   ISBN 13: 978-0-325-03786-8 (Kit)

Composition: Publishers' Design and Production Services, Inc.
Cover photos: Bill Miller

Printed in the United States of America on acid-free paper

16   15   14   13   12   VP   1   2   3   4   5

Explorations *in* Nonfiction Writing

CONTENTS

• •

• •

VL Indicates Power Writes that focus on visual literacy

Introduction to
Explorations in *Nonfiction Writing*

from Tony and Linda

We undertook the creation of this resource because we both have devoted many years to opening the door to nonfiction for teachers and students. We believe that children should be surrounded by nonfiction reading and writing from the very beginning. Not only does nonfiction reflect real-world demands—to meet standards, to communicate information, to build world knowledge—but exploring nonfiction can also capitalize on our learners' curiosity and their fascination and willingness to learn about the world around them.

In a climate of inquiry and research, nonfiction writing flourishes. Facts and information provide an infinite pool of ideas to write about. Writing for a specific audience and purpose—to inform, narrate or retell, instruct or lay out a procedure, respond, or persuade—gives momentum to those ideas.

Immersion in nonfiction writing does not happen by chance. It requires a dynamic teaching environment in which nonfiction writing is regularly and explicitly taught, not touched upon occasionally or extrapolated from a creative writing process. The unique features and thinking that go into creating nonfiction texts demand teacher modeling and gradual release of responsibility for writing and learning to the students.

Perhaps most important, nonfiction writing has the power to transform a classroom: to generate energy and excitement in all learners and to meet every writer where he or she is, no matter how experienced or inexperienced. When children are constantly engaged in thinking and drawing and writing about what they are learning, knowledge sticks.

Tony Stead

Linda Hoyt

We believe that young writers deserve:

▸ Extended, in-depth writing projects that allow them iterative practice of the entire writing process

▸ Brief, intensive writing tasks that build their fluency in writing a variety of text types

▸ Opportunities to study mentor texts— professional models and models constructed with their teacher—in order to discover the characteristics and features of a variety of written forms

▸ Authentic writing experiences—messages they want to communicate to an audience they care about for a real purpose—that infuse them with enthusiasm for writing

▸ Time to research topics they are passionate about—to immerse themselves in print and other media, to ask and answer questions, to explore collaboratively and independently

▸ Clearly scaffolded instruction that begins with teacher guidance and culminates in the students' independent approximation of a form

▸ Assessment with explicit expectations that makes students partners in their own learning: self-assessment for writers, formative and summative assessment for teachers

▸ Frequent opportunities to share and celebrate their accomplishments as writers

The Extended Writing Units (EWUs) and Power Writes you will find in each section of this lesson book are meant to be teaching models, not prescriptions. It is essential to remember that the topics presented in each are simply suggestions—possibilities for you to consider. You may want to take advantage of the organization and content provided and use them just as they are written. However, we also encourage you to personalize them and make them your own!

The real goal of this resource is to give you examples that assist you in linking nonfiction writing to the interests of your students and your curriculum. The following walk-throughs will highlight the teaching framework for all the lessons. By all means, use this framework to teach whatever content works for your class. If an Extended Writing Unit is on the planets but you have terrific resources and a curriculum goal that focuses on life cycles of insects, change it! Slip your own topic into the session framework, and go for it! The structure and focus points of the Extended Writing Unit will work just as well with your topic as the topic you find here. If a Power Write is about writing directions on how to build a circuit board, feel free to switch it to how to solve a math problem, how to play safely on the playground, or how to read a book.

We would love nothing more than to hear how you have personalized the EWUs and Power Writes to create a powerful support system that is finely tuned to the needs of your students and your curriculum. When you infuse a strong writing emphasis into content learning, your students will remember more while at the same time thriving in an atmosphere where writing is a tool for content retention.

Tony Stead and Linda Hoyt

Getting Ready to Teach
Explorations in Nonfiction Writing

To make informed decisions about how to use this resource, what to teach first, and how to integrate nonfiction writing into your classroom practice, you need to know that the *Explorations in Nonfiction Writing* lessons are organized by writing purpose and that you have two kinds of lessons to choose from.

WRITING PURPOSES

The first thing you'll notice as you thumb through this resource is its organization around critical nonfiction writing *purposes*. (See *A Guide to Teaching Nonfiction Writing, Grades 3–5*, for an expanded discussion.) The lessons in each of the tabbed sections focus clearly on one of these purposes.

▸ INFORM to provide information: describe, explain, give the reader facts, tell what something looks like, summarize.

▸ INSTRUCT to tell the reader how to do something: outline a process, detail a procedure.

▸ NARRATE to draw the reader into an event or sequence of events to provide insights into the life of a person, other living thing, or situation: Personal narratives are about the writer's own experience; nonfiction narratives are about a person, thing, or event outside the writer.

▸ PERSUADE to influence the reader to take action or to subscribe to a belief.

▸ RESPOND to express ideas about a text or topic: engage in critical, evaluative thinking; may include a specific prompt or format.

EXTENDED WRITING UNITS AND POWER WRITES

Next, you'll find that within each of these tabbed sections, there are two kinds of exploration.

1. Extended Writing Units

Each Extended Writing Unit (EWU) outlines a two-week writing project during which children research, write, and publish a particular form for a given purpose. Each unit comprises ten 40- to 60-minute sessions. You may adapt EWUs to any topic for which you have resources or a curriculum need.

Every unit presented here follows the same gradual-release teaching model: each session is rich in teacher modeling and coaching as well as student-to-student collaboration, but students then work independently to apply what they've learned in the whole-class minilesson to their own writing projects. Throughout the EWU sessions, you will notice the familiar routines you expect to see in a writing workshop. After the unit, you will find suggestions for planning and implementing follow-up units in which students have more control over their choice of topic. These personal writing projects also encourage greater independence for student writers.

2. Power Writes

Following the EWU in each section is a collection of Power Writes. These brief cross-curricular writing experiences are designed to be taught in a single teaching session and linked to your curriculum in science, social studies, math, language arts, and so on. Power Writes offer opportunities for increasing cross-curricular writing volume through brief experiences with a wide variety of text types. Power Writes serve as a springboard for using the target text type again and again as a tool for solidifying cross-curricular understandings.

Like EWUs, Power Writes gradually release responsibility to the student. They begin with explicit teacher modeling and think-alouds before moving to guided and then independent practice.

INFUSING *EXPLORATIONS* INTO YOUR CURRICULUM

The lessons in *Explorations in Nonfiction Writing* can be used to support a variety of instructional purposes in the content areas as well as in language arts. The important goal is to provide your writers with the full spectrum of purposes and text types for nonfiction writing—across the curriculum. Doing a single report on animals is simply not enough to build nonfiction writing power in your students.

Following are three models for ways you might integrate *Explorations* into your classroom. No matter which way you choose, it is critical to note that the order of the tabbed sections (alphabetical) and the lessons within them (Extended Writing Units first, then Power Writes) is not meant to be prescriptive; that is, you are not meant to work from beginning to end in this collection, starting your year with the report in the Inform Extended Writing Unit and ending your year with a Respond Power Write, nor do you need to start a unit on narration, for example, with the

EWU. These are resources from which you may pick and choose depending on the requirements of your curriculum.

USE *EXPLORATIONS* AS THE FOUNDATION OF YOUR WRITING CURRICULUM

If you want to strengthen your students' nonfiction writing, it is helpful to begin with Extended Writing Units and identify those you plan to teach. Then, map out a yearlong plan for how they will fit into your curriculum. There are six EWUs in your resource guide, so if you do one per month, you can select at least two units to revisit—with a new topic as the focus. You can arrange the units in any order that best matches your learners and your curriculum.

The sample year-long plan that follows lays out one possible scenario. As you review it, notice that this plan provides two EWUs for personal narrative and informational report, as these two text types are of high utility for writers. The combinations you create and the order in which you present them to your students have endless possibilities.

	OCTOBER	NOVEMBER	DECEMBER	JANUARY	FEBRUARY	MARCH	APRIL	MAY
EWUs	Persuasive Letters	Directions	Description	Personal Narrative	Persuasive Article	Response	Information-al Narrative	Explanation
Power Writes	Throughout the year to teach, reinforce, and refresh							

Sample Year-Long Plan: Using Extended Writing Units and Power Writes to Teach One Purpose per Month

Note: Samples of grade-specific year-long plans can be found on the *Resources* CD-ROM.

If you are making *Explorations in Nonfiction Writing* your core writing curriculum, you have a choice of where to start. Some teachers like to start with an Extended Writing Unit and then use Power Writes to ensure that skills and strategies built during the EWU are supported all year long. Power Writes keep writers tuned up and ready to go with a wide variety of text types, ensuring that nonfiction writers don't forget the writing traits and understandings they developed during an EWU.

Other teachers like to begin nonfiction writing through Power Writes, as these lessons are quick and easy, yet they are filled with intentional instruction that launches writers into the text type. Power Writes provide explicit teacher modeling of the features and the form and then propel writers into guided practice as they generate nonfiction writing in response to their learning. Once writers have done several Power Writes, you will find that they have developed momentum that will launch them easily into an in-depth Extended Writing Unit.

So, you can start with an Extended Writing Unit and use Power Writes to extend and secure learning, or you can start with Power Writes to build momentum for a longer study with an Extended Writing Unit. You are in the driver's seat!

SLIP *EXPLORATIONS* INTO YOUR EXISTING WRITING WORKSHOP

Both Extended Writing Units and Power Writes can slide easily into your existing writing workshop, providing rich diversity within your existing workshop format. If you have a writing workshop up and running already, you might:

Use an Extended Writing Unit as a change-of-pace replacement for a unit of study

Try out an EWU between two established units of study

Teach Power Writes to add depth to a unit of study

Again, map out the year-long plan for your writing workshop, and identify the places that a nonfiction *Explorations* unit might contribute to what you are already doing or provide some variation. In the sample year-long plan below, we matched EWUs to an established writing workshop curriculum and specified a choice of Power Writes with the same writing purpose. Once mapped this way, all your choices will align with your core writing curriculum. You can choose to use *Explorations* as additional enhancements or as alternatives to your established plan.

	OCTOBER	NOVEMBER	DECEMBER	JANUARY	FEBRUARY	MARCH	APRIL	MAY
Writing Workshop	Argument		Writing Craft	Author Study	Procedures		Persuasion	Fiction
EWUs	Persuasive Letter	Informational Narrative	Explanation	Response	Procedural Text	Description	Persuasive Poster	Narrate
Power Writes	Any from the Persuade section	Any from the Narrate section	Any from the Inform section	Any from the Respond section	Any from the Instruct section	Any from the Inform section	Any from the Persuade section	Any from the Narrate section

Sample Year-Long Plan: Using Power Writes and EWUs as Alternatives or Additions in Writing Workshop

EMBED *EXPLORATIONS* INTO EVERY LEARNING EXPERIENCE

Nonfiction writing is a natural and important aspect of content-area learning, and *Explorations in Nonfiction Writing* lends itself to enhancement of all curriculum activities. Extended Writing Units can go hand in hand with social studies or science units, providing a platform for expressing new concepts and ideas. In addition to the traditional science or social studies report (the Inform EWU), writers might *narrate* a bit of the history they are studying, create a flyer to *persuade* the school to care for the environment, *respond* to a historical fiction read-aloud, or *instruct* another class on how to do a science experiment. Embedding an ongoing EWU into a content-area unit does triple duty. It provides sustained writing instruction; it consolidates content-area learning; and perhaps most important, it provides a purposeful learning experience. Students have reasons to write. Writers have reasons to learn.

Power Writes are especially easy to infuse into every dimension of the learning day. Most Power Writes can be completed in a single session, so you will find that they merge easily into math, science, social studies—even read-aloud and snack time. The goal with Power Writes is to create opportunities for short bursts of writing in every subject area, every day. If you set aside just five minutes of every time segment and write to remember, write to wonder, write to understand—you will see a difference in both content retention and writing expertise.

Note: See grade-specific examples of ways you might integrate Power Writes and Extended Writing Units into your learning day on the *Resources* CD-ROM.

SETTING UP YOUR CLASSROOM FOR *EXPLORATIONS*

To optimize your teaching of nonfiction writing, you will want to plan your space, set up a system for keeping track of your writers' work, find and organize resources to support research, and establish "thinking partners" to give each student a writing buddy. The "Setting the Stage for Nonfiction Writing: Scaffolds for Success" section of *A Guide to Teaching Nonfiction Writing, Grades 3–5,* provides a wealth of practical, classroom-savvy management ideas. In addition, for a look into an inquiry-based classroom where all of these structures are in play, check out the two DVDs in *Nonfiction Writing: Intentional, Connected, and Engaging,* also published by Heinemann.

SPACE

Explorations in Nonfiction Writing operates best in a classroom that supports students' curiosity, talk, collaboration, and concentration as well as your own teaching flexibility.

You need space:

▸ To gather the whole class for focused instruction

▸ To pull a small group together for a differentiated lesson

▸ To circulate among writers, coaching and encouraging

▸ To confer with individuals about their writing

Writers need space:

▸ To research their topics

▸ To work together in pairs and small groups

▸ To write on their own

▸ To confer one-on-one with their teacher

Plan for your whole-group instruction first, making sure you can seat the class comfortably for a focused minilesson, and then plan an area for your own small-group lessons or individual writing conferences. Next, seat writers at tables to encourage collaboration and sharing. Finally, organize the space for your students to have access to different resources, and carve out some corners for students to write on their own or share with a friend.

RESEARCH OPPORTUNITIES

When gathering resources, make available different types of resources, and organize them for easy access when students are researching. Disperse resources across several areas of your classroom to provide spaces in which writers can productively engage with a variety of media tools to collaborate, share information, and learn together. Ensure that your librarian knows about the topics you are studying so that he or she can help students locate information when they are researching in the library.

Some useful resources include:

‣ Books and magazines

‣ Pictures, photographs, and models

‣ Realia or observations

‣ Computer and Internet access

‣ DVDs and websites

The Resources section at the back of this book provides extensive guidance in selecting, managing, and teaching students to use research materials, including setting up task management boards and using research notebooks and organizers.

WRITING AND RESEARCH FOLDERS OR NOTEBOOKS

If a sustained writing effort is part of your classroom, you probably already have a system for keeping track of writers' ongoing work and for archiving finished pieces in a portfolio. If not, *A Guide to Teaching Nonfiction Writing, Grades 3–5,* provides a mini-course in organizing a writing workshop. You'll at least want to set up and teach students to manage their own writing folders—and to store them in a central location where you can regularly review their work (and keep the work safe from hazard and loss!).

A specially designated research notebook, folder, or organizer is a good idea for each project explored in the nonfiction writing classroom. State standards as well as the Common Core standards make it clear that nonfiction writers are expected to develop a wide array of strategies for researching and organizing nonfiction information. In an Extended Writing Unit especially, significant amounts of time are dedicated to research so that your writers are empowered with facts and data to infuse into their writing projects. In the Resources section at the back of this lesson book, you'll find specific descriptions of a variety of research tools— notebooks, folders, concept webs, organizers, and so on—that will enhance your writers' information gathering.

RESEARCH STRATEGIES

Both the Extended Writing Units and Power Writes in this resource are rich in opportunities for students to learn, practice, and apply a range of effective research strategies. For example, the R.A.N. (Reading and Analyzing Nonfiction) strategy (first explored in *Reality Checks: Teaching Reading Comprehension with Nonfiction*) is a tool for organizing information gathered from research during Extended Writing Units. Students can use this strategy throughout a research project to record and categorize information on the go. The R.A.N. strategy helps writers in three critical ways: first, to be aware of and critically examine their thinking; second, to raise questions that spur further inquiry about a given topic; and third, to organize their research information in preparation for writing. The Resources section at the end of this book contains a fuller description of the R.A.N. strategy as well as other research strategies students will apply to their writing projects.

THINKING PARTNERS

TURN &TALK *You'll notice in the following sample lessons that writers are asked to turn and talk at key moments during the focused minilesson or during sharing and reflecting.*

Whether you assign thinking partners yourself or let writers choose their own, it helps to establish the partnerships before the lesson so that partners can sit together. The moment of turning and talking is then completely focused on the target learning. There is no time wasted searching for a conversation partner. The distributed discourse of a Turn and Talk—first between thinking partners and then shared with the group—empowers language use and improves content retention.

Thinking partners can also be useful collaborators during researching, peer editors during revising and editing, and colleagues during publishing. If you choose to make significant use of thinking partnerships, you might want to pair students for social reasons (for example, a more focused learner with a more active one) or for instructional reasons (a strong writer with a challenged one).

Teaching
Explorations in Nonfiction Writing

Explorations in Nonfiction Writing provides teaching tools and models the methodology for integrating nonfiction writing into your school day. As you roll up your sleeves and prepare to utilize *Explorations* with your students, you'll want to become familiar with what it offers.

THE RESOURCES

Explorations in Nonfiction Writing provides four key resources:

▸ This book drives instruction with classroom-based teaching models.

▸ The *Resources* CD-ROM packaged with this book contains printable versions of support materials for students and teachers.

▸ The *Book of Mentor Texts* supports the sessions with exemplary writing models for students to emulate, six of which are full-size, four-color posters.

▸ *A Guide to Teaching Nonfiction Writing, Grades 3–5,* lays out the professional underpinnings of effective teaching of nonfiction writing with primary-grade writers.

EXPLORATIONS IN NONFICTION WRITING LESSON BOOK

In this tabbed, spiral-bound lesson book, you will find Extended Writing Units (EWUs) and Power Write lessons organized according to the major purposes for which nonfiction writing is created: Inform, Instruct, Narrate, Persuade, and Respond. Behind each purpose tab is an EWU (two EWUs in the narrative section) and a collection of Power Writes, all focused on writing a particular form to meet that writing purpose.

Extended Writing Units

Each Extended Writing Unit (EWU) outlines a two-week writing project during which students research, write, and publish a particular form for a given purpose. Each unit comprises ten 40- to 60-minute sessions. You may adapt EWUs to any topic for which you have resources or a curriculum need.

Every unit presented here follows the same gradual-release teaching model: each session is rich in teacher modeling and coaching as well as student-to-student collaboration, but students then work independently to apply what they've learned in the whole-class minilesson to their own writing projects. Throughout the EWU sessions, you will notice the familiar routines you expect to see in a writing workshop.

Power Writes

Following the EWU in each section is a collection of Power Writes. These brief cross-curricular writing experiences are designed to be taught in a single teaching session and linked to your curriculum in science and social studies, with a wide variety of text types. They serve as a springboard for using the target text type again and again as a tool for solidifying cross-curricular understandings.

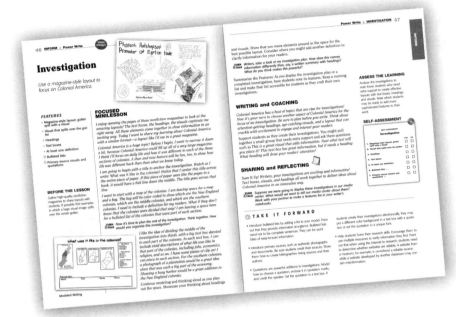

At least two Power Writes in each purpose section highlight visual sources of communication—photographs, labeled diagrams, drawings, and the like—in the mentor texts and in the nonfiction writing that writers construct. Look for the visual text label in this lesson book's organizing charts and table of contents to locate these important lessons.

Like EWUs, Power Writes gradually release responsibility to the student. They begin with explicit teacher modeling and think-alouds before moving to guided and then independent practice.

BOOK OF MENTOR TEXTS

This richly crafted collection of texts is used throughout the EWUs and Power Writes to show writers exemplary models of various text forms. The texts showcase beautiful visuals so your young writers can easily access high-quality linguistic features, text features, visuals, and nonfiction content. Six of these mentors are full-size, four-color posters. With these models, your writers will soon be writing like experts!

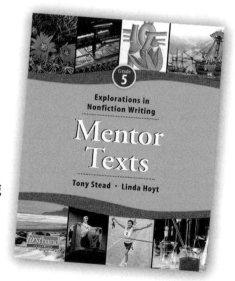

RESOURCES CD-ROM

All of the selections in the *Book of Mentor Texts* are on the *Resources* CD-ROM so you can easily print the selections for the enjoyment of your students both at school and at home. Stored on this disk you will also find a wide array of ready-to-use, printable writing tools like a personal R.A.N. chart, word lists, and editing and revising checklists, as well as teaching tools like Ongoing Monitoring Sheets and Self-Assessment forms.

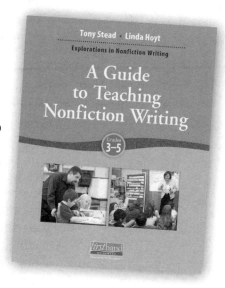

A CD-ROM icon at the corner of a facsimile tells you this resource is printable from the *Resources* CD-ROM.

A GUIDE TO TEACHING NONFICTION WRITING, GRADES 3–5

This guide is loaded with tips and tools for helping you launch an exciting adventure with nonfiction writing. You will find a rationale for why nonfiction writing is so important to the future of the students we serve, explanations of the unique features of nonfiction texts, help with setting up and managing a writing workshop, ideas for conducting effective writing conferences, and a vast array of additional information to make your class's nonfiction writing experiences powerful.

THE LESSONS

As you take a look at the following pages from an Extended Writing Unit and a Power Write, you will notice the harmony in their routines. The three-part lesson structure is identical in both EWUs and Power Writes and follows the gradual release of responsibility model: Focused Minilesson (teacher-directed, student-engaged); Writing and Coaching (student-driven, teacher-guided); and Sharing and Reflecting (student-centered, teacher-supported).

1. Focused Minilesson

The lesson guides you to set the stage for your writers and focus attention on specific learning tasks. This may be done by interacting with the *Book of Mentor Texts* or the posters, by thinking aloud and creating a piece of modeled writing, or by engaging nonfiction writers more deeply with their research or writing strategies.

2. Writing and Coaching

There is no replacement for time to write. For our learners to become proficient writers, they need lots of writing time. During Writing and Coaching, children research, draw, write, meet with partners, confer, and join guided-writing or shared-writing sessions. They are active, engaged—and writing! And there is no replacement for your own time to circulate among your writers, observing, praising, questioning, giving hints, making notes for future minilessons, or calling small groups together. You will find many tips for management and conferring in *A Guide to Teaching Nonfiction Writing*, Grades 3–5.

3. Sharing and Reflecting

This is a time to consolidate the learning. Partners or individuals share the drawing, writing, and research they have done; consider the learning goals of the session; and consider how they can continue to move forward as nonfiction writers. You will want to take this opportunity to summarize and restate the teaching points in the lesson as well as ask partners to turn and talk about their work. In the Power Writes, a summary chart icon reminds you to create a chart of the text features (listed at the beginning of the lesson) that you have taught.

TURN & TALK *EWUs and Power Writes also share abundant opportunities for partners to turn and talk. This is important. If you call on only one student, only one learner is thinking, using language, and taking responsibility for understanding. On the other hand, if you pose a question and ask all students to turn to a thinking partner, suddenly all writers are engaged—thinking, using language, and taking responsibility for understanding.*

Extended Writing Units (EWUs)

An Extended Writing Unit is designed to be taught over approximately two weeks. It first guides writers through discovery of a specific text structure and its features and then models the writing process in minilessons that may focus on research strategies, writing traits and craft elements, mechanics, or presentation strategies. Then, the focus shifts to the students as they apply what the teacher has just taught and modeled to their own writing. An EWU can be planned to support any unit of study—in math, science, or social studies—that requires collecting and organizing information in order to convey it to an audience.

The *overview* to each EWU provides:

▸ A description of what this particular unit is about, a chart laying out the teaching and learning tasks in each three-part session, and suggestions on how to pre-assess students' writing strengths and weaknesses

▸ Specific guidance for advance preparations: charts to make, research stations and notebooks to set up, a standards rubric to plan for, and the like

▸ Ways to make the unit most effective before, during, and after teaching

The *afterward* to each EWU provides:

▸ Suggestions for planning and implementing personal writing projects in which students cement their understandings from the model unit and apply them to their own writing lives through writing projects of personal interest that encourage greater independence

▸ Suggested topics and forms for personal writing projects

A SESSION FROM AN EXTENDED WRITING UNIT

Headers tell you where you are in the Extended Writing Unit.

The **lesson title** and a **brief description** let you know what happens in the session.

The **Session Snapshot** helps you focus your instruction on the stages of the writing process, writing traits, and the recommended mentor text.

At the beginning of every session, a teacher-directed **Focused Minilesson** invites writers to explore the features of a text and models some aspect of the writing process.

A **mentor text** from the *Book of Mentor Texts* provides the initial model for text features, language features, and conventions. Most minilessons begin with examination of the mentor text.

Suggested think-aloud language helps you model the steps in the writing process as you focus on key writing traits. See *A Guide to Teaching Nonfiction Writing, Grades 3–5*, for a full explanation of each stage and some sample lessons.

Teaching language in italics gives you a model for how you might think aloud, explain, or guide students' participation.

SESSION 4
Turning Notes into Running Text

Writers turn research notes and sketches into a draft.

SESSION SNAPSHOT

Process Focus: Drafting

Trait(s): Organization, Voice

Mentor Text: "A Breathtaking Body System," by Amy Gilbert

BEFORE THE LESSON

Provide copies of the mentor explanations on the *Resources* CD-ROM and additional mentors that you have gathered. Give partners time to read several examples, noticing how they are written. Then, guide a conversation comparing and contrasting the explanations. Note: Copies of Explanations needed for CD ROM

FOCUSED MINILESSON

Review the learning goals from the previous session. If time allows, have students turn and talk about what they have learned so far.

Summarize the learning goals for today's session: *The focus today is on turning notes and the flow chart into an explanation by beginning to write in paragraph form.*

Using the Mentor Text

■ Read the beginning of the mentor text. *"Every cell in your body needs oxygen—but how does it get there? You take about 20,000 breaths a day, but you probably don't think too much about how the oxygen finds its way to your cells. The answer is the respiratory system."*

■ *Do you notice how the author began this piece? She started with a question that would get us actively thinking about her topic and also gave us a fascinating fact: that we take in 20,000 breaths a day. This powerful opening really makes me want to read more.*

Modeling

■ *To write my explanation on the heart, I also need a great lead. Watch as I write.* Your heart is the most incredible pump ever created! Stay tuned, because I am going to explain how every minute of every day, your heart propels. . . .

> **TURN &TALK** *Analyze my lead. Does it make you want to read more? Did I make it exciting and also make it clear that this is an explanation? Get ready to tell why this lead works or what we could do to make it better.*

■ *Now I am ready to take the first box on my flow chart and use it in my writing. It says,* blood flows to the atrium. *I want to be sure to start a new paragraph. I also want to be sure to use the heading that I inserted in my flow chart. Watch as I leave a line blank and then write my heading:* The Journey Begins. *I return to the left margin and here comes my next paragraph:* The amazing story of how blood moves through our bodies begins when. . . .

■ Continue modeling how to take phrases from your flow chart and research notes and turn them into sentences. Emphasize words of sequence such as *then, next, if, when, because,* and so on. (See the *Resources* CD-ROM for a list of words and phrases that show sequence.)

■ Demonstrate how you use illustrations with labels to support your explanation.

- Emphasize the understanding that this is a draft, so it is okay to draw lines through words, start over, insert new ideas in the margins, and so on. Discourage students from using erasers as they draft and revise.

WRITING and COACHING

- Support writers as they begin to draft using information from their flow charts, writer's notebooks, and research notebooks. Guide them in being fearless as they experiment with language and invite their readers to join them in celebrating the information they are sharing. Be sure partners are aware that although they have researched together, they will each be creating their own drafts.

- As writers begin to draft, some may realize that they need more research and need to return to that phase of the writing process.

- Help writers remember that nonfiction writing needs to have visual supports. Even though this is just a draft, it can be a powerful time to consider where to include a heading, a labeled diagram, a boldfaced word, and so on.

SHARING and REFLECTING

TURN &TALK *Drafting is messy work. It is a time when notes, sketches, and graphic organizers fuel our thinking and help us create the final pieces of writing that will wow our readers. Find a partner and talk about your drafts. What went well? What challenges did you face today? How are you doing at converting your notes and flow charts into sentences?*

- Lead a class discussion about converting research notes, graphic organizers, and sketches into powerful pieces of writing: What worked well? What was difficult? What can be done tomorrow to improve the process?

- Gather the drafts and analyze your students' attempts to turn notes into running text. Identify writers who may need additional modeling as well as those who are ready for higher levels of sophistication.

> Your heart is the most incredible pump ever created! Stay tuned, because I am going to explain how every minute of every day, your heart propels...
>
> **The Journey Begins**
>
> The amazing story of how blood moves through our bodies begins when blood flows to the atrium.

Modeled Writing

TIP Some students may need additional coaching as they convert phrases to sentences and use their writer's notebooks to experiment with leads, wording, transition words, and so on. These students would greatly benefit from a small-group guided writing experience.

Sample **Modeled Writing** is provided throughout, but you may want to customize the models to make them your own.

During **Writing and Coaching,** students research and write their own texts. Over time they collect, organize, write, revise, and edit information for the texts they are creating. During this independent work time, you confer with individuals and small groups as needed.

Teaching **Tips** provide explanations, advice, and ideas for managing and tailoring the session to all students.

At the close of each day's lesson, the **Sharing and Reflecting** section prompts writers to discuss progress, lingering questions, and goals for the next step in the process. Facilitate this conversation, helping students consolidate knowledge and summing up important teaching points for the day

Regular **Turn & Talks** give writers a chance to consolidate and share understandings.

CONSIDERATIONS FOR IMPLEMENTING EXTENDED WRITING UNITS

Teachers who have piloted the Extended Writing Units (EWUs) in their classrooms have shared valuable insights. Following is their advice for managing efficient, effective Extended Writing Units.

Collaborate.

‣ Where possible, team up with colleagues and implement the units at the same time. This will enable you to share resources as well as plan and evaluate the units together. Your students will also be able to share their class and individual projects with other classes that have explored similar text types and topics.

‣ Take advantage of the expertise of your school or town librarian. Alert your librarian in advance so he or she can assemble a cart of related books and periodicals—and perhaps videos and a website list—that can support your writers' research.

Plan ahead.

‣ Read the entire series of sessions ahead of time so you know what's coming up. This will assist you in assembling resources, choosing teaching priorities, and planning the timing of your sessions.

‣ Initially, there may be a lot of prep work with gathering resources, but once they are up and running, they will be a powerful means to have students locate information for themselves, rather than being spoon-fed facts. Give yourself a pep talk as you organize your learning environment: you are helping your students become curious, self-motivated learners. Inform your school librarian about topics you are exploring, and visit the local library/media center in your area to collect additional resources.

‣ If your EWU is centered on a science or social studies topic, be familiar with the content. This will enable you to help students gather relevant and accurate information.

Teach routines.

‣ If this is your students' first time working with an Extended Writing Unit, they will need time to get used to the process of investigation. You may need extra sessions to assist them with researching, recording information, and using the writing process. Once students are familiar with the routine, you will find that the EWUs will run smoothly.

▸ During every EWU session, there are many opportunities for students to
turn and talk. To ensure this works successfully, make sure each writer has a
learning partner, and guide partners to sit together during focused minilessons
and sharing/reflection time. Demonstrate to students how to both share their
thinking and listen to their partners.

Focus on teaching priorities.

▸ Remember that you are not trying to accomplish
all of your writing goals in one EWU. Be selective
about what you concentrate on, and go deep rather
than trying to achieve too much.

▸ When using the mentor texts for writing
instruction, keep the students focused on the
strategy or feature you are teaching. Avoid getting
lost in the content of the text. The posters and
selections in the *Book of Mentor Texts* have been
designed to represent the text structure and
language features of specific text types. If you want
to explore the content of the mentor texts further,
use your reading and/or content time to achieve
this.

▸ When students are writing, many may need assistance at one time. Throughout
independent writing time, coach for independence. Teach writers strategies for
working on their own instead of waiting for help. For example, when writers
are unable to spell a word, show them how to write the letter for the beginning
sound, then draw a blank line for the rest of the word, and keep going. This will
keep writers writing and on the path toward success.

▸ When students are researching, make sure they are not spending all their time
finding information. They need quality time to discuss and record their findings.
Don't skip the sharing and reflecting time at the end of each session. Often this is
the most valuable opportunity for consolidating knowledge.

Be flexible.

▸ Although each EWU session is designed to be accomplished in forty to fifty
minutes, it is likely that you'll need to adjust the number of sessions or their
duration to fit your students' needs. Use the unit's sessions as the foundation of
your teaching, adjusting the time frames as necessary to give your students time
to research, draft, revise, edit, and publish.

▸ If something suggested in an EWU doesn't work well, ask yourself what
adjustments you can make to ensure it works better next time.

▸ If you find your students are already knowledgeable about something suggested
in an EWU, extend their understandings with deeper demonstrations and
discussions.

▸ When students are publishing, don't expect perfection. Celebrate their attempts,
but also stretch them to produce their best and take pride in their work.

Integrate writing across the curriculum.

▶ The topics explored in these model EWUs are only suggestions. They are a vehicle for showing how to develop students' skill with and understanding of different text types. Many other topics that suit your students and your curriculum can be substituted for what you see here. With this said, if you select an EWU on a topic from your science or social studies curriculum, you will also be able to develop key content understandings through the units.

▶ Although these are writing units, the emphasis on reading is strong. Integrating the reading/writing process is important. Use your shared, guided, and independent reading times to support your Extended Writing Units.

▶ You will find that each time you implement an EWU, you will become more confident and knowledgeable in providing a wonderful series of lessons that will help your students grow as nonfiction writers. Each year, it helps if you select some of the same topics as in past years but also do a couple of new ones based on the class's interests or your curriculum. That way you begin creating another great set of explorations you can repeat in the future. This means you will gradually accumulate resources and become familiar with the supports and challenges of implementing a variety of units.

Power Writes

A Power Write is an introductory lesson designed to be taught in a single thirty- to forty-minute block. The lesson begins with your on-the-spot creation of a mentor text accompanied by a think-aloud narrating your thinking process as you write. This focused minilesson allows young writers to see and hear the process of writing a specific form and has the added potential to directly reflect something that is going on in their own school lives. It is easy to see how you might substitute a topic you just studied or an audience (the librarian in place of the principal?) or even a purpose (narrate instead of instruct?) in the lessons provided.

Power Writes are designed to slip into your day as a natural part of your curriculum. When students engage with manipulatives during math, with a multimedia experience in art, with the science experiment conducted as a group, or with the books and videos shown to help social studies come to life, they are engaging in research that can be turned immediately into a written form. The Power Writes give you ideas for following your curriculum activities with writing lessons that give students a chance to work in a meaningful way with the information they have just learned. Power Writes help you link to the content of your curriculum so that nonfiction writing can become a part of every subject, every day.

Some Power Writes in each section focus on creation of a visual text—a cross section, graph, map, table, labeled diagram, and so on. In addition, each section always includes investigations in which writers work with the layout of a magazine-like "spread" that requires pleasing, informative placement of pictures, captions, diagrams, and the like to develop students' visual literacy as it develops their ability to create the form.

A POWER WRITE

The **lesson title** names the writing and relates the form to the purpose.

The **Features** list calls out the distinctive features of the form that you will want to emphasize for writers. Arrows indicate features not explored in the main lesson but addressed later in the Take It Forward section

Brief opportunities to use **Turn & Talk** keep students on task, provide access to others' ideas, and give them time to think about what they want to say or write.

The think-aloud model that begins every Power Write narrates the process of creating a **Modeled Writing** sample. This becomes the mentor text for the lesson.

---

44 INFORM : Power Write

VISUAL LITERACY

Flowchart

Use a flowchart to show how the body processes foods.

FEATURES
- Title
- Boxes with arrows to show time/order
- Caption
- Explanations
- Summative paragraph to explain the process
- Linking words to show time/order

FOCUSED MINILESSON

The parts of the digestive system move food through a sequence of events that nourish our bodies. Today I want to create an explanation of how our bodies process food. I am going to create a flowchart, a visual snapshot of a process. A flowchart is a great tool to show any sequence at a glance. Watch as I begin with a title so that my readers will know the purpose of the flowchart: How does the body process foods?

Now I can begin the flowchart. Watch as I draw a box on the far left side of the paper. I want to leave plenty of room for the rest of the events. In the box, I am writing the first part of the process: Saliva in the mouth breaks down food. *Notice that my writing is pretty simple and straightforward. I want to create a visual that a reader can easily scan, so I am not focusing on rich description. Instead, I am making sure that each part of the process is accurate and that I put the boxes in the correct order from beginning to end. Now I am drawing an arrow, creating another box, and then writing the next part of the explanation in the second box:* Food moves down the esophagus to the stomach.

TURN & TALK *Partners, think together. The next part of the process happens in the stomach, where the stomach breaks down the food into smaller pieces. Give me some advice! How should I reflect this part of the process in the flowchart?*

Continue modeling and thinking aloud as you complete the flowchart. Demonstrate how you enclose each step in a box, writing it succinctly. You connect the boxes to show the order. You might show a revision after placing the box in the wrong order. Emphasize the importance of checking your work to be sure the steps in the process are in the correct order in your flowchart.

Writers, my flowchart captures the steps in food's journey through the body! Now I want to write a paragraph to summarize the information. This process is sequential, so I am going to focus on using linking words that show time order to keep my writing organized. Right at the beginning, I am going to use a linking word: As food enters the mouth, . . .

Sea Turtle Flow Chart

How does the body process food?

Saliva in the mouth breaks down food	Food moves down the esophagus to the stomach.	The stomach breaks down food.

The large intestines prepare waste to eliminate it from the body.	The body absorbs vitamins, minerals, proteins, carbohydrates, and fats from the small intestines.

As food enters the mouth, teeth grind up the food and saliva breaks it down, turning it into a liquidy mixture. Then the tongue pushes the food toward the esophagus, a stretchy tube that reaches down toward the stomach. Chemicals in the stomach further break down the food. From the small intestines, the body absorbs life-giving nutrients, like vitamins, minerals, and proteins. Meanwhile, the materials the body does not need move to the large intestines, where they will be eliminated.

Modeled Writing

Power Write : FLOWCHART 45

INFORM

Continue writing your paragraph, using a variety of linking words to show time order. Point out that, because you are writing a paragraph, your sentences are enriched with deeper description—the small boxes don't confine you. *Writers, I have a flowchart that gives an at-a-glance view of a process and a paragraph that sums up the flowchart with more detail. Together, these elements explain a process so that readers can understand it.*

TURN & TALK *Writers, take a look at the paragraph and the flowchart. Do they reflect the same content? What features of a flowchart will you need to remember to create flowcharts of your own?*

Summarize the Features: Have pairs work together to list the features of flowcharts in their writer's notebooks. Check their lists to be sure they've included all the features. They can save their lists as they develop flowcharts in the future.

WRITING and COACHING

A flowchart can capture a variety of sequences and processes. Use a flowchart to show how another body system works. How does the skeletal system help the body move? How does the circulatory system bring oxygen to your blood? Don't forget to put each step in a box and use arrows to show the flow of the steps. Then write a paragraph to explain the process.

As writers create flowcharts, confer with them to be sure they are writing concise sentences in each box. Distribute the "Linking Words to Show Time/Order" resource for students who need support as they write their summative paragraphs.

SHARING and REFLECTING

Sum It Up! *Your flowcharts are visuals that offer a snapshot of a process from beginning to end. As you wrote your summative paragraphs, you masterfully chose linking words to explain how a process works.*

TURN & TALK *Get ready to share your flowcharts with partners. First, review the features list. Be sure you have everything in place in both your flowchart and paragraph. Then you'll be ready to talk with your partner about your work.*

▶ TAKE IT FORWARD

▸ Students can use flowcharts throughout the year to record various processes such as the steps in a science experiment, the events that happen to trigger an earthquake, important events in the life of a historical figure—any topic that flows in sequential order.

▸ Have students revisit other explanations they have written to revise for strong sequential order using linking words that reflect time. The lists of linking words from the *Resources* CD-ROM can serve as references as they write.

▸ Students might examine informational texts with sequential details and create flow charts that could be inserted into those resources. Take the opportunity to discuss with students how visuals and text work together to assist readers in fully understanding ideas.

ASSESS THE LEARNING

Provide writers with the Self-Assessment Checklist from the *Resources* CD-ROM so they can review their work. Then have them record their flowcharts in their writer's notebooks as a resource for other flowcharts they may create in the future.

SELF-ASSESSMENT

SELF-ASSESSMENT
Flowchart

	YES	NO
1. Title	☐	☐
2. Boxes with arrows to show time/order	☐	☐
3. Caption	☐	☐
4. Explanations	☐	☐
5. Summative paragraph to explain the process	☐	☐
6. Linking words to show time/order	☐	☐

Headers tell you the purpose and the form the lesson addresses.

A **teacher think-aloud** is the heart of every focused minilesson. Think aloud as you create a writing model that captures the features of the form you are introducing. In keeping with the gradual release of responsibility, this part of the lesson is the most teacher-supported.

An **Assess the Learning** feature in every Power Write frames your evaluation of student work. The accompanying **Self-Assessment** provides a way to focus writers' attention on key conventions and elements of the form.

Hand over the writing to students as you provide guidance and, if needed, additional teaching during **Writing and Coaching**.

A summary chart icon reminds you to create a classroom chart of the text features in the lesson for writers to use as a resource.

Each Power Write ends with a distilled summary of the important teaching points for the day in **Sharing and Reflecting**. Think about giving children the last word here, too, with a **Turn & Talk** that lets them share what they have learned.

A **Take It Forward** feature with every Power Write nudges you to extend students' experiences to include explorations of additional features and forms.

Assessment in
Explorations in Nonfiction Writing

Assessing and monitoring students' competencies as writers is a critical component in planning and implementing a focused, balanced nonfiction writing program. In *Explorations in Nonfiction Writing,* it is a daily occurrence. Pre-assessment, ongoing monitoring, and final assessment enable you to:

▸ Plan Extended Writing Units, Power Writes, and focused minilessons based on the common needs of the class

▸ Tailor instruction to the needs of each writer through conferences and small-group instruction

▸ Document each student's growth as a writer

▸ Give students an opportunity to see their own growth as writers

WHAT WILL I ASSESS?

You may be embedding nonfiction writing into your content curriculum—writing letters to town officers in a Power Write or writing a persuasive essay to the school principal in a social studies EWU—but resist the temptation to confuse students' content learning with their writing performance. Judge the merits of their writing by how well it reflects the text features and writing traits you have taught.

Identifying the specific traits that students need as nonfiction writers is critical. It enables you to provide targeted formal and informal assessments and look at specific attributes and strategies while monitoring students' growth and planning instruction.

Purpose-Centered Writing Rubrics

Every section of this book begins with an introduction to the writing purpose and contains a rubric, Key Skills and Understandings, that is specific to the type of text being studied. This rubric is a helpful tool that will guide your pre-assessment, help you choose focused minilessons, direct your individual student conferences, and help you assess the progress of your writers. Keep the rubric at your fingertips—or use the Ongoing Monitoring Sheet that is a direct copy of the rubric on a tracking form—when teaching Extended Writing Units and when assessing writing products that result from Power Writes. (Full-size copies of the Ongoing Monitoring Sheet can be printed from the *Resources* CD-ROM or found in the Resources section at the back of this book.)

In addition, each Power Write begins with a notation of the critical features of the form or text type that students will be writing and ends with a focused summation and assessment of these same features. You always know what is important for students to know and for you to teach and assess.

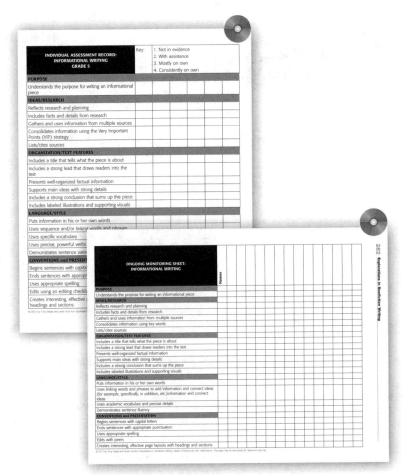

The Individual Assessment Record and the Ongoing Monitoring Sheet are tools for tracking and teaching for writing progress.

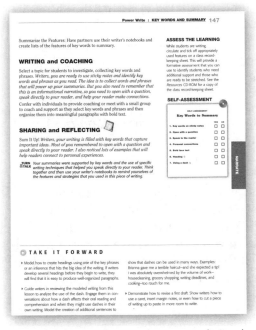

Focusing instruction on the text and visual features of each text type ensures writers' effective creation of that text.

WHEN SHOULD I ASSESS?

Explorations in Nonfiction Writing puts the emphasis on formative assessment—ongoing assessment that informs instruction—so assessment permeates every session of an EWU and every Power Write. Instead of building on separate test performances that distract writers from the important business of moving forward in their writing development, *Explorations in Nonfiction Writing* integrates daily, explicit, natural opportunities to gather data, assess understanding, and make plans for specific demonstrations in whole-class, small-group, and individual settings based on identified needs.

ONGOING MONITORING SHEET: INFORMATIONAL WRITING	Names	Katia	Michael	Carson	Shannon	Eva	Shem	Tamar	Malik	Juliet	Mark	Maria	Jamal
PURPOSE													
Understands the purpose for writing an informational piece		3/8	3/7	3/7	3/8	3/7	3/7		3/8	3/9		3/7	
IDEAS/RESEARCH													
Reflects research and planning		3/8	3/7		3/8		3/7		3/8	3/9		3/7	3/7
Includes facts and details from research		3/9	3/9		3/9			3/9					
Gathers and uses information from multiple sources													
Consolidates information with key words													
Lists/cites sources													
ORGANIZATION/TEXT FEATURES													
Includes a title that tells what the piece is about		3/8	3/7	3/9	3/9	3/9	3/7		3/8	3/9		3/9	
Includes a strong lead		3/8	3/7	3/9	3/8	3/9	3/7		3/8	3/9		3/9	
Presents well-organized factual information													
Supports main ideas with strong details													
Includes a strong conclusion													
Includes illustrations and supporting visuals		3/9			3/9			3/9				3/9	
LANGUAGE/STYLE													
Puts information in his or her own words		3/9		3/9			3/9				3/9		
Uses linking words (for example, specifically, in addition, etc.) to add information and connect ideas		3/9		3/9			3/9					3/9	
Uses precise nouns and powerful verbs		3/9											
Creates a variety of sentences		3/9			3/9							3/9	
CONVENTIONS and PRESENTATION													
Begins sentences with capital letters		3/4	3/4	3/4	3/4	3/4	3/4	3/4	3/4	3/4	3/4	3/4	3/4
Ends sentences with appropriate punctuation													
Uses appropriate spelling		3/10		3/10						3/10		3/10	
Edits with peers													
Creates interesting, effective page layouts with headings and sections													

This teacher uses her Ongoing Monitoring Sheet to record what students can do and to identify small groups and individuals for additional instruction.

Before, During, and After an Extended Writing Unit

You can assess students' strengths and needs during each unit in an additional session beforehand or by analyzing student work that you already have on hand.

Formal Pre-Assessment: After a basic introduction to each writing purpose and form as well as a review of various examples, have students write in the same form about a topic they already know a lot about. Encourage students to use as many of the features of the particular writing form as possible, but don't provide direct support. The goal here is to find out how much students already know about the writing purpose and form so you can tailor your teaching accordingly.

Experimentation in Writer's Notebooks: You might want to stop short of a formal pre-assessment and instead ask students to experiment with writing in their writer's notebooks at the end of the first session. This exercise may be less unnerving for some students and should yield enough information to form the basis of your pre-assessment.

Looking Back at Previous Work: Whether you choose to assess students' writing skills before beginning an Extended Writing Unit or during the first session, we recommend that you also consider unrelated writing projects that you've already collected from students. These may not reveal much about your students' ability to write a coherent procedure, for example, but should tell you a great deal about their grasp of writing conventions and other traits such as focus, organization, voice, and sentence fluency. Depending on how much student work you already have on hand, you might not have to devote any class time to pre-assessment.

Your analysis of students' strengths and weaknesses will tell you what they already know—thus, what you do not need to teach—and what they don't know about a particular form and purpose. This information scaffolds and supports planning of minilessons to specifically target learner needs while providing a way to celebrate the understandings that writers bring to the unit of study.

Use the class Ongoing Monitoring Sheet (copy the full-size version from the Resources section at the back of this book, or print a copy from the *Resources* CD-ROM) or a recording form of your own to record the results of your analysis and keep track of the key skills and understandings students need to learn. Use whatever notation system works for you to monitor student performance and to identify what you need for whole-class and small-group instruction or for individual teaching conferences in order to ensure understanding. Record observations on your Ongoing Monitoring Sheet, and update it throughout the EWU as you collect and review student work. (If you want to keep a separate record of each student's understanding, use copies of the Individual Assessment Record on the *Resources* CD-ROM and in the Resources section at the back of this book.)

At the conclusion of the unit, analyze each student's individual piece, and use the Ongoing Monitoring Sheet or the Individual Assessment Record to track individual growth. Use these results to inform future units.

With Every Power Write

The Assess the Learning feature of every Power Write lesson provides you with specific tips for looking at students' writing. You can make your assessment part of your observational notes as you circulate among writers, helping them during the Writing and Coaching part of your lessons. Or you might use the tips either to establish the final step in children's daily writing or to guide Sharing and Reflecting.

During Sharing and Reflecting, Assess the Learning offers students a variety of self-assessment opportunities. Children may be asked to compare their writing to the model you created to be sure that their work includes all the features of the target text type. They may be invited to meet with a partner and identify the elements they are most proud of in their writing. In addition, each Power Write contains a self-assessment checklist designed for children. You'll note that this checklist reflects the precise features and understandings that are the focus of instruction. Read more about checklists under Self-Assessment on page xxxii.

HOW SHOULD I ASSESS?

The ongoing assessment embedded in *Explorations* assumes that you'll want to collect and evaluate student writing often (*formative assessment* to inform your instructional plans), that you'll want to encourage children to look at and become constructive critics of their own writing (*self-assessment* to build writer confidence and independence), and that in the end you'll want to have clear evidence that students are becoming more powerful and flexible writers (*summative assessment* to provide a record of growth).

Formative Assessment

Make it a point every day or two to look at the writing or the research created by your students so you can assess understanding and decide if some writers need support through additional modeling, reteaching, a writing conference, and so on. This kind of regular informal review of work will quickly tell you if all students, or just a few, need additional support in implementing a nonfiction writing strategy. It will tell you what to bring up in the next one-on-one conference, with a small group needing special support, or in a whole-class focus lesson. As noted above, the Ongoing Monitoring Sheet is a convenient place to record and store your ongoing observations for both EWUs and Power Writes.

It is especially important to use what you find in students' writing as an opportunity to celebrate writer strength and see the positives in the work of each child. Even if you only take a few samples per afternoon from Power Writes or EWUs and review them to identify points of growth and learner need, you will be well informed about the progress of your students and the steps you need to take in lifting them as nonfiction writers.

In addition, writing conferences during the Writing and Coaching part of each day are perfect forums for observing, evaluating, recording, and teaching. A clipboard loaded with your Ongoing Monitoring Sheet or a stack of sticky notes or some other convenient data collector of your choice on which to write notes about each child will set you up to make the most of your side-by-side talks with students. Your review of a child's writing the day before, your notes, or your Ongoing Monitoring Sheet may suggest what you want to examine. Alternatively, you may simply sit down and see what the writer is working on, seizing the moment to praise what he or she is already doing and to suggest one more step toward writing excellence. Consult the Focus on Conferring section in *A Guide to Teaching Nonfiction Writing, Grades 3–5*, for tips on effective writing conferences.

Self-Assessment

We know that self-reflection and self-assessment are among the most powerful tools we utilize in education. There are many opportunities for student reflection and self-assessment built into *Explorations*.

▸ Sharing and Reflecting: In both Extended Writing Units and Power Writes, writers pause at the end of each day to consider their learning for the session. They self-assess the facts they gathered, the quality of the revisions they made, the kinds of edits they inserted into their work, or the quality of headings that were featured in their nonfiction writing, monitoring their growth as writers. To facilitate this kind of self-reflection, you will find a Student Self-Assessment Sheet for each writing purpose on the *Resources* CD-ROM.

▸ Self-Assessment Checklists: Every Power Write has a self-assessment checklist that you may elect to have students discuss or fill out and save in their writing folders for ongoing reflection on personal growth. You may elect to read the checklist aloud and have children think about and discuss it, or you may have writers actually fill it out (a full-size copy is on the *Resources* CD-ROM) and save it in their writing folders for ongoing reflection on personal growth. The interactive nature of the self-assessment increases self-reflection and writers' observation of their own work.

▸ Revising and Editing Checklists: These encourage writers to look critically at their own work. Choose from or adapt the collection of writing and editing checklists on the *Resources* CD-ROM.

Self-assessment checklists at the end of every Power Write highlight the key elements writers should be sure to include.

Summative Assessment

As suggested in *A Guide to Teaching Nonfiction Writing, Grades 3–5,* you will want to maintain a storage folder for children's writing as well as a folder for ongoing work. The storage folder can house the various compositions that result from Power Write lessons as well as final EWU projects. After a few months, writers (and their parents!) can glance through and see the array of different text types they have written, and more important, you and the writers can look for evidence of growth. Is the child writing more in January than he did at the beginning of the school year? Is she trying more spellings and more features? Are mechanics becoming more conventional? Do later pieces look more "finished"—detailed, neat, illustrated—than earlier pieces, showing that the child has become engaged as a real writer? Document the changes. Comparing work from month to month should give you summative evidence of improvement.

If you have been sure to keep writers' pre-assessment writing samples from your earlier analysis of their writing skills, you have the perfect vehicle for demonstrating growth. Look at the writer's pre-assessment sample and final writing side by side. Consult the Key Skills and Understandings rubric or the Ongoing Monitoring Sheet. What does the writer do now that he or she did not do before? How many elements on the rubric has the writer added to her or his repertoire? Has the writer moved from beginning to use a skill to developing it or from developing a skill to using it with confidence? If you need to give grades, rubrics and the writer's ongoing work will give you plenty of data to inform them.

There is one added benefit to before-and-after writing samples. When writers are presented with their "before" samples and asked to compare them and their final writing with the "Features of a Great _____" chart that was built throughout the unit of study, students see for themselves how much they now know about the form of writing under study. The comparison of the writing pieces often results in astonishment for the writers but usually ends in joyful celebration as they recognize their own progress.

Grade 5
Overview of Learning Objectives

Inform

Extended Writing Unit: Explanation

- Purpose (to explain)
- Features
- Choosing a topic
- Using a research notebook
- Using multiple sources
- Very Important Points Strategy (VIP)
- Organizing with a flowchart
- Sequence
- Cause-and-effect
- Writing a strong lead
- Drafting paragraphs
- Adding labeled illustrations
- Varying sentence length
- Using powerful verbs
- Writing a satisfying conclusion
- Adding titles and headings
- Focused edits
- ● Editing Checklist
- Laying out pages

Mechanics

- Paragraphs
- Sequence words
- Linking words
- Sentence fluency
- Spelling
- Punctuation

Features of a Great Explanation

- Opens with a statement or question about the topic to be explained
- Focuses on sequence or order; may use words such as *when, if, first, next, then, finally*
- Includes cause-and-effect connections
- Generalized nouns (*the muscles, the nerves*)
- Powerful verbs
- Exact and important details
- May include a supportive diagram or illustration
- Includes a concluding statement
- List of sources

Power Write: Pass-Around Explanation

- Summarize content with a group.
- ● Checklist for Pass-Around Summary

Features of a Pass-Around Explanation

- Recaps understandings
- Uses subject-specific vocabulary
- Includes main idea and details

Power Write: Dictionary of Terms

- Create a dictionary of terms related to a concept.
- ● Checklist for Dictionary of Terms

Features of a Dictionary of Terms

- Alphabetical arrangement
- Terms central to the subject
- Definition for each term
- Guide words at the top of each page
- ◉ Illustration or labeled diagram

Power Write: Partner Description: List Poem

- Create a description in the form of a list poem.
- ● Checklist for Partner Description: List Poem

Features of a Partner Description: List Poem

- Facts
- Physical description
- Precise nouns and adjectives
- Conclusion that supports sensory images
- ◉ Photograph with caption and labels

Power Write: Scientific Description

- Write a description based on science.
- ● Checklist for Scientific Description

Features of a Scientific Description

- Precisely-worded description
- Present-tense verbs
- Descriptive adjectives
- ◉ Boldface words
- ◉ Magnification or close-up
- ◉ Scientifically correct labels

Power Write: Summary with Headings		*Features of a Summary with Headings*
	• Write a summary with a gist statement supported by details. • ▶ Linking words to connect ideas • ● Checklist for Summary with Headings	• Opening with a gist statement • Headings • Descriptive words • Title • ▶ Conclusion • ▶ Linking words to connect ideas: *because, so, when, since, also, and, besides, in addition, for example* • ▶ Photographs
Power Write: Explanation Focused on Why		*Features of an Explanation Focused on Why*
	• Write an explanation telling what happened and why. • ● Linking Words That Add Information • ● Checklist for Explanation Focused on Why	• Focus on why • Opening statement • Linking words that add information: *in addition, it is also true that, because, in order to, furthermore* • Labeled diagram • ▶ Headings • ▶ Conclusion
Power Write: Explanation Focused on Why and How		*Features of an Explanation Focused on Why and How*
	• Write an explanation focusing on why and how. • Linking words to provide specific examples • ● Checklist for Explanation Focused on Why and How	• Focus on why and how • Shows relationship between ideas • Opening statement: gist • Linking words to provide specific examples: *specifically, for example, in fact, of course, to illustrate, for instance* • Headings • ▶ Conclusion: Restatement of the gist • ▶ Quote
VL **Power Write:** Diagram with Key		*Features of a Diagram with Key*
	• Label a line drawing to convey information. • ▶ Linking words that show summation or addition of information • ● "Skin" • ● Checklist for Diagram with Key	• Line drawing • Heading • Labels • Arrows to link labels with diagram • Key • Color coding • ▶ Caption • ▶ Concluding paragraph with linking words that show summation or addition of information
VL **Power Write:** Flowchart		*Features of a Flowchart*
	• Use a flowchart to show how the body processes food. • ● Temporal Words and Phrases to Show Sequence • ● Checklist for Flowchart	• Title • Boxes with arrows to show time order • Caption • Explanations • Summative paragraph to explain the process • Linking words to show time order

VL **Power Write:** Investigation: Colonial America	• Use a magazine-style layout to focus on colonial America. • ▶ Primary source visuals and quotations • ◉ Checklist for Investigation	*Features of an Investigation* • Magazine-style layout: gutter spill with a visual • Headings • Text boxes • At least one definition • ▶ Bulleted lists • ▶ Primary source visuals and quotations

Instruct

Extended Writing Unit: Procedural Text • Purpose (to instruct) • Features • Choosing a topic • Researching steps • Taking notes from multiple sources • Writing an introduction • Turning notes into running text • Words that signal time order • Precise vocabulary • Labeled diagrams • Satisfying conclusion • Precise present-tense verbs • ◉ Editing Checklist • Laying out pages	*Mechanics* • Sequence words • Present-tense verbs • Commas • Capital letters	*Features of a Great Procedural Text* • Title that tells what the procedure is • Includes a brief introduction • Information that is organized in sequence • Words and phrases that signal the passage of time • Powerful present-tense verbs in imperative voice • Precise vocabulary • Labeled diagrams • Text features, such as headings and bold words • May include a conclusion • May include a list of sources
Power Write: Instructions	• Write instructions to tell how to jump rope. • ◉ Checklist for Instructions	*Features of Instructions* • Title • Numbered steps • Verb first in each step • ▶ Bold words • ▶ Supporting visuals
Power Write: Partner Explanation	• Explain with a partner how an extreme weather pattern works. • Linking words to show order • ◉ Checklist for Partner Explanation	*Features of a Partner Explanation* • Opening statement of what is to be explained • Precise vocabulary • Exact details • Clear sequence of steps • Linking words to show order: *as soon as, finally, afterward, meanwhile, now, since, soon, then, while, when* • ▶ Passive voice • ▶ Timeless present-tense verbs • ▶ Conclusion

Power Write: Problem-Solving Guide	• Write a procedural text to solve a math problem. • Math Problem Stories • Computation Clue Words • Problem-Solving Framework • Checklist for Problem-Solving Guide	*Features of a Problem-Solving Guide* • Problem is highlighted or presented in boxed text • Linking words to show order • Precise mathematical language • Mathematical computation presented along with explanation • Conclusion
VL **Power Write:** Oral Presentation	• Create an oral presentation to explain how to do something. • Tips for Giving a Great Speech • Checklist for Oral Presentation	*Features of an Oral Presentation* • Formal spoken language with present-tense verbs • Visual display with title and headings, showing steps in order • Handout provided to audience with steps written out in numbered order or with words of sequence • Handout includes a storyboard or flow-chart of steps • ▶ Precise vocabulary
VL **Power Write:** Partner Line Graph	• Create a line graph to compare. • Checklist for Partner Line Graph	*Features of a Partner Line Graph* • Title • Vertical grid with caption • Horizontal grid with caption • Two distinct colors to show lines for regions being compared • Labels to name what is being compared • Key • ▶ Narrative conclusion

Narrate

Extended Writing Unit: Personal Narrative • Purpose (to describe an event in the writer's life) • Features • First-person point of view • Choosing a topic • Personal Narrative Organizer (topic, setting, main event, sensory details, emotions and reactions, ending) • Drafting from notes • Crafting a lead that establishes the situation • Using temporal words • Infusing concrete words and sensory details • Visualizing • Adding powerful verbs • Ending with thoughts and feelings • Revising for varied sentence beginnings and fluency • Editing Checklist • Laying out pages	*Mechanics* • First-person pronouns • Temporal words and phrases • Sensory details • Verbs • Sentence beginnings and fluency • Punctuating dialogue • Commas • Spelling strategies	*Features of a Great Personal Narrative* • Introduction that sets the scene • Precise and powerful words • Sensory details • Ending that shows the author's response to the situation • May include illustration or photography • First-person point of view • Use of temporal words and phrases to show sequence or passage of time

Extended Writing Unit: Informational Narrative

- Purpose (to tell about a real person, thing, or event)
- Features
- Third-person point of view
- Choosing and narrowing a topic
- Researching in multiple sources
- Taking brief notes
- Citing sources
- Organizing information in time order
- ⊙ Timeline
- Turning notes into running text
- Writing an inviting lead
- Using temporal words and phrases
- ⊙ Temporal Words and Phrases
- Infusing descriptions and details
- Crafting a satisfying ending
- Revising for sentence variety and fluency
- Editing with a focus on using past-tense verbs
- ⊙ Editing Checklist
- Adding supportive visuals
- Laying out pages

Mechanics
- Third-person pronouns
- Temporal words, phrases, and clauses
- Varying sentence beginnings
- Past-tense verbs
- Irregular verbs
- Editing for conventions

Features of a Great Informational Narrative
- Opening that establishes the situation
- Third-person point of view
- Temporal words and phrases that show sequence
- Rich descriptions and strong details
- Powerful language that engages the reader
- Strong ending

Power Write: Personal Narrative with Suspense

- Use a variety of words, phrases, or clauses to create suspense and highlight details.
- ⊙ Personal Narrative Planning Page
- ⊙ Checklist for Personal Narrative

Features of a Personal Narrative with Suspense
- Enticing title
- Lead establishes a tone or mood
- Settings and events are tightly linked
- Sensory details
- ▷ Concrete words make details stand out
- ▷ Variety of sentence types
- ▷ Variety of connectives
- ▷ Distinct ending

Power Write: Personal Narrative of a Single Focused Moment in Time

- Use sensory details to describe a situation and the subject's response to the situation.
- ⊙ Personal Narrative Planning Page
- ⊙ Checklist for Personal Narrative of a Single Focused Moment in Time

Features of a Personal Narrative of a Single Focused Moment in Time
- Introduction
- Sensory details
- Variety of sentence patterns
- Speak directly to the reader
- ▷ Relevant details situate events in a time or place
- ▷ Connective words and phrases
- ▷ Significance or importance of situation is established
- ▷ Illustration or photo

Power Write: Informational Narrative

- Use simile and action to bring a reader close to a subject.
- ⦿ Informational Narrative Planner
- ⦿ Checklist for Informational Narrative

Features of an Informational Narrative
- Simile
- Onomatopoeia
- Action
- Accurate facts
- ▷ Focus on one
- ▷ Varied sentence structure
- ▷ Clear ending

Power Write: Key Words and Summary

- Use key words to support a summary.
- ⦿ Checklist for Key Words to Summary

Features of Key Words and Summary
- Key words on sticky notes
- Open with a question
- Speak to the reader
- Personal connections
- Boldface text
- ▷ Heading
- ▷ Using a dash

Power Write: Narrative Poetry with a Partner

- Craft a narrative nonfiction poem.
- ⦿ Checklist for Narrative Poetry

Features of Narrative Poetry
- Phrases and/or short sentences
- Descriptive detail
- Metaphor
- No punctuation
- Justify left or center
- Conclusion
- ▷ Title

Power Write: Partner News Article

- Write a news article using an inverted pyramid structure.
- ⦿ "Conquering the Canyon"
- ⦿ News Article Planning Sheet
- ⦿ Checklist for Partner News Article

Features of a Partner News Article
- Inverted pyramid structure
- Tells who, what, when, where, why
- Lead statement with main idea
- Opens with a question or surprising statement
- Most important facts in first paragraph
- ▷ Quotation
- ▷ Byline

VL **Power Write:** Flowchart

- Sequence historical events with a flowchart.
- ⦿ "The Eruption of Mt. St. Helens"
- ⦿ Checklist for Flowchart and Narrative

Features of a Flowchart
- Text boxes
- Arrows to show order
- Explanatory narrative
- Introduction
- Sources are cited
- ▷ Title
- ▷ Linking words

VL **Power Write:** Team Investigation: Photo Essay

- Craft a photo essay.
- ⦿ Photo Essay "Ruby Bridges"
- ⦿ Checklist for Team Investigation: Photo Essay

Features of a Team Investigation: Photo Essay
- Magazine-style layout
- Captions
- Photographs
- Quotations
- ▷ Impact statement
- ▷ Linking words
- ▷ Citations

Persuade

Extended Writing Unit: Persuasive Letter

- Purpose (to persuade)
- Features
- Choosing a topic
- Writing an opinion statement
- Asking and answering questions to focus research
- Finding relevant information
- Using multiple sources
- Organizing reasons and facts
- ⊙ Persuasive Text Graphic Organizer
- Writing a strong introduction
- Writing the body
- Using linking words to connect reasons and facts
- ⊙ Linking Word Lists
- Writing a summarizing conclusion
- Revising for sentence variety and fluency
- Revising for logical organization
- ⊙ Revision Checklist for Persuasive Text
- Editing with a focus on contractions
- ⊙ Editing Checklist
- Publishing the letter
- Persuasive visuals

Mechanics

- Linking words and phrases to connect ideas
- Persuasive language
- Sentence variety
- Contractions
- Capital letters
- End punctuation
- Spelling
- Subject-verb agreement

Features of a Great Persuasive Text

- Clear introduction that states an opinion or position
- Reasons logically ordered to support the opinion or position
- Facts and details that support reasons
- Linking words, phrases, and clauses that connect facts and reasons
- Persuasive language
- Strong conclusion that summarizes the opinion or position

Power Write: Maybe

- Use a framework to compare and contrast arguments to draw a conclusion.
- ▷ Linking words of summation
- ⊙ Maybe Framework
- ⊙ Checklist for Maybe

Features of Maybe Framework

- Controversial statement
- Two perspectives on the same topic
- ⊙ Conclusion that includes linking words of summation such as *because, since, in conclusion, based on the evidence*
- ▷ Linking statements that acknowledge an opposing view such as *it could be said that, some people suggest, the opposing view might argue that*

Power Write: Public Service Announcement

- Use persuasive techniques to focus the public on health, safety, the environment, or national spirit.
- Connecting phrases
- ⊙ Persuasive Framework
- ⊙ Checklist for Public Service Announcement

Features of a Public Service Announcement

- Call to action (a question, a statement, or an emotionally engaging image)
- Directly address the reader
- Details support call to action
- Connecting phrases: *it should be noted, in addition, based on the evidence, for example, to illustrate, you see, research has shown, as a result*
- Conclusion restates the call to action
- ▷ Integrate the opposing view

Power Write: Electronic Slide Show		*Features of a Slide Show*
	• Create a slide show to show support for an argument. • 💿 Checklist for Slide Show	• Statement of opinion • Build supporting evidence with visuals and text • Anticipate and respond to the opposing view • 💿 Conclusion
Power Write: Video Commercial (Infomercial)		*Features of a Video Commercial*
	• Create a plan for an engaging video commercial. • ▷ Comparisons • 💿 Exaggerations! • 💿 Commercial Planning Tool • 💿 Checklist for Infomercial	• Enticing title • Convincing argument • Exaggeration • Speak directly to the viewer • Action and visuals • Conclusion with linking words of summation such as *as you can see, because, since, based on the evidence, in conclusion* • ▷ Comparisons: metaphor, simile, analogy
Power Write: Debate Plan		*Features of a Debate Plan*
	• Work with a partner to plan for a persuasive debate. • ▷ Linking words of comparison • 💿 Debate Organizer • 💿 Common Debate Sentence Frames • 💿 Checklist for Debate Plan	• Statement of opinion or call to action • Detailed evidence supports call to action • Strong emotional appeal • Acknowledge the opposing view • Summary and restatement of call to action • ▷ May use a hypothetical situation • ▷ Linking words of comparison: *however, but, although, on the other hand, similarly, likewise, in contrast to*
Power Write: Formal Letter		*Features of a Formal Letter*
	• Write a persuasive letter to the editor. • 💿 Checklist for Formal Letter	• Greeting, body, closing • Position statement • Facts to support position • Linking words to support specific examples: *for example, in fact, of course, consequently, specifically to illustrate, for instance* • Voice is formal and respectful • Restatement of position in conclusion • Call for action • ▷ Emotive words make the reader feel an emotional connection • ▷ Anticipate reader questions

Power Write: Multi-Paragraph Essay

- Write a multi-paragraph essay support-ing a position.
- ▷ ⬤ Comparisons
- ⬤ Multi-Paragraph Essay Organizer
- ⬤ Checklist for Multi-Paragraph Essay

Features of a Multi-Paragraph Essay
- Enticing title
- Clear organizational structure
- Facts and details support each paragraph
- Writing appeals to emotions
- Repetition solidifies message
- Strong emotional ending that repeats premise
- ▷ Comparisons are used: metaphor, simile, analogy
- ▷ Potential objections are addressed
- ▷ Prognosticate—offers a glimpse into the future

VL **Power Write:** Persuasive Framework

- Create a persuasive framework to show how reasons support a position.
- ⬤ Persuasive Framework
- ⬤ Checklist for Persuasive Framework

Features of a Persuasive Framework
- Visual layout
- Facts and reasons arranged in a logical sequence
- Arrows connect sections and show order of thinking
- Concise phrases present facts
- Linking words: *so, therefore, if, then, as a result, because, since, as, in conclu-sion*
- ▷ Conclusion restates problem and key points
- ▷ Call to action uses imperative language

VL **Power Write:** Investigation: Important Time in History

- Convince readers of an argument using a magazine-style layout.
- ⬤ Checklist for Investigation

Features of an Investigation
- Magazine-style layout with text boxes and visuals
- Title states a position
- Text boxes with headings include points of support for position, including specific examples
- ▷ Linking words to connect ideas
- ▷ Conclusion that restates position

Respond

Extended Writing Unit: Analytical Response • Purpose (to respond critically to a text or prompt) • Features • Writing an opinion statement • Supporting opinions with evidence • Discussing texts • Using specific vocabulary • Selecting main ideas for the response • Organizing opinions and linking to text evidence • ⊙ Spider Map Organizer • Writing a strong introduction • Drafting from notes • Connecting opinions to evidence • ⊙ Linking Words That Add Information • Writing a strong conclusion • Revising for effective punctuation • ⊙ Revision Checklist • Using editing symbols • ⊙ Editing Checklist • Pull quotes and visuals • Laying out pages	*Mechanics* • Linking words and phrases to connect evidence to opinions • Varied sentence lengths and types • Commas • Quotations and references • Capitalization of proper nouns • Spelling • Using editing symbols	*Features of a Great Analytical Response* • Introduction that clearly states an opinion • An organization with logically grouped ideas • Reasons supported by facts and details from the text • Words, phrases, and clauses that link opinions to examples *(for example, consequently, specifically, such as)* • Specific vocabulary • Conclusion that summarizes and reinforces the opinion
Power Write: Quote It!	• Draw inferences from quotations. • ⊙ "A Car for the Masses" • ⊙ Quote It! Planner • ⊙ Checklist for Quote It!	*Features of Quote It!* • Quotation • Inferences derived from the quotation • Support for inferences • Citation • ▷ Summarizing paragraph
Power Write: Summary: Main Ideas	• Determine two or more main ideas, and support them with details from the text. • ⊙ "Antarctica: Frozen Desert" • ⊙ Main Idea Response Organizer • ⊙ Checklist for Summary: Main Ideas	*Features of a Summary: Main Ideas* • Opening statement: gist • Paragraph headings represent main ideas • Evidence from text under headings • Linking words to add information: *because, so, when, since, also, and, besides, in addition, for example, it is important to note, to illustrate* • ▷ Concluding statement that recaps main idea(s)
Power Write: Compare and Contrast	• Compare and contrast two or more subjects, settings, or events. • ▷ Quotation • ⊙ Linking Words That Signal Comparison • ⊙ Checklist for Partner Comparison	*Features of Compare and Contrast* • Opening: gist statement • Linking words of comparison: *however, but, although, on the other hand, similarly, likewise, in contrast to, both* • Specific details • Conclusion • ▷ Supporting graphic or visual

Power Write: Summarizing from Multiple Sources

- Determine main ideas in multiple texts, and support them with details from the text.
- 💿 "A Brilliant Idea"
- 💿 "Out of Darkness"
- 💿 Main Idea Response Organizer
- 💿 Citation Formats
- 💿 Checklist for Summarizing from Multiple Sources

Features of a Summary from Multiple Sources
- Open with a gist statement
- Headings
- Details using justification from multiple sources
- Linking words to connect ideas: *because, so, when, since, also, and, besides, in addition, for example*
- ▶ Conclusion
- ▶ Visuals
- ▶ List sources

Power Write: Partner Book Review

- Compare text structures and information.
- 💿 Nonfiction Book Review
- 💿 Text Structures
- 💿 Checklist for Nonfiction Book Review

Features of Partner Book Review
- Linking words of comparison: *however, but, although, on the other hand, similarly, even though, still, though, yet, also, likewise*
- Signal words are identified for target text types
- Specific examples from texts
- Rating for each book
- Justification for rating
- ▶ Introduction

Power Write: Two-Word Strategy: Lewis and Clark

- Choose two words that describe the traits of significant historical figures.
- 💿 Checklist for Two-Word Strategy

Features of Two-Word Strategy
- Two words that offer inferences based on details in a text
- Justification with real events or factual content
- Bold words
- ▶ Supporting visuals

VL **Power Write:** Sketch to Stretch

- Respond to a poem with a Sketch to Stretch.
- 💿 "Waterworld"
- 💿 Checklist for Sketch to Stretch

Features of a Sketch to Stretch
- Series of sketches to reflect images brought forward by different sections of the poem
- Caption for each sketch
- ▶ Summative paragraph

VL **Power Write:** Venn Diagram (Three-Circle)

- Use a diagram to analyze multiple accounts of the same event or topic.
- 💿 "The Courage to Learn"
- 💿 Checklist for Venn Diagram: Three-Circle

Features of a Venn Diagram: Three-Circle
- Overlapping circles
- Key words and phrases
- Summative paragraph
- Linking words of comparison: *however, but, although, similarly, even though, still, yet, also, in contrast to*
- Description of similarities and differences
- ▶ Precise language

Informational Writing Projects

Informational texts describe and classify our world. Their purpose is to describe a place, thing, or group of things, rather than to retell a happening or series of events. Often informational texts give details about such topics as animals, space, plants, weather, geographical features, machines, places, industries, housing, and medicine. Students are most likely to encounter informational text in the form of nonfiction books and reports, but informational text may appear in many formats, including signs, posters, charts, lists, notes, and informational poetry. Informational text often includes illustrations.

CONTENTS

The Big Picture

. . . .

During the model unit that follows, students will write a detailed explanation of how a human body system or organ works. The mentor text, "A Breathtaking Body System," provides a model of the structure and features of a great explanation. Students begin by observing features of the mentor text and then work in pairs or small groups to gather and organize information about the system of their choice, using a research notebook. (You will probably want to remove the lungs and heart from the list of choices so students will not be tempted to copy from the mentor text or your modeled writing.) From their notes, students then write and illustrate pages for their explanation. They revise, edit, and publish the explanation in a format of their choice. Finally, they share their publications with classmates and others and reflect on what they have learned about writing an explanation.

Session	Focused Minilesson	Writing and Coaching	Sharing and Reflecting
1	Identifying the purpose and features of an explanation	Begin to record facts in your research notebook.	What did you find out about a body system or organ? Share information with partners.
2	Using the Very Important Points (VIP) strategy	Work with partners to use the VIP strategy.	Share sentences with another partner pair.
3	Organizing ideas with a flowchart	Create flowcharts from VIPs.	Share and analyze flowcharts with a partner.
4	Turning notes into running text	Draft using information from your flowchart and research notebook and using sequence words.	Talk about your draft with a partner. What went well? What challenges did you face?
5	Varying sentence length	Focus on monitoring sentence length and fluency.	Share your thinking about fluency with a partner. Share a place in your writing that has sentence fluency.
6	Using powerful verbs	Focus on using verbs that offer action and precision.	Share sentences from your writing that have precise, powerful verbs.
7	Revising for a satisfying conclusion	Revise and write a satisfying ending.	Share your thinking about your ending.
8	Revising to add titles and headings	Revise or draft, inserting enticing titles and headings.	Share your thinking about titles and headings with a partner.
9	Focused edits	Edit, focusing on one convention at a time.	Share your editing work with a partner. What changes did you make?
10	Publishing and adding supportive visuals	Format page layouts.	What advice would you give about writing a great explanation?

Assessing Students' Needs

The model unit is designed to teach students about the structure and features of a specific type of informational writing as they apply basic writing strategies. Each of the focused minilessons provides you with suggested demonstrations, but you may want to tailor your instruction based on the common needs of your own students. You can assess students' strengths and needs during each unit, in an additional session beforehand, or by analyzing student work that you already have on hand.

Formal Pre-Assessment: After a basic introduction to each writing purpose and form as well as a review of various examples, have students write in the same form about a topic they already know a lot about. Encourage students to use as many of the features of the particular writing form as possible, but don't provide direct support. The goal here is to find out how much students already know about the writing purpose and form so you can tailor your teaching accordingly.

Experimentation in Research Notebooks: You might want to stop short of a formal pre-assessment and instead ask students to experiment with writing in their research notebooks at the end of the first session. This exercise may be less unnerving for some students and should yield enough information to form the basis of your pre-assessment.

Looking Back at Previous Work: Whether you choose to assess students' writing skills before beginning an Extended Writing Unit or during the first session, we recommend that you also consider unrelated writing projects that you've already collected from students. These may not reveal much about your students' ability to write a coherent explanation, for example, but should tell you a great deal about their grasp of writing conventions and other traits such as focus, organization, voice, and sentence fluency. Depending on how much student work you already have on hand, you might not have to devote any class time to pre-assessment.

Focusing on Standards

Before introducing this model unit, carefully review the key skills and understandings below so you can keep the lesson objectives in mind as you teach, coach, and monitor students' growth as writers of informational texts.

KEY SKILLS AND UNDERSTANDINGS: INFORMATIONAL WRITING GRADE 5
Purpose
Understands the purpose for writing an informational piece
Ideas/Research
Reflects research and planning
Includes facts and details from research
Gathers and uses information from multiple sources
Consolidates information using the Very Important Points (VIP) strategy
Lists/cites sources
Organization/Text Features
Includes a title that tells what the piece is about
Includes a strong lead that draws readers into the text
Presents well-organized factual information
Supports main ideas with strong details
Includes a strong conclusion that sums up the piece
Includes labeled illustrations and supporting visuals
Language/Style
Puts information in his or her own words
Uses sequence and/or linking words and phrases
Uses specific vocabulary
Uses precise, powerful verbs
Demonstrates sentence variety and fluency
Conventions and Presentations
Begins sentences with capital letters
Ends sentences with appropriate punctuation
Uses appropriate spelling
Edits using an editing checklist
Creates interesting, effective page layouts with headings and sections

This list is the basis for both the Individual Assessment Record and the Ongoing Monitoring Sheet shown in Figure 1.1. (Both forms can be found in the Resources section at the back of this book and also on the *Resources* CD-ROM.) Use the Individual Assessment Record if you want to keep separate records on individual students. The Ongoing Monitoring Sheet gives you a simple mechanism for recording information on all your students as you move around the class, evaluating their work in progress. Use this information to adapt instruction and session length as needed.

At the end of these and any additional units you may teach on informational writing, compare students' final publications with their initial attempts at writing in the text type. Use the Ongoing Monitoring Sheet and/or the Individual Assessment Record to record students' growth as writers.

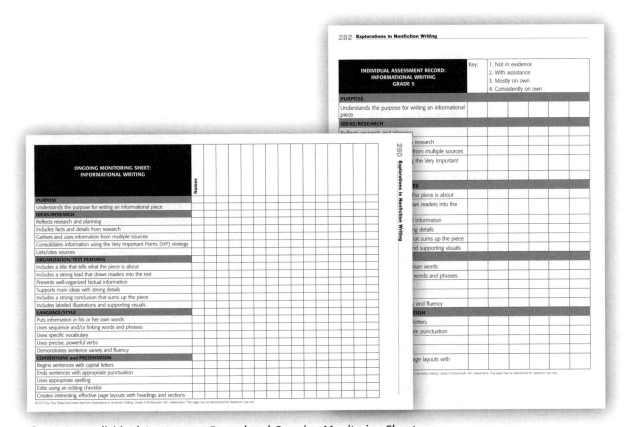

Figure 1.1 Individual Assessment Record and Ongoing Monitoring Sheet

Planning and Facilitating the Unit

Students will need preparation, coaching, prompting, and support as they move through this and other Extended Writing Units. Use the following tips and strategies as needed to ensure each student's success.

Before the Unit:

▶ When planning your teaching, bear in mind that each lesson in the model unit that follows is designed to be completed in one session. However, you will likely find that your students need more time for certain activities. Take the time you need to adequately respond to the unique needs of your students, and remember that they will likely progress through the writing process at their own pace.

▶ Begin building background knowledge about the text type and writing topics in advance. Shared reading, guided reading, and read-aloud experiences as well as group discussions will ensure that students are not dependent exclusively on their own research.

▶ For the research component, you may want to gather suitable books, magazine articles, encyclopedia entries, and websites in your classroom or work with the media center teacher to assemble a collection in advance. Make sure the research materials you gather are at a range of difficulty levels and include plenty of text features such as close-up photographs, captions, bold headings, and diagrams.

During the Unit:

▶ Begin each session with a focused minilesson to demonstrate the traits of writing the particular type of text you're exploring. Tailor the suggested minilesson to suit the needs of your students. The mentor texts on the *Resources* CD-ROM and in the *Book of Mentor Texts* are models you can use to show students the structure and features of each text type. You may want to use other mentor texts to assist you with your demonstrations.

▶ Be sure to model note-taking for students as you think aloud about information in reference materials. Use chart paper and sticky notes to capture your thinking, and display the models prominently as students work on their own research and note-taking.

▶ As students work independently on their writing and publishing, note those who are struggling and bring them together for small-group instruction. Use the Individual Assessment Record and/or the Ongoing Monitoring Sheet to assist in tailoring instruction to the needs of your students.

▶ Students who seem very confident and who have clearly grasped all of the concepts taught so far can be brought together in a small group to extend their understanding to more challenging work.

▶ Provide templates for students who need extra support when writing. You'll find a variety of graphic organizers on the *Resources* CD-ROM from which to choose.

After the Unit:

▸ Be sure to give students opportunities to share and celebrate their individual writing projects.

▸ Distribute copies of the Personal Checklist for Informational Writing shown in Figure 1.2. (This form can be found on the *Resources* CD-ROM and in the Resources section at the end of this book). Students will benefit greatly from the chance to reflect on their progress during the unit and to hear their classmates' feedback.

▸ Compare students' final writing products with pre-assessments and past work to evaluate their growth as writers of informational texts.

▸ Reflect on the strengths and challenges of implementing this series of lessons. How might it be adjusted to maximize student learning?

▸ Look at common needs of the class, and address these when planning future explorations or when using the Power Writes.

Personal Checklist for Informational Writing

Process Reflections:
Research:
I used the following resources in gathering facts: _____

Drafting:
I solved the following problems in my writing: _____

Revising:
When revising, I focused on improving my message by: _____

Editing:
To ensure that I edited effectively, I used an editing checklist and concentrated on: _____

Presentation:
I chose the following format to present my writing: _____

I am most proud of: _____

I have checked the following:
- ☐ My title tells what will be explained or described.
- ☐ There is a strong lead that draws the reader in.
- ☐ The information is clearly organized in paragraphs and sections.
- ☐ My paragraphs have main ideas and supporting details.
- ☐ Depending on my topic, I have included cause-effect words or words that show passage of time.
- ☐ I have used linking words such as *for example, specifically,* and *in addition* to connect ideas.
- ☐ I have included facts and details throughout my writing.
- ☐ I have used precise vocabulary to describe or explain.
- ☐ A conclusion emphasizes the main ideas and provides a satisfying ending.
- ☐ My writing has sentence fluency and I have used a variety of sentence lengths.
- ☐ The published presentation includes thoughtful page layout and interesting visuals.
- ☐ I have listed my sources.

© 2012 by Tony Stead and Linda Hoyt from *Explorations in Nonfiction Writing, Grade 5* (Portsmouth, NH: Heinemann). This page may be reproduced for classroom use only.

Figure 1.2 Personal Checklist for Informational Writing

SESSION 1
Identifying the Purpose and Features of an Explanation

Writers analyze an explanatory text, identify its structure and features, and then begin researching to write their own.

SESSION SNAPSHOT

Genre Focus: Features of an Explanation

Process Focus: Prewriting

Trait(s): Ideas

Mentor Text: "A Breathtaking Body System," by Amy Gilbert

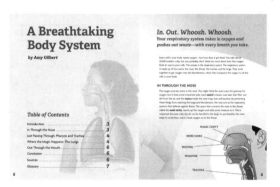

FOCUSED MINILESSON

Summarize the learning goals: *We are going to focus on a nonfiction genre called explanation. These are texts that explain how or why something happens. For example, if I were to explain why it rains, I would talk about how warm air turns the water from rivers, lakes, and oceans into water vapor that rises into the air. That water vapor forms clouds, which contain small drops of water.*

If I were to explain how a bicycle works, I would say that "When you push on the pedals, the gear assembly begins to turn. Then, teeth hook into the chain, and the chain rotates." I could also write an explanation of how the Union was formed or how the Titanic *sank.*

To write a great explanation, we first need to learn about the features and structure of a good explanation. Let's take a look at a mentor text that explains about how the lungs work.

Using the Mentor Text

■ The mentor text for this unit is "A Breathtaking Body System." You will find it on page 2 of the *Book of Mentor Texts* and in the Inform section on the *Resources* CD-ROM. Make enough copies for every student or group of students to have one, or use an electronic projection device to display the mentor for whole-class viewing.

Modeled Writing

■ Read the opening sentence. *I have already noticed a feature of an explanation. The title and the first paragraph clearly tell us that this explanation is about the respiratory system.* Read an additional portion of the text. *I am noticing that because this explanation tells how something works, there are words that suggest order or sequence. Notice where it says "After passing through the nose. . . ." As we read on, watch for more features that make an explanation different from other kinds of nonfiction texts.*

■ As you guide writers in moving through the explanation about the respiratory system, help them notice the features of an explanation. Guide them to understand that sequence and cause-and-effect order are important features of an explanation.

- *Over the next ten sessions, we are going to write explanations of how different body systems or organs work.* Have each student select an element of the human body such as the digestive system, the nervous system, the muscular system, the cardiovascular system, or an individual organ. Pair the students so that they have a partner to research with. Ensure that not too many students are working on the same body system or organ so that there are adequate resources.

TURN &TALK *Think together. When you write your explanations about your selected body system or organ, what features will you include?*

- Guide students as they share their observations, and record their thinking on a chart labeled "Features of a Great Explanation."

Modeling

- *Writers, I am going to begin an explanation about the heart. To do this, I am first going to need to do some research. I have books, magazines, and some information from the Internet that I am going to use to assist me with my research.*

- *Watch as I record information about a wonderful website I found, using this three-column chart that helps me stay organized. I write the name of the organization, or source, that sponsors the website in the first column. Under "Location," I'll write the URL so I can easily find the site again. And then, I'll jot down a few thoughts about the website and the kind of information it contains.*

- *Today you will write notes about the resources you think will be most helpful in your own research.*

WRITING and COACHING

- Provide students with resources about the body system or organ they are explaining, including nonfiction books, photographs, or articles.

- Guide students in using their research notebooks to note important details. You may want to organize the notebooks into categories in advance to help students identify important information to include as they research, such as the source title, the location of the information (page number or URL), and relevant notes. Alternatively, you may have students record their information on a Personal R.A.N. Organizer as described on page 266 and on the *Resources* CD-ROM.

- Focus guided-writing groups on assisting students who struggle with researching their particular body system or organ.

SHARING and REFLECTING

TURN &TALK *Partners, share some of the information you have discovered about your body systems or organs.*

- Lead a discussion about explanations, reviewing the list of features. Revisit the mentor text to help students consolidate their understandings about the genre.

- Gather the research notebooks, and analyze students' attempts to research. Identify writers who may need additional modeling as well as those who are ready for higher levels of sophistication.

Features of a Great Explanation

- Opens with a statement or question about the topic to be explained.
- Focuses on sequence or order. May use words such as: when, if, first, next, then, finally.
- Includes cause-and-effect connections
- Generalized nouns (the muscles, the nerves)
- Powerful verbs
- Exact and important details
- May include a supportive diagram or Illustration.
- Includes a list of sources

TIP The research will be better facilitated if you collect resources on systems of the body and/or organs in advance of this lesson. As writers begin to fine-tune their research, they will surely expand their research to the Internet, to the library, and so on.

SESSION 2
The Very Important Points Strategy (VIP)

Writers research and identify important points to include in their explanations.

SESSION SNAPSHOT

Research Strategy: VIP

Process Focus: Prewriting

Trait(s): Ideas, Organization

Mentor Text: "A Breathtaking Body System," by Amy Gilbert

FOCUSED MINILESSON

Review the learning goals from the previous session. If time allows, have students turn and talk about what they have learned so far.

Summarize the learning goals for today's session: *Today we will continue researching. You will be working with your partner to gather information and begin organizing facts for the explanations that you will each be writing. To help us be very strategic in identifying important facts to include in our explanations, we will be using strips of sticky note material to mark very important points in our resources.*

Using the Mentor Text

- Display the mentor text, and read a portion of it aloud. *Writers, can you see how the author has included only the most important facts about how the respiratory system works? As you research your body system or organ, you will read lots of facts. You will have to ask yourself if these facts are important when explaining how your body system works.*

Modeling

- *To use the VIP strategy, I begin by tearing sticky notes into thin strips that each has a bit of the adhesive on the bottom. Then, as I find points that I think are important, I can tear off strips and attach them to the side of the page so that each fact is easy to find again. I have a limited number of strips, so I can't mark everything. I need to choose wisely.*

Make a fist. This is about the size of your heart. Sixty to one hundred times every minute your heart muscles squeeze together and push blood around your body through tubes called blood vessels.

Try squeezing a rubber ball with your hand. Squeeze it hard once a second. Your hand will get tired in a minute or two. Yet your heart beats every second of every day. In one year your heart beats more than thirty million times. In an average lifetime a heart will beat over 2,000,000,000 (two thousand million) times.

The heart works hard when we relax or sleep and even harder when we work or exercise. It never stops for rest or repair. The heart is a most incredible pump.

In this computer-enhanced photograph, the heart is pictured in the center of the chest surrounded by blood vessels in the lungs, neck, and arms.

4

Modeled Writing

- *Listen as I read and think aloud.* Use a document camera to display a page from a resource on the heart. *On the first page of this book, it says that the heart is about the size of a fist. That is important, but my goal is to write an explanation of how the heart works. I don't think this fact will help me do that, so I am not going to use one of my VIPs on this fact right now. I just want to focus on how the heart works. I can come back later and add details. Next, it says that when the heart muscles squeeze together, they push blood out into the blood vessels. This fact is perfect for a VIP because it will help me explain how the heart functions. Watch as I tear off a strip and attach it to the side of the page so it sticks out a bit and I can find this fact again quickly.*

TURN &TALK *Listen as I read the next paragraph, and help me decide if there is a VIP that should be marked that will help me explain how the heart works. Analyze this passage and think about how the heart works. Is there a VIP here?*

■ *It is important to pause every now and then to summarize the facts you have collected with VIPs and jot down a sentence or two in your writer's notebooks. This is a time when you can experiment with different sentences that make your facts come alive and really tell how something works. Watch as I jot a sentence in my own words to summarize the VIPs I have so far:* "The muscles of the heart squeeze together and act like a pump pushing blood from the heart into the blood vessels."

■ Guide a conversation to recap the process of determining importance during research—matching facts to the purpose for your writing and marking them with VIPs.

■ Encourage writers to pause frequently and summarize their VIPs in their writer's notebooks. This will provide an opportunity to experiment with ways to include facts in an explanation.

WRITING and COACHING

■ Have partners work with selected resources to use the VIP strategy.

■ Coach partners as they research and selectively mark VIP points that will support an explanation about their topics.

■ Confirm that all writers are pausing at regular intervals to jot summaries of their learning in their writer's notebooks.

SHARING and REFLECTING

TURN &TALK *Partners, you have collected some great research facts using your VIP points. And I see that many of you have been using your writer's notebooks to experiment with sentences that might showcase your facts in an explanation. Meet with another partner pair so you create teams of four, and share your learning with each other. Make a point to share the best sentences you have generated during your research.*

■ Bring writers back together to sum up the learning. *Today we learned how to use the VIP strategy to collect interesting facts for our explanations, and we've begun to generate great sentences using those facts. We are on our way to writing some fascinating explanations!*

■ Collect the students' notebooks, and analyze their attempts to mark the most important facts about their topic. Note students who may need additional modeling in turning VIPs into sentences and those who may be ready for higher levels of sophistication. Use the class writing development rubric or the individual student rubric on the *Resources* CD-ROM to track writing proficiencies.

TIP You will need to provide students with many demonstrations over the year on the VIP strategy to help them internalize what facts are important to include in their writing.

TIP Some students may be challenged by the process of determining importance and need additional guided practice in a small-group setting before working independently. Others may need explicit modeling of how to take a fact marked as a VIP and turn it into a lively sentence in their writer's notebooks.

SESSION 3
Organizing Ideas with a Flowchart

Writers organize facts on a flowchart in preparation for writing.

SESSION SNAPSHOT

Process Focus: Prewriting, Planning

Trait(s): Organization

FOCUSED MINILESSON

Review the learning goals from the previous session. If time allows, have students turn and talk about what they have learned so far.

Summarize the learning goals for today's session: *Today we will be using flowcharts as tools for organizing facts into a logical sequence. This will help you write clear, well-organized explanations. Flowcharts help you gather your facts and keep them in order. Watch as I use one to organize the facts that I collected about the heart.*

Modeling

■ Display a page in a book or magazine about the heart in which you have marked VIP points. *Today I am going to use a flowchart to arrange facts (VIPs) in an order that helps me explain how the heart works. Here is a VIP that says blood enters the heart through the atrium and then the atrium pumps it down to the ventricles. To create the flowchart, I will write my facts on strips of paper, and then I will organize the strips into an order that makes sense and connect them with arrows. Here is my first fact: "blood flows to the atrium." On my second strip, I will write "blood goes into the ventricle." Notice that these are not complete sentences. When we are researching, phrases or notes are fine. One of my VIPs reminds me that there is a valve that closes when the blood leaves the ventricles so the blood can't flow backward. I will write that on the third strip. Now I need to decide how to organize my strips. It is important to get the order correct when writing an explanation.* Think aloud as you arrange the strips, taking time to recheck references to model checking for accuracy. *These strips tell how blood moves through the heart, so I am going to add a heading for this group of strips: "The Journey Begins." Adding headings will help me have organized paragraphs.*

TURN &TALK *Writers, examine my flowchart and talk about the way it is helping me organize my facts as I prepare to write an explanation. What are the benefits of a flowchart? Why is it helpful to write phrases and draw arrows when you are researching?*

Flowchart

Heading: the journey begins

> blood flows to the atrium

↓

> blood goes into the ventricle

↓

> a valve closes when when blood leaves the ventricles so blood can't flow backward

↓

Heading:

>

↓

>

Modeled Writing

■ Continue modeling writing VIPs on rectangles and then continuously check the order and accuracy of the sequence you are creating. You may want to show that sometimes arrows in a flowchart go out to the side and sometimes they are vertical.

■ *Once I have all the important facts on strips and I feel confident about the order I have created, I paste or tape the rectangles in position and draw arrows between them. This puts an emphasis on what happens first, second, and so on. Order is important in an explanation about how something works. If I was working on why something happened, a flowchart would also help me because it would show elements of cause and effect.*

WRITING and COACHING

■ Guide partners as they continue with their research and create their flowcharts from their VIPs. Encourage them to experiment with rearranging their strips and thinking about sequence and cause and effect.

■ Support and extend the thinking of your writers by helping them be very clear about focusing on **how their subject works** for their explanations. Cue their thinking with questions such as *And how will this fact help you explain the way that _____ works? Where does this fact fit in the order of the ways things happen with the _____ you are explaining?*

■ Extend understanding by showing writers how to cluster the strips into groups that would make a good paragraph, organizing strips on the flowchart under headings—just as they will do when they write paragraphs.

SHARING and REFLECTING

TURN &TALK *Partners, this is a good time to pause and think together about your research. Analyze your flowcharts. Do they show a clear order or sequence? Do they have enough information, or do you need to continue adding research?*

■ Guide a conversation that returns student attention to the overall goal of writing an explanation, and explain that when they feel their research is complete, they will begin turning their flowcharts and notes into a written explanation.

■ Gather the students' flowcharts, and analyze their attempts to show sequence and cause-and-effect elements. Identify writers who may need additional modeling as well as those who are ready for higher levels of sophistication. Use the class writing development rubric or the individual student rubric on the *Resources* CD-ROM to track writing proficiencies.

TIP Using multiple resources and/or the Internet will help students remember that researchers turn to many sources for their information. Many student-friendly websites such as kidshealth.org offer passages in English and in Spanish. Be sure to have students keep track of the websites they access so they can use the information in their reference lists if you are having them keep one.

TIP Some students may benefit from a small-group experience to provide additional assistance in extracting facts and organizing them in a logical sequence to support an explanation.

SESSION 4

Turning Notes into Running Text

Writers turn research notes and sketches into a draft.

SESSION SNAPSHOT

Process Focus: Drafting

Trait(s): Organization, Voice

Mentor Text: "A Breathtaking Body System," by Amy Gilbert

BEFORE THE LESSON

Provide copies of mentor explanations that you have gathered. Give partners time to read several examples, noticing how they are written. Then, guide a conversation comparing and contrasting the explanations.

FOCUSED MINILESSON

Review the learning goals from the previous session. If time allows, have students turn and talk about what they have learned so far.

Summarize the learning goals for today's session: *The focus today is on turning notes and the flowchart into an explanation by beginning to write in paragraph form.*

Using the Mentor Text

■ Read the beginning of the mentor text. "Every cell in your body needs oxygen—but how does it get there? You take about 20,000 breaths a day, but you probably don't think too much about how the oxygen finds its way to your cells. The answer is the respiratory system."

■ *Do you notice how the author began this piece? She started with a question that would get us actively thinking about her topic and also gave us a fascinating fact: that we take in 20,000 breaths a day. This powerful opening really makes me want to read more.*

Modeling

■ *To write my explanation on the heart, I also need a great lead. Watch as I write.* "Your heart is the most incredible pump ever created! Stay tuned, because I am going to explain how every minute of every day, your heart propels. . . ."

> **TURN &TALK** *Analyze my lead. Does it make you want to read more? Did I make it exciting and also make it clear that this is an explanation? Get ready to tell why this lead works or what we could do to make it better.*

■ *Now I am ready to take the first box on my flowchart and use it in my writing. It says,* "blood flows to the atrium." *I want to be sure to start a new paragraph. I also want to be sure to use the heading that I inserted in my flowchart. Watch as I leave a line blank and then write my heading:* "The Journey Begins." *I return to the left margin, and here comes my next paragraph:* "The amazing story of how blood moves through our bodies begins when. . . ."

■ Continue modeling how to take phrases from your flowchart and research notes and turn them into sentences. Emphasize words of sequence such as *then, next, if, when,* and *because.* (See the *Resources* CD-ROM for a list of temporal words and phrases that show sequence.)

■ Demonstrate how you use illustrations with labels to support your explanation.

■ Emphasize the understanding that this is a draft, so it is okay to draw lines through words, start over, insert new ideas in the margins, and so on. Discourage students from using erasers as they draft and revise.

WRITING and COACHING

■ Support writers as they begin to draft using information from their flowcharts, writer's notebooks, and research notebooks. Guide them in being fearless as they experiment with language and invite their readers to join them in celebrating the information they are sharing. Be sure partners are aware that although they have researched together, they will each be creating their own drafts.

■ As writers begin to draft, some may realize that they need more research and need to return to that phase of the writing process.

■ Help writers remember that nonfiction writing needs to have visual supports. Even though this is just a draft, it can be a powerful time to consider where to include a heading, a labeled diagram, a boldface word, and so on.

> Your heart is the most incredible pump ever created! Stay tuned, because I am going to explain how every minute of every day, your heart propels...
>
> <u>The Journey Begins</u>
>
> The amazing story of how blood moves through our bodies begins when blood flows to the atrium.

Modeled Writing

TIP Some students may need additional coaching as they convert phrases to sentences and use their writer's notebooks to experiment with leads, wording, transition words, and so on. These students would greatly benefit from a small-group guided-writing experience.

SHARING and REFLECTING

TURN &TALK *Drafting is messy work. It is a time when notes, sketches, and graphic organizers fuel our thinking and help us create the final pieces of writing that will wow our readers. Find a partner and talk about your drafts. What went well? What challenges did you face today? How are you doing at converting your notes and flowcharts into sentences?*

■ Lead a class discussion about converting research notes, graphic organizers, and sketches into powerful pieces of writing: What worked well? What was difficult? What can be done tomorrow to improve the process?

■ Gather the drafts and analyze your students' attempts to turn notes into running text. Identify writers who may need additional modeling as well as those who are ready for higher levels of sophistication.

SESSION 5
Varying Sentence Length

Writers focus on writing sentences of varying lengths.

SESSION SNAPSHOT

Process Focus: Drafting, Revising

Trait(s): Sentence Fluency

Mentor Text: "A Breathtaking Body System," by Amy Gilbert

FOCUSED MINILESSON

Review the learning goals from the previous session. If time allows, have students turn and talk about what they have learned so far.

Summarize the learning goals for today: *One of the ways writers achieve sentence fluency is by making sure their sentences differ in length and that the writing sounds smooth when read aloud. Our focus today is making sure that our explanations include some sentences that are long and complex mixed in with short and medium-length sentences.*

Using the Mentor Text

■ Revisit the mentor text. Read aloud the first paragraph. "Every cell in your body needs oxygen. But how does it get there? You take about 20,000 breaths a day but you probably don't think too much about how that oxygen finds its way to your cells. The answer is the respiratory system. . . ."

> **TURN &TALK** *Tell your partner which sentences the author has used that are complex. Where has she used short or simple sentences? How has she joined information? Read some of her sentences out loud. Notice how the different sentence lengths make her writing flow more smoothly and sound more pleasing.*

■ Invite students to share their thinking with the class.

Modeling

■ *As I draft my explanation about the heart, I am going to focus on writing some short sentences and some that are longer. My first sentence,* "The ventricles are the lower chambers of the heart," *is pretty short. That's okay as long as I follow it with a longer complex sentence. I remember how Seymour Simon uses comparisons in his books, so I am going to start my next sentence with* "Like a giant machine. . . ." *I want to help my reader understand that the heart has to be so powerful it can send blood out of the heart with enough pressure that it can travel to every part of the body.*

> **TURN &TALK** *Writers, think together. My sentence begins with* "Like a giant machine. . . ." *It needs to be pretty long because my first sentence was short. Identify some options for completing the sentence so it is longer.*

- *I've got it!* "Like a giant machine, these powerful muscles must send blood away from the heart with enough power that it can travel around the entire body." *Starting my sentence with a comparison and a comma helped me create a longer complex sentence. Let's read it aloud and see how it sounds. The best test is to see how it sounds when you read it aloud.*

- Continue modeling the addition of sentences with varying lengths, including a bit of onomatopoeia (dupp-lup), which is very helpful for sentence fluency.

> The ventricles are the lower chambers of the heart. Like a giant machine, these powerful muscles must send blood away from the heart with enough power that it can travel around the entire body.

Modeled Writing

WRITING and COACHING

- As writers return to drafting, support them in remembering to read their work aloud to see how it sounds to the ear and to consciously monitor sentence lengths as they draft sentences.

- Remind writers to read aloud to each other as they draft and share thinking about sentence fluency while they are in the process of drafting and revising.

- Coach writers with questions such as *What length of sentence are you planning next? How is the sentence fluency in this piece? Does it flow and sound smooth when you read it aloud?*

SHARING and REFLECTING

- Return to the mentor text, your own modeled writing, or an exemplary piece of student writing, and focus on sentence fluency with an expressive oral reading of one section. Guide students in noticing how naturally sentence fluency occurs when short and longer sentences are woven together.

  TURN &TALK *Identify a partner you haven't worked with yet, and share your thinking about sentence fluency. What do you know about it? Then, select a place in your own writing where you think you have sentence fluency, and share it with your partner.*

- Gather the drafts and analyze your students' attempts to vary sentence length. Identify writers who may need additional modeling as well as those who are ready for higher levels of sophistication. Use the class writing rubric or the individual student rubric on the *Resources* CD-ROM to track writing proficiencies.

TIP Writers are likely to be in different places in the writing process by this point—some researching while others are nearly finished drafting. A Workshop Organizer as shown in *A Guide to Teaching Nonfiction Writing*, page 49, is a great tool to help you monitor the stages of the process for your students.

SESSION 6
Using Powerful Verbs

Writers reflect on and integrate powerful verbs into their explanations.

SESSION SNAPSHOT

Process Focus: Drafting, Revising

Trait(s): Word Choice

Mentor Text: "A Breathtaking Body System," by Amy Gilbert

FOCUSED MINILESSON

Review the learning goals from the previous session. If time allows, have students turn and talk about what they have learned so far.

Summarize the learning goals for today's session: *Verbs are often called the engines of sentences. They bring action and help make descriptions come to life. Today our focus is on using verb choices that sizzle.*

Using the Mentor Text

■ Revisit the mentor text on the respiratory system. *Let's begin by looking once again at the mentor text and noticing the verbs. See how the author used the verb* thrusted? *He could have used the verb* pushed, *but listen how the verb* thrusted *sounds so much better.*

> **TURN &TALK** *Identify with your partner some of the verbs in this piece. Which ones do you think are powerful?*

Modeling

■ *As I draft today, I am going to focus on the verbs that I select to make sure they are precise and powerful. I am ready to tell that when the blood pushes out of the left ventricle and goes into the aorta, our biggest blood vessel, the blood has to come out with so much power that it can travel all the way around the body. To get ready to write, I will make a list of verbs that reflect this amazing power: surge, jet, rocket, push, propel, shoot, thrust, smash, burst, explode.*

> **TURN &TALK** *Think together. Discuss the verbs that would make it clear that the blood moves from the ventricle to the aorta with enormous power.*

surge	jet
rocket	push
propel	shoot
thrust	smash
burst	explode

Like water erupting through a bursting dam, blood _____ from the ventricle into the aorta.

Modeled Writing

■ *Watch as I try several different verbs in the sentence. Then, we can think together about which verb is the most precise and offers a reader the clearest mental picture of the powerful river of blood that exits from the heart into the aorta. Writers, notice that I am not writing on my draft. I am experimenting on a separate piece of paper. When you experiment with verbs and word choice, you may want to do this in your writer's notebooks or on a separate piece of paper and then select your best sentence to use in your drafts.*

- Continue thinking aloud and inviting students to experiment with different verbs to see which deliver the most precision in meaning and offer the best sensory imaging for your sentence: "Like water erupting through a bursting dam, blood _____ from the ventricle into the aorta."
- Show students how you play with language while drafting and sometimes experiment writing sentences several ways before you select the one you like the best.

WRITING and COACHING

- As writers return to drafting, remind them to experiment with different verbs as they draft and revise, selecting the ones that offer action and precision in the writing.
- Remind students that a thesaurus can be a helpful tool when focusing on word choice.
- Coach writers with questions such as *Which verbs are your strongest? Why did you select them? What other verbs did you consider for that sentence?*

SHARING and REFLECTING

- *Research partners, please sit together and take a minute to examine the verbs in one of the resources you have used for research. Evaluate them. Are they precise with action and strong visual images? Next, examine the verbs in the sentences you wrote today. Share your thinking about the verbs you used and why precise and powerful verbs make writing stronger.*
- After partners share, guide your community of writers in reflecting about verbs and precision in word choice.
- Gather the writer's notebooks, and analyze your students' attempts to use precise and powerful verbs. Identify writers who may need additional modeling as well as those who are ready for higher levels of sophistication. Use the rubrics on the *Resources* CD-ROM to track writing proficiencies.

TIP Making a list of powerful verbs with students and having them displayed in the classroom will help them in selecting the ones they want to use when writing their own explanations.

TIP While most writers are likely to have moved beyond research at this point, some may feel that they are close to finishing their drafts. For these students, a craft lesson on precise nouns or adjectives and adverbs can lead to more sophisticated revision, including the addition of rich and detailed new sentences.

SESSION 7
Revising for a Satisfying Conclusion

Writers identify features of a satisfying ending and then confirm that those elements are present in their own explanations.

SESSION SNAPSHOT

Process Focus: Drafting, Revision

Trait(s): Organization, Voice

Mentor Text: "A Breathtaking Body System," by Amy Gilbert

FOCUSED MINILESSON

Reflect on the learning goals from the last session. If time allows, have students turn and talk about what they have learned so far.

Summarize the learning goals for this session: *Revision is a time when writers challenge themselves to reach deeper and think about their writing through the eyes of a reader. One of the important steps in revision is to check the conclusion. That is our focus for today.*

Using the Mentor Text

■ Read the ending of the mentor text.

> **TURN &TALK** *Share with your partner what makes the ending powerful. What do you think are the attributes of a good ending?*

■ Have writing partners examine the endings of the books they have been using for their research and evaluate them. Which ones do they like? Which ones are not very satisfying? What are the attributes of a strong ending?

Modeling

■ *We have discovered that we like endings that make us think, give us an emotional connection to the topic, make us wonder, and speak directly to us. Let's look at draft 1 of my ending. "The heart. . . ."* I definitely need to revise. I think I'm going to start over. Draft 2: "The heart—mysterious, magical." *Did you notice that I have tied in my title, "The Mysterious Heart"? Now I want to speak directly to a reader, so I will add a question:* "What have you done for your heart today?"

> **TURN &TALK** *Writers, analyze my second draft. Evaluate this ending and prepare to share your thinking. Is this a better ending? Could I improve it even more? What else could I do to revise so I have a terrific ending to my explanation?*

■ Continue guiding a discussion about alternative options that would strengthen the ending. Then, create a list of the attributes of a great ending that you can post for your writers.

Draft 1

The heart has many parts and acts like a big pump for our blood. The end.

Draft 2

The heart is mysterious, magical, and life-sustaining. What have you done for your heart today?

Modeled Writing

WRITING and COACHING

■ As writers return to their writing to revise and consider endings, remind them to use the posted list of attributes of an ending. They also may want to look at more nonfiction selections by authors they like and see what those authors have done to create satisfying endings.

■ Coach writers who are revising through questions such as *Which revisions have you made that you think improved your writing and/ or clarified the message for your reader? Which revisions are you still planning to do?*

■ Remind authors who are still in the drafting phase of their writing that they do not need to abandon their work but can continue to draft and work on their endings when they are ready to revise. You will need to provide additional time for these learners to complete their drafts.

■ For writers who have moved on to editing, remind them that the writing process is one in which they are constantly moving forward and backward. Even though they may have started to edit, they can still reread and be reflective about their endings.

SHARING and REFLECTING

TURN &TALK *Writing partners, we have a lot to celebrate. Everyone has exciting drafts, and most people have begun to revise and edit. Today we focused on drafting and revising our endings to be sure they are satisfying, speak directly to the reader, and make us wonder. Share your thinking about your ending. If you have written it, read it to your partner. If you haven't written it yet, share your thoughts about what you might say at the end.*

■ Remind writers to keep an eye out for terrific endings, and create a bulletin board of great nonfiction endings that have strong attributes.

■ Gather the drafts and analyze your students' attempts to revise and craft enticing conclusions. Identify writers who may need additional modeling as well as those who are ready for higher levels of sophistication. Use the rubrics on the *Resources* CD-ROM to track writing proficiencies.

TIP Revision is multifaceted and can take a long time for writers to control. It may be helpful to post a list of revision strategies or to offer revision checklists such as those on the *Resources* CD-ROM.

SESSION 8
Revising to Add Titles and Headings

Writers analyze titles and headings and then select ones that will entice their readers.

SESSION SNAPSHOT

Process Focus: Revising, Drafting

Trait(s): Text Features: Titles and Headings, Organization

Mentor Text: "A Breathtaking Body System," by Amy Gilbert

FOCUSED MINILESSON

Have students reflect on the learning goals from the last session. If time allows, have students turn and talk about what they have learned so far.

Summarize the learning goals: *You finished the full draft of your explanation in our last session, and now it's time to think about what you will call it and how you will help readers work their way through it. Titles and headings are really important. They tell readers about the topic and often make a difference in whether or not we pick up a book or magazine and enter its pages. Since many of you are getting close to the end of your drafts, this is a good time to begin to think about titles and headings.*

Using the Mentor Text

■ If possible, use an electronic projection device to display the mentor text for whole-class viewing. *When we look at the title of the mentor text, we can see that the author has used a very enticing and amusing title. We can also see that she has used headings such as* "In Through the Nose" *and* "Out Through the Mouth" *to show how her piece is organized.*

Modeling

■ Display a wide range of nonfiction books and magazines with a range of titles and headings—some intriguing and some not. *As I look at the titles of these books, it is pretty easy to make two piles—boring titles and interesting titles. For example, I love this one:* "The Sticky Secret of Gecko Toes." *Who wouldn't want to read that! I also find myself drawn to* "Walk with a Wolf, "Think of an Eel," *and* "Wilma Unlimited"—*I want to know what makes Wilma Rudolph "unlimited." When I look at this heading about tornadoes that says* "Destroyed in Less Than a Minute," *I am immediately drawn in and want to read that section.*

> **TURN &TALK** *What are the attributes of titles and headings that draw you in and make you want to read more?*

■ *You had some great ideas about titles and headings, and here is one more. Sometimes a title or a heading can offer a sense of mystery and help you realize that if you read on, you may learn something fascinating—like* "The Sticky Secret of Gecko Toes." *With that in mind, I am going to make a list of possible titles for my explanation about the heart. I will start with* "Mysteries of the Heart." *Does that make you wonder and want to read? How about* "Marvelous Mystery: The Heart"? *Let's keep going. Now I'm going to think about some great headings for each of the sections in my explanation.*

■ Continue focusing on interesting titles and headings. Explore the possibilities of such literary devices as alliteration and onomatopoeia.

WRITING and COACHING

■ As writers return to their drafting, encourage them to reread their work and begin thinking about titles and headings that might entice a reader into their writing. Some may find it helpful to keep their writer's notebooks close at hand so they can add title ideas as they come to mind while working on their drafts.

■ For writers who have completed their drafts and are moving forward with revision and editing, this may be a perfect time to direct their attention to title and heading selection before they make a final choice.

■ Headings are essential building blocks of organization. Remind writers to be consistent in inserting headings in the body of their work to help their readers mentally organize the material. Like titles, headings should be carefully chosen to both summarize the content and intrigue a reader.

SHARING and REFLECTING

TURN &TALK *Writers, work with a thinking partner who has been writing on a topic that is different than yours. Think together about titles and headings for each of your pieces, sharing your possible ideas with each other and deciding together which titles and headings are most enticing to a reader.*

■ Guide your community of writers in coming together to share their thinking about titles and headings. Enjoy a quick sharing of titles and headings that excite and entice!

■ Gather the drafts and analyze your students' attempts at using enticing titles and headings. Identify writers who may need additional modeling as well as those who are ready for higher levels of sophistication. Use the rubrics on the *Resources* CD-ROM to track writing proficiencies.

TIP During individual conferences and small-group writing sessions, double-check to be sure writers have selected headings and titles that effectively reflect the content. Headings, in particular, should represent the main idea of each section.

SESSION 9
Focused Edits

Writers reread for specific editing points.

SESSION SNAPSHOT

Process Focus: Editing

Trait(s): Conventions

TIP It may be helpful to post a list of conventions to remind writers of targets they might set for each reading.

FOCUSED MINILESSON

Reflect on the learning goals from the last session. If time allows, have students turn and talk about what they have learned so far.

Summarize the learning goals for this session: *Once our messages are clear and as concise as possible, it is time to turn our attention to editing—looking at spelling, punctuation, and the surface structures that help readers navigate our writing. Today we are going to draw our attention to focused edits in which we reread for each editing point.*

Modeling

■ *In a focused edit, I want to think about one editing point at a time. That helps me notice details that I might miss if I were thinking about too many things at once. In a focused edit, I select a single editing point and ignore everything else. My first reading will focus on just subject-verb agreement. I want to be sure that nouns and verbs work together. There may be other conventions in the writing that need attention, but I am only going to think about subject-verb agreement in this reading. "The ventricle are"—Ooops. Ventricle is singular and the verb* are *is only used with plural nouns. I need to add an* s *to* ventricle *so it reads, "The ventricle*s *are. . . ." That sounds much better.*

■ *Did you notice that I didn't focus on spelling or spacing or capital letters? I only looked at one aspect of my writing.*

> **TURN &TALK** *Can you help me with another focused edit? Read the passage I have written again. In this focused edit, we are looking only at spelling. Look closely at my spelling, and be ready to report on the findings of your focused edit.*

■ Continue guiding students in focused edits with a single goal for each reading of the piece you have crafted. You will need to have some spelling mistakes and punctuation errors in your piece so that students are able to identify mistakes that need fixing.

Like water erupting through a bursting dam, blood surge^s from the ventricle into the aorta.

Modeled Writing

WRITING and COACHING

■ Have writers engage in focused edits with their work—focusing on only one convention at a time.

■ For writers who are still drafting and revising, remind them that when they are ready to edit, you will expect them to focus their edits so they can notice more detail.

■ Coach editors with questions such as *What is the editing focus of this reading? What is your single editing point? What will you read for on your next reading?*

SHARING and REFLECTING

TURN &TALK *Work with a partner, and share the work you have done in editing your work. Identify the editing points you used for each reading and the result of your editing work. What did you change? What elements did you have in place that made you feel accomplished today?*

■ Guide a discussion among writers about the power of focused editing and rereading for each editing point.

■ Gather the drafts and analyze your students' attempts to edit. Identify writers who may need additional modeling as well as those who are ready for higher levels of sophistication. Use the rubrics on the *Resources* CD-ROM to track writing proficiencies and tailor future instruction.

TIP Students may find it difficult to remember focus points for editing. You may want to provide editing checklists that guide their thinking such as those on the *Resources* CD-ROM.

SESSION 10
Publishing and Adding Supportive Visuals

SESSION SNAPSHOT

Process Focus: Presenting, Publishing

Trait(s): Conventions

Mentor Text: "A Breathtaking Body System," by Amy Gilbert

FOCUSED MINILESSON

Before the lesson: Decide what format you would like to use for publishing the modeled writing you have done. You may want to use a cut-and-paste technique to assemble a handwritten, bound book. You may want to turn it into a PowerPoint presentation or a video presentation. You may want to make a display inside or outside the classroom on a bulletin board. The lesson that follows utilizes projecting the information from your computer to a screen or electronic whiteboard. If you are unable to project from your computer to a viewing screen, use chart paper or publishing paper to demonstrate to your students skills used in publishing and presenting a finished piece of writing.

Review the learning goals from the last session, and summarize the learning goals for today. *In our last session, we looked at focused edits. This means it's time for publishing and presenting. These are exciting times for writers as we get to take our drafts and embellish them with visuals, photographs, and interesting page layouts.*

Using the Mentor Text

■ Display a copy of the mentor text, and guide students to identify the visual and text supports this author has included, such as labeled diagrams, photographs, a table of contents, and a glossary.

■ *Published texts like this one rarely have only words. They are filled with interesting images, charts, and so on that support the writing.*

Modeling

■ *When presenting my writing for others, I first want to think about page layout and visuals that will help make the information understandable to a reader. A helpful trick is to place sections of your writing into text boxes on the computer. Once they are in a text box, you can move the writing around on the page, change the size and shape of the text box, insert photographs or diagrams, and so on. Watch as I take my cursor and drag the text box of my writing to a new position and enlarge the diagram that I downloaded from the Internet. Notice that I added a smaller text box at the right to serve as a caption for the diagram.*

TURN &TALK *Think about the way the page looks. Do you like the text boxes where I have placed them? What do you think about the size of the visual? What can I do to make this look really professional? Take a look at the books, magazines, and web pages you have been using for research, and see if they give you any helpful ideas about page layout.*

■ Continue modeling options with page layout and visuals, highlighting the way you can rearrange spaces and text boxes to create a visually pleasing arrangement. Also, show your writers how to add a page number in the footer section of the page so that their pages are automatically numbered.

WRITING and COACHING

■ For writers who are ready to present and publish, provide access to computers so they can begin to format interesting page layouts and experiment with rearranging text boxes on the page. If you don't have access to computers, have students experiment with page layouts using publishing paper.

■ For writers who may still be drafting or revising, assure them that they can think about their layout and presentation while they move forward with their writing.

■ Remind writers that flowcharts make great additions to the writing. If theirs are too large to include in their published works, they could use a digital camera or scanner to capture the image of the flowchart and digitally install them in their writing.

SHARING and REFLECTING

■ *Presenting and publishing is a very exciting time. This is when our hard work blossoms into a finished piece. This is a time when we can celebrate and take great pride in our hard work. To help us celebrate your explanations and the beautiful publications you have created, I have invited the class next door to join us and become your learning partners. When they arrive, each of you will have an opportunity to meet with at least two individuals from that class to share your learning and your publication.*

TURN &TALK *Partners, think together for a few minutes. Our guests are going to want to learn about both your topic and how to write an explanation. Make a plan and list the key points you want to share so that the guests you work with will learn about both the topic and the features of an explanation. What advice would you give them if they had to write their own?*

■ Gather the students' final pieces, and analyze their attempts at presentation. Identify writers who may need additional modeling as well as those who are ready for higher levels of sophistication. Use the rubrics on the *Resources* CD-ROM to track writing proficiencies and tailor future instruction.

TIP Some students may need additional support in considering page layout and would benefit from a small-group writing session in which you guide them in examining the pages of several nonfiction resources for ideas on layouts and visuals.

In the rainforest, there are layers of vegetation from the understories shade-loving plants to the sun-drenched leaves of the canopy.

At the lowest levels, there are mosses, trees and shrubs. Since there is little light and a lot of water the mosses are strong but bushes and small trees are weak.

Animal life at each level is different too. Tree climbers like monkeys can take advantage of the sunlit canopy. Ground-animals must adapt to the dark, wet surroundings or die.

Pass-Around Explanation

Summarize content with a group.

FEATURES

- Recaps understandings
- Uses subject-specific vocabulary
- Includes main idea and details

BEFORE THE LESSON

To model a pass-around explanation, you'll need to enlist three students to model with you. Prepare them for the modeled writing, and sit in a circle with the students, with the rest of the class in a larger circle around you.

FOCUSED MINILESSON

Today I want to explain important ideas about math. I want to use a special kind of explanation called a pass-around explanation. Just like its name sounds, I am going to pass the explanation around to teammates so we can work on it together. I have a group of four, and we're going to work together to explain why it's important to understand fractions. Gather your group around you. We will each start with a piece of paper with the same math question at the top: "Why is it important to understand fractions"?

The first thing we will each do in our group is write the same question at the top of our papers. Each member of the group will do the same thing: "Why is it important to understand fractions"?

Now we are each going to pass the paper to our right. To start the explanation, each of us will write our ideas about why it is important to understand fractions. I love sports, and fractions are part of my favorite games! There are two halves in a basketball game and four quarters in a football game. One inning is a ninth of a baseball game. Knowing fractions helps me understand sports better.

TURN & TALK *Now we're going to pass the papers around to our right again. We'll write reasons on our papers for why fractions are important. While we write in our group, turn to your partner and identify what you would write to answer the question.*

Let's take a look at my next explanation of what makes fractions important. Notice that I use the content-specific word "fraction." I am also including main ideas and details. The main idea is that fractions are important. I have added details about real-life situations in which fractions play a part.

Why is it important to understand fractions?

I love sports, and my favorite games are played in halves and quarters. Knowing fractions helps me understand these games better.

When I am dividing a pizza between my two brothers, and myself it's important to know which fraction of the pizza we should each get so that it's fair.

I've used fractions to divide food, like birthday cake. I think fractions are very important for food for other reasons, too. When cooking, for example, if you don't know the right fractions, you can really mess up a recipe! If a recipe calls for half a cup of milk but you don't know what a half is, you could add the wrong amount.

Modeled Writing

Pass the paper one more time, and show your modeled writing to students. *Notice how I am adding to the thoughts of the writers before me? That's an important reason why we pass the explanation around. We could write a list of reasons ourselves, but it's very important that we consider what the writer or writers before us have written as we add our thoughts to the explanation.*

TURN &TALK *Writers, take a look at this pass-around explanation. Four of us worked together to create this. Does it make sense? What do you think are the benefits of writing an explanation this way?*

Summarize the features: Place students in the groups in which they'll work to pass around an explanation. Have group members work together to generate features checklists for this kind of explanation. They can keep their features checklists handy as they work together.

WRITING and COACHING

Writers, let's try this with another question about math—"Why is it important to know geometric shapes? How do they affect our daily lives"? Work in your group to pass around an explanation that answers the question.

As students pass around their explanations, circulate to note those who need extra support with using domain-specific words and including details in their writing.

SHARING and REFLECTING

Sum it up! *Writers, you have learned how to use a unique collaboration tool! You included details that reflect your understanding of math concepts.*

TURN &TALK *Get ready to share your pass-around explanations with another group. As you share in your team, what features of these explanations will be important in your discussions? List them together.*

ASSESS THE LEARNING

Analyze the explanations to identify writers who need assistance in supporting main ideas with details and working with classmates to reflect on concepts.

SELF-ASSESSMENT

SELF-ASSESSMENT

Pass-Around Explanation

	YES	NO
1. **Recaps understandings**	☐	☐
2. **Uses subject-specific vocabulary**	☐	☐
3. **Includes main idea and details**	☐	☐

▶TAKE IT FORWARD

▸ Pass-around explanations are great tools for capturing main ideas and details in any content area. Use this tool throughout the year to give students the opportunity to reflect on content—and to reflect on teammates' responses.

▸ Students will enjoy using the pass-around format to write fictional stories or to create sequential nonfiction, such as biographies. Each student adds to the sequence as the paper comes around to him or her. The pass-around format is also well suited for response writing.

▸ You can have students regroup after the papers have traveled around the entire team to write paragraphs of summation. Encourage students to use linking words of summation as they craft summary paragraphs.

Dictionary of Terms

*Create a dictionary of terms
related to a concept.*

FEATURES

- Alphabetical arrangement
- Terms central to the subject
- Definition for each term
- Guide words at the top of each page
- Illustration or labeled diagram

BEFORE THE LESSON

Brainstorm a list of content-specific words and phrases on a chart. Cut them apart and work with students to place them in alphabetical order in a pocket chart. Choose a cluster for your modeled writing. Then, have students work in groups with clusters of words as they move into writing and coaching.

FOCUSED MINILESSON

Today I want to create a dictionary to capture important content about forces and motion. A dictionary may be many pages or a whole book. I am going to choose just four words from our chart for a page in a dictionary: mechanical advantage, potential energy, pulley, *and* ramp.

Words in dictionaries are in alphabetical order so that readers can easily find them. Watch as I write the words on sticky notes and then arrange them in alphabetical order along the side of the paper. I am leaving space to write a definition for each word.

I'll start the dictionary page by defining the first word. Watch as I leave a bit of space and then write the definition of mechanical advantage: *"the advantage created by a machine that allows people to do work while using less force." I'm not sure if this definition is enough information. I think to truly understand mechanical advantage, readers will need an example. I remember trying to lift bricks to make a path in my garden. It was hard to lift more than one brick by myself, but when I used a wheelbarrow, I could carry a whole load of bricks at once. That's a great example of mechanical advantage that my readers will understand.*

I have noticed that in most dictionaries, the entry words are bold. I am using a marker to make the words mechanical advantage *bold. Now my entry is complete!*

TURN & TALK *Writers, next I want to craft a definition for* potential energy. *What advice would you give me?*

Forces and Motion Dictionary

mechanical advantage   ramp

mechanical advantage	the advantage created by a machine that allows people to do work while using less force. Using a wheelbarrow to move a heavy load, for example, provides a mechanical advantage over lifting the heavy load yourself.
potential energy	the energy stored in an object because of its position. A boulder perched on the edge of a cliff has potential energy because of gravity.
pulley	a simple machine consisting of a wheel that rotates around a stationary axle. The outer rim of the pulley is grooved to accommodate a rope or chain.
ramp	an inclined plane. Movers use ramps to make it easier to move a load over a distance.

Continue the modeled writing of your dictionary page. Think aloud as you write definitions and examples. Showcase your thinking as you craft definitions that are simple, concise, and factual and that will help readers truly understand the words in the dictionary.

Dictionary pages have one additional feature to help readers navigate the pages—guide words. The guide word on the left of the page shows the first word on the page, and the guide word on the right shows the last word. Watch as I add mechanical advantage *and* ramp *to the top of the page.*

TURN &TALK *Writers, what features stand out as you look at the model? What might you suggest to make this dictionary page even better?*

Summarize the features: Display your modeled writing, and have students identify the features of a dictionary. As they list features, label these on the model. Students can copy this information into their writer's notebooks.

WRITING and COACHING

We only have one page of a dictionary for forces and motion. Work in a team to create another page. Choose words that you think are important for understanding forces and motion. Then, arrange the words in alphabetical order, and assign each team member a word or two. Double-check your definitions to be sure they are correct. Add examples to any words that might benefit from a little more explanation.

Provide dictionaries for students to use as mentor texts in writing definitions and examples.

SHARING and REFLECTING

Sum it up! *Your work is just like a published dictionary! Alphabetical entries with guide words help readers find just what they were looking for. And your accurate definitions include the kinds of examples that will make this content crystal clear for anyone using your dictionary.*

TURN &TALK *Writers, we are going to place our dictionaries in the media center's reference section. When we present our dictionaries, what features will we want to mention? List them with your team.*

ASSESS THE LEARNING

Analyze dictionary pages to check for alphabetical order, correct dictionary form, concisely worded definitions, and illustrative examples. Note students who are ready to add sophisticated features to their writing.

SELF-ASSESSMENT

SELF-ASSESSMENT
Dictionary of Terms

	YES	NO
1. Alphabetical arrangement	☐	☐
2. Terms central to the subject	☐	☐
3. Definition for each term	☐	☐
4. Guide words at the top of each page	☐	☐
5. Illustration or labeled diagram	☐	☐

▶ TAKE IT FORWARD

▸ Students may want to add illustrations or diagrams to their dictionary entries. Think aloud, for example, as you add a labeled diagram of a pulley to your modeled writing. Students may also want to download clip art and/or photographs to include in their dictionaries. Model how to label a diagram and how to write a caption for a photograph.

▸ Provide presentation options, such as electronic slide shows that feature a word and definition with a corresponding

visual on each slide or a picture dictionary for younger readers that includes words with simple definitions and striking visuals.

▸ As you begin a new unit of study, leave space on a bulletin board for a dictionary of terms to which students can contribute throughout the unit. They can write individual entries on large index cards so that they can be placed in alphabetical order as they are added to the display.

Partner Description: List Poem

Create a description in the form of a list poem.

Polar Bear

Huge

Blubbery

Predator

Weighs as much as ten grown men

Dedicated hunter

Master of icy survival

King of the Arctic

FEATURES

- Facts
- Physical description
- Precise nouns and adjectives
- Conclusion that supports sensory images
- Photograph with caption and labels

FOCUSED MINILESSON

Writers, today I want to describe a tadpole and a frog. It's fascinating to me that a tiny wriggling fish-like animal turns into a frog! I am going to create my description in the form of a poem. A poem can evoke images while also conveying facts. It's important when creating a nonfiction poem to use accurate details. My poem is going to hone in on the physical characteristics of tadpoles and frogs, because a tadpole undergoes striking changes to become a frog.

I want to start by writing about how tadpoles move. I could just write a line: "Tadpoles move in the water." But that's not very descriptive. A lot of animals move in the water! What's so special about how tadpoles move?

TURN &TALK *Writers, think together. Picture in your minds how tadpoles move. What verbs do you think best describe their movements? Identify a few and be ready to share.*

As I picture a tadpole in the water, I visualize it darting and wiggling. Watch as I write each of those precise verbs as a line in the poem: "Dart./Wiggle." Now I am going to write another line about tadpoles: "Tadpoles breathe through gills." Notice that I used a precise noun, gills. *I focused on gills because frogs are different than tadpoles. Once tadpoles grow into frogs, they don't use their gills to breathe anymore. I thought that was an interesting fact to emphasize.*

Now I am ready to focus on frogs! Model writing a few concise lines with precise nouns and adjectives to describe frogs. Emphasize that your lines, although descriptive and poetic, are still factual. Your poetry is nonfiction.

Writers, I want to conclude my poem with a strong sensory image. I am picturing a frog in my mind, and I'm particularly thinking about how different a frog is from a tadpole. I think it's interesting how long a frog can stay still, waiting for food to come by, and then dart its sticky tongue out to capture a fly. Watch as I continue with a line with a strong sensory image: "Statue on a rock."

Now my poem is complete. It's a list of words and phrases that describe the subject in an accurate way.

From Tadpole to Frog

Dart.

Wiggle.

Tadpoles breathe through gills.

Powerful legs.

Sticky tongue.

Statue on a rock.

Modeled Writing

TURN &TALK *Writers, evaluate my writing. How is a list poem different from other kinds of descriptions? What images do you think are particularly powerful? What other precise words might you use to describe tadpoles and frogs?*

Summarize the features: Display your list poem, and have students name features as you write them on a chart for students' reference.

WRITING and COACHING

Writers, it's your turn! Work with a partner to create a list poem of your own. Choose a subject, such as an animal, and then consider precise nouns and adjectives that will help you create a poem that is both factual and engaging.

As writers develop their poems, confer with individuals or small groups to support and scaffold understanding. Encourage students to experiment with the placement of lines, reading and rereading until they achieve the desired effect in their writing.

SHARING and REFLECTING

Sum it up! *Writers, your list poems contain precise nouns and adjectives that create sensory images while conveying facts. What an engaging way to concisely present information and create strong images!*

TURN &TALK *We are going to share our poems with your families in a poetry reading. What features should we highlight as we explain to our families how we created these poems? Think together as you and your partner list features.*

ASSESS THE LEARNING

Analyze list poems to identify writers who need extra support in using precise nouns and adjectives to support sensory images. Note students who may be ready to add more sophisticated features to their writing.

SELF-ASSESSMENT

SELF-ASSESSMENT
Partner Description: List Poem

	YES	NO
1. Facts	☐	☐
2. Physical description	☐	☐
3. Precise nouns and adjectives	☐	☐
4. Conclusion that supports sensory images	☐	☐
5. Photograph with caption and labels ⊙	☐	☐

▶TAKE IT FORWARD

▸ Students may want to add photographs to their poems. Show students how to add photographs to your list poem about tadpoles and frogs. Add captions to the photographs, and label the gills, writing the word *gills* and connecting it with a line to the gills in the photograph.

▸ Provide a variety of presentation options. Students may want to find music to complement readings of their poems. They could also create electronic slide shows with images that match their poems, or they could turn their list poems into posters to display in a class reading or writing corner.

▸ Encourage students to return to descriptions they have already written with an eye toward adding more precise nouns and adjectives. You may need to provide example sentences with "tired" words and have students work with you to replace them to work up to this task.

▸ Students may want to experiment with other poetic devices or poetic forms. They could insert a carefully crafted phrase that includes onomatopoeia or a simile or metaphor. They might choose a form for a poem other than a list, such as a haiku.

Scientific Description

Write a description based on science.

Tornado

A tornado is a powerfully twisting column of air that begins as a funnel cloud and then makes contact with the ground. During the funnel cloud stage, it begins as an invisible force of air that twists and spins in a narrow column. As the funnel cloud races across the ground, it collects water droplets, dust, and debris... evolving into a tornado.

The initial step is usually a thunderstorm. Warm, humid air rises upward and cools. The water droplets in the rising air condense and then grow bigger. As these droplets fall, they create downdrafts that meet the continuing warm updrafts and create the unique spinning action that defines a tornado. The internal speed of a tornado has been measured at up to 300 miles per hour.

FEATURES

- Precisely worded description
- Present-tense verbs
- Descriptive adjectives
- Boldface words
- Magnification or close-up
- Scientifically correct labels

BEFORE THE LESSON

Share books with students that offer rich descriptions of topics in science. You might share Walter Wick's *A Drop of Water,* any books by Seymour Simon (such as *The Heart* or *Animals Nobody Loves*), or Stephen Kramer's *Caves* or *Hidden Worlds.*

FOCUSED MINILESSON

Wasn't Seymour Simon's description of the human heart fascinating? I have a fresh perspective and understanding of the heart because of his description. Today I want to write a scientific description about the lungs. My goal is to use words that are precise and engaging to help my readers picture the lungs and understand what they do.

Watch as I begin by engaging my readers with a question. "You might take . . . without them"? This question is going to get my readers thinking. They'll want to know, "What do we take for granted? Why are they so essential?"

Next, I want to write that the lungs get bigger and get smaller—I could just say that, but that wouldn't be very engaging or descriptive. I want to use more precise verbs. When the lungs go in, they squeeze. When they go out, they inflate. Those words are so much more precise—they will help my readers picture what the lungs do. Watch as I capture these words in my next sentence: "Safely encased . . . every minute."

TURN &TALK *Writers, take a close look at this sentence. What adjectives do you notice? How do they create a vivid description?*

*There's another important thing to notice about scientific descriptions. Take a close look at the verbs in the sentence—*squeeze *and* inflate. *The verbs are in the present tense. That's because a description is timeless—lungs always squeeze and inflate. Now I'll continue writing, each sentence describing the lungs and what they do.*

Continue writing, thinking aloud as you use precise words, descriptive adjectives, and present-tense verbs to show the timeless quality of a scientific description.

TURN &TALK *Writers, evaluate the description together. What words and phrases do you think are particularly powerful? What suggestions would you make to strengthen this description even further?*

You might take them for granted, but what would you do without them? Safely encased inside the bones of your rib cage, your spongy, stretchy lungs tightly squeeze and re-inflate 15 to 25 times every minute. Airways lead from your mouth and nose to these twin organs. As the airways open, they take in oxygen-rich air. The lungs transfer that oxygen to waiting cells. As the lungs constrict, they push out waste—carbon dioxide. In. Out. Whoosh. Whoosh. The cycle repeats endlessly, with each breath you take.

Modeled Writing

Summarize the features: Have students use your modeled writing for reference as they note features of descriptions in their writer's notebooks. Encourage them to use the features lists as they create descriptions of their own.

WRITING and COACHING

There are many topics in science you can write about in a rich description, from a body organ or system to a misunderstood animal to an intriguing plant to a science "extreme"! Describe it in details with precise words. Remember that your description should be timeless, with present-tense verbs.

Gather small groups together for those students who need additional support. Students may benefit from examining the mentor text to note precise words. You might also need to provide support to help students differentiate between present-tense and past-tense verbs.

SHARING and REFLECTING

Sum it up! *Your descriptions capture the timeless feel of scientific descriptions with your present-tense verbs. And your precise words bring your topics to life for your readers!*

TURN &TALK *Get ready to share your description with a fellow scientist. Mark on your writing with sticky notes places where you deliberately inserted features of scientific descriptions so that you are ready to share. List the features together as you share your work.*

ASSESS THE LEARNING

Analyze the scientific descriptions to identify writers who may need additional instruction in using precise words and keeping verbs consistently in the present tense.

SELF-ASSESSMENT

SELF-ASSESSMENT Scientific Description	YES	NO
1. Precisely worded description	☐	☐
2. Present-tense verbs	☐	☐
3. Descriptive adjectives	☐	☐
4. Boldface words	☐	☐
5. Magnification or close-up	☐	☐
6. Scientifically correct labels	☐	☐

◐TAKE IT FORWARD

▸ Bold words emphasize important content. Show students mentor texts with bold words, and have them consider how they enhance reader understanding. Then, encourage them to strategically bold words in their descriptions. Remind them not to overdo—bold words lose their impact if too many are bold.

▸ Students may want to add close-ups or magnified views of content, in either photographs or sketches. In your model, for example, you could show a close-up of the air sacs in the lungs or the bronchial tubes. Be sure to build students'

understanding with a variety of mentor texts. Encourage them to use close-ups to intrigue readers, who will want to know "What is this?" Then, they'll read the description to find out more!

▸ Emphasize the importance of using scientifically correct labels for visuals and precise academic words in descriptions. Students may need to cull facts from research to write accurate descriptions about science. Show them how to take notes from reference sources to infuse accurate facts into their writing.

Summary with Headings

Summarize with a gist statement supported by details.

FEATURES

- Opening with a gist statement
- Headings
- Descriptive words
- Title
- Conclusion
- Linking words to connect ideas: *because, so, when, since, also, and, besides, in addition, for example*
- Photographs

FOCUSED MINILESSON

The Underground Railroad changed the lives of numerous slaves who made the dangerous journey from the South toward freedom in the North. Not only were the slaves in constant danger, but so were the people who assisted them. I want to answer the question "What was the Underground Railroad"? I am going to answer the question in a summary with headings. I'll write the question as a title.

To begin, I need a gist statement. A gist statement previews the content. It does so in a way that will engage readers so that they want to read on. Watch as I write a gist statement to begin my summary: "It is called a railroad, but it had no tracks or cars. It is called underground, but it was mostly above the ground. Yet the Underground Railroad ushered slaves from bondage to freedom."

TURN &TALK *Partners, read the gist statement together, and analyze it. How will this statement pull readers into the summary? What might you do to strengthen it?*

What was the Underground Railroad?

It is called a railroad, but it had no tracks or cars. It is called underground, but it was mostly above the ground. Yet the Underground Railroad ushered slaves from bondage to freedom.

Why It's Called Underground

The trackless Underground Railroad crisscrossed forests, rivers, roads, fields, and even networks of people's own homes—it wasn't really underground. Slaves escaping from the South and the brave "engineers" who shepherded them to freedom were breaking the law. That meant they had to stay out of sight, living "underground." Slaves were concealed in innovative ways. One abolitionist hired a hearse and disguised a group of slaves as a group at a funeral. Another slave, Henry "Box" Brown, was shipped from Richmond to Philadelphia in a box.

Modeled Writing

Now that I have readers wondering how the Underground Railroad got its name, I am ready to begin writing my summary. I want to organize it using headings. I mentioned in my gist statement the idea that the Underground Railroad wasn't really underground. That's a great place to start my summary with a heading, so I'll create a heading: "Why It's Called Underground." *Notice the heading is on its own line. I am going over the heading with a marker to make it stand out from the rest of the text.*

I could begin this section by simply writing "The Underground Railroad was not really underground." That's an accurate summary, and it's actually pretty interesting because it seems odd to name something in a way that doesn't accurately describe it! But I want my summary to be even more descriptive. I am going to use the adjective trackless *to describe this unique railroad. I will describe where it was so that readers will understand it wasn't underground. Watch as I write:* "The trackless Underground Railroad crisscrossed . . . it wasn't really underground."

Exploring the Rainforest

things that bite crawl near your feet. things that fly around you. Grab your bug spray! You are in the rain forest, a place with alot to explore.

orangutans Live in the forest

The orangutans travel through trees in search of food. collect everything they need from plants and trees mostly fruit. use sitiks and branches as tools

The madidi in brazil is a wild forest

The bright and colorful bird live here. sloths and wild pigs live here. poisonus snake, biting insects, & blood sucking flies.

Continue writing this part of the summary. Showcase your thinking as you stretch to discover descriptive words that will truly capture your readers' interest. Note how you carefully consider whether each detail in the section truly supports the heading to keep your summary cohesive and organized.

TURN &TALK *Writers, think together as you examine this summary. What text features are great organizational tools for readers? What descriptive words and details create vivid pictures of the Underground Railroad, and why it's called "underground"?*

Summarize the features: As students examine your modeled writing, have them name features of summaries with headings. List the features and then display them in a conspicuous spot for student reference.

WRITING and COACHING

We identified big ideas about the Underground Railroad, crafted a heading, and then wrote information to tell more about it. Now it's your turn. You can write more headings about the Underground Railroad to add to our summary, or you can start with a new topic related to the Civil War. If you start with a new topic, don't forget to include an intriguing gist statement!

Circulate as students work, tallying those who may need more scaffolded instruction on creating an intriguing gist statement or organizing information with headings. Note those who have mastered these strategies and can add sophistication to their summaries.

SHARING and REFLECTING

Sum it up! *Your gist statements got your summaries off to a strong start. Once you intrigued your readers and left them wanting more, you organized your writing to deliver information in a powerful way.*

TURN &TALK *You will be sharing your summaries with buddies in another class. Before we visit the other class, meet with a partner. Use the features list to check each other's work to ensure that all features are in place. Do you notice anything missing or anything that could be stronger? Offer your advice!*

ASSESS THE LEARNING

Have students use the self-assessment checklist to look for features before meeting with you in writing conferences. As you examine the writing together, look for opportunities to praise students' work to reinforce their strategy use as well as for opportunities to assist students in including elements of strong summaries organized with headings.

SELF-ASSESSMENT

SELF-ASSESSMENT **Summary with Headings**	YES	NO
1. Opening with a gist statement	☐	☐
2. Headings	☐	☐
3. Descriptive words	☐	☐
4. Title	☐	☐
5. Conclusion ⊘	☐	☐
6. Linking words to connect ideas: *because, so, when, since, also, and, besides, in addition, for example* ⊘	☐	☐
7. Photographs ⊘	☐	☐

▶TAKE IT FORWARD

▸ As students wrap up the headings that are previewed in their gist statements, work with them to craft strong conclusions. Model adding a conclusion that restates the gist statement or a conclusion that ends with a quotation or a fascinating fact culled from research.

▸ Photographs are strong additions to summaries of nonfiction. If you create your model on the computer, you might consider having a photograph on your desktop that you can copy and then paste into your model. Showcase your thinking as you consider where to place the photograph and what caption to write.

▸ You might add linking words to your model that connect ideas. Consider using linking words such as *because, so, when, since, also, and, besides, in addition*, and *for example*. Then, encourage students to follow your lead. As you model using the linking words, show students that some can be used in strong openings, while others can be used to combine shorter sentences. Display properly punctuated sentences with these linking words in a variety of positions for students' reference as they draft and revise.

Explanation Focused on Why

Why Do Polar Bears Have Blubber?

Polar bears have blubber, a thick layer of insulating fat, in all seasons of the year. In the spring and summer, the blubber is a fairly thin layer that has been depleted by winter survival. In the fall, blubber can grow to a depth of 3-4 inches as a polar bear prepares for winter. This thick wall of blubber is essential to survival as it keeps the bear warm through the intense cold of winter ice flows and icy waters. It also offers a sustained source of calories when the bear faces long periods without a meal during the harshest challenges of winter. Bears intuitively know that they must eat aggressively during the summer and fall when there is easier access to seals, their favorite food. Blubber is essential to winter survival.

Tell what happened and why.

FEATURES

- Focus on why
- Opening statement
- Linking words that add information: *in addition, it is also true that, because, in order to, furthermore*
- Labeled diagram
- Headings
- Conclusion

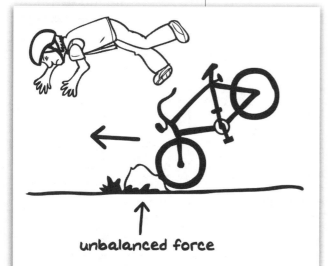

unbalanced force

You are riding your bicycle and—unfortunately—crash into a rock. The bicycle stops abruptly, yet you keep on going, flying through the air and landing a few feet away. What explains why this happens? Newton's First Law of Motion gives you the answer. Newton's First Law states that an object at motion continues in motion with the same speed and in the same direction unless acted upon by an unbalanced force. This means that most objects will just keep on doing what they're doing. If your bicycle were on a path free from obstructions, it would just keep on going. The rock in the road is an unbalanced force, acting on your bicycle. Newton's First Law of Motion is just one reason to wear a helmet on a bike ride. Furthermore, the Law of Motion explains why it's important to always wear a seatbelt in the car. Can you explain why—using Newton's Law?

Modeled Writing

FOCUSED MINILESSON

If I roll a ball and the ball hits another soccer player on my team, the ball stops rolling. What explains why the ball stops? Newton's First Law of Motion explains the ball's behavior. Today I want to write an explanation that focuses on why. My explanation will focus on Newton's Law.

I want to begin with an opening statement that helps readers understand why Newton's First Law of Motion affects them directly. So, I am posing a scenario in the opening. Watch as I begin: "You are riding your bicycle and—unfortunately—crash into a rock. The bicycle stops abruptly, yet you keep on going, flying through the air and landing a few feet away." *This opening captures my readers' attention. Many of us have had this happen or know someone to whom it's happened. And this statement sets up the readers for a scientific explanation focused on why.*

Now I want to get a little deeper into my explanation. Watch as I continue: "What explains why this happens? . . . keep on doing what they're doing."

TURN &TALK *Partners, take a look at the sentences I wrote. How do these sentences work together to answer the question "Why?"*

Continue modeling as you think aloud. Showcase your thinking as you focus your explanation on why. *Writers, I've written a sentence about why Newton's Law of Motion is one reason to wear a bike helmet. I want to add another example of how Newton's First Law affects our daily lives. When I add information this way, I often use a linking word to show that I am adding information. Watch as I begin with a linking word and add another example:* "Furthermore, the Law of Motion explains. . . ."

My explanation tells why Newton's First Law of Motion explains the stopping of the bicycle when it hits a rock. But I think a labeled diagram would add to my readers' understanding even more! Watch as I add a diagram. I am sketching a rock and a cyclist. The bicycle is running into the rock. I am drawing an arrow to show the direction in which the cyclist was headed. I am labeling the rock "unbalanced force." Notice that the bicycle is stopped—and the cyclist is in the air past the bike and headed toward the ground.

TURN &TALK *Writers, take a look at the explanation. How does the labeled diagram support the text? What features of the labeled diagram do you think are important to note to create labeled diagrams of your own?*

Summarize the features: Have partners work together to create features checklists for explanations focused on *why.* They can each create checklists on large sticky notes to have them on their desks as they write.

WRITING and COACHING

Writers, choose another science topic to explain with an emphasis on why. You could focus, for example, on why the sky looks blue from Earth or why there is so much more salt water on Earth than freshwater. Consider what linking words you might use to show that you are adding information in your writing.

As students work, circulate to be sure they are using linking words that add information and are focusing their writing on *why.* Provide the linking words resource for those students who need more assistance.

SHARING and REFLECTING

Sum it up! *Your explanations focused on* why, *with strong opening statements that engaged readers and let them know the focus of your writing. Labeled diagrams supported your texts to show* why *even more clearly than the text could show alone.*

TURN &TALK *You are going to share your explanations with your reading buddies. What features of an explanation focused on why make this kind of writing different from other explanations you've created? List a few ideas in your writer's notebooks before you get together with your buddies.*

ASSESS THE LEARNING

Assess students' work to note those writers who need support to write an explanation that is focused on *why* and uses linking words that add information. Note those who may need additional instruction on creating labeled diagrams.

SELF-ASSESSMENT

SELF-ASSESSMENT

Explanation Focused on Why

	YES	NO
1. Focus on why	☐	☐
2. Opening statement	☐	☐
3. Linking words that add information: *in addition, it is also true that, because, in order to, furthermore*	☐	☐
4. Labeled diagram	☐	☐
5. Headings	☐	☐
6. Conclusion	☐	☐

▶ TAKE IT FORWARD

▸ Conclusions will provide strong endings to students' work. Model how to create a conclusion that leaves the reader with an intriguing question to ponder. A conclusion can also end with a fascinating fact or a thought-provoking statistic or simply restate the opening in a new way.

▸ If students' explanations become long, they may want to add headings. An explanation on Newton's laws, for example, might have three headings—one for each law of motion. Encourage students to create headings to organize their ideas.

▸ Students may want to create question-and-answer books. Each page can be an intriguing question followed by an explanation that is focused on *why.* An electronic slide show could be crafted the same way, with each student responsible for creating two slides—one with a question, and one with a heading followed by an explanation.

Explanation Focused on Why and How

Write an explanation focusing on why and how.

> ### Wall of Water
> Imagine a 20-foot wave that weighs over 1000 pounds. This wave is the destroyer of cities, the flooder of towns, and the killer of thousands. This is a tsunami! First, continental plates shift under water causing an earthquake. Then, the vibrations underwater create a tsunami. Finally, the tsunami speeds to land destroying everything in its path.

FEATURES

- Focus on why and how
- Shows relationship between ideas
- Opening statement: gist
- Linking words to provide specific examples: *specifically, for example, in fact, of course, to illustrate, for instance*
- Headings
- Conclusion: restatement of the gist
- Quote

FOCUSED MINILESSON

Today I want to write an explanation that focuses on why *and* how. *I want to answer a question: How do carbohydrates and fats affect the body?*

Watch as I begin with a gist statement. I could simply start by saying "Today I want to explain carbohydrates and fats." *But that statement is boring! In a gist statement, I want to preview the content and the main ideas while also intriguing my readers. The purpose of the gist statement is to get them thinking about the content so they want to read on. Watch as I write:* "Are carbohydrates and fats the enemy? While . . . for you—they are essential."

TURN & TALK *Writers, take a close look at the gist statement and analyze it. How does the gist statement preview the content? How does the gist statement capture readers' attention?*

Carbohydrates and fats affect the body in different ways, and they are both big topics. I want to focus first on carbohydrates, so I am going to indicate that I am beginning a section by creating a heading. Watch as I write "Carbohydrates" *as my first heading. Now I can move to another line to begin writing about carbohydrates:* "Almost every food . . . carbohydrates." *My readers may not know what foods are rich with carbohydrates, so I will list a few. To show that I am providing examples of carbohydrates, I want to use linking words that indicate examples. Watch as I use the phrase* for example *to highlight certain foods that contain carbohydrates:* "Fruits, vegetables, milk, and sugar, for example, are rich with carbohydrates."

Now I am explaining how, telling how carbohydrates affect the body: "Both simple carbohydrates . . . are better than others." *Even though I've explained how, I am not satisfied that I've explained why some carbohydrates are better than other ones. Watch as I add a specific example starting with another linking word:* "To illustrate. . . ."

Are carbohydrates and fats the enemy? While many diet books seem to blame both of these substances for poor health and fitness, fats and carbohydrates in moderation are not only acceptable for you--they are essential.

Carbohydrates

Almost every food you put in your mouth has carbohydrates. Fruits, vegetables, milk, and sugar, for example, are rich with carbohydrates. Both simple carbohydrates, like the sugar in your sugar bowl, and complex carbohydrates, like the carbohydrates in breads, crackers, and rice, break down in the blood stream to create energy-giving sugar. But some carbohydrates are better than others. To illustrate, the sugar from a lollipop will give you energy for a short time. The sugar from fruit will keep you feeling more full and satisfied for longer, and fruit has fiber and vitamins. In fact, doctors are linking big jumps in sugar in the bloodstream to heart disease and diabetes.

Modeled Writing

Finish your model, using another linking word to provide a specific example of the impact that doctors believe excessive carbohydrates may have on the body.

TURN &TALK *Writers, think together as you analyze the writing. What linking words indicate examples? How does this summary tell both why and how?*

Summarize the features: Have students contribute features for a list of explanations focused on *why* and *how*. Be sure the list is in a visible place as students focus on explanations of their own.

WRITING and COACHING

Have students craft other explanations related to health issues. They may want to explain, for example, how the sun can damage the skin or why it is necessary to regularly brush and floss teeth. Point to your model as you remind students to begin with a heading formatted as a question. Provide research time or references as needed.

As students work, use a running checklist to note those who have mastered the features and those who may benefit from scaffolded instruction. You might pull together a small group for instruction on gist statements, closing statements, or linking words that sum up.

SHARING and REFLECTING

Sum it up! *Your explanations focused on* how *and* why *started with questions. Then, you answered those questions using powerful facts along with linking words that organized ideas for your readers.*

TURN &TALK *As you share your explanations with your reading buddies in fourth grade, they may want to know how you created them. Before you meet with your buddies, jot down a features list in your writer's notebooks. What features do you want to be prepared to share?*

ASSESS THE LEARNING

As you read students' explanations, determine who may need further assistance with formatting headings as questions and answering those questions in their explanations. Note those who are ready to take it forward with additional features.

SELF-ASSESSMENT

SELF-ASSESSMENT

Explanation Focused on Why and How

	YES	NO
1. Focus on why and how	☐	☐
2. Shows relationship between ideas	☐	☐
3. Opening statement: gist	☐	☐
4. Linking words to provide specific examples: *specifically, for example, in fact, of course, to illustrate, for instance*	☐	☐
5. Headings	☐	☐
6. Conclusion: Restatement of the gist ☺	☐	☐
7. Quote ☺		

⏵TAKE IT FORWARD

▸ Students may want to add closure to their explanations with strong conclusions. Provide examples of strong closings from mentor texts. Show a variety of ways to close—a powerful statistic, a quotation, a question, or a restatement of the gist.

▸ Students may do research to craft their explanations. Encourage them to use quotes from experts to support their explanations. Show them how to properly punctuate a quotation and credit the source, for example, "Nutritionist Ima B. Healthway asserts, 'Children's diets should consist mostly of vegetables, fruits, whole grains, and lean sources of protein.'"

▸ Encourage students to return to their writing folders to find explanations that would benefit from the infusion of linking words that provide specific examples. Show students how you revise a piece of previously completed writing by using a caret mark to insert new words and sentences.

Diagram with Key

Label a line drawing to convey information.

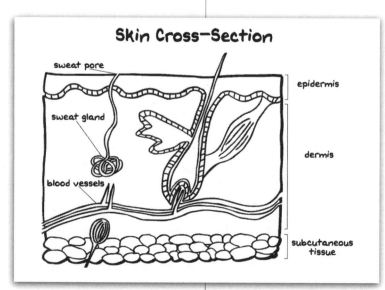

FEATURES

- Line drawing
- Heading
- Labels
- Arrows to link labels with diagram
- Key
- Color coding
- Caption
- Concluding paragraph with linking words that show summation or addition of information

FOCUSED MINILESSON

Today I want to create a labeled diagram of an important organ—the skin. A labeled diagram is a great way to capture information visually, especially of things that we cannot see easily. My diagram will be a special kind of diagram called a cross section. It will look almost as if I was able to take a piece of skin and then look at it sideways and close up!

It's important for diagrams to be factually accurate, so I am creating this diagram based on research I've done about the skin. I've done research on skin so that I know my diagram will be accurate. It's important for diagrams to be backed up with research. Watch as I start by drawing a piece of skin from a sideways view. This shows the top layer of the skin and the layers that would be below the surface if we could see them.

Now it's time to draw the parts of the skin and label them. One of the skin's most important functions is to help regulate body temperature by sweating. Because this is so important, I am drawing a sweat pore and a sweat gland. The sweat gland is under the surface. We can't normally see this. That's why a cross section is perfect for capturing the important structures of the skin. I am adding labels for both parts. Notice that I am not writing long descriptions, like "The sweat pore is an opening in the skin that allows the skin to cool off when the body is too warm." I just wrote "sweat pore" and drew an arrow from the pore to the structure in the diagram.

TURN &TALK *Writers, I want to show the blood vessels under the skin. Give me some advice. What should I do to clearly show my readers the location of the blood vessels?*

Continue labeling the diagram, writing clear labels and thinking aloud as you draw arrows from labels to the structures of the skin. Be careful to include only essential parts. Showcase your thinking as you determine which structures are most important to viewers in helping them understand the skin and how it functions.

The skin has three different layers. Instead of just labeling the layers, I want to add color. This will make the layers stand out so they are clear to readers. First, I need to

Modeled Writing

create a key. Then, readers will know which layer is which based on the colors. Watch as I create a key. In this column, I'm writing the colors I will use. In this column, I'm writing the body parts. Looking at my key, the epidermis will be pink. Watch as I return to the diagram, draw a line that indicates the relative size and location of the epidermis, and color the epidermis pink. Continue using the key to color code the layers of the skin.

TURN &TALK *Writers, evaluate my diagram. What about it makes it easy to understand? If you were going to create a similar diagram, how would you ensure that the information on the diagram is accurate?*

Summarize the features: Have students work with partners to create features checklists for diagrams with keys. Be sure they keep their checklists handy as they create their diagrams.

WRITING and COACHING

Create a labeled diagram with a key to create a visual snapshot of another body part, such as the brain, the heart, or even a diagram of the tongue's taste centers. Include labels, linking them to the sketch with lines. If you color code your diagram, be sure to include a key.

Confer with writers who need support to create labeled diagrams. Remind them to create clear labels and to link the labels with the sketch. Be sure that colors don't obscure important details.

SHARING and REFLECTING

Sum it up! *Diagrams are powerful tools to show information at a glance, and you created diagrams with clear labels connected to your sketches. Color coding added another visual cue to assist your readers in understanding parts of the body.*

TURN &TALK *You are going to take your diagrams home to share with your families. Get ready to tell your families about your diagrams. What features will you share? Make a list on a sticky note to attach to your diagrams.*

ASSESS THE LEARNING

Analyze labeled diagrams to determine writers who may need extra support to create labeled diagrams and to make accurate keys connected to their visuals. Some students may be ready to sum up information in their diagrams with summative paragraphs.

SELF-ASSESSMENT

SELF-ASSESSMENT **Diagram with Key**	YES	NO
1. Line drawing	☐	☐
2. Heading	☐	☐
3. Labels	☐	☐
4. Arrows to link labels with diagram	☐	☐
5. Key	☐	☐
6. Color coding	☐	☐
7. Caption ☉	☐	☐
8. Concluding paragraph with linking words that show summation or addition of information ☉		

▶TAKE IT FORWARD

▸ Show students labeled diagrams in various resources, and ask what additional features students notice. They may notice captions. Discuss the characteristics of captions, and then add a caption to your model: *The skin is the body's first defense against intruders.*

▸ Think aloud as you model writing a paragraph based on the diagram of the skin. Use linking words that sum up or add information, such as *in brief, in summary, throughout, in all, in addition, on the whole, to sum up, overall, finally, to conclude, to recap,* and *in the end.* Example: *To sum up, the*

skin protects the body and helps regulate its temperature. It's the body's largest organ!

▸ Have students examine a variety of nonfiction texts and list various uses for diagrams that they notice. They can compile a running list and examples on a wall of diagrams to use as inspiration for their own work—labeled diagrams in science experiments or for science topics, diagrams to make or build something, maps with keys, diagrams of playing fields for games, and so on.

VISUAL LITERACY

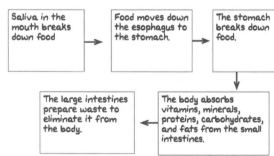

Flowchart

Use a flowchart to show how the body processes food.

FEATURES

- Title
- Boxes with arrows to show time/order
- Caption
- Explanations
- Summative paragraph to explain the process
- Linking words to show time/order

FOCUSED MINILESSON

The parts of the digestive system move food through a sequence of events that nourish our bodies. Today I want to create an explanation of how our bodies process food. I am going to create a flowchart, a visual snapshot of a process. A flowchart is a great tool to show any sequence at a glance. Watch as I begin with a title so that my readers will know the purpose of the flowchart: "How does the body process food?"

Now I can begin the flowchart. Watch as I draw a box on the far left side of the paper. I want to leave plenty of room for the rest of the events. In the box, I am writing the first part of the process: "Saliva in the mouth breaks down food." Notice that my writing is pretty simple and straightforward. I want to create a visual that a reader can easily scan, so I am not focusing on rich description. Instead, I am making sure that each part of the process is accurate and that I put the boxes in the correct order from beginning to end. Now I am drawing an arrow, creating another box, and then writing the next part of the explanation in the second box: "Food moves down the esophagus to the stomach."

TURN &TALK *Partners, think together. The next part of the process happens in the stomach, where the stomach breaks down the food into smaller pieces. Give me some advice! How should I reflect this part of the process in the flowchart?*

Continue modeling and thinking aloud as you complete the flowchart. Demonstrate how you enclose each step in a box, writing it succinctly. You connect the boxes to show the order. You might show a revision after placing the box in the wrong order. Emphasize the importance of checking your work to be sure the steps in the process are in the correct order in your flowchart.

Writers, my flowchart captures the steps in food's journey through the body! Now I want to write a paragraph to summarize the information. This process is sequential, so I am going to focus on using linking words that show time order to keep my writing organized. Right at the beginning, I am going to use a linking word: "As food enters the mouth, . . ."

How does the body process food?

```
Saliva in the    →   Food moves down   →   The stomach
mouth breaks         the esophagus to       breaks down
down food            the stomach.           food.
                                               │
                                               ↓
The large intestines  ←  The body absorbs
prepare waste to          vitamins, minerals,
eliminate it from         proteins, carbohydrates,
the body.                 and fats from the small
                          intestines.
```

As food enters the mouth, teeth grind up the food and saliva breaks it down, turning it into a liquidy mixture. Then the tongue pushes the food toward the esophagus, a stretchy tube that reaches down toward the stomach. Chemicals in the stomach further break down the food. From the small intestines, the body absorbs life-giving nutrients, like vitamins, minerals, and proteins. Meanwhile, the materials the body does not need move to the large intestines, where they will be eliminated.

Modeled Writing

Continue writing your paragraph, using a variety of linking words to show time order. Point out that because you are writing a paragraph, your sentences are enriched with deeper description—the small boxes don't confine you. *Writers, I have a flowchart that gives an at-a-glance view of a process and a paragraph that sums up the flowchart with more detail. Together, these elements explain a process so that readers can understand it.*

TURN &TALK *Writers, take a look at the paragraph and the flowchart. Do they reflect the same content? What features of a flowchart will you need to remember to create flowcharts of your own?*

Summarize the features: Have pairs work together to list the features of flowcharts in their writer's notebooks. Check their lists to be sure they've included all the features. They can save their lists as they develop flowcharts in the future.

WRITING and COACHING

A flowchart can capture a variety of sequences and processes. Use a flowchart to show how another body system works. How does the skeletal system help the body move? How does the circulatory system bring oxygen to your blood? Don't forget to put each step in a box and use arrows to show the flow of the steps. Then, write a paragraph to explain the process.

As writers create flowcharts, confer with them to be sure they are writing concise sentences in each box. Distribute the Temporal Words to Show Sequence resource for students who need support as they write their summative paragraphs.

SHARING and REFLECTING

Sum it up! *Your flowcharts are visuals that offer a snapshot of a process from beginning to end. As you wrote your summative paragraphs, you masterfully chose linking words to explain how a process works.*

TURN &TALK *Get ready to share your flowcharts with partners. First, review the features lists. Be sure you have everything in place in both your flowcharts and paragraphs. Then, you'll be ready to talk with your partners about your work.*

ASSESS THE LEARNING

Provide writers with the Self-Assessment Checklist from the *Resources* CD-ROM so they can review their work. Then, have them record their flowcharts in their writer's notebooks as a resource for other flowcharts they may create in the future.

SELF-ASSESSMENT

SELF-ASSESSMENT **Flowchart**	YES	NO
1. Title	☐	☐
2. Boxes with arrows to show time/order	☐	☐
3. Caption	☐	☐
4. Explanations	☐	☐
5. Summative paragraph to explain the process	☐	☐
6. Linking words to show time/order	☐	☐

▶ TAKE IT FORWARD

▸ Students can use flowcharts throughout the year to record various processes such as the steps in a science experiment, the events that happen to trigger an earthquake, important events in the life of a historical figure—any topic that flows in sequential order.

▸ Have students revisit other explanations they have written to revise for strong sequential order using linking words that reflect time. The list of temporal words from the *Resources* CD-ROM can serve as references as they write.

▸ Students might examine informational texts with sequential details and create flowcharts that could be inserted into those resources. Take the opportunity to discuss with students how visuals and text work together to assist readers in fully understanding ideas.

Investigation

Use a magazine-style layout to focus on Colonial America.

FEATURES

- Magazine-style layout: gutter spill with a visual
- Headings
- Text boxes
- At least one definition
- Bulleted lists
- Primary source visuals and quotations

BEFORE THE LESSON

Gather high-quality nonfiction magazines to share layouts with students. If possible, find examples in which a large visual image spills over the center gutter.

FOCUSED MINILESSON

I enjoy opening the pages of these nonfiction magazines to look at the amazing layouts! The text boxes, the headings, the visuals captivate me right away. All these elements come together to show information in an inviting way. Today I want to share my learning about Colonial America with a similar format—a layout like I'd see in a great magazine.

Colonial America is a huge topic! Before I begin, I want to narrow it down a bit, because Colonial America could fill up all of a very large magazine. I think I'll focus on daily life and how it was different in each of the three sections of colonies. A then and now feature will be fun, too, to show how life was different back then than what we know today.

I am going to begin with a title to anchor the investigation. Watch as I write: "What was it like in the colonies?" Notice that I center this title across the entire piece of paper. If this piece of paper were like the pages in a book, it would have a fold line down the middle. The title goes across that line.

I want to start with a map of the colonies. I am leaving space for a map and a key. The key will be color coded to show which are the New England colonies, which are the middle colonies, and which are the southern colonies. I need to include a definition for my readers. What if they don't know that the colonies were divided that way? I am leaving a space here for a bulleted list of the colonies that were part of each section.

TURN &TALK Now it's time to plan the rest of the investigation. Think together. How would you organize this investigation?

I like the idea of dividing the middle of the investigation into thirds, with a big text box devoted to each part of the colonies. In each text box, I can include vivid descriptions of what life was like in that part of the colonies, including jobs, economics, religion, and so on. I have some pieces of clip art I can place in each section. For the southern colonies, a photograph of a plantation would be a great idea since that was such a big part of the economy. Showing a busy harbor would be a great addition to the New England colonies.

Continue modeling and thinking aloud as you plan out the space. Showcase your thinking about headings

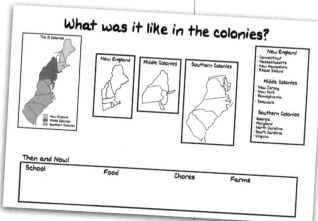

Modeled Writing

and visuals. Show that you move elements around in the space for the best possible layout. Consider where you might add another definition to clarify information for your readers.

TURN &TALK *Writers, take a look at my investigation plan. How does this convey information differently than, say, a written summary with headings? What do you think makes this powerful?*

Summarize the features: As you display the investigation plan or a completed investigation, have students note its features. Keep a running list, and make that list accessible for students as they craft their own investigations.

WRITING and COACHING

Colonial America has a host of topics that are ripe for investigations! Now it's your turn to choose another aspect of Colonial America for the focus of an investigation. Be sure to plan before you write. Think about attention-getting headings, eye-catching visuals, and a layout that can crackle with excitement to engage and interest your readers.

Support students as they create their investigations. You might pull together a small group that needs extra support and ask them questions such as *This is a great visual that adds information. Near what text will you place it? This text box has great information, but it needs a heading. What heading will draw your readers' attention?*

SHARING and REFLECTING

Sum it up! *Writers, your investigations are exciting **and** informative! Text boxes, visuals, and headings all work together to deliver ideas about Colonial America in an innovative way.*

TURN &TALK *Suppose we were going to display these investigations in our media center. What would we want to tell our media center about them? Work with your partners to make a features list in your writer's notebooks.*

ASSESS THE LEARNING

Analyze the investigations to note those students who need extra support to create effective layouts with text boxes, headings, and visuals. Note which students may be ready to add more sophisticated features to their work.

SELF-ASSESSMENT

SELF-ASSESSMENT **Investigation**	YES	NO
1. Magazine-style layout: gutter spill with a visual	☐	☐
2. Headings	☐	☐
3. Text boxes	☐	☐
4. At least one definition	☐	☐
5. Bulleted lists ⊙	☐	☐
6. Primary source visuals and quotations ⊙	☐	☐

▷TAKE IT FORWARD

▸ Introduce bulleted lists by adding a list to your model. Point out that they provide information at a glance. Bulleted lists need not be complete sentences. They can be quick bites of easy-to-scan information.

▸ Introduce primary sources, such as authentic photographs and documents. Be sure students credit their sources. Show them how to create bibliographies listing sources and their authors.

▸ Quotations are powerful additions to investigations. Model how to choose a quotation, enclose it in quotation marks, and credit the speaker. Set the quotation in a text box. If

students create their investigations electronically, they may put a different color background in a text box with a quotation or set the quotation in a unique font.

▸ Help students hone their research skills. Encourage them to use multiple resources to verify information they find. Point out that when using the Internet to research, students need to determine whether websites are reliable. A website from a museum, for example, is considered a reliable source; a website developed by another classroom may contain misinformation.

Taking It Forward: Personal Writing Projects

. . . .

After they have had the opportunity to work through the model unit and lessons in this section, cement your students' understandings about informational writing by having them complete one or more *personal* writing projects on topics of their choice. This is an important follow-up to the model unit because it allows students to apply their new understandings to their own writing lives based on personal interests.

For example, the teaching processes outlined in the model unit on human body systems and organs can easily be adapted to personal projects on a variety of topics and in a variety of forms. If students have trouble deciding what to write about, you might want to suggest topics and forms such as the ones that follow. Otherwise, give students the freedom to choose the topics they find most interesting—provided you deem them appropriate.

Possible Topics for Informational Writing

Science	**Social Studies**
Insects	Community resources
Birds	Cities
Reptiles	States
Plants	Regions
Trees	Countries
Life cycles	Cultures
Deserts	Careers
Oceans	Holidays
Ecosystems	Clothing
Rocks	Food
Pollution	Transportation
Machines	Heroes
Weather	Historical events
Matter and energy	Social issues
Forces and motion	

Possible Forms for Informational Writing

Lists	Signs	Labeled diagrams
Tables	Poems	Illustrations
Charts	Letters	Websites
Flowcharts	Dictionary	Glossary
Posters	Magazine articles	Travel guides
Reports	Slide presentations	Field guides
Documentaries	Descriptions	Scientific observations
Summaries	Explanations	Information equations

Planning and Implementing Personal Writing Projects

Your students will need preparation, coaching, prompting, and varying amounts of support as they move through their own personal explorations. The ten-session structure presented in the model unit may be too long for personal projects that assume less time spent on instruction and modeling. Give students the time they need to fully develop their topics and to move through the stages of the writing process, but don't be surprised if many students require fewer than ten sessions.

Use the following tips and strategies as needed to ensure each student's success.

Before the Personal Projects:

▸ Help students select topics that they are interested in, and provide research materials if needed.

▸ Continue to use information you gather from the Individual Assessment Record or your Ongoing Monitoring Sheet to provide specific instruction in whole-class, small-group, and individual settings as needed. Use the Daily Planner to lay out each day's lesson.

During the Personal Projects:

▸ Give students the personal checklists from the *Resources* CD-ROM to use as samples for creating their own checklists. A blank checklist can be found on the *Resources* CD-ROM and in the Resources section at the end of this book. Explain to the students that you will also be checking to see if they have included key features on the checklist.

▸ If needed, begin each session with a focused minilesson. Tailor the suggested minilesson to suit the needs of your students.

▸ Continue to provide high-quality mentor texts. Display mentor texts prominently, and allow students time to read them before they begin to write their own. Continue to call students' attention to the features list created during the model unit.

▸ You may want to write your own text along with the students as you did during the model unit to provide an additional model.

▸ Have writing partners conference with each other often to check one another's work for sense and clarity.

▸ As students work independently on their writing and illustrations, note those who are struggling and bring them together for small-group instruction. Use the Individual Assessment Record and/or the Ongoing Monitoring Sheet to assist in tailoring instruction to the needs of your students.

▸ Students who seem very confident and who have clearly grasped all of the concepts taught so far can be brought together in a small group to extend their understanding to more challenging work.

After the Personal Projects:

▸ Be sure to give students opportunities to share and celebrate their writing projects.

▸ Compare students' final writing products with their earlier attempts in order to evaluate their growth as writers.

▸ Distribute copies of the Student Self-Reflection Sheet (on the *Resources* CD-ROM). Students will benefit greatly from the chance to reflect on their progress and to hear their classmates' feedback.

▸ Reflect on the strengths and challenges of implementing the personal projects. How might the process be adjusted to maximize student learning?

▸ Look at common needs of the class, and address these when students are working on future projects.

Procedural Writing Projects

Procedural or instructional texts tell the reader how to make something, do something, complete a process, or accomplish any task that requires several steps. Students are most likely to encounter procedural text in the form of directions on schoolwork, instructions on how to use something, or procedures for scientific experiments. Procedural text may appear in many formats, including directions on schoolwork or forms, rules for games, recipes, map directions, care directions, instructions for assembly, and user guides.

CONTENTS

EXTENDED WRITING UNIT

▸ Using Science Equipment

POWER WRITES

▸ Instructions

▸ Partner Explanation

▸ Problem-Solving Guide

▸ Oral Presentation

▸ Partner Line Graph

The Big Picture

During the model unit that follows, students will write a procedure for using a piece of science equipment. The mentor text, "How to Use a Telescope," provides a model of the structure and features of a great procedural text. Students begin by observing features of the mentor text and then work in pairs or small groups to gather and organize information about how to use a piece of science equipment of their choice, using their research notebooks and a procedural text graphic organizer. (You will probably want to remove using a telescope or graduated cylinder from the list of choices so students will not be tempted to copy from the mentor text or your modeled writing.) From their notes, students then write their procedures. They revise, add labeled visuals, edit, and publish their procedures in a format of their choice. Finally, they share their publications with classmates and reflect on what they have learned about writing a procedure.

Session	Focused Minilesson	Writing and Coaching	Sharing and Reflecting
1	Identifying the purpose and features of a procedural text	Begin to research and take notes in your research notebook.	What did you learn about your science equipment? Share information with a partner.
2	Writing an introduction	Work in pairs to locate and note ideas to include in an introduction.	Share your introduction with a partner, and ask for feedback.
3	Turning notes into running text	Begin to draft sentences from notes.	Talk with a partner about how you crafted sentences from your notes. What strategies helped you? What was challenging?
4	Organizing sentences in time order	Use time-order words and phrases to show sequence.	Share sections you worked on today. What time-order words did you use? Did you number steps? What strategies helped you most?
5	Using precise domain-specific words	Add precise scientific terms and definitions to the procedure.	Share a section where you used precise vocabulary. Do you have suggestions for your partner?
6	Adding labeled diagrams	Add diagrams and labels that match the text.	Share diagrams with a partner, and offer feedback.
7	Revising to create a satisfying conclusion	Revise or draft to create a strong conclusion.	Share conclusions with a partner working on another topic, and offer feedback.
8	Revising for verb tense	Use precise present-tense verbs.	Share drafts with a partner, and focus on the verbs. Do you have suggestions for your partner?
9	Using an editing checklist	Edit for one point at a time, using a checklist.	How did using an editing checklist help you?
10	Publishing the procedures	Format page layouts.	Share procedures with learning partners. What advice would you give for writing a procedure?

Assessing Students' Needs

The model unit is designed to teach students about the structure and features of a specific type of procedural writing as they apply basic writing strategies. Each of the focused minilessons provides you with suggested demonstrations, but you may want to tailor your instruction based on the common needs of your own students. You can assess students' strengths and needs during each unit, in an additional session beforehand, or by analyzing student work that you already have on hand.

Formal Pre-Assessment: After a basic introduction to each writing purpose and form as well as a review of various examples, have students write in the same form about a topic they already know a lot about. Encourage students to use as many of the features of the particular writing form as possible, but don't provide direct support. The goal here is to find out how much students already know about the writing purpose and form so you can tailor your teaching accordingly.

Experimentation in Research Notebooks: You might want to stop short of a formal pre-assessment and instead ask students to experiment with writing in their research notebooks at the end of the first session. This exercise may be less unnerving for some students and should yield enough information to form the basis of your pre-assessment.

Looking Back at Previous Work: Whether you choose to assess students' writing skills before beginning an Extended Writing Unit or during the first session, we recommend that you also consider unrelated writing projects that you've already collected from students. These may not reveal much about your students' ability to write a coherent procedure, for example, but should tell you a great deal about their grasp of writing conventions and other traits such as focus, organization, voice, and sentence fluency. Depending on how much student work you already have on hand, you might not have to devote any class time to pre-assessment.

Focusing on Standards

Before introducing this model unit, carefully review the key skills and understandings below so you can keep the lesson objectives in mind as you teach, coach, and monitor students' growth as writers of procedural texts.

KEY SKILLS AND UNDERSTANDINGS: PROCEDURAL WRITING GRADE 5
Purpose
Understands the purpose for writing a procedural piece
Ideas/Research
Reflects research and planning
Includes facts and details from research
Gathers information from multiple sources
Lists/cites sources
Organization/Text Features
Includes a title that tells what the procedure is
Includes a clear introduction
Presents steps or tips in sequence
Includes labeled diagrams that support the text
May include a conclusion
Language/Style
Puts information in his or her own words
Uses powerful present-tense verbs
Uses specific vocabulary and precise details
Uses words and phrases that signal the passage of time
Demonstrates sentence variety and fluency
Conventions and Presentation
Begins sentences with capital letters
Uses correct end punctuation
Uses appropriate spelling
Edits using an editing checklist
Creates clear and interesting page layouts, depending on form

This list is the basis for both the Individual Assessment Record and the Ongoing Monitoring Sheet shown in Figure 1.1. (Both forms can be found in the Resources section at the back of this book and also on the *Resources* CD-ROM.) Use the Individual Assessment Record if you want to keep separate records on individual students. The Ongoing Monitoring Sheet gives you a simple mechanism for recording information on all your students as you move around the class, evaluating their work in progress. Use this information to adapt instruction and session length as needed.

At the end of these and any additional units you may teach on procedural writing, compare students' final publications with their initial attempts at writing in the text type. Use the Ongoing Monitoring Sheet and/or the Individual Assessment Record to record students' growth as writers.

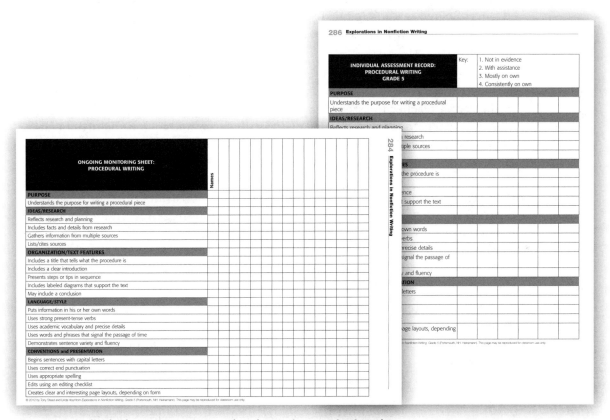

Figure 1.1 Individual Assessment Record and Ongoing Monitoring Sheet

Planning and Facilitating the Unit

Students will need preparation, coaching, prompting, and support as they move through this and other Extended Writing Units. Use the following tips and strategies as needed to ensure each student's success.

Before the Unit:

▸ When planning your teaching, bear in mind that each lesson in the model unit that follows is designed to be completed in one session. However, you will likely find that your students need more time for certain activities. Take the time you need to adequately respond to the unique needs of your students, and remember that they will likely progress through the writing process at their own pace.

▸ Begin building background knowledge about the text type and writing topics in advance. Shared reading, guided reading, and read-aloud experiences as well as group discussions will ensure that students are not dependent exclusively on their own research.

▸ For the research component, you may want to gather suitable books, magazine articles, encyclopedia entries, and websites in your classroom or work with the media center teacher to assemble a collection in advance. Make sure the research materials you gather are at a range of difficulty levels and include plenty of text features such as close-up photographs, captions, bold headings, and diagrams.

During the Unit:

▸ Begin each session with a focused minilesson to demonstrate the traits of writing the particular type of text you're exploring. Tailor the suggested minilesson to suit the needs of your students. The mentor texts on the *Resources* CD-ROM and in the *Book of Mentor Texts* are models you can use to show students the structure and features of each text type. You may want to use other mentor texts to assist you with your demonstrations.

▸ Be sure to model note-taking for students as you think aloud about information in reference materials. Use chart paper and sticky notes to capture your thinking, and display the models prominently as students work on their own research and note-taking.

▸ As students work independently on their writing and publishing, note those who are struggling and bring them together for small-group instruction. Use the Individual Assessment Record and/or the Ongoing Monitoring Sheet to assist in tailoring instruction to the needs of your students.

▸ Students who seem very confident and who have clearly grasped all of the concepts taught so far can be brought together in a small group to extend their understanding to more challenging work.

▸ Provide templates for students who need extra support when writing. You'll find a variety of graphic organizers on the *Resources* CD-ROM from which to choose.

After the Unit:

▸ Be sure to give students opportunities to share and celebrate their individual writing projects.

▸ Distribute copies of the Personal Checklist for Procedural Writing as shown in Figure 1.2. (This form can be found on the *Resources* CD-ROM and in the Resources section at the end of this book). Students will benefit greatly from the chance to reflect on their progress during the unit and to hear their classmates' feedback.

▸ Compare students' final writing products with pre-assessments and past work to evaluate their growth as writers of procedural texts.

▸ Reflect on the strengths and challenges of implementing this series of lessons. How might it be adjusted to maximize student learning?

▸ Look at common needs of the class, and address these when planning future explorations or when using the Power Writes.

Personal Checklist for Procedural Writing

Process Reflections:

Research:
I used the following resources in gathering facts: _____

Drafting:
I solved the following problems in my writing: _____

Revising:
When revising, I focused on improving my message by: _____

Editing:
To ensure that I edited effectively, I used an editing checklist and concentrated on: _____

Presentation:
I chose the following format to present my writing: _____

I am most proud of: _____

I have checked the following:
- ☐ My title tells what the procedure is.
- ☐ I have included a clear introduction.
- ☐ The information is organized in sequence.
- ☐ The steps are complete and accurate.
- ☐ I have used words and phrases that show sequence or passage of time.
- ☐ I have used strong present-tense verbs.
- ☐ I have included precise vocabulary and details.
- ☐ My writing has sentence fluency, and I have used a variety of sentence lengths.
- ☐ I have included labeled visuals that help readers understand the procedure.
- ☐ The published procedure has a clear, organized layout.
- ☐ I have listed my sources.

Figure 1.2 Personal Checklist for Procedural Writing

SESSION 1

Identifying the Purpose and Features of a Procedural Text

Writers analyze a procedural text, identify its structure and features, and then begin researching to write their own.

SESSION SNAPSHOT

Genre Focus: Features of a Procedural Text

Process Focus: Prewriting

Trait(s): Ideas

Mentor Text: "How to Use a Telescope," by Amy Gilbert

Modeled Writing

Smallest you need
Level surface
Pour in liquid

FOCUSED MINILESSON

Summarize the learning goals: *We are going to focus on a nonfiction genre called procedural text. These are texts that explain how to make or do something. For example, if I wanted to explain how to use a camera, I'd explain, step-by-step, how to aim the camera and focus to take a picture. I might include a labeled diagram to help my readers understand the parts of the camera they need to use.*

To write a great procedural text, we first need to learn about the features and structure of a strong procedure. Let's take a look at a mentor text that explains how to use a telescope.

Using the Mentor Text

■ The mentor text for this unit is "How to Use a Telescope," by Amy Gilbert. You will find it on page 16 of the *Book of Mentor Texts* and in the Instruct section on the *Resources CD-ROM.* Make enough copies of the mentor text for each student to have one. You may also want to use an electronic projection device to display it for whole-class viewing.

■ Distribute or display the mentor text, and read the title aloud. *I have already noticed a feature of a procedural text. The title is clear and simple—it tells what the procedure is about.*

■ Draw students' attention to the introduction. *Sometimes a procedure can begin with an introduction. This author begins by telling us about the function of a telescope. Not all procedures have introductions, but sometimes it's a good idea to include them.*

> **TURN &TALK** *What other procedural texts can you think of? Think about the types of procedural writing you have seen. Share your thinking with your partner.*

■ *Partners, continue looking through the mentor text. What other features of a procedural text do you notice?* Encourage students to self-discover the features. As needed, guide them to understand that information organized in sequence, words that signal the passage of time, present-tense verbs, and precise vocabulary are other important features of a procedural text.

■ *Over the next ten sessions, we are going to write our own procedural texts explaining how to use various pieces of science equipment.*

■ Have each student select a piece of equipment, such as a balance scale, a microscope, a spring scale, or a thermometer. Pair the students so they will have partners for their research. Ensure that not too many students are working on the same equipment, so there will be adequate research materials available.

■ Guide students as they share their observations, and record their thinking on a chart labeled "Features of a Great Procedural Text."

> **TURN &TALK** *Think together. When you write your procedural text about your chosen science equipment, what features will you be sure to include?*

Modeling

■ *Writers, I am going to begin a procedure on how to use a graduated cylinder. To make sure my procedure is accurate, I first need to do some research. I have a book that shows how to use a graduated cylinder. Watch as I record some notes from each step. In addition, our science text has some photographs that show how to get an accurate reading of volume. I also found an instructional video on the Internet. Here I have a graduated cylinder and a beaker with some water in it so that I can practice using it. I might even make some sketches so I can keep track of terms I'm learning about.*

> **Features of a Great Procedural Text**
>
> · Title that tells what the procedure is
> · Usually a brief introduction
> · Information that is organized in sequence
> · Words and phrases that signal the passage of time
> · Powerful, present tense verbs in imperative voice
> · Precise vocabulary
> · Labeled diagrams
> · Text features, such as headings and bold words
> · May include a list of sources

WRITING and COACHING

■ Guide students in using their research notebooks to take notes. You may want to suggest that they organize their notebooks to capture notes both from the research they do in books and online and from their own use of the equipment. In addition to jotting words and phrases, encourage students to include sketches and visual notes as they research.

■ Focus guided-writing groups on assisting students who struggle with researching their particular pieces of science equipment. You might model choosing important facts and recording key words that capture that information, so students don't copy reference sources word for word. You might also suggest that one student demonstrates using the equipment and talking about the process while the partner jots down notes.

SHARING and REFLECTING

■ Lead a discussion about procedural texts, reviewing the list of features. Revisit the mentor text to help students consolidate their understandings about the genre.

> **TURN &TALK** *Partners, share some of the information you have discovered about your science equipment. What are some of the steps you need to know when using it?*

■ Gather the research notebooks, and analyze students' attempts to research. Be sure they are using correct terminology for their pieces of equipment. Identify writers who may need additional modeling to locate appropriate information as well as those who are ready for a broader range of research materials.

TIP The research will be better facilitated if you collect resources in advance. You might do demonstrations with the equipment in small groups and give students the chance to use the equipment themselves. Videos are also great resources for procedural texts.

SESSION 2
Writing an Introduction

Writers craft an introduction using research and notes.

SESSION SNAPSHOT

Process Focus: Prewriting, Drafting

Trait(s): Ideas, Organization

Mentor Text: "How to Use a Telescope," by Amy Gilbert

FOCUSED MINILESSON

Review the learning goals from the previous session. Have students turn and talk about the features of a procedural text. *Why are procedural texts important?*

Summarize the learning goals for this session: *Today you will use your research and notes to craft an introduction for your procedural texts.*

Using the Mentor Text

■ Display the mentor text, and read the introduction out loud. *Writers, I noticed that this procedural text has great organization and wonderful facts. The author begins with an introduction that tells us why we would use a telescope.*

Modeling

■ Use an electronic projection device to display a page from a resource on using a graduated cylinder. *Here is a website that says that graduated cylinders are used to accurately measure liquids. That's great information for my introduction. It doesn't tell me how to use a graduated cylinder but rather **why** I would use one. I am going to save that information by jotting down some facts. Watch as I write the words "to measure liquids." Notice that when taking notes, I do not try to write in complete sentences. I only write a couple of words that will help me remember the fact. While reading through my research, I noticed several other important words:* different sizes, base, tube, *and* lines. *These are key words that I'll want to include in my introduction.*

> **TURN &TALK** *Writers, think together as you look at the information in this resource. Are there any other facts I could use for my introduction?*

■ *Now watch as I take my notes and put them into sentences that will make up my introduction. How about* "Graduated cylinders have a base, tube, and lines for measuring liquids. They come in different sizes." *These sentences tell about the parts of a graduated cylinder, but they tell nothing about each part. The reader will have no idea how these parts work together, or what a graduated cylinder is used for—and the sentences aren't particularly engaging, either. Listen as I try a different way:* "When measuring liquids, try a graduated cylinder.

When measuring liquids, try a graduated cylinder. This tube-shaped tool comes in different sizes and has lines like a ruler down the side for accurate measuring.

Modeled Writing

This tube-shaped tool comes in different sizes and has lines like a ruler down the side for accurate measuring." *I think these sentences provide helpful, engaging information that really lets my readers know what this piece of equipment is used for.*

■ Guide a conversation to recap the process of determining which information is suitable to include in an introduction.

TURN &TALK *Writers, tell your partner some information you might include in your introductions.*

WRITING and COACHING

■ Have partners work with selected resources to locate ideas that are important to include in the introduction of their procedural texts. Coach them as they record those ideas in their notebooks.

■ Confirm that writers are summarizing the facts they find rather than copying directly from resources. Some students may find this challenging—consider pulling them into a small group for instruction on how to record key words or phrases when they are researching.

■ Students who have completed their introductions can return to researching how to use the piece of science equipment they have selected.

SHARING and REFLECTING

TURN &TALK *Partners, share your introductions. Ask your partner if your introductions are clear and informative.*

■ Discuss students' ideas about the introduction. Allow time for students to meet with new partners who have selected a different piece of science equipment and share what they found.

■ Gather the research notebooks and introduction drafts, and analyze students' understanding of the purpose of their chosen equipment. Look for brief notes that capture important facts about the use of the equipment. Identify students who may need additional modeling on note-taking and those who are ready for higher levels of sophistication.

TIP Some writers will have more success than others in clearly identifying the information that describes or explains the function of the equipment as opposed to information that tells the reader how to use it. If you find your students are struggling to differentiate between the two, provide additional demonstrations as needed.

TIP Emphasize the value of using multiple sources when researching. Some students may be tempted to rely on one reference source. Point out that there may be other methods for using the equipment and that different resources might provide different tips or perhaps clearer instructions. If students find the same information in more than one source, you might have them place check marks next to facts or ideas the sources have in common.

Turning Notes into Running Text

Writers use their notes to begin drafting their procedures.

SESSION SNAPSHOT

Process Focus: Drafting

Trait(s): Organization, Ideas, Voice

Mentor Text: "How to Use a Telescope," by Amy Gilbert

FOCUSED MINILESSON

Review last session's learning goals. If time allows, have students turn and talk about how their introductions help the reader understand the purpose of the procedures.

Summarize the learning goals for this session: *When we took notes, we used words and phrases to capture our ideas. But for procedural texts, we need to create smooth, clear sentences. Our focus for today is to continue to research and then turn our notes into sentences that will explain to our readers how to use the science equipment we chose.*

Using the Mentor Text

■ Display a copy of the mentor text, and ask student volunteers to point out some of the many facts it contains.

■ *We can tell that this procedure was well researched because it contains so many facts and details. But do you notice that the facts are not just listed, one by one? The writer has woven her facts into clear sentences that flow smoothly and lead us easily through the steps of the procedure.*

Modeling

■ *Today I'm going to use the notes I have collected to craft complete instructional sentences. My first set of notes is about how to select the right graduated cylinder. I have the words* "smallest you need." *This is the first step in my procedure. Watch as I use these notes to craft a sentence. I could say* "Select the smallest graduated cylinder that you think can hold the amount of liquid you need."

■Continue modeling how you use phrases and words from your notes to craft informative and complete sentences. Emphasize how you try using the phrases in different ways. Explain that carefully considering the way your sentences "sound" before writing them helps you as you draft.

Notes
smallest you need

Draft
Select the smallest graduated cylinder that you think can hold the amount of liquid you need.

Modeled Writing

WRITING and COACHING

- Support writers as they review their notes and put them into sentences. Encourage them to be fearless as they experiment with different sentences. Be sure that partners are aware that although they have researched together, they will each be creating their own drafts.

- As writers begin to draft their procedures, some may realize that they need more research and need to return to that phase of the writing process.

SHARING and REFLECTING

TURN &TALK *Find a partner and talk about how you crafted your sentences. How did you experiment with words from your notes to put sentences together? What strategies helped you? What did you find challenging?*

- Invite a few students to share powerful sentences with the class.

- Gather the research notebooks and drafts. Note which students may need assistance with turning notes into complete informative sentences. Note, also, those students who may be ready for additional challenges, such as using precise words and combining sentences. Plan your instruction based on students' needs.

TIP Note students who are at ease turning notes into sentences, and provide additional challenges, such as adding more precise words or focusing on powerful verbs. You might also gather those who need more scaffolding to write sentences that contain subjects and verbs.

SESSION 4
Organizing Sentences in Time Order

Writers focus on drafting and organizing sentences in time order, using temporal words and phrases to show sequence.

SESSION SNAPSHOT

Process Focus: Drafting

Trait(s): Organization, Ideas

Mentor Text: "How to Use a Telescope," by Amy Gilbert

TIP While some procedural texts use temporal words to show sequence, others use numbers to track the steps. Be sure students are proficient with both methods of writing procedural texts. Should they choose to use numbered steps, model how to use time-order words within the steps themselves so that students are able to use multiple methods to create a well-organized text.

FOCUSED MINILESSON

Review the learning goals from the previous session. Have students turn and talk about strategies for turning notes into running text.

Summarize the learning goals for today: *Procedural texts explain how to do something. For our readers to follow the steps correctly, we need to make sure our sentences are in an order that makes sense and that they are clearly linked together.*

Using the Mentor Text

■ *Let's look again at the mentor text. See how the writer used the words* first, now, *and* then? *These words tell the reader exactly when to do each step. If you want your procedures to be followed correctly, the order in which you place the steps needs to be correct. And you need to use words that signal time order. We call these "temporal words."*

Modeling

■ *As I draft my procedure on how to use a graduated cylinder, I am going to make sure I have all of my steps in the correct order. When I do this, I often speak directly to my readers and tell them what to do, just as if I were standing next to someone, helping him or her to use a graduated cylinder for the first time. Look at these steps in my draft:* "Select the smallest cylinder that can hold the amount of liquid you need. Place the cylinder on a flat surface. Pour in your liquid slowly." *Though these are in the right order, it will be hard for the reader to keep track of what step he or she is on.*

■ *I want to make it clear for my reader what the first step is. To do that I am going to add the word* first: "First, select the smallest cylinder that can hold the amount of liquid you need." *Now my reader will know exactly where to begin.*

TURN &TALK *Writers, think together as you evaluate the next two steps. What time-order words or phrases could we add to those steps?*

■ Continue thinking aloud as you experiment with different temporal words and phrases at the beginning of steps.

Draft 1

Select the smallest cylinder that can hold the amount of liquid you need.

Draft 2

First, select the smallest cylinder that can hold the amount of liquid you need.

Modeled Writing

■ Together with your students, you may want to construct a chart displaying temporal words and phrases. Encourage your students to use the chart as a reference while they are writing. You can also refer to the list of temporal words and phrases to show sequence in the Instruct section of the *Resources* CD-ROM.

WRITING and COACHING

■ As writers return to drafting, remind them to begin by making sure they have their steps in the right order. Encourage them to experiment with different time-order words and phrases and to select the ones that show the right order.

■ Provide additional support as needed in small-group or individual settings, and remind students to refer to the class chart for ideas.

■ No matter how precise students' time-order words are, their steps need to be in the correct order for the procedural text to be effective. Students may want to ask a partner to pantomime the steps to be sure they are in the correct order.

SHARING and REFLECTING

TURN &TALK *Partners, share the sections you worked on today. How did you add temporal words and phrases to your drafts? What temporal words did you use? Did you choose to number your steps? What strategies helped you most?*

■ Invite a few students to share their thinking with the class.

■ Gather the drafts and analyze your students' attempts to write procedural steps that contain temporal words and phrases. Consider which students may need assistance with using time-order words and which may need assistance in putting their steps in the correct order.

TIP Writers are likely to be in different places in the writing process by this point. Some may be close to finishing their drafts, while others might still be turning notes into running text. A Workshop Organizer as shown in *A Guide to Teaching Nonfiction Writing*, page 49, is a great tool to help you monitor the stages of the process for your students.

SESSION 5
Using Precise Domain-Specific Words

Writers use precise scientific vocabulary to create informative and accurate text.

SESSION SNAPSHOT

Process Focus: Drafting, Revising

Trait(s): Ideas, Word Choice

Mentor Text: "How to Use a Telescope," by Amy Gilbert

FOCUSED MINILESSON

Review what students learned in the previous session. Invite them to share the strategies they used for organization.

Summarize the learning goals for today: *When writing a procedure, it is important to use the correct terms for things. You want to make sure the reader can follow each step precisely. This is especially helpful in a procedure using a piece of science equipment. When we use the correct terms, it helps the reader follow each step.*

Using the Mentor Text

■ Revisit the mentor text, pointing out words and phrases such as *magnification, finderscope,* and *light pollution* that are specific to science and science equipment.

> **TURN & TALK** *Partners, think together. Why did the author include all these scientific terms? How do these terms help you understand and follow the procedure?*

■ Invite students to share their thinking with the class.

Modeling

■ *Precise words are important in procedures, especially in scientific ones. Can you imagine trying to follow steps without specific words? For example, if we wrote "turn that thing" and "adjust that wheel," our readers would be lost. Watch as I read to make sure that I used precise and specific terms when referring to each piece of my graduated cylinder: "Check the measurement by reading the bottom of the curved line." Since I am talking about science equipment, I am going to check my notes to see if that curved line has a scientific name.*

■ *I see here that the curved line is called a meniscus. Watch as I change my sentence to include that specific term. I'll write, "Check the measurement by reading the bottom of the curved line, which is called the meniscus." This revised sentence is more clear and precise.*

■ *Did you notice how I included a definition of the term right in my text? I did that so readers who are unfamiliar with the term will know what it means. From now on, anytime I refer to that curved line, I need to make*

Draft 1

Check the measurement by reading the bottom of the curved line.

Draft 2

Check the measurement by reading the bottom of the curved line, which is called the meniscus.

Modeled Writing

sure I call it the meniscus. If I switch from meniscus *to* curved line *and back again, I will confuse my readers.*

■ Continue to model until you feel your students have internalized the concept. Show students how you use your resources to gather and define domain-specific words.

> **TURN &TALK** *Writers, think about your procedures. Are there terms you could use that are more precise and specific? Why are specific terms needed in procedures?*

WRITING and COACHING

■ As writers start adding precise domain-specific terms, remind them that they can use their notes or their reference materials.

■ If students aren't able to find specific vocabulary to use, provide the terminology for them.

■ Explain that in the next session, students will have time to focus on creating diagrams that will match these terms exactly, to provide their readers with additional information about any unfamiliar terms.

SHARING and REFLECTING

■ Return to the mentor text, your modeled writing, or an exemplary student description. Focus on how the right words help with visualization. Guide students in noticing how using precise vocabulary aids in the understanding of their procedures.

> **TURN &TALK** *Identify a partner you haven't worked with yet, and share some of your revisions. Partners, what feedback can you offer? What suggestions would you make?*

■ Gather the drafts and analyze your students' attempts to include precise domain-specific vocabulary. Be sure students naturally weave these terms and their definitions into their procedural texts. Even when using scientific words, the sentences should flow smoothly.

TIP Some students may need additional coaching as they attempt to add scientific words and phrases in their procedures. These students might benefit from a small-group guided-writing experience. Model several ways to incorporate definitions of domain-specific vocabulary. You might also have students examine the science terminology in various procedural texts that you've gathered and in the reference materials they are using for this Extended Writing Unit.

SESSION 6
Adding Labeled Diagrams

Students examine the role of diagrams in procedural writing and add labeled diagrams to their works in progress.

SESSION SNAPSHOT

Process Focus: Drafting, Revising

Trait(s): Organization, Text Features

Mentor Text: "How to Use a Telescope," by Amy Gilbert

FOCUSED MINILESSON

Review the learning goals from the previous session. If time allows, have students turn and talk about what they have learned so far.

Summarize the learning goals for this session: *Diagrams are very useful in a procedure because they help readers understand information and follow instructions correctly. Today we'll focus on creating diagrams that will support our procedures.*

Using the Mentor Text

■ Revisit the mentor text, inviting students to examine the diagrams that were included.

> **TURN &TALK** *Partners, think together. Why did the author include diagrams in this procedure? How do the diagrams help you understand the procedure?*

■ Invite students to share their thinking with the class.

Modeling

■ *In one of my steps, I say* "Place the graduated cylinder on a flat surface, being sure the base is level." *Because the base is important, I'm drawing and labeling it. Watch as I write the word* base *and then draw a line from the label to that part of the cylinder. Did you notice that I didn't write the procedure in the diagram? I didn't write* "Place the graduated cylinder on a flat surface, being sure the base is level." *That sentence will go into my procedure. I don't want to clutter the diagram. I don't need to label other parts of the graduated cylinder right now because that's not what this step in my procedure is about.*

> **TURN &TALK** *Writers, think together. What other information should be included in my diagram?*

■ Continue modeling how you add information to your diagram, asking students for their input. Think aloud as you decide which labels to add and where to place them. Show students that after considering a fact from your research, you may decide it's not important or doesn't belong in the diagram.

■ *Take a look at your own procedural texts and the sketches you created in your notebooks and organizers. Today you'll use those sketches to create diagrams.*

Modeled Writing

WRITING and COACHING

▪ As writers create their diagrams, emphasize that the diagrams and labels in a procedure must closely match the text for each step. Remind them that they may have some vocabulary terms to add as labels.

▪ Coach writers with questions such as *Do you think you need a diagram for each step? What might your reader need to see to be able to understand what to do? Is this diagram clear? Does it really match the text? What labels might you use?*

▪ Remind writers to share their diagrams with each other to ensure they are clear and contain as much detail as needed.

SHARING and REFLECTING

▪ Return to the mentor text, your own modeled diagrams, or an exemplary student diagram, and focus on the diagrams and labels. Guide students in noticing how a well-designed diagram that precisely matches the text can significantly help readers understand a procedure.

> **TURN &TALK** *Work with a partner, and share your diagrams. Partners, what feedback can you offer? What do you like about the diagrams? What suggestions would you make?*

▪ Gather the drafts and analyze your students' attempts to create clearly labeled diagrams. Identify writers who may need additional modeling as well as those who are ready for higher levels of sophistication. Use the class writing rubric or the individual student rubric on the *Resources* CD-ROM to track writing proficiencies.

TIP Having students sketch and label the important parts of their diagrams will help them focus their procedures and remind them of how the science equipment is used. Remind them that their sketch does not have to be perfect, but the parts should be easily identifiable.

TIP Some students may need additional coaching as they attempt to create diagrams to go with the steps in their procedures. Consider inviting these students to examine diagrams in various procedural texts that you've gathered and in the reference materials they are using for this Extended Writing Unit. What features do they find in common in the diagrams? What makes some diagrams particularly effective?

SESSION 7

Revising to Create a Satisfying Conclusion

Students focus on writing a strong conclusion for their procedural text.

SESSION SNAPSHOT

Process Focus: Drafting, Revising

Trait(s): Ideas, Organization, Voice

Mentor Text: "How to Use a Telescope," by Amy Gilbert

FOCUSED MINILESSON

Review the learning goals from the previous session. If time allows, have students turn and talk about what they have learned so far.

Summarize the learning goals for this session: *Today we'll think about our conclusions and make sure they wrap up our procedures in a way that brings closure. We want to make sure our writing flows and doesn't end abruptly.*

Using the Mentor Text

■ Display the mentor text, and read the ending aloud.

> **TURN &TALK** *Tell your partner what you think about this conclusion. Why do you think the author ended the procedure this way?*

■ Lead a discussion about the traits of a strong conclusion. *Did you notice that this author used her conclusion to remind us that using a telescope is simple? She also gives a very compelling reason for using a telescope—to bring faraway sights into view. This author has written a hardworking conclusion that makes the reader want to follow her procedure.*

Modeling

■ *I have told my readers all that I want them to know about using a graduated cylinder, but as I read over my draft, I see that I need to think about the ending. I wrote "And that is how you measure liquids with a graduated cylinder." I am sure I can do better than this. I want to make the ending sound like using a graduated cylinder is easy and fun. How about "By following these simple steps, you can feel confident that you will make accurate measurements of liquids each and every time."*

> **TURN &TALK** *Writers, what do you think about this ending? Is it satisfying? Is it interesting? Can you think of another way to end this piece?*

■ *How about this ending? "Now that you know how to use a graduated cylinder, you will certainly measure liquids with ease." I want to make sure that I try several different endings until I find the one I think sounds best.*

Draft 1

And that is how you measure liquids with a graduated cylinder.

Draft 2

By following these simple steps, you can feel confident that you will make accurate measurements of liquids each and every time.

Draft 3

Now that you know how to use a graduated cylinder, you will certainly measure liquids with ease.

Modeled Writing

■ *You may want to try out different endings in your writer's notebooks and then add the one you like best to the bottom of your drafts.*

WRITING and COACHING

■ As writers work on their conclusions, remind them to look at your examples. They will want to experiment with several different conclusions before they pick one.

■ Coach writers through questions such as *How can you make this more interesting? Does your ending feel abrupt? What are some different ways you could end this?*

■ Remind students who are still in the drafting phase of their writing that they do not need to abandon their work but can continue to draft and work on adjusting their conclusions when they are ready to revise. You will need to provide additional time for these writers to complete their drafts.

■ For writers who have moved on to editing, remind them that the writing process is ongoing and that they revisit their drafts often. Even though they may have started to edit, they can still reread and be reflective about the conclusion in their writing.

SHARING and REFLECTING

TURN &TALK *Find a partner who is working on a different piece of equipment, and share your conclusions. What do you like best about your partner's work? What might make his or her conclusion more satisfying?*

■ Give students time to share their reflections and talk about what they might do in the next session to improve their writing. Have one or two students share their conclusions with the class.

■ Gather the writer's notebooks and drafts, and analyze your students' attempts to write engaging, effective conclusions. Identify students who would benefit from additional modeling or a guided-writing session.

TIP It may be helpful to post examples of conclusions to aid students in crafting their own. Remind them that there is no need to erase—drafts are sloppy! There will be plenty of time to revise before publishing.

TIP It may be helpful to pair students who struggle with students who appear competent in drafting strong conclusions. Create a community of writers by encouraging students to assist each other in the writing process.

SESSION 8
Revising for Verb Tense

Writers revise their drafts to check that verbs are in the present tense.

SESSION SNAPSHOT

Process Focus: Revising

Trait(s): Conventions

Mentor Text: "How to Use a Telescope," by Amy Gilbert

FOCUSED MINILESSON

If necessary, review verb tense, focusing on the difference between present and past tense. Make a chart of past- and present-tense verbs with your students, and encourage them to use it as a reference.

Reflect on the learning goals from the last session. Have students turn and talk, sharing the qualities of powerful endings in procedural texts.

Summarize the learning goals for this session: *We have crafted procedures that make sense, include helpful visuals, and contain precise scientific terms. Before we present our work to an audience, we'll want to check for many elements, including the correct use of verbs. That is our focus for today.*

Using the Mentor Text

■ Revisit the mentor text. *Let's begin by noticing the verbs the author chose. See how she uses verbs such as* remove, choose, look, *and* repeat *in her procedure? These verbs tell the reader exactly what to do. And here's something else to notice: the verbs are in the present tense. Notice how the author is not describing how she used the telescope in the past. For procedures to be followed correctly, the verbs need to be exact and in the present tense. In this way, the author speaks directly to the reader, another feature of a great procedure.*

■ Refer students back to the chart of past- and present-tense verbs you created. Add additional present-tense verbs from the mentor text to the list if they are not included.

Modeling

■ *Watch as I reread my procedure. As I do this, I have a few goals in mind. I am going to make sure my verbs are precise and in the present tense. I will pretend that I am speaking directly to my readers and telling them what to do, just as if I were standing next to someone and telling him or her what to do. Let's examine this sentence:* "First, I placed my graduated cylinder on a flat surface."

TURN &TALK *Writers, think together as you evaluate this step. How do you think we could improve it?*

■ *Many of you noticed that this sentence does not have a present-tense verb. Instead, it tells what I did when I used a graduated cylinder. This makes it a retell, not a procedure. Watch as I revise:* "First, place the

Draft 1

First, I placed my graduated cylinder on a flat surface.

Draft 2

First, place the cylinder on a flat and level surface.

Modeled Writing

graduated cylinder on a flat and level surface." *Now this sounds more like directions and less like I am describing what I did. This is the tone that a procedure should take.*

■ Continue to model how you examine each of the verbs in your procedure. Some students may need additional scaffolding to understand the difference between present-tense and past-tense verbs. Pull those students together for small-group instruction.

WRITING and COACHING

■ As writers return to drafting and revising, remind them to experiment with different verbs as they draft, selecting the ones that are the most precise and ensuring that they are in the present tense.

■ Coach writers by posing questions such as *How do we begin steps in a procedural text? Why do we need to have present-tense verbs? Why do we need to put the verbs first? Have you chosen verbs that tell your readers what to do? How can you improve them?*

■ Have students refer to the list you created. If they find they are using a new present-tense verb, invite them to add it to the list.

■ Provide additional assistance through small-group instruction as needed.

SHARING and REFLECTING

TURN &TALK *Partners, share your drafts and look closely at the verbs. Do they clearly convey what you should do? Are they in the present tense? Do you have any suggestions for your partner?*

■ Gather the drafts and analyze students' use of present-tense verbs. Be sure they have chosen strong verbs and have written them in the present tense. Note which students are ready to add more sophistication to their drafts. Use the class writing rubric or the individual student rubric on the *Resources* CD-ROM to track writing proficiencies.

TIP Point out that reading procedures aloud can help writers notice their verb tenses and ensure that their directions are clear. Encourage students to choose a partner and read their drafts aloud.

Using an Editing Checklist

Writers follow a checklist to edit for one editing point at a time.

SESSION SNAPSHOT

Process Focus: Editing

Trait(s): Conventions

FOCUSED MINILESSON

Make enough copies of the editing checklists from the *Resources* CD-ROM to give one to each student. Replicate the checklists for your modeling.

Reflect on the learning goals from the last session. If time allows, have students turn and talk about what they have learned so far.

Summarize the learning goals for this session: *We have worked hard to craft procedures that make sense, are organized in sequence, use precise vocabulary, and include helpful visuals. Before we present our work to an audience, we'll want to edit to check our conventions. This last step helps us present work that our readers can understand.*

Modeling

■ *I am going to use an editing checklist as I review my writing. This will help me make sure my procedure is ready to be shared with others. The first thing I am going to check for is my use of commas. As I do this check, I am not going to look at capital letters, spelling, or anything else—just my comma use. Here I have a run-on sentence.* "Look at the meniscus at eye level read the bottom part of the curve and then record the number you see there." *This sentence needs some corrections; it sounds really confusing. Watch as I make some slight adjustments:* "Look at the meniscus at eye level, reading the bottom part of the curve, and then record the number you see there."

TURN &TALK *Writers, what do you think? Does it sound better when I add commas?*

■ *I am going to continue to check my sentences for comma use. I added time-order words in some of the steps in my procedure. Now I need to make sure that each of those words is followed by a comma. Watch as I examine this sentence:* "Next slowly pour the liquid to the correct line." *I notice that I left out the comma after the word* next. *I'll add that here. I'll read on to the next sentences:* "Kneel down to read the meniscus at eye level." *This helps you stay accurate. Watch as I edit:* "By kneeling down to eye level, you will have an accurate measurement." *Notice that I placed the comma after* level. *This separates the sentence into two parts—the introduction followed by a comma and the main sentence.*

Draft 1

Look at the meniscus at eye level read the bottom part of the curve and then record the number you see there.

Draft 2

Look at the meniscus at eye level, reading the bottom part of the curve, and then record the number you see there.

Modeled Writing

TURN &TALK *Writers, what steps would you need to follow to create a sentence like this?*

■ Have a few students share their thinking with the class.

■ Now that I have checked for comma use, I am going to look at my use of capital letters and other punctuation. When I have done that, I will go back and check my spelling.

WRITING and COACHING

■ Have writers use the editing checklists to focus on one editing point at a time.

■ Provide small-group instruction as needed for students who struggle with editing.

■ For writers who are still drafting and revising, remind them that when they are ready to edit, you will expect them to follow the checklists and edit their procedural texts. You can also encourage students to use the editing checklists for guidance as they draft.

■ If students are overwhelmed, consider focusing on just a few key points on the editing checklists. You can adapt the editing checklists from the *Resources* CD-ROM according to the needs of your students. Be sure to match your editing checklists to the focus lessons you have demonstrated for students.

SHARING and REFLECTING

TURN &TALK *Partners, how did using an editing checklist help you make your procedures ready to share with readers? What did you find challenging?*

■ Guide a conversation to help students summarize what they learned by using the editing checklists.

■ Gather the drafts and analyze your students' attempts to edit. Identify writers who may need additional modeling in editing for a single editing point as well as those who may know how to identify errors in their writing but not how to fix them. Use the rubrics on the *Resources* CD-ROM to track writing proficiencies and tailor future instruction.

TIP Editing checklists are not meant to be used for teaching. Students should only use them to edit their work. Be sure the editing checklists you share with students include only the focus points from this or previous instruction and do not introduce any new strategies or skills.

SESSION 10
Publishing the Procedures

Writers add text features to their procedures and then work to publish and share their work.

SESSION SNAPSHOT

Process Focus: Publishing

Trait(s): Presentation

Mentor Text: "How to Use a
Telescope," by Amy Gilbert

FOCUSED MINILESSON

Decide what format you would like students to use in publishing their writing. You may want them to create a poster that can be placed over the equipment whenever it is being used in class. The lesson that follows describes creating a poster and displaying it with an electronic projection device. Alternatively, you may want to use chart paper or publishing paper to demonstrate presentation skills.

Review the learning goals from the last session, and summarize the learning goals for this session. *In our last session, we edited with a checklist to prepare our work for our readers. This means it's time for publishing and presenting. This is an exciting time for writers. We get to combine our drafts and our visuals to create interesting and helpful page layouts.*

Using the Mentor Text

■ Display the mentor text, and ask students what they notice about the layouts and visuals.

> **TURN &TALK** *Writers, talk about the mentor text with your partners. Why are the layouts and visuals so important in a procedural text?*

■ Give students time to share their thinking with the class.

Modeling

■ *When presenting my writing for others, I want to think about certain features that will help improve it. When I look at published procedures, they typically do not have just words. Many are filled with interesting images, headings, and so on that support the procedure. To make my writing more understandable to a reader, I am going to include some headings and bold words.*

■ *I am planning on creating a poster; there are many different ways to set one up. For this one, I will begin by adding the title to the top of my poster. Then, my introduction should appear as the first part of the text, in a spot that readers can easily identify as the starting point. For the steps of my procedure, I am going to write the word "Procedure" as a bold heading. This will help my readers distinguish between my introduction and my set of steps.*

■ *As you can see, I can pick and choose where I want to place my information and where I want to place my diagrams and any photographs I have selected.* Model moving your text around and rearranging your page layout, so students can see how one might experiment with layouts.

■ *A helpful strategy is to place each part of your procedure into its own text box on the computer. Once the steps are in text boxes, you can move them around on the page and change the size and shape of the text boxes and diagrams. Watch as I take my cursor and drag the text box containing my first section to a new position and enlarge the diagram I created to match this section.*

> **TURN &TALK** *Think about the way the page looks. Do you like the text boxes where I placed them? Do you think the size of the visual is good? Is my information in a clear sequential order? What can I do to make this poster really easy to follow? Take a look at the sources you have been using for research, and see if they give you any helpful ideas about page layouts.*

■ Continue modeling options with page layouts, visuals, font sizes, colors, and bold words. Highlight the way you can rearrange spaces and text boxes to create a professional, easy-to-follow procedure.

WRITING and COACHING

■ For writers who are ready to publish, provide access to computers so they can begin to format interesting page layouts and experiment with rearranging text boxes on the page. If you don't have access to computers, have students experiment with page layouts using publishing paper.

■ For writers who may still be drafting or revising, assure them that they can think about their layouts and presentations while they move forward with their writing.

■ Remind writers that either the visuals they created to go with their procedures can be pasted on after printing or they can use a digital camera or scanner to capture the images and digitally import them in their writing.

■ Consider adding another session or two to the unit if students need more time to create published work that really makes them proud.

SHARING and REFLECTING

■ *I have invited the class next door to join us and become your learning partners. When they arrive, each of you will have an opportunity to meet with at least two individuals from that class and share your learning. You'll also invite them to try out your procedures.*

> **TURN &TALK** *Partners, think together for a few minutes. Our guests are going to want to learn about both what your topics are and how you write a procedure. Make a plan and list the key points you want to share so that the guests you work with will learn about both the topic and the features of a procedure. What advice would you give them if they had to write their own procedures?*

■ At the end of the session, gather the students' final pieces, and analyze their attempts at presentation. Identify writers who may need additional modeling as well as those who are ready for higher levels of sophistication. Use the rubrics on the *Resources* CD-ROM to track writing proficiencies and tailor future instruction.

TIP Some students may need additional support in considering text features and page layouts and would benefit from a small-group writing session in which you guide them in examining the pages of several nonfiction resources for ideas on layouts and features.

Instructions

Write instructions to tell how to jump rope.

FEATURES

- Title
- Numbered steps
- Verb first in each step
- Bold words
- Supporting visuals

FOCUSED MINILESSON

Jumping rope is great exercise! I want to create a poster today with instructions for jumping rope. The gym teacher is going to hang the poster as part of Healthy Heart Month, which will encourage students to exercise. Watch as I begin with a title: "How to Jump Rope." Notice that I write the title on its own line. The title isn't very long or descriptive, either. Instructions are simple and to the point.

Now it's time to list the steps. Just like in a recipe and other instructions, I am going to start the first step with the number 1. Watch as I begin: "1) Choose the right-sized rope. With the rope folded in half, it should reach from the floor nearly to your shoulders."

Notice that I started the step with a verb, choose. *Instructions sound the way we would speak to someone if we were telling someone how to do something. When we write instructions, we simply begin with a verb with language that almost sounds bossy! It's also important to be specific. I wrote how long the jump rope should be. That information is so important to people who want to jump rope. Having the wrong size rope makes jumping rope impossible!*

TURN &TALK *Writers, once a properly sized jump rope is chosen, the jumper needs to grab the rope and get ready to jump. Put your heads together and think. What should I list next in my instructions?*

I am beginning this step with the number 2 and a verb: "2) Grab. . . ." Notice that my steps are concise. If I make the steps too long, the instructions will be difficult to follow. Since I am creating these instructions on a poster, it's even more important that they be brief. Too much text will clutter the poster.

Continue thinking aloud as you write the rest of the instructions. Point out that each step starts with a number to keep the steps in order, begins with a verb, and includes precise language so that readers know exactly what to do.

How to Jump Rope

Instructions:

1) Choose the right-sized rope. With the rope folded in half, it should reach from the floor nearly to your shoulders.

2) Grab the rope with one end or one handle in each hand.

3) Put the jump rope behind you and let the loop hang even with your knees.

4) Throw the jump rope over your head. When it meets your feet, jump over it.

5) Repeat these steps. It might help at first to do a small hop between bigger jumps.

Modeled Writing

How to Tie a Bowline Knot

You will need a rope of any length.

1. Loop one side of the rope and make sure the short part is underneath the long part.

2. Take the other side of the rope and thread it through the loop.

3. Make a loop around the short part from step 1 and take it back through the loop from step 1.

4. Pull tight. Only pull on the two ends.

TURN &TALK *Partners, evaluate my instructions together. What suggestions would you have for making these instructions even easier to follow?*

Summarize the features: Display your instructions as a reference as students work independently to list features of instructions. Then, students can volunteer features for a class checklist that you can display and then duplicate for students' writing folders.

WRITING and COACHING

Writers, now it's your turn. Choose a form of exercise or a game. Maybe your instructions will be about stretching before exercise. Write instructions for whatever you choose! Use direct verb-first language in your instructions.

As writers create their instructions, work with individuals and small groups who may need your support. Students may need assistance to write with verbs first. Help them locate the verbs in their sentences to check their placement. Provide instructions for students to use as mentor texts.

SHARING and REFLECTING

Sum it up! *Writers, your instructions are crystal clear because you used numbers to keep steps in order and started each step with a verb so that it's clear what your readers should do. Your instructions are concise, so your readers will not be confused.*

TURN &TALK *Suppose we are going to present our posters to our gym teacher. Think about the features you used in your instructions. What features do you want to mention to our gym teacher? Work with a partner to list them.*

ASSESS THE LEARNING

Analyze the instructions and identify writers who need additional support in putting steps in order, beginning steps with verbs, and using direct, to-the-point language. Note which students are ready to add more sophisticated features to their writing.

SELF-ASSESSMENT

SELF-ASSESSMENT **Instructions**	YES	NO
1. Title	☐	☐
2. Numbered steps	☐	☐
3. Verb first in each step	☐	☐
4. Bold words ⊙	☐	☐
5. Supporting visuals ⊙	☐	☐

⊳TAKE IT FORWARD

▸ Discuss bold words, explaining to students that writers often use bold words that are important. Have them analyze their instructions to identify which words might be bold. Model using bold words in your own instructions first. In the first step, for example, you might make *shoulders* bold to show students that the length of the rope is important.

▸ Labeled diagrams or storyboards are strong support for these instructions. Think aloud as you add visuals to your model, and then encourage students to follow your lead.

▸ Give students publishing options. They may want to create posters as you did for the model or demonstrate their instructions, either "live" or on videos you can post on the school or district website.

▸ Students might create posters or guidelines for a variety of purposes, such as how to write a newspaper article, how to use a piece of science equipment in the classroom, or how to do a tornado drill.

Partner Explanation

Explain with a partner how an extreme weather pattern works.

The Very Unweak Wave

Did you know that underwater earthquakes cause more than you think? They actually cause another serious natural disaster called a Tsunami. First, Two plates collide under the ocean floor. Next the collision of the plates causes a minor earthquake underwater. Therefore, the quake causes waves to occur. These waves form to be very big, causing fish and other sea life to wash up on shores and locations near oceans. Many structures are damaged and sometimes destroyed.

FEATURES

- Opening statement of what is to be explained
- Precise vocabulary
- Exact details
- Clear sequence of steps
- Linking words to show order: *as soon as, finally, afterward, meanwhile, now, since, soon, then, while, when*
- ◖ Passive voice
- ◖ Timeless, present-tense verbs
- ◖ Conclusion

BEFORE THE LESSON

Display a list of linking words that indicate sequence on chart paper, or project a list with a document camera.

Falling Balls of Ice

It's hard to believe that ice can fall from the sky in warm weather! But hail can form during a summer thunderstorm.

First, a small cluster of water droplets or snow near the top of a tall storm cloud clumps together to make a small ball of ice called an ice nucleus. While the ice nucleus is bounced around by winds called an updraft, it gathers moisture around it to grow larger until it's no longer an ice nucleus, but a piece of hail. Finally, when it is heavy enough, the hail falls toward Earth.

Modeled Writing

FOCUSED MINILESSON

Today I am going to write an explanation about a special weather phenomenon—hail. I'm going to focus on how hail forms and what happens that makes it fall to Earth. I want to capture my readers' attention in the introduction. I know I am surprised when ice falls from the sky when it's hot outside, so I am going to start with that idea. Watch as I begin: "It's hard to believe that ice can fall from the sky in warm weather! But hail can form during a summer thunderstorm." *I've captured my readers' attention, and they will know what process I am describing.*

Now I'm ready to write my explanation. To form hail, the first thing that happens is that a small ball of ice called a nucleus forms in a storm cloud. I want to signal that this happens before anything else, so watch as I begin with the time-order word first: *"First, a small cluster of. . . ."*

TURN &TALK *Partners, at the same time that the ice nucleus is bouncing around in the clouds, ice and water gather around the nucleus. Take a look at the list of linking words. Identify a word that shows that two things are happening at the same time.*

I think while *is a great word to show that two things happen at once. Watch as I begin my next sentence:* "While the ice nucleus is bounced around. . . ."

Continue thinking aloud as you finish the modeled writing. Showcase your thinking about the precise vocabulary and the linking words you are using. Conclude the last step with the word *finally* and a summation that wraps up the explanation.

TURN &TALK *Partners, think together as you evaluate this explanation. How does the explanation reflect a process? What might you do to make the writing even stronger?*

Summarize the features: Have partners work together to generate features checklists for explanations. As students work together, circulate to be sure no important features are missing from the lists.

WRITING and COACHING

Work with a partner to create an explanation. You might explain how another form of severe weather works. You could also explain how a simple machine works, how a sedimentary rock forms, or some other process with a sequence. Be sure you include linking words and precise vocabulary as you explain the process.

As partners write their explanations, confer with pairs as needed to support and scaffold understanding. You might pull together a small group for instruction with linking words. Encourage students to strive for variety in their linking words rather than starting every sentence with the word *next*.

SHARING and REFLECTING

Sum it up! *Writers, your explanations are clear. Your precisely worded sentences and linking words take readers through a process and make it easy to understand.*

TURN &TALK *We've been asked to teach how to write an explanation to fourth graders. What features of explanations do you want to be sure to share? Think together as you make a list.*

ASSESS THE LEARNING

Analyze the explanations to identify writers who need additional support in using linking words to convey a sequence in an explanation of how something happens.

SELF-ASSESSMENT

SELF-ASSESSMENT
Partner Explanation

	YES	NO
1. Opening statement of what is to be explained	☐	☐
2. Precise vocabulary	☐	☐
3. Exact details	☐	☐
4. Clear sequence of steps	☐	☐
5. Linking words to show order: *as soon as, finally, afterward, meanwhile, now, since, soon, then, while, when*	☐	☐
6. Passive Voice ○	☐	☐

▷TAKE IT FORWARD

▸ Have students add a conclusion to their explanations. A conclusion can leave the reader with a fascinating fact or an intriguing question. A conclusion can also summarize the process.

▸ Students who want to revise their explanations can examine them for passive voice. Have students consider changing passive verbs to timeless present-tense verbs. You will need to model this process for it to become intuitive.

▸ Have students add a visual with a caption to their explanations. You might add to your model, for example, a sketch

of a storm cloud in which hail typically forms or a labeled cutaway diagram of a piece of hail in which the nucleus is clearly labeled.

▸ Have students look through their writing folders for other explanations they have written that would benefit from a closer look at linking words. Have them use the linking words resources as they infuse their writing with organizational guideposts.

Problem-Solving Guide

Write a procedural text to solve a math problem.

FEATURES

- Problem is highlighted or presented in boxed text
- Linking words to show order
- Precise mathematical language
- Mathematical computation presented along with explanation
- Conclusion

BEFORE THE LESSON

If necessary, build background by sharing math problems with students. (See the *Resources* CD-ROM for Math Problem Stories.) Then, work with students to write a math problem.

FOCUSED MINILESSON

*Today I want to create a problem-solving guide that we can use to solve math problems. We solved a problem today, so I want to create the problem-solving guide side by side with the problem so that we show **and** tell our readers how to solve math problems.*

When we solved our problem, we first wrote the problem in the top box of the organizer. Watch as I write that step: "First, write. . . ." Notice that I started with the linking word first. *That linking word is a signal to my readers. The step is simple and to the point so that readers can follow it. I am simply telling my readers what to do.*

TURN &TALK *The next thing we did was read the entire math problem. Think together. Identify how you would you write that step.*

I was thinking about writing "Read the problem." *But I want to be sure my readers can keep the steps in order, so I am starting with a linking word: "Then, read. . . ." The next thing we did was to look for details that would help us solve the problem. I want to use a variety of linking words in my problem-solving guide, so I am going to choose another word to start the next step: "Next, ..." Notice that the steps are short and direct and that each begins with a linking word.*

Continue modeling and thinking aloud as you finish the problem-solving guide. Be sure that the steps are clear and that they apply to all word problems and not just the sample problem. Link the steps to the sample problem, and use a linking word to begin each step.

TURN &TALK *Writers, analyze the guidelines. What makes this guide easy to follow? What would you suggest to make it even clearer for readers?*

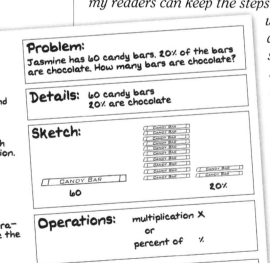

First, write the problem in the top box.

Then, read the whole problem to get the gist.

Next, look for details and list them.

Fourth, create a sketch to illustrate the situation.

Next, identify the operation you need to solve the problem.

Finally, solve it.

Problem: Jasmine has 60 candy bars. 20% of the bars are chocolate. How many bars are chocolate?

Details: 60 candy bars 20% are chocolate

Sketch:
60   20%

Operations: multiplication X or percent of %

Solve: 60 X 20% = 12

Modeled Writing

Summarize the features: Have partners work in groups to generate features checklists for problem-solving guides. They can use the checklists as a reference as they write and can save their checklists for future writing.

WRITING and COACHING

You know how to solve lots of problems—crossword puzzles, brain teasers, number puzzles, and so on. Work with a partner to write a problem-solving guide that would help readers with your selected problems. Use linking words to keep the steps organized, and be sure your steps are simple—speak directly to your readers.

As partners write problem-solving guides, help those who need assistance.

SHARING and REFLECTING

Sum it up! Writers, you created clear and helpful guidelines that use linking words and simple steps. With these guides in hand, your readers will be able to solve all sorts of problems!

TURN &TALK *We're going to teach our guidelines for solving math problems to another class. What features of guidelines do you want to be sure to share? Think together about what is most important to include.*

ASSESS THE LEARNING

Analyze the guides to identify writers who need additional support in organizing a procedural text and using precise language to convey a procedure. Note those who are ready for higher levels of sophistication.

SELF-ASSESSMENT

SELF-ASSESSMENT
Problem-Solving Guide

	YES	NO
1. Problem is highlighted or presented in boxed text	☐	☐
2. Linking words to show order	☐	☐
3. Precise mathematical language	☐	☐
4. Mathematical computation presented along with explanation	☐	☐
5. Conclusion	☐	☐

▷TAKE IT FORWARD

▸ Students can create guidelines for procedures they might follow outside of school, such as how to do laundry or pack a healthy lunch.

▸ Have students create another sample problem that can accompany the guidelines. They can show the problem with the steps on poster board or in electronic slides as presentation options for their work.

▸ Students can create guidelines with accompanying visuals as the basis for a demonstration speech. As they detail the steps in a process, they can show a flowchart or actually do the process as they explain it. Suggest simple topics, such as lacing a shoe, preparing a snack, or making a simple musical instrument like a drum.

▸ Have students create problem-solving guides for younger students, using age-appropriate math problems to illustrate how to use the guides.

VISUAL LITERACY

Oral Presentation

Create an oral presentation to explain how to do something.

FEATURES

- Formal spoken language with present-tense verbs
- Visual display with title and headings, showing steps in order
- Handout provided to audience with steps written out in numbered order or using words of sequence
- Storyboard or flowchart of steps in handout

▶ Precise vocabulary

FOCUSED MINILESSON

Today I want to capture the steps of planting a tomato in an oral presentation. My presentation will combine words with pictures to clearly show readers how to grow a tomato like a professional gardener!

First, I want to create visuals for reference. I can refer to these visuals as I speak and also use them for a handout I'll give to audience members. I am going to sketch the first step—putting a tomato seed in water. Watch as I sketch the seed in the water and add a caption to be sure my readers know how much water to use and how long to keep the seed in the water. Now watch as I create the second sketch. I am including a caption to tell how many days later I need to remove the seed and put it in direct sunlight.

TURN & TALK *Writers, there are a few more steps to growing a tomato seed. What advice would you give me for sketching these last few steps?*

Finish the sketches, adding captions to them. Showcase your thinking as you go back to add any labels that might be crucial to understanding the process.

Now for the exciting part, I am going to use my drawings as I give a speech. A speech is a talk for an audience. I want to think very carefully about how I will speak. The tone of a speech is friendly, but not the way I would talk with friends in an informal setting. In a speech, I speak formally, without slang. I make sure I speak loudly enough for people to hear but not so loudly that it's irritating! I keep the tempo slow and even. If I speak too quickly, I'll lose my audience. Of course, speaking too slowly could make them tune out as well. There's a lot to think about when giving a speech!

My goal in this speech is to teach a process. Linking words are perfect to keep the steps in order as I speak. Listen as I speak about the first sketch:

How to Plant a Tomato

1.

Place a tomato seed in **3** tablespoons of water for **7** days.

2.

After seven days, remove the seed and place it in a mulch pellet. Gently mist the pellet and keep it in direct sunlight.

3.

When the seed has sprouted one inch above the pellet, transfer it to an empty yogurt container. Make sure that the container will not tip over.

4.

When the tomato has grown six inches and several leaves have emerged, transfer the plant to the ground.

Modeled Writing

"First, place a tomato seed. . . ." *I used* first *to tell my readers how to get started. I kept this step nice and short so that my readers will remember it after the speech.*

TURN &TALK *Partners, choose a sketch. How would you capture the ideas of the sketch in a speech? Choose a linking word to start the step.*

Continue your speech. Match the words to your sketches. Be sure to use linking words, keeping steps short and direct.

Summarize the features: Have partners work in groups to generate features checklists for oral presentations of processes. They can practice their speeches with partners. Partners can use the checklists to offer feedback.

WRITING and COACHING

Now choose a procedure, and create a presentation to explain how to do it. You could choose a science project, a craft, a game, or some other procedure you know how to do. It is important that you create a handout with the steps in your procedure written out and accompanied by sketches. This will help your audience to follow along during your presentations and even to complete the processes themselves.

As writers develop their sketches and speeches, confer with individuals or small groups as they need support. Listen in as students speak to be sure their language is appropriate for a speech. You might give students the Tips for Giving a Great Speech resource from the *Resources* CD-ROM.

SHARING and REFLECTING

Sum it up! *Together, your sketches and speeches were powerful ways to explain procedures. Linking words kept things in order, and you were able to both show and tell.*

TURN &TALK *Suppose you wanted to share your oral presentations with family members. What features would you want to point out from your work? Think with your partners as you list the most important ones.*

ASSESS THE LEARNING

Analyze the presentations to identify writers who need additional support in using language appropriate for a speech. Use familiar examples to make sure students know the difference between formal and informal language.

SELF-ASSESSMENT

SELF-ASSESSMENT
Oral Presentation

	YES	NO
1. Formal spoken language with present-tense verbs	☐	☐
2. Visual display with title and headings, showing steps in order	☐	☐
3. Handout provided to audience with steps written out in numbered order or using words of sequence	☐	☐
4. Handout includes a storyboard or flowchart of steps	☐	☐
5. Precise vocabulary ⊙	☐	☐

▷ TAKE IT FORWARD

▸ Have students strive to include precise domain-specific vocabulary in their presentations. As you model, for example, include words that pertain to plants and what plants need to grow. Students can list important content-area words they should include in their presentations and plan to include each one.

▸ Encourage students to return to procedural texts they have already crafted to add a handout that shows in addition to tells. How can visuals enhance their procedural texts?

▸ Place students in groups of four, and have each group work on sketches and an oral presentation for a process such as playing a game, making a craft, or using a recipe to prepare a dish. Have the groups teach their procedures to the class. The class can evaluate the procedures to make sure presentations include clear steps and linking words.

▸ Students may want to publish their sketches in different formats, such as slides in an electronic slide show or posters that can be presented and then displayed. Have them speak as they show their slides or posters.

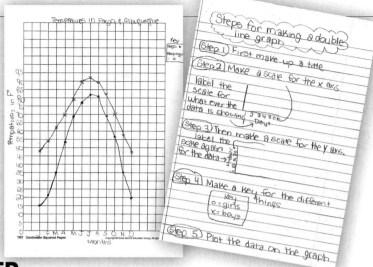

Partner Line Graph

Create a line graph to compare.

FEATURES

- Title
- Vertical grid with caption
- Horizontal grid with caption
- Two distinct colors to show lines for regions being compared
- Labels to name what is being compared
- Key
- Narrative conclusion

FOCUSED MINILESSON

We can use graphs to compare and contrast data. Today we will create line graphs and then craft guidelines for making them. You can use the line graphs you complete to compare data.

TURN &TALK *What are the elements of a line graph? Think back to graphs we've created in math and science. Talk with a partner as you identify some parts of a graph.*

The title tells readers what the visual conveys. Watch as I write the title of my graph: "Snowfall in the Midwest and Rocky Mountain Regions."

Now that I have a title, I'll label the axes. The x axis is the horizontal axis. Watch as I write a clear, concise label for it: "months." I am labeling the months across the axis. Now for the y axis. I am creating a label for it: "snowfall in inches." Watch as I use the data we collected about snowfall to plot a line. I'm starting with the Midwest. I am using blue to plot the lines because I'll show the Rocky Mountain region with another color.

Continue modeling and thinking aloud as you create a line for the Rocky Mountain region. *How will my readers know which line is which? I need to create a key to show which color represents which region. Now my graph is complete! What if my readers wanted to create a graph themselves? I want to craft directions for creating a graph.*

Showcase your thinking as you match directions to your graph. Include simple numbered steps to make the process easy for readers to follow.

Summarize the features: Have partners work in groups to generate features checklists for line graphs. Let students know that they will use their checklists to create graphs they will use to compare data with partners.

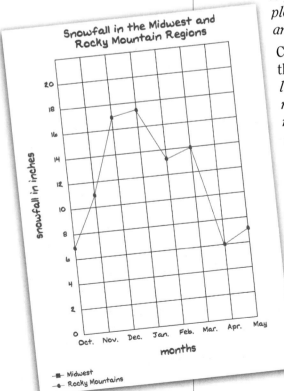

Modeled Writing

WRITING and COACHING

Work with a partner. Each of you will create a line graph and then compare your data. You might choose snowfall, rainfall, and/or overall precipitation. You could each create line graphs showing the change in your height over the years. Find data points, decide on your units, and add headings and labels.

As partners create their graphs, confer with individuals or small groups to support and scaffold understanding. Some students may need additional support in how to create graphs using data, including how to label each axis and create a key.

SHARING and REFLECTING

Sum it up! *Writers, your graphs include clear labels for each axis along with a title and key. You have displayed data in a way that makes it easy for viewers to understand.*

TURN &TALK *We're going to present our graphs to math buddies in another class. What features of graphs do you want to be sure to share? Think together about the most important features.*

ASSESS THE LEARNING

Analyze the graphs and directions for making them to identify writers who need support to include the features of a graph and to explain how to make one. Identify writers who are able to add more sophisticated features to their graphs or their writing about them.

SELF-ASSESSMENT

SELF-ASSESSMENT
Partner Line Graph

	YES	NO
1. Title	☐	☐
2. Vertical grid with caption	☐	☐
3. Horizontal grid with caption	☐	☐
4. Two distinct colors to show lines for regions being compared	☐	☐
5. Labels to name what is being compared	☐	☐
6. Key	☐	☐
7. Narrative conclusion ☺	☐	☐

▶TAKE IT FORWARD

‣ Students can write a narrative conclusion of their graphs. Students should include the conclusion they reached based on the data gathered and the way that the data are displayed in the graph.

‣ Have partners each create one graph about a similar topic and then compare their graphs. They can use linking words for comparisons to draw conclusions about their data.

‣ Have students present their graphs for the class. Classmates can ask questions about the data points and the subjects. Partners can discuss why they chose the subjects they did.

‣ Students can create graphs for science or math problems or data. In science, for example, students might graph the growth of a plant over time. Have them use the guidelines they learned to decide on units, find data points, and write captions. Have students present their findings to small groups or partners.

Taking It Forward: Personal Writing Projects

....

After they have had the opportunity to work through the model unit and lessons in this section, cement your students' understandings about procedural writing by having them complete one or more *personal* writing projects on topics of their choice. This is an important follow-up to the model unit because it allows students to apply their new understandings to their own writing lives based on personal interests.

For example, the teaching processes outlined in the model unit on how to use science equipment can easily be adapted to personal projects on a variety of topics and in a variety of forms. If students have trouble deciding what to write about, you might want to suggest topics and forms such as the ones that follow. Otherwise, give students the freedom to choose the topics they find most interesting—provided you deem them appropriate.

Possible Topics for Procedural Writing

Topics may correlate with content in your science and social studies standards, current events, or class interests.

- How to make a favorite food
- How to make a sandwich
- How to play a game
- How to get to a destination
- How to have a good book discussion
- How to take care of something (a pet, your bike, etc.)
- How to look up a word
- How to wrap a gift
- How to entertain a younger child
- How to be a good classmate or friend
- How to do a science experiment
- How to clean your bedroom
- How to grow a flower
- How to make or do a project
- How to solve a problem

Possible Forms for Procedural Writing

Signs	Illustrations	Guidelines
Recipes	Flowcharts	Demonstrations
Brochures	Advertisements	Timelines
Maps	Notes	Presentations
Directions	Letters	Explanations
Diagrams	Posters	Storyboards
Guides	Scientific procedures	Rules
Instructions	Graphs	

Planning and Implementing Personal Writing Projects

Your students will need preparation, coaching, prompting, and varying amounts of support as they move through their own personal explorations. The ten-session structure presented in the model unit may be too long for personal projects that assume less time spent on instruction and modeling. Give students the time they need to fully develop their topics and to move through the stages of the writing process, but don't be surprised if many students require fewer than ten sessions.

Use the following tips and strategies as needed to ensure each student's success.

Before the Personal Projects:

▸ Help students select topics that they are interested in, and provide research materials if needed.

▸ Continue to use information you gather from the Individual Assessment Record or your Ongoing Monitoring Sheet to provide specific instruction in whole-class, small-group, and individual settings as needed. Use the Daily Planner to lay out each day's lesson.

During the Personal Projects:

▸ Give students the personal checklists from the *Resources* CD-ROM to use as samples for creating their own checklists. A blank checklist can be found on the *Resources* CD-ROM and in the Resources section at the end of this book. Explain to the students that you will also be checking to see if they have included key features on the checklist.

▸ If needed, begin each session with a focused minilesson. Tailor the suggested minilesson to suit the needs of your students.

▸ Continue to provide high-quality mentor texts. Display mentor texts prominently, and allow students time to read them before they begin to write their own. Continue to call students' attention to the features list created during the model unit.

▸ You may want to write your own text along with the students as you did during the model unit to provide an additional model.

▸ Have writing partners conference with each other often to check one another's work for sense and clarity.

▸ As students work independently on their writing and illustrations, note those who are struggling and bring them together for small-group instruction. Use the

Individual Assessment Record and/or the Ongoing Monitoring Sheet to assist in tailoring instruction to the needs of your students.

▸ Students who seem very confident and who have clearly grasped all of the concepts taught so far can be brought together in a small group to extend their understanding to more challenging work.

After the Personal Projects:

▸ Be sure to give students opportunities to share and celebrate their writing projects.

▸ Compare students' final writing products with their earlier attempts in order to evaluate their growth as writers.

▸ Distribute copies of the Student Self-Reflection Sheet (on the *Resources* CD-ROM). Students will benefit greatly from the chance to reflect on their progress and to hear their classmates' feedback.

▸ Reflect on the strengths and challenges of implementing the personal projects. How might the process be adjusted to maximize student learning?

▸ Look at common needs of the class, and address these when students are working on future projects.

Narrative Writing Projects

Narrative writing projects focus on two areas: personal narrative and informational narrative. The purpose of both is to entertain and inform the reader. A *personal narrative* is written in the first person. It often focuses on a brief episode and includes personal reflection. The purpose is to retell events in order, including details and words that show the writer's feelings. Personal narrative can take many forms including autobiographies, personal reflections, diary entries, diagrams, illustrations, and poetry. An *informational narrative* is written in the third person. The events are factual and told in time order, but the information is woven into a narrative format with a beginning, middle, and end. Informational narrative can take many forms including true stories, news reports, observation logs, diagrams, illustrations, and poetry.

CONTENTS

EXTENDED WRITING UNIT

▸ Personal Narratives

▸ Informational Narratives

POWER WRITES

▸ Personal Narrative with Suspense

▸ Personal Narrative of a Single, Focused Moment in Time

▸ Informational Narrative

▸ Key Words and Summary

▸ Narrative Poetry with a Partner

▸ Partner News Article

▸ FlowChart

▸ Team Investigation

The Big Picture

During the model units that follow, students will write a personal narrative and an informational narrative.

PERSONAL NARRATIVE

The mentor text, "The Night I Started Stargazing," provides a model of the structure and features of a great personal narrative. Students begin by observing features of the mentor text and then choose a memorable moment in their own lives to be the topic for their personal narrative. Students use their writer's research notebooks and a personal narrative graphic organizer to collect ideas and plan their writing and then use their notes to write their narrative. They revise, edit, and publish the narrative in the form of pages for a class anthology, adding a title and visuals. Finally, they share their publications with classmates and others and reflect on what they have learned about writing a personal narrative.

Personal Narrative

Session	Focused Minilesson	Writing and Coaching	Sharing and Reflecting
1	Identifying the purpose and features of a personal narrative	Brainstorm topic ideas, share memories with a partner, and list possible topics.	Share your topic list. What topics stand out as great ideas?
2	Planning for writing	Use a graphic organizer to plan and organize the narrative.	How did the organizer help you today? How do you think it will support you as you begin drafting?
3	Crafting a lead that establishes the situation	Use the graphic organizer to begin drafting; focus on writing a descriptive lead.	Analyze your draft with a partner. Does your lead establish the situation?
4	Using temporal words	Use words that show order and sequence.	Share a place where you used temporal words. Why did you choose the words?
5	Infusing concrete words and sensory details	Write or revise sentences that include strong sensory images.	Share a section where you infused some concrete words and sensory details. Tell what you learned about yourself as a writer.
6	Adding action words	Use powerful verbs to enhance the narrative.	Find a place where you infused powerful action verbs. Find a place to replace a "tired" verb.
7	Revising for a satisfying conclusion	Revise or draft a conclusion that strengthens the piece.	Share your ending with your partner.
8	Revising sentences	Reread and revise, focusing on sentence beginnings and flow. Tally beginnings.	What revisions did you make? What did you learn about sentence fluency?
9	Focused edits	Use a checklist to edit for one point at a time.	Share the edits you made and why you made them.
10	Making publishing decisions	Add a title and publish the narrative.	What did you learn about writing a personal narrative? What features should it include?

INFORMATIONAL NARRATIVE

The mentor text, "Battle at Hampton Roads: A Turning Point in Naval History," provides a model of the structure and features of a great informational narrative. Students begin by observing features of the mentor text and then work in pairs or small groups to gather and organize information about an important moment in history, using their research notebooks and an informational narrative graphic organizer. From their notes, students then write their own informational narrative. They revise, edit, and publish the narrative in the form of pages for a class anthology, including supportive visuals such as photographs and timelines. Finally, they share their published pieces with classmates and others and reflect on what they have learned about writing an informational narrative.

Informational Narrative

Session	Focused Minilesson	Writing and Coaching	Sharing and Reflecting
1	Identifying the purpose and features of an informational narrative	Begin to take notes in your research notebook, using a variety of research materials.	What did you learn about your historical event? Share new information with your partner.
2	Citing multiple sources	Continue to take notes, citing sources.	Share with another partner pair. How did you go about finding and using information today?
3	Organizing information in time order	Research and use facts to create a timeline for the event.	Analyze timelines with a partner. Do you need to continue researching?
4	Turning notes into running text	Begin to draft using notes from the timeline and your research notebook; choose quotes.	Share what you wrote today. What was difficult? What can you do to improve the process?
5	Using temporal words and phrases	Add words that provide a clear sequence of events.	Share with a new partner. Where did you include words to help your reader understand the sequence?
6	Infusing descriptions and details	Experiment with adding interesting details.	Share a section of your draft. Where have you added interesting details?
7	Crafting a strong ending	Craft or revise for a strong ending.	Share your ending or thoughts about how you might end your narrative.
8	Revising to add variety to sentence beginnings	Reread and revise to provide variety in sentence beginnings.	Share your revisions. What kinds of sentence beginnings did you try?
9	Focused edits	Edit for one convention at a time; focus on using past-tense verbs.	Identify the editing points you used for each reading. What did you change?
10	Publishing and adding supportive visuals	Publish the narrative, adding visuals.	What did you learn about writing an informational narrative? What advice would you give about writing one?

Assessing Students' Needs

The model units are designed to teach students about the structure and features of specific types of narrative writing as they apply basic writing strategies. Each of the focused minilessons provides you with suggested demonstrations, but you may want to tailor your instruction based on the common needs of your own students. You can assess students' strengths and needs during each unit, in an additional session beforehand, or by analyzing student work that you already have on hand.

Formal Pre-Assessment: After a basic introduction to each writing purpose and form as well as a review of various examples, have students write in the same form about a topic they already know a lot about. Encourage students to use as many of the features of the particular writing form as possible, but don't provide direct support. The goal here is to find out how much students already know about the writing purpose and form so you can tailor your teaching accordingly.

Experimentation in Research Notebooks: You might want to stop short of a formal pre-assessment and instead ask students to experiment with writing in their research notebooks at the end of the first session. This exercise may be less unnerving for some students and should yield enough information to form the basis of your pre-assessment.

Looking Back at Previous Work: Whether you choose to assess students' writing skills before beginning an Extended Writing Unit or during the first session, we recommend that you also consider unrelated writing projects that you've already collected from students. These may not reveal much about your students' ability to write a coherent narrative, for example, but should tell you a great deal about their grasp of writing conventions and other traits such as focus, organization, voice, and sentence fluency. Depending on how much student work you already have on hand, you might not have to devote any class time to pre-assessment.

Focusing on Standards

Before introducing this model unit, carefully review the key skills and understandings below so you can keep the lesson objectives in mind as you teach, coach, and monitor students' growth as writers of narrative texts.

KEY SKILLS AND UNDERSTANDINGS: NARRATIVE WRITING GRADE 5
Purpose
Understands the purpose for writing a narrative piece
Ideas/Research
Generates ideas
Focuses on an event or sequence of events
Organizes ideas and plans writing
Provides factual information
Includes engaging related details
Lists/cites sources
Organization/Text Features
Includes a title that relates closely to the narrative
Includes an engaging lead
Relates an event or sequence of events in time order
Presents information in paragraphs with main ideas and supporting details
Has a conclusion that includes thoughts and feelings and wraps up the piece
Includes illustrations and/or visuals that support the narrative
Language/Style
Uses first person for personal narratives
Uses third person for informational narratives
Uses a consistent verb tense
Includes precise, powerful words
Includes vivid descriptions and images
Uses temporal words and phrases (*at first, finally*, etc.)
Demonstrates sentence variety and fluency
Conventions and Presentation
Uses complete sentences
Begins sentences with capital letters
Ends sentences with correct punctuation
Uses appropriate spelling
Creates interesting, effective page layouts

This list is the basis for both the Individual Assessment Record and the Ongoing Monitoring Sheet shown in Figure 1.1. (Both forms can be found in the Resources section at the back of this book and also on the *Resources* CD-ROM.) Use the Individual Assessment Record if you want to keep separate records on individual students. The Ongoing Monitoring Sheet gives you a simple mechanism for recording information on all your students as you move around the class, evaluating their work in progress. Use this information to adapt instruction and session length as needed.

At the end of these and any additional units you may teach on narrative writing, compare students' final publications with their initial attempts at writing in the text type. Use the Ongoing Monitoring Sheet and/or the Individual Assessment Record to record students' growth as writers.

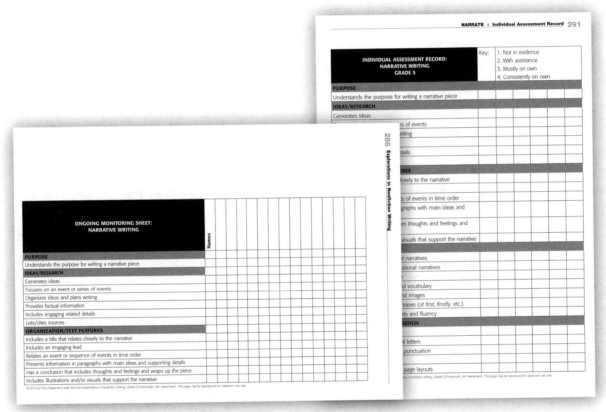

Figure 1.1 Individual Assessment Record and Ongoing Monitoring Sheet

Planning and Facilitating the Unit

Students will need preparation, coaching, prompting, and support as they move through this and other Extended Writing Units. Use the following tips and strategies as needed to ensure each student's success.

Before the Unit:

▸ When planning your teaching, bear in mind that each lesson in the model units that follow is designed to be completed in one session. However, you will likely find that your students need more time for certain activities. Take the time you need to adequately respond to the unique needs of your students, and remember that they will likely progress through the writing process at their own pace.

▸ Begin building background knowledge about the text type and writing topics in advance. Shared reading, guided reading, and read-aloud experiences as well as group discussions will ensure that students are not dependent exclusively on their own research.

▸ For the research component, you may want to gather suitable books, magazine articles, encyclopedia entries, and websites in your classroom or work with the media center teacher to assemble a collection in advance. Make sure the research materials you gather are at a range of difficulty levels and include plenty of text features such as close-up photographs, captions, bold headings, and diagrams.

During the Unit:

▸ Begin each session with a focused minilesson to demonstrate the traits of writing the particular type of text you're exploring. Tailor the suggested minilesson to suit the needs of your students. The mentor texts on the *Resources* CD-ROM and in the *Book of Mentor Texts* are models you can use to show students the structure and features of each text type. You may want to use other mentor texts to assist you with your demonstrations.

▸ Be sure to model note-taking for students as you think aloud about information in reference materials. Use chart paper and sticky notes to capture your thinking, and display the models prominently as students work on their own research and note-taking.

▸ As students work independently on their writing and publishing, note those who are struggling and bring them together for small-group instruction. Use the Individual Assessment Record and/or the Ongoing Monitoring Sheet to assist in tailoring instruction to the needs of your students.

▸ Students who seem very confident and who have clearly grasped all of the concepts taught so far can be brought together in a small group to extend their understanding to more challenging work.

▸ Provide templates for students who need extra support when writing. You'll find a variety of graphic organizers on the *Resources* CD-ROM from which to choose.

After the Unit:

▸ Be sure to give students opportunities to share and celebrate their individual writing projects.

▸ Distribute copies of the Personal Checklist for Narrative Writing as shown in Figure 1.2 (This form can be found on the *Resources* CD-ROM and in the Resources section at the end of this book). Students will benefit greatly from the chance to reflect on their progress during the unit and to hear their classmates' feedback.

▸ Compare students' final writing products with pre-assessments and past work to evaluate their growth as writers of narrative texts.

▸ Reflect on the strengths and challenges of implementing this series of lessons. How might it be adjusted to maximize student learning?

▸ Look at common needs of the class, and address these when planning future explorations or when using the Power Writes.

Personal Checklist for Narrative Writing

Process Reflections:

Research:
I used the following resources in gathering facts: _____

Drafting:
I solved the following problems in my writing: _____

Revising:
When revising, I focused on improving my message by: _____

Editing:
To ensure that I edited effectively, I used an editing checklist and concentrated on: _____

Presentation:
I chose the following format to present my writing: _____

I am most proud of: _____

I have checked the following:
- ☐ My title tells who or what the narrative is about.
- ☐ There is an inviting lead that draws the reader in.
- ☐ The information is organized and separated into paragraphs with main ideas and supporting details.
- ☐ I have included factual information throughout.
- ☐ I have included words and phrases such as *at first* and *finally* that show the passage of time.
- ☐ I have included descriptive details and vivid images.
- ☐ I have used precise, powerful words.
- ☐ I have used the first-person or third-person point of view consistently.
- ☐ The closing includes my thoughts and feelings and wraps up the narrative.
- ☐ My writing has sentence fluency, and I have used a variety of sentence beginnings.
- ☐ I have included visuals that support the narrative.
- ☐ The published narrative has an organized and engaging layout.
- ☐ I have listed my sources.

Figure 1.2 Personal Checklist for Narrative Writing

SESSION 1

Identifying the Purpose and Features of Personal Narrative

Writers analyze a personal narrative, identify its structure and features, and then brainstorm topic ideas for personal narratives of their own.

SESSION SNAPSHOT

Genre Focus: Features of a Personal Narrative

Process Focus: Prewriting

Trait(s): Ideas

Mentor Text: "The Night I Started Stargazing," by James Cronce

My Ideas for a Personal Narrative

· Learning to ride two-wheeler
· First day at college
· Seeing sunset at lake
· Yesterday's perfect swim

Modeled Writing

FOCUSED MINILESSON

Summarize the learning goals: *We are going to focus on a type of nonfiction writing called personal narrative. A personal narrative describes an incident or a series of incidents that happened over a short period of time. It's a true story about something that happened to you and how you felt about it.*

To write quality personal narratives, it will help us to first learn about what makes a personal narrative great—what are its features and its structure?

Using the Mentor Text

■ The mentor text for this unit is "The Night I Started Stargazing," by James Cronce. You will find it on page 29 of the *Book of Mentor Texts* and in the Narrate section on the *Resources* CD-ROM. Make enough copies of the mentor text for each student to have one. You may also want to use an electronic projection device to display the mentor for whole-class viewing.

■ Read the first paragraph. *Right away, I can identify one important feature of a personal narrative. Do you notice the pronoun I? This pronoun shows that the narrative is written from the first-person point of view. The author is part of the narrative, so he refers to himself as I.*

■ *I also notice that the author focuses on one memorable moment in his life. He pulls us into the narrative by setting the scene and telling us about where and when the event takes place. The vivid sensory details help us visualize the scene. Then, he tells us that the moon comes into focus through his telescope, and we're hooked—we want to find out what will happen next. As we continue to read, be on the lookout for more features of a great personal narrative.*

■ Guide writers in examining the mentor text, perhaps by having them work in small groups to discover its features. If necessary, point out that in a personal narrative, authors use precise, powerful words and write about the events in the order in which they occur.

■ *Writers, over the next ten sessions, we are going to write our own personal narratives about memorable moments from our own lives.*

TURN &TALK *Think together. When you craft your personal narratives about episodes from your own lives, what features will you include?*

■ Guide students as they share their observations, and record their thinking on a chart labeled "Features of a Great Personal Narrative."

Modeling

■ *To write a great personal narrative, it helps to list ideas. I'll start by thinking about some memorable moments in my life and listing them on paper.*

■ *Keep in mind that a personal narrative is not a story that starts with the day you were born and then tells about all the major things that happened to you between then and now. Instead, a great personal narrative hones in on a single episode and draws it out with rich descriptions and insights that make the incident come alive.*

■ *Watch as I write my list of possible topics for my personal narrative. My list includes "learning to ride two-wheeler; first day at college; seeing sunset at lake; and yesterday's perfect swim." Any one of these moments would make a great topic for my personal narrative, but I'm not going to decide on my topic today. Right now I am just listing ideas in my writer's notebook.*

> ### Features of a Great Personal Narrative
>
> · Introduction that sets the scene
> · Precise and powerful words
> · Sensory details
> · Ending that shows the author's response to the situation
> · May include illustration or photography
> · First-person point of view
> · Use of temporal words and phrases to show sequence or passage of time

WRITING and COACHING

■ To get students thinking about topics, you might tell about a memorable moment of your own. For example, you might tell about finding a nest of baby rabbits under your back porch. Or you might tell about a time when you had to do something you were dreading and how you felt when it was finally over. Your narrative should be brief and memorable.

■ Students can share their ideas for personal narratives with partners. You might offer a topic: *I told you about seeing a beautiful sunset while I was staying at the lake last summer. Have you ever seen anything unexpected outside? Tell your partner about it.*

■ After giving students time to share their memories, encourage them to brainstorm a list of possible topics for their personal narratives.

SHARING and REFLECTING

TURN &TALK *Writers, share your topic lists with your partner. What ideas stand out to you as great ideas for personal narratives?*

■ If students are ready to use their partners' feedback to choose their topic, encourage them to put a star beside it on their list of topics.

■ Lead a discussion about personal narratives, reviewing the list of features. Revisit the mentor text to solidify students' understanding of this purpose for writing.

■ Gather the writer's notebooks, and analyze each student's attempts to create a list of topics. Identify writers who need additional support in choosing a topic for their narratives as well as those who are ready to extend their thinking.

TIP Students may struggle with listing ideas, or they may lists ideas that are very broad. Help them narrow their lists to ideas that will result in a tightly focused narrative. If, for example, a student lists "my trip to Disney World," ask narrowing questions to hone in on a great episode from the trip, such as riding the Tower of Terror or watching the fireworks in the park. If they struggle to list ideas, continue to tell stories of your own that focus on brief memorable moments.

SESSION 2
Planning for Writing

Writers use graphic organizers to plan their personal narratives.

SESSION SNAPSHOT

Research Strategy: Organizing with a Graphic Organizer

Process Focus: Prewriting

Trait(s): Ideas, Organization

Mentor Text: "The Night I Started Stargazing," by James Cronce

TIP It is important for students to remember that graphic organizers can be useful tools when preparing to write. Emphasize that an organizer can help bridge the gap between thinking about a true story from their own lives and writing about it. Be sure to think aloud as much as possible as you model working with a Personal Narrative Graphic Organizer such as the one on the *Resources* CD-ROM.

FOCUSED MINILESSON

This unit includes modeled writing about an incident involving a community service project. Most likely you will want to replace this with an authentic personal narrative about an episode or event in your own life.

Review the learning goals from the previous session. If time allows, have students turn and talk about what they have learned so far.

Summarize the learning goals for today's session: *In our last session, you created a list of topics for personal narratives and chose a topic you most want to write about. Today you will hone in on that idea and consider how to develop it into a strong personal narrative. You'll use an organizer to plan the narrative so that it will draw readers in, sparkle with detail, and end with your feelings or observations.*

Using the Mentor Text

- Display the mentor text, and discuss how the writer may have planned in advance. *Writers, do you notice that this narrative focuses on just one event? The writer does a great job of pulling us into the story, including details that make us feel like we are there, and then closing by describing his feelings about the stargazing episode. Writing that is this well focused takes careful planning. Before we start writing our own personal narratives, we're going to do some careful planning, too.*

Modeling

- *Graphic organizers are great tools for helping us gather the thoughts and ideas we want to include in our writing. I am going to use this special graphic organizer for a personal narrative.* Display the Personal Narrative Graphic Organizer (from the Narrate section on the *Resources* CD-ROM) on chart paper or with an electronic projection device.

- *Today I'm going to use this graphic organizer to help me think about a special moment in my life. Watch as I use the organizer to plan my narrative about the time that I volunteered to help clean up the beach near my home and found a glass fishing float stuck in the sand. I will start by recording my topic, "Beach Clean-up," in this first box. Next, I'll jot down some words that describe the setting. I will write "Cannon Beach" since that is the name of the beach where I was working. I will also write the phrases "bright sun; white, crashing waves; sand dollars." These phrases help me remember just what the day was like when I volunteered to help clean up the beach. Notice that I didn't record complete sentences. When you are using a graphic organizer, you can use phrases or sentence fragments to represent your thinking. You'll be able to write complete sentences later as you draft.*

TURN &TALK *Partners, examine my graphic organizer, and think about how it might help me as I begin to draft my personal narrative. Talk together.*

■ *I heard many of you say that a graphic organizer like this might help me develop my topic and remember the details that would make the event come to life for my readers. I agree! When I stop and try to visualize the event, it helps me map out a clear and cohesive narrative.*

■ Continue to model as you fill in the other sections of the graphic organizer. Be sure students understand that their organizers are not "final." As they continue to draft, they may add more details or decide to leave out some of the details that are listed. The organizer is a planning tool, not the final product.

■ *This graphic organizer is a great tool for jotting down details that will lead to a focused and creative narrative that engages readers. As you are writing, you might scratch out some ideas, write new ones, draw arrows to new boxes—it's okay for your organizers to be messy.*

Personal Narrative Organizer

Topic

Beach Clean-up

Setting: Place and Time

Cannon Beach

Main Event

Sensory Details

bright sun; white, crashing waves; sand dollars

Emotions, Feelings, and Reactions

Ending

Modeled Writing

WRITING and COACHING

■ Invite students to use a graphic organizer to plan and organize their personal narrative. Encourage students to take the time to visualize the event and include as much information about the event as they can.

■ Coach students as they include phrases, sentences, or sentence fragments in each section of their graphic organizers.

■ You might need to model looking over the notes from your writer's notebook to help you consider what details to place in the organizer. As you model, pick and choose from the notes to show that you need not include everything in the organizer. Instead, you are choosing the details that will assist your readers in visualizing the events.

■ Remind students that their organizers are working documents. They can always return to them to add more details, cross out ideas that aren't working, and so on.

SHARING and REFLECTING

TURN &TALK *How did the graphic organizer help you today? How do you think this tool will support you as you begin drafting?*

■ Bring writers back together to review how to use a graphic organizer to organize and plan for writing.

■ At the end of the session, collect the organizers and review your students' attempts to plan their writing. Note students who have not yet found their focus and those who are ready to begin drafting.

TIP The graphic organizer focuses on the features of a great personal narrative that were identified in the first session, and it includes topics that will be covered in future sessions. For this reason, you may want to have students complete the organizer in this session or fill it in session by session as you cover the various features.

TIP Some writers might experience difficulty in narrowing their topics to one moment in time. Help students understand that powerful narratives don't tell about an entire vacation from beginning to end. Instead, a powerful narrative might focus on one memorable part of that trip.

SESSION 3
Crafting a Lead That Establishes the Situation

Writers begin to draft leads that orient the reader by establishing the situation.

SESSION SNAPSHOT

Process Focus: Prewriting, Planning

Trait(s): Ideas, Organization

Mentor Text: "The Night I Started Stargazing," by James Cronce

FOCUSED MINILESSON

Review the learning goals from the previous session. Consider having students take another look at their organizers with partners to be sure they are prepared to move into drafting.

Summarize the learning goals for today's session: *We have begun to focus on the details that will make our personal narratives sparkle. Today we'll draw readers into our narratives so that they will understand the situation and want to read more.*

Using the Mentor Text

■ Read the beginning of the mentor text.

TURN &TALK *Writers, what do you notice about how the author began his narrative?*

■ Guide students to understand that a powerful personal narrative draws readers in by establishing the setting or situation right away.

Modeling

■ *To craft a powerful personal narrative, I need to create a lead that will establish the situation and make my readers want to read on. I could begin with "You're getting ready to read about a time I helped to clean up a beach. It was cool!" However, I think I can do much better than that. As I browse through some of the nonfiction books in our classroom library, I notice that some authors begin by describing the setting in detail. I'm going to try that.*

■ *As I examine my graphic organizer, I notice that I recorded some descriptions of that day. Perhaps I can use some of those images to begin my narrative.*

TURN &TALK *Partners, think together. How could I use the description of that day to begin my writing? Do you think it would help to establish the situation for my reader? What suggestions do you have?*

■ *I heard some great suggestions. I think I'll begin by describing how the beach looked when I arrived early that morning. Watch as I write: "The sky was a bright cobalt blue, and the waves were high and foamy on the morning that I learned a valuable lesson." Notice that I use a specific description of the setting to help readers feel that they were right*

Draft 1

The sky was a bright, cobalt blue and the waves were high and foamy on the morning that I learned a valuable lesson.

Draft 2

When I set out to clean up Cannon Beach on that bright, sunny morning so long ago, I had no idea that I was about to find something that would teach me the lesson of a lifetime.

Modeled Writing

there on the beach with me. I also cued my readers in to the fact that I learned something from the experience.

- Emphasize that there are multiple ways to begin a personal narrative, and consider modeling others so that not every student begins with the same lead that you created: "When I set out to clean up Cannon Beach on that bright blue morning so long ago, I had no idea that I was about to find something that would teach me the lesson of a lifetime."

WRITING and COACHING

- Guide your students as they use their graphic organizers to begin drafting. Encourage them to examine other nonfiction texts to see how they begin.

- Students may benefit from reading their leads aloud to partners. Have partners close their eyes to see if they can visualize the situations. What tips can partners offer to make these narratives even more cohesive and descriptive?

- As you confer with individual writers, cue their thinking with questions such as *How does this lead establish the situation of this narrative? Have you tried another lead? What are you learning about yourself as a writer today?*

SHARING and REFLECTING

TURN &TALK *Partners, analyze what you have written so far. Are you satisfied that you have written a lead that will establish the situation for your reader? Share your thinking with a partner.*

- Lead a class discussion about creating a lead that "worked." What worked well? What was more challenging?

- Collect students' graphic organizers and drafts, and analyze their attempts at writing an effective lead. As you identify students who may need additional instruction to draft a lead, consider which strategies you might use. Show more models? Have students write as a group? Work with them to rewrite a beginning? Consider also which students may be ready for additional craft elements in their leads, such as powerful opening elements set off by commas.

TIP Some students may benefit from additional support in crafting a lead that establishes the situation. Consider collecting several nonfiction books that utilize these kinds of leads. Lead a discussion about why these leads are powerful. Help students utilize the same strategies as they begin their narratives.

TIP Modeling a variety of leads will ensure that you don't read the same opening in each narrative. Encourage students who need extra support to examine leads with you and evaluate their effectiveness. What makes some leads powerful while others are weak? Consider displaying leads on a bulletin board and/or creating a features list for powerful beginnings that students can use as a reference as they write.

SESSION 4
Using Temporal Words

Writers continue to draft their personal narratives, focusing on selecting words that show time order or sequence.

SESSION SNAPSHOT

Process Focus: Drafting, Revising

Trait(s): Organization, Word Choice

Mentor Text: "The Night I Started Stargazing," by James Cronce

FOCUSED MINILESSON

Review the learning goals from the previous session—crafting an engaging lead. If time allows, have students turn and talk about the strategies they used to draw readers into their narratives.

Summarize the learning goals for today's session: *A narrative is unlike many other kinds of nonfiction writing because it describes events in time order, from beginning to end. Because this is such an important feature of narrative writing, today we'll focus on infusing our drafts with words and phrases that show time order and sequence. These words and phrases are called* temporal *words and phrases.*

Using the Mentor Text

■ Read the beginning of the mentor text.

■ *Do you notice how the author uses temporal words and phrases such as* now, then, *and* this time *to signal sequence and show the passage of time?*

■ Read aloud the second-to-last paragraph. *As I read this section, I can easily understand when the events took place. It helps me as a reader. I can see how the author has used the phrase* "for another half-hour" *and the word* "finally" *to show the passage of time.*

TURN &TALK *Partners, think together. Identify temporal words and phrases that signal sequence and show the passage of time.*

■ As students identify temporal words and phrases from the mentor text, record them on a chart so students can refer to it later as they write.

Modeling

■ Display the chart of temporal words and phrases your students created, or print the list titled Temporal Words and Phrases to Show Sequence from the *Resources* CD-ROM.

■ *Writers, we have created a list of temporal words and phrases. These words alert our readers that we are describing a sequence of events. In a narrative, that's really important. A narrative describes events in order, but it's not like a procedural text in which every sentence starts with a word like* first, next, *and* last. *We want our writing to be more powerful than that. I am going to challenge myself to use a variety of sequence words and phrases that show the passage of time.*

■ *I am working on the section of my draft in which I describe how I walked along the beach picking up trash and found a treasure. I have written,* "I was eager to begin cleaning my assigned section of the beach, so as soon as I grabbed the plastic garbage bag, I started down the deserted stretch of rocky coastline."

> **TURN &TALK** *Writers, examine this section of my personal narrative. Identify a word or phrase that shows time order.*

■ Continue demonstrating how you infuse temporal words to show the sequence of events. *Now I want to smooth out my writing a bit and show the progression of events in my narrative. Watch as I write:* "I walked a few steps, I saw a sparkly, a round object sticking out of the sand." *These sentences are a bit choppy, and they don't show time order. On our list of temporal words and phrases, I see the word* after. *This would work perfectly to combine the two sentences and make them flow more smoothly:* "After I walked a few steps, I saw. . . ." *Now I am satisfied I have helped my readers with time order while also making a sentence that sounds better!*

> I was eager to begin cleaning my assigned section of the beach, so as soon as I grabbed the plastic garbage bag, I started down the deserted stretch of rocky coastline. After I walked a few steps, I saw a sparkly, round object sticking out of the sand.

Modeled Writing

WRITING and COACHING

■ As writers return to drafting their personal narratives, support them in selecting words that show order and sequence.

■ Remind writers that they are focusing on one powerful event. While adding temporal words and phrases to their drafts, they need to maintain a tight focus and hone in on the actions and feelings surrounding one episode.

■ Coach writers with questions such as *What happens next? What word or phrase might you add to keep the events in order?*

■ Writers who are ready for extra challenges can begin to use other types of linking words, such as those that add information or signal comparisons. See the *Resources* CD-ROM for these word lists.

■ Encourage students to strive for variety as they work to infuse temporal words and phrases. You might consider modeling various placements of temporal words—at the beginning of sentences, in the middle, or even toward the end.

■ Remind students to refer back to their graphic organizers as they continue to draft.

TIP Emphasize a variety of temporal words and where students place them to avoid dull constructions such as *First, we . . . Then, we . . . Next, we. . . .* Through modeling and practice, students' use of temporal words and phrases will become more sophisticated and their writing more fluent. By reading models aloud, you'll help train your students' ears to notice smooth, flowing writing.

SHARING and REFLECTING

■ Return to the mentor text, an exemplary piece of student writing, or your own modeled writing. Ask students to focus on temporal words and phrases and discuss how they propel the narrative forward.

> **TURN &TALK** *Find a place in your writing where you wrote or revised to include temporal words. Share with your partner why you chose the words that you did. What did these words or phrases add to the narrative?*

■ Gather the drafts and analyze your students' attempts to include temporal words and phrases. Identify writers who are stuck on "tired transitions" and direct them to the class list of temporal words and provide supplemental teaching as needed. Use the class writing rubric or the individual student rubric on the *Resources* CD-ROM to track writing proficiencies.

SESSION 5
Infusing Concrete Words and Sensory Details

Writers use concrete words and sensory details to create vivid images for their readers.

SESSION SNAPSHOT

Process Focus: Drafting, Revising

Trait(s): Ideas, Word Choice

Mentor Text: "The Night I Started Stargazing," by James Cronce

FOCUSED MINILESSON

Review the learning goals from the previous session. If time allows, have students turn and talk about the various temporal words and phrases they used and how they infused them into their writing.

Summarize the learning goals for today: *One of the ways authors create rich images for their readers is by using concrete words and sensory details that help readers visualize the action and feel like they are experiencing the events. This is our focus for today.*

Using the Mentor Text

■ Display a copy of the mentor text, and draw students' attention to the third paragraph, which is particularly rich in imagery and details.

> **TURN &TALK** *Partners, take a look at this portion of the text. What words appeal to your senses? What can you hear when you read this text? What can you see and feel? What words bring the narrative to life for you? What sensory images and concrete details has the author used to help us create a vivid mental image of what is happening?*

■ Invite partners to share their thinking with the class. Guide students to discuss the image of the moon as a "silver sliver" or a "crescent cookie."

Modeling

■ *As I continue to write my personal narrative about the time I volunteered to clean up a section of beach and learned a lesson in the process, I want to focus my attention on choosing words and phrases that will help my readers feel as though they are right there with me. One way I can do this is to include concrete words that involve my five senses.*

> The hot sand squished between my toes as I reached down to pick up the shimmering, colorful object. I was so mesmerized by what I saw that I barely heard the seagulls screeching overhead . . .

Modeled Writing

■ *Let's examine this sentence: "I bent down to pick up the shimmering object." I want to tell more about the moment when I found a glass fishing float in the sand. Watch me as I close my eyes and try to relive that moment, focusing on what I heard, saw, felt, and touched.*

> **TURN &TALK** *Close your eyes and think about what it would feel like to be on a beach on a warm day. What sensory images come to mind? What words could I include that would involve my five senses?*

■ *I heard some fantastic words and images. I could write:* "The hot sand squished between my toes as I reached down to pick up the shimmering, colorful object. I was so mesmerized by what I saw that I barely heard the seagulls screeching overhead."

- Continue demonstrating how you add concrete words and sensory details. Show students how your narrative links back to your graphic organizer, especially to the section where you recorded sensory details.

- Draft or revise another sentence or two, sharing your thinking as you appeal to the senses with strong words and phrases that evoke imagery.

WRITING and COACHING

- As writers return to drafting, encourage them to write or revise sentences that include strong sensory images. Have them go back to their organizers for details they may have overlooked.

- Coach writers as they use words to describe sight, sound, smell, taste, and touch in their narratives. Assist them as they craft descriptive writing with sensory images.

- Remind them of their goal: *Remember, you are helping your readers visualize. Use your senses to help your readers see what you saw and hear what you heard.*

- If students struggle to add concrete words and sensory images, ask questions such as *How hot was it outside when you were planting that tree? How can you capture what it felt like so your readers can experience it, too?*

SHARING and REFLECTING

- Return to the mentor text, an exemplary piece of student writing, or your own piece of modeled writing. Ask students to focus on the concrete words and sensory details that are included in the piece. Lead a discussion about how these additions help create vivid images.

  TURN &TALK *Find a place in your writing where you infused some concrete words and sensory details. Share the section with your partner, and tell what you learned about yourself as a writer today.*

- Gather writer's notebooks to do a quick assessment of students' work. Use the class writing rubric or the individual student rubric on the *Resources* CD-ROM to track writing proficiencies as you note which students may need extra assistance to write richly detailed sensory images and which ones may be ready for modeling of more sophisticated methods.

TIP Students may benefit from combing through mentor texts for examples of words that appeal to all the senses. Have them sort words and phrases on a wall chart that has spaces designated for each of the senses. Encourage students to use the chart for inspiration and to add other examples of sensory words they find.

TIP Less experienced writers might benefit from additional support in identifying sensory images. Read a few brief and richly detailed poems with the students. Invite them to categorize the images according to the five senses. Lead a discussion about how using sensory images can improve their writing.

TIP Students may benefit from reading with partners. Challenge partners to listen with an ear for sensory images and clear mental pictures. Have partners describe the mental pictures they create. Do any of the images need adjusting? Partners can offer feedback for revision.

SESSION 6
Adding Action Words

Writers use powerful verbs to enhance their personal narratives.

SESSION SNAPSHOT

Process Focus: Drafting, Revising

Trait(s): Ideas, Word Choice

Mentor Text: "The Night I Started Stargazing," by James Cronce

TIP Show students how to underline the verbs in their narratives so they can focus more fully on them. Then, help them identify passive verbs that show no action, and encourage them to replace these verbs with more dynamic choices. Identifying and recording sentences with powerful verbs from mentor texts might also assist students as they internalize the process of making strong verb choices.

FOCUSED MINILESSON

Review the previous session's learning goals. Have students turn and talk about the strategies they used to create powerful sensory images in their writing.

Summarize the learning goals for today: *One of the ways authors make their writing come to life is by infusing verbs that are strong and vivid. Our focus today is making sure our narratives are chock-full of powerful action verbs.*

Using the Mentor Text

■ Revisit the mentor text with students. Draw their attention to particularly strong verbs, such as *jolted, crunched, leapt,* and *tramped.*

> **TURN &TALK** *Partners, think together. What impact do the verbs in this section have on you as a reader?*

■ Invite partners to share their thinking with the class. Guide students to self-discover that strong verbs propel the action forward and add excitement to the narrative.

Modeling

■ *As I write my narrative, I want to focus more closely on the glass fishing float that I found and what it was like to discover this treasure. Here is my first attempt at describing this moment:* "I saw the shimmering glass in the sand. I made a noise because I was surprised. I picked up the orb to show my friends, who took a close look at the orb in my wet, sandy hands."

■ *I have a great start with some descriptive words like* shimmering, wet, *and* sandy *and even a very descriptive and specific noun,* orb, *which is another word for a round object. But my verbs need some help. In the first sentence, the word* saw *doesn't really capture what happened. The orb was partially hidden, so it's almost like I caught a glimpse of it by accident. The verb* spied *captures that action really well. Watch as I revise:* "I spied the shimmering glass, just one part sticking out of the sand."

> **TURN &TALK** *Writers, think together as you take a look at the next sentence:* "I made a noise because I was surprised." *What are some other ways that you could say "made a noise" that might be more powerful and descriptive?*

- Continue modeling how you think of options and include verbs that are powerful and descriptive as you revise your writing: "I gasped in surprise at the sparkling object." "Carefully extracting the orb from the sand, I shared it with my friends, who gazed at the object in my wet, sandy hands."

- Let students know that whether they are writing or revising, they can consider powerful verbs to add to their personal narratives today.

WRITING and COACHING

- As writers return to drafting, support them in adding powerful verbs to their narratives. If your students have experience working with a thesaurus, invite them to use one to help with verb choices.

- Coach writers with questions such as *What verbs have you added? How have they strengthened your narrative? You used the word said three times in these sentences. How did you say something? Did you whisper, gasp, cry out, or squeal? Think of how the verbs you use affect your reader, reflect what really happened, and set the tone for your narrative.*

- Pull together students who are struggling with verb choices, and try a visualization exercise. Ask students to visualize flat verbs such as *ran*, *said*, and *saw*. What did they see in their mind's eye? Now have them visualize stronger verbs like *sprinted*, *stammered*, and *stared*. Which verbs are easier to "see"?

SHARING and REFLECTING

- Return to the mentor text, an exemplary piece of student writing, or your own piece of modeled writing. Ask students to focus on the action verbs that are included in the piece. Lead a discussion about how these verbs propel the action, create feelings, and help readers visualize the action.

  TURN & TALK *Find a place in your writing where you infused powerful action verbs. Identify another place where you might replace a tired verb with one that shows more action.*

- Gather the writer's notebooks, and take a closer look at students' verb choices. Identify students who may need assistance to craft writing with strong, powerful verbs and those who may be ready for more sophisticated features such as adverbs. Use the class writing rubric or the individual student rubric on the *Resources* CD-ROM to track writing proficiencies.

Draft 1

I saw the shimmering glass in the sand. I made a noise because I was surprised. I picked up the orb to show my friends, who took a close look at the orb in my wet, sandy hands.

Draft 2

I spied the shimmering glass, just one part sticking out of the sand. I gasped in surprise at the sparkling object. Carefully extracting the orb from the sand, I shared it with my friends, who gazed at the object in my wet, sandy hands.

Modeled Writing

TIP Some writers will struggle with choosing powerful verbs for their narratives. Gather those students into a small group, and provide them with a model that you can revise together. Consider also creating a class chart that displays a list of "tired" verbs along with strong verb alternatives for them. For example, you might list the word *walk* along with alternatives such as *saunter, strut, creep, step, stride, tramp, dawdle,* and *limp*.

SESSION 7
Revising for a Satisfying Conclusion

Writers craft endings that wrap up their narratives by including thoughts and feelings about the episode or event.

SESSION SNAPSHOT

Process Focus: Drafting, Revising

Trait(s): Organization, Voice

Mentor Text: "The Night I Started Stargazing," by James Cronce

---

Conclusion #1

Cleaning up the beach was a lot of fun. You should try it!

Conclusion #2

When I volunteered to clean up a section of the beach, I knew I would be picking up trash. What I didn't realize is that I would also be picking up treasure, and a new respect for our amazing environment.

Modeled Writing

FOCUSED MINILESSON

Reflect on the learning goals from the last session. Students might turn and talk about the strategies they used to ensure that their narratives are full of powerful verbs.

Summarize the learning goals for this session: *We have written some powerful personal narratives. Today we'll focus on writing endings that leave our readers with strong impressions about our feelings and thoughts about the events we have described.*

Using the Mentor Text

■ Display the mentor text again, and read the conclusion aloud.

> **TURN &TALK** *Partners, analyze the ending that this author wrote. What does it do for the piece? How does it showcase the author's response to the event that was described in the narrative?*

■ Invite partners to share their thinking with the class.

Modeling

■ *I've written my personal narrative describing the time I helped clean a section of the beach and found a beautiful glass fishing float. I am feeling finished, but I need to consider some options for my conclusion. I could say,* "Cleaning up the beach was a lot of fun. You should try it!" *Here is another ending I could try:* "When I volunteered to clean up a section of the beach, I knew I would be picking up trash. What I didn't realize is that I would also be picking up treasure, and a new respect for our amazing environment."

> **TURN &TALK** *Evaluate both of the conclusions I have written. Which one do you prefer? Why?*

■ Demonstrate how you experiment with several endings by saying each of them out loud and then choosing the one that sounds best.

■ As you talk about endings, consider creating or adding to a features chart to guide students as they write. Students might consider various methods for ending, such as ending with a question or restating the lead in new words. Be sure students avoid ending a narrative with a phrase like "in conclusion" or "to sum it up." Students may simply end a narrative by describing the final event, and that works as a narrative ending—just caution students not to leave their readers "hanging" at the end without a satisfying conclusion.

TIP If you have students who are struggling with drafting or revising an ending, consider using a shared text that is familiar to the students. Invite pairs to craft new endings for the selection. Then, encourage pairs to share the new ending with the rest of the group.

WRITING and COACHING

■ Support students who are drafting their conclusions as well as those who are revising. Cue their thinking with questions such as *What endings have you tried? How did you go about picking an ending that worked for you? How has this revision strengthened your piece?* Refer students to the features chart you created. Assure them that there is no one right way to end a personal narrative, but their readers will want to know how the episode ended and what effect it had on them.

■ If students need extra support, gather them in a small group to have them add an ending to a narrative that you provide. Talk about what feelings or reactions the author might have and the best way to "wrap up."

■ Encourage students to orally share their endings with a partner before they begin drafting and to give each other advice on how to make the writing powerful.

SHARING and REFLECTING

TURN &TALK *Today we focused on revising to make sure we have crafted a satisfying ending. The ending gives us one last chance to make a good impression on our reader, so it's important to take time and think carefully when we craft the ending. Share your ending with your partner.*

■ After partners share, coach the students as they reflect on what they learned about creating a satisfying ending.

■ Gather the drafts and analyze your students' attempts to craft a satisfying ending. Did they conclude the action, include the writer's feelings, and sum up a response to the events? Identify writers who may need additional modeling as well as those who are ready for higher levels of sophistication. Use the rubrics found on the *Resources* CD-ROM to track writing proficiencies.

SESSION 8
Revising Sentences

Writers examine their sentence beginnings and revise to improve sentence fluency.

SESSION SNAPSHOT

Process Focus: Revising

Trait(s): Sentence Fluency

FOCUSED MINILESSON

Have students reflect on what they learned about crafting satisfying endings. If time allows, have students turn and talk about the strategies they used to create powerful endings for their narratives.

Summarize the learning goals: *Your narratives have really taken shape! Today we're going to focus on sentence beginnings to make sure we have variety. This kind of variety engages our readers and makes for more satisfying narratives.*

Modeling

■ *When I think I'm finished with a draft, one of my important jobs is to focus on how my sentences are crafted. When I do that, I create a piece that is a joy to read aloud. I want my writing to have rhythm and to flow smoothly. Are my sentences of different lengths? Do I use a variety of words to begin my sentences, or do they all start the same way? These are the questions I will ask myself as I read over my draft with an ear for sentence fluency.*

■ *Listen as I read this section of my personal narrative. Pay close attention to the first word in each sentence. Using a sticky note, I am going to jot down the first word in each sentence. If I repeat a word, I will add a tally mark next to the word.*

■ Read a section of your modeled writing aloud, pausing to record the first word of each sentence.

TURN &TALK *Partners, what did you notice about my piece? What are you thinking? Have I used a variety of words to begin my sentences?*

■ *I heard some of you say that I have a bit of a problem. Many of my sentences begin with the same word, and all my sentences are fairly short. I need to revise! I think I could combine a couple of my sentences, and that might help. Let's try that.*

■ Show students how you work to combine sentences and find alternate ways to begin some sentences so that there is variety. Use different ways to begin sentences, such as with an opening element followed by a comma or a prepositional phrase. Consider combining sentences as well to add variety to beginnings and to make the writing flow more smoothly.

Draft

The fishing float was made of light green glass. The glass had been etched by the sand. The fishing float sparkled in the bright, morning sun. I picked it up carefully. I turned it over in my hand slowly. Light bounced off it in all directions. I couldn't believe what I had found.

Revision

The light green glass, etched by the sand, sparkled in the bright, morning sun. Carefully, I picked it up and turned it over in my hand, as the light bounced off it in all directions. I couldn't believe what I had found.

Modeled Writing

■ *Let's read this section again now that I have made some revisions. Have I improved the flow of my writing and injected some variety? Do you think revising in this way strengthened my narrative? Using the tally sheet helped me discover the problem with this section, and it led me to revise.*

WRITING and COACHING

■ As writers return to their narratives, encourage them to reread their writing in order to focus on sentence beginnings and flow. Remind them how to record the first word of each sentence and use tally marks to denote repeated words.

■ Confer with writers who are still in the drafting phase. Encourage them to focus on how each of their sentences begins **as they are writing** and to write long, short, and medium-length sentences.

■ Help your students as they work to revise the beginnings of their sentences. Celebrate with them as they read the revised sentences aloud and appreciate the smooth flow they create.

SHARING and REFLECTING

TURN &TALK *Partners, meet together and talk about your work today. What did you notice when you tallied your sentence beginnings? What revisions did you make? What did you learn about sentence fluency today?*

■ Bring together your community of writers, and ask them to share their thinking about how to revise with a focus on sentence fluency.

■ Gather the writer's notebooks, and analyze your students' attempts at rereading and revising for sentence fluency. Identify writers who may need additional modeling as well as those who are ready for higher levels of sophistication. Use the rubrics on the *Resources* CD-ROM to track writing proficiencies.

TIP Lead students to examine sentence beginnings in mentor texts. Which techniques do authors use to begin their sentences? Have students record some powerful beginnings to make to an "inspiration bulletin board" of strong sentences. Encourage them to use these sentence beginnings for reference as they write.

SESSION 9
Focused Edits

Writers reread their narratives for specific editing points.

SESSION SNAPSHOT

Process Focus: Editing

Trait(s): Conventions

Mentor Text: "The Night I Started Stargazing," by James Cronce

TIP You can use one of the editing checklists from the *Resources* CD-ROM or create a custom checklist for your class. Be sure your checklist does not introduce any new skills. A checklist should never be used to teach and should include only those conventions that you have explicitly modeled in class.

FOCUSED MINILESSON

If time allows, reflect on the last session as you have students turn and talk about strategies they used to achieve variety in sentence beginnings.

Summarize the learning goals for this session: *You have crafted personal narratives that are enjoyable to read. Now it's time to focus our efforts on editing. As editors, we examine those items that any proofreader would attend to—punctuation, spelling, capitalization, and the surface structures that enable our readers to focus on our content and not on our mistakes. While our edits will take into account all of these editing points, today we are going to focus on one point at a time.*

Using the Mentor Text

■ Display the mentor text again, and invite partners to examine punctuation and capitalization, particularly in sentences that included opening elements.

> **TURN &TALK** *Partners, think together. What kinds of punctuation marks do you see in sentence openings? What patterns or rules did the author follow?*

Modeling

■ Before the lesson, gather resources students might use to edit. You might use students' personal word banks, personal dictionaries, sample sentences on a chart, spell-check programs, and so on. Use resources that you have taught students to use, and tailor this lesson to what students already know.

■ *When I edit, I focus on one editing point at a time, and I ignore everything else. My first reading will focus on punctuation. There may be other conventions in my narrative that need correction, but for this reading, I am only going to think about punctuation.*

■ *When we examined the mentor text, we noticed that the author always used a comma after an opening element. Let's look at a section of my narrative and see if I have some editing to do.*

■ Display a short section of your modeled writing where you have purposefully inserted punctuation errors: "Pulling on the rubber gloves I felt my spirits fall at the prospect of picking up garbage all day."

> **TURN &TALK** *Partners, think together. Do you see any punctuation errors in the opening element of this sentence?*

Pulling on the rubber gloves͜ I felt my spirits fall at the prospect of picking up garbage all day.

Modeled Writing

■ *Aha! I left out a comma. Listen as I read the sentence aloud—that's a great way to identify where the comma should be placed because you'll hear a slight pause. Now I know where to put the comma. Watch as I use a caret mark to show that I need to place a comma between* gloves *and* I.

■ Continue demonstrating how you reread to check for punctuation errors and then other editing points from your checklist. Show that your editing makes your writing look "messy" because you aren't erasing and rewriting. Instead, you are using copyediting marks to show the corrections you need to make before you publish.

WRITING and COACHING

■ Invite writers to examine their writing with editing checklists in hand. Remind them to edit for one point at a time to ensure their full attention and to focus on creating an error-free draft. Doing so allows readers to focus on the message rather than figuring out what the writer is trying to say.

■ Remind students who are still drafting and revising that when they are ready to edit, you will expect them to focus on one editing point at a time. Alternatively, you may encourage them to edit the sections of their drafts that they consider "final" and then to edit again when the rest is complete.

■ Coach editors with questions such as *What did you notice as you examined the punctuation of your opening elements? Did you change anything? For what point are you editing now? What strategies are you using to be sure your spelling is correct?*

■ Remind writers to use tools such as word lists, lists of frequently misspelled words, and dictionaries to check their spelling.

SHARING and REFLECTING

TURN &TALK *Writers, share the edits you made to your personal narratives. Show your partner what you changed and why.*

■ Give students a chance to share some of their edits with the whole class, and then lead a discussion among writers about the various resources they can use as they edit. Which resources did they find most helpful? What did they like about them?

■ Gather the drafts and analyze your students' attempts to edit. Use the rubrics on the *Resources* CD-ROM to track writing proficiencies and tailor future instruction. Consider which students may need to focus on fewer editing points to be successful and which ones can expand their editing to include more elements. You might need to provide specific instruction on certain editing points, such as capitalizing proper nouns or including commas after introductory clauses.

TIP Correctly punctuating introductory clauses may be difficult for some students. You may need to provide additional demonstrations using a variety of sentences that you have found in mentor texts or that you have written yourself.

SESSION 10
Making Publishing Decisions

Writers examine a variety of presentation options as they prepare their personal narratives to share with an audience.

SESSION SNAPSHOT

Process Focus: Publishing, Presenting

Trait(s): Ideas, Conventions

Mentor Text: "The Night I Started Stargazing," by James Cronce

FOCUSED MINILESSON

Before the lesson: Gather various examples of published texts. These might include electronic books, spiral-bound books, PowerPoint presentations, and so on.

Review the learning goals from the last session, and summarize the learning goals for today. *During our last session, we focused on editing. Now we are ready to publish and share our personal narratives. Today you'll have the opportunity to choose how you would like to present your narrative.*

Using the Mentor Text

■ Display the mentor text again, and have students comment on how the narrative is presented. Call attention to the strong font used for the title and to the callouts that draw attention to the piece, and highlight important parts and the illustrations that leave us with a strong impression of the author's feelings about this event.

Modeling

■ *As I prepare to publish and share my personal narrative, I want to think about all of the options I have for publishing. The author of our mentor text chose to use a magazine-style layout with callouts, illustrations, and a strong typeface. I have some other examples of published personal narratives from other authors. Some of them chose to publish e-books, some simply wrote a single page, and others used an electronic slide show to tell their stories.*

■ *I need to decide how I would like to present my personal narrative about the day I found a fishing float on the beach. I think I am going to use my computer to make an electronic slide show.*

■ *Watch me as I create the first slide in my presentation. This slide should include the title of my narrative and my name, since I'm the author. I also want to include a photograph or illustration to grab the reader's attention and make the slide pleasing to look at. Because my narrative takes place during a volunteer beach clean-up, I think I'll include this photograph I took of the beach that day. It shows people holding garbage bags and walking with their heads down, looking for trash. I click on Insert and then choose Picture. I am going to include this picture from a file, so I'll click on that and then choose the picture. You can see that the picture is now included in my slide.*

TURN &TALK *Think together. What did you notice about how I created this first slide? What might I add to my next slide?*

■ Continue modeling how you create your presentation, showing students how you experiment with different slide layouts. Think aloud as you decide how to break the narrative into a series of slides.

WRITING and COACHING

■ When writers are ready to publish, provide tools and resources depending on their publishing choices. If you have access to several computers, allow students to use these to create electronic slide shows or word processing documents. Other students may want to create books by handwriting and binding pages with illustrations. Gather materials that will help your writers be successful.

■ Encourage students to experiment with different titles for their personal narratives. Offer assistance to students who struggle to come up with a compelling and representative title.

■ Give students time to publish their work. Remind them to set their titles apart from the narratives with bold letters or color. Students may want to add illustrations to their narratives.

■ Some students may still be drafting or revising their narratives. Assure these writers that they can think about how they would like to publish their work when they have finished.

■ Many students will need more than one publishing session. Provide the time for students to produce their best work.

SHARING and REFLECTING

■ *We have created some powerful personal narratives that allow our readers to picture the action and leave them with a strong impression of our thoughts and feelings about these events. I think our families would enjoy reading our published pieces. Let's invite members of our families to come to our school next week so we can celebrate our hard work together. When our family members arrive, each of you will have the opportunity to meet with them to share your narrative **and** what you have learned about writing personal narratives.*

TURN &TALK *What did you learn about writing a personal narrative? If you were asked to teach someone how to write a personal narrative, what things would you share? Work with a partner to create a list of the key features that should be included in a quality personal narrative.*

■ Gather the students' final pieces, and analyze their attempts at publishing and presentation. Identify writers who may need additional modeling as well as those who are ready for higher levels of sophistication. Use the rubrics on the *Resources* CD-ROM to track writing proficiencies and tailor future instruction.

SESSION 1

Identifying the Purpose and Features of an Informational Narrative

Writers analyze an informational narrative, identify its structure and features, and then begin researching to write their own.

SESSION SNAPSHOT

Genre Focus: Features of an Informational Narrative

Process Focus: Planning, Researching

Trait(s): Ideas

Mentor Text: "Battle at Hampton Roads," by Cynthia Nye

Battle at Hampton Roads:
A Turning Point in Naval History
BY KAREEM RANDALL

When two ironclad ships joined in battle, they changed naval history, if not the course of the Civil War.

21

Source	Location	Notes
Remember the Little Big Horn by Paul Robert Walker	Classroom library	Includes great eyewitness accounts

Modeled Writing

FOCUSED MINILESSON

Summarize the learning goals: *Today we are going to focus on a type of nonfiction writing called informational narrative. An informational narrative describes real people and events in the order in which they happened. The rich descriptive language in an informational narrative and the emphasis on time order can make you feel like you're reading a story—a true story, that is!*

If we're going to craft a powerful informational narrative, we need to learn about the features and structure of these kinds of texts. Let's examine this mentor text that tells about a pivotal event that took place during the Civil War.

Using the Mentor Text

■ The mentor text for this unit is "Battle at Hampton Roads," by Cynthia Nye. You will find it on page 21 of the *Book of Mentor Texts* and in the Narrate section on the *Resources* CD-ROM. Make enough copies for every student or group of students to have one, or use an electronic projection device to display it for whole-class viewing.

■ Read the opening paragraph. *After reading this opening section, I can already identify one important feature of an informational narrative. The lead establishes the situation so that the reader is ready for the rest of the narrative.*

■ Read an additional portion of the text. *I am also noticing that the episode is told from the third-person point of view. That means the author is detached from the topic, and she will describe the thoughts and actions of all of the people mentioned in the text.*

■ As you guide writers in examining the mentor text, help them self-discover and notice the features of this kind of narrative, such as an enticing beginning that sets the scene and an ending that is powerful and satisfying. Help students self-discover that an informational narrative must contain accurate facts.

■ *Writers, over the next ten sessions, we are going to write our own informational narratives that describe important historical events.* Provide students with several choices, such as the bombing of Pearl Harbor, the assassination of Martin Luther King, Jr., Lee's surrender at Appomattox, or the moon landing. To ensure that there are adequate resources for all students, monitor the choices so that there are not too many students working on the same subject.

TURN &TALK *Partners, think together. When you write your informational narrative about your chosen episode, what features will you want to be sure to include?*

■ Guide students as they share their observations, and record their thinking on an anchor chart labeled "Features of a Great Informational Narrative."

Modeling

■ *Writers, I am going to begin an informational narrative about the Battle of Little Bighorn, an important event that took place in our region in 1876. To do this, I am first going to need to do some research. I have books, magazines, and some information from the Internet that I can use to help me do my research.*

■ *Watch as I record information about a wonderful book I found, using this three-column chart that helps me stay organized. I write the name of the book under "Source." Under "Location," I'll write "classroom library" so I can easily find the book again. I know from paging through it that this book contains some awesome eyewitness accounts of the battle. I'll put this information under "Notes" so I will know why this book will be good to include in my research.*

■ *Today you are going to make some brief notes about the resources you think will be most helpful to your research.*

WRITING and COACHING

■ Provide students with a variety of reliable research materials, including books, magazines, websites, encyclopedias, and online sources.

■ Coach students as they research and record notes in their research notebooks or on the organizer on the *Resources* CD-ROM.

■ Confer with individual students or gather a small group of writers who are experiencing difficulty with researching. Support the learning by demonstrating how you read a short section from a reliable source and then record the key words or phrases that capture your thinking.

SHARING and REFLECTING

TURN &TALK *Writers, what did you learn about the historical events that you chose to write about? Share some new information with your partner.*

■ Lead a discussion about informational narratives, reviewing the list of features. Return to the mentor text, and have students locate the features in the mentor text to reinforce their understanding of informational narratives.

■ Gather the research notebooks, and look over the information that students gathered. Use your observations of students' work to note those who need more explicit modeling of locating and noting information. Identify students who are ready to extend their thinking, for example, by using more sophisticated research sources.

Features of a Great Informational Narrative

· Opening that establishes the situation
· Third-person point of view
· Temporal words and phrases that show sequence
· Rich descriptions and strong details
· Powerful language that engages the reader
· Strong ending

TIP Some historical topics are too far-reaching for an informational narrative. Students may need more explicit modeling on how to narrow the focus of their research to find a pivotal episode about which to write. If students choose the Civil War as a focus, for example, you might show a timeline of several events such as the start of the war at Fort Sumter, the signing of the Emancipation Proclamation, or Lincoln's Gettysburg address, and ask them to choose one event.

SESSION 2
Citing Multiple Sources

Writers use multiple reference materials and cite their sources.

SESSION SNAPSHOT

Research Strategy: Using a Variety of Resources

Process Focus: Prewriting

Trait(s): Ideas, Organization

Mentor Text: "Battle at Hampton Roads," by Cynthia Nye

FOCUSED MINILESSON

Review the previous session, noting features of informational narratives and discussing the research students have done so far.

Summarize the learning goals for today's session: *Today we will continue researching to find out more about the historical events we've chosen. To help us collect a wide range of reliable facts, we're going to look at multiple sources, and as we select information from our research materials, we will note their titles and authors. This way, our readers will know where we found our facts.*

Using the Mentor Text

■ Display the bibliography provided in the mentor text. *Writers, do you notice how the author lists several sources in this bibliography? This makes it clear that the information in her narrative is well researched and reliable. Today as you research your historical episodes, you may find a single source that seems to contain all the information you need for your narrative. Don't stop there! The more sources you consult, the better able you'll be to verify your information and collect the most interesting facts.*

Modeling

■ *Writers of nonfiction need to use multiple sources for their information. I'm researching facts to include in my informational narrative about the Battle of Little Bighorn. I have a couple of books that I found in our classroom library and a page that I printed off the Internet. My goal is to gather information from each of these that I can use in my writing. I'm sure there will be information about the actual battle, but for now I'm just going to focus on who was involved in the battle and collect ideas in my research notebook.*

■ Open the first book to a pre-identified point. Use a document camera to display the page. *Here is a page that tells about who was involved in the battle. It says that the Lakota and Cheyenne tribes had joined forces. I'm going to save that information in my research notebook. Watch as I write:* "Who: Lakota and Cheyenne tribes." *Notice that I don't write a full sentence. I simply jot down a few words that will help me remember the information.* Be sure to model how you write the title and author of this resource in your notebook, too.

■ Display and read a short passage from a second book with information about the topic. Continue modeling how you extract important information and cite the source.

TURN &TALK *Partners, this magazine article has some great information about who took part in the Battle of Little Bighorn. If you were going to use some facts from this resource, what would you want to remember? Think together about what I should jot down in my writer's notebook.*

■ Repeat the process with the third source, integrating information with the facts collected from the first and second sources and noting the title and author.

WRITING and COACHING

■ Coach and mentor students as they research and record simple notes about a historical episode. Check to be sure they are recording notes in their own words or enclosing exact words in quotation marks and giving credit to sources.

■ Provide support to students who are struggling to narrow the focus of their research. If the topics are too large, ask leading questions to help students narrow their topics.

■ Circulate as students work to ensure that all writers are citing their sources. You may want to suggest that students keep a running list of sources on a separate page in their research notebooks so the information is easy to retrieve later.

SHARING and REFLECTING

TURN &TALK *Writers, I noticed that you worked hard at finding multiple sources from which to collect information. I also saw that you were only using facts that were important and that you cited all your sources. Find another partner pair so that you form a group of four. Share your thinking from today's session. How did you go about finding and using important information from a variety of sources?*

■ Bring writers back together to sum up the learning. *Today we learned that using multiple sources allows us to check our facts and to find the most interesting facts. We also learned that when we cite our sources, we show readers that our information is well researched and accurate.*

■ Collect the students' research notebooks, and analyze their attempts to gather facts from multiple sources and to cite the resources they've used. Note students who may need additional modeling in recording notes from multiple sources and those who may be ready for higher levels of sophistication. Use the class writing development rubric or the individual student rubric on the *Resources* CD-ROM to track writing proficiencies.

TIP The trick for most students will be to focus on a single idea and not all of the information in each source. This will require repeated teaching and modeling experiences. Be sure also that you model how you verify facts from one source to another. For students who are ready, consider discussing how you evaluate a source to be sure that it is a reliable one.

TIP Some writers can become overwhelmed by facts if they don't have a system for organizing the information they are collecting. Consider showing them how to dedicate one page of their writer's notebooks to each subtopic within the general topic. Their writer's notebooks, then, serve as a multi-page graphic organizer. Other students may want to take notes on note cards that they can organize by topic.

Organize Information in Time Order

Writers organize notes in timelines to focus on sequential order in preparation for writing.

SESSION SNAPSHOT

Process Focus: Prewriting, Planning

Trait(s): Organization

Mentor Text: "Battle at Hampton Roads," by Cynthia Nye

FOCUSED MINILESSON

Review the learning goals from the previous session. If time allows, have students turn and talk about what they have learned so far.

Summarize the learning goals for today's session: *Today we will be using timelines to help us organize our facts into a logical sequence for our readers. These timelines will help you keep your facts organized and will support you when you begin to write your informational narratives. Watch me as I create a timeline to organize the sequence of events in the Battle of Little Bighorn.*

Using the Mentor Text

■ Display a copy of the mentor text, and draw students' attention to the words and phrases that signal time order, such as *before, meanwhile, at noon,* and *for four hours.* If possible, use markup tools to circle any dates that appear in the text. Emphasize for students that informational narratives describe events in the order in which they happened.

Modeling

■ Display a page in your writer's notebook where you have written facts and dates. *Today I am going to use a timeline to arrange my facts in an order that helps me tell the story of the Battle of Little Bighorn. Here in my research notebook, I jotted down some important events that led up to the battle. I included dates for the most important events. It's important to get the order correct when I'm writing an informational narrative. To help me do this, I will write the important dates and events on this timeline. Here is my first date: "December 3, 1875: Government orders Native Americans to return to reservation."*

■ *You'll notice that I didn't write complete sentences. When you are researching, you can jot down phrases or words. As I peruse all of the important dates and events, it looks like the December 3 date is the first one I'll want to include. I'll write that on the first box in my timeline. I'll probably only want to include four or five of the most important events leading up to the actual battle.* Think aloud as you reference your notes from your writer's notebook, taking time to double-check references to check for accuracy.

TURN &TALK *Partners, look closely at my timeline. How might it help me when I begin to write? Why is it helpful to write dates and events on a timeline when you are researching?*

■ Continue demonstrating how you record dates and events on the timeline, pausing to check the order and accuracy of the sequence you are creating. You may want to show how you decide which dates and events are showcased and which ones are not as important. Model considering and then rejecting a date that is not essential in telling about the events.

■ *I have some important dates and events recorded on my timeline, and I feel confident about the sequence I have created. I know that as I tell a factual story, the order will be important to my reader.*

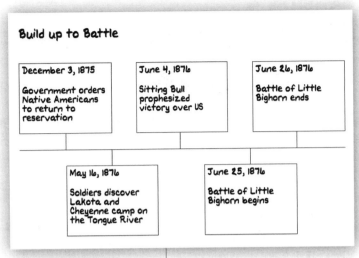

Modeled Writing

WRITING and COACHING

■ Coach partners as they continue to research and use the facts they have gathered to create timelines for their events. Encourage them to limit the events in their timelines so that their writing will be rich yet concise.

■ Help students learn how to be selective in the facts they are recording in their research notebooks. Cue their thinking by asking questions such as *Where will this date fit in your informational narrative? How will this fact help you to tell the story of this event? Is this one of the most important facts concerning this event?*

SHARING and REFLECTING

TURN &TALK *Writers, now is an ideal time to pause and think together about your research. Analyze your timelines. Do they show a clear order and sequence? Have you gathered enough information on your events, or do you need to continue researching?*

■ Guide a conversation that returns students' attention to the overall goal of writing an informational narrative. Explain that when they feel their research is complete, they will begin turning their timelines and notes into written narratives.

■ Collect the students' timelines, and analyze their attempts to show sequence and order. Identify writers who may need additional modeling as well as those who are ready for higher levels of sophistication. Use the class writing development rubric or the individual student rubric on the *Resources* CD-ROM to track writing proficiencies.

TIP Some students may benefit from additional support in using their notes to create a timeline. Consider gathering these students in a small group and providing additional teaching and modeling. Partners or small groups might also write timeline entries on sticky notes and work together to place them in order on timelines. Using sticky notes will allow students to easily confirm and reject timeline entries and to add other entries as necessary.

TIP Consider showing students how authors of informational narratives sometimes include timelines either at the beginning or at the end of their texts. Encourage students to consider experimenting with adding photographs or drawings to final copies of their timelines.

Turning Notes into Running Text

Writers turn research notes and notes from their timelines into running text.

SESSION SNAPSHOT

Process Focus: Drafting

Trait(s): Ideas, Organization, Voice

Mentor Text: "Battle at Hampton Roads," by Amy Gilbert

BEFORE THE LESSON

Provide a variety of informational narratives from the *Resources* CD-ROM or from your own personal collection, and give partners time to read several examples, noticing how they are written. You might also provide examples of other texts, such as biographies, informational picture books in the narrative style, and narratives from nonfiction magazines. Guide a conversation comparing and contrasting the informational narratives.

FOCUSED MINILESSON

Review the learning goals from the previous session. If time allows, have students turn and talk about what they have learned so far.

Summarize the learning goals for today's session: *Today we'll be using our timelines and notes to begin writing informational narratives in paragraph form.*

Using the Mentor Text

■ Read the beginning of the mentor text. *Do you notice how the author has started the piece?*

■ *This beginning really draws me in! The author has crafted the lead in a way that makes me want to read more. I can't wait to read more to find out how the* Virginia *and the* Monitor *changed naval history. I also like the rich descriptive language this author uses. For example, describing the* Virginia *as a* "turtle with a chimney on its back" *and saying that both ships* "struck terror in the hearts of Civil War soldiers" *set the scene and make me feel like part of the action right away.*

Modeling

■ *I've filled several pages in my research notebook with the most interesting facts I could find about the Battle of Little Bighorn, and I've plotted the most important information on a timeline that will help me order my narrative. I'm ready to start drafting, and my goal is to turn my brief notes and timeline entries into rich descriptive sentences that flow smoothly and help my readers picture the action at Little Bighorn. Watch as I start to write a beginning that I hope will draw my readers into the narrative:* "It would eventually be known as 'Custer's Last Stand,' but on the hot, dry morning of June 25, 1875, Lieutenant Colonel George Armstrong Custer couldn't have known that he would not survive the fierce battle ahead."

TURN &TALK *Partners, examine my beginning. What about it makes you want to read more? What advice do you have for making it even stronger?*

■ *Now that I've set the scene, I want to tell about the events that led up to the battle. I am ready to look at the first event on my timeline and use it in my writing. It says,* "December 3, 1875: Government says Native Americans must return to reservations." *I'll want to be sure to start a new paragraph here as I write a bit about that. Here's how I'll begin the paragraph:* "Months previously, on December 3, 1875, the

U.S. government had ordered Native Americans to return to their reservations or be considered hostile enemies. News of the government's orders spread through the Lakota and Cheyenne tribes like wildfire as General Custer and his troops began to round up the anguished native people."

■ Continue demonstrating how you collect phrases from both the timeline and research notes and turn them into sentences.

■ Model how you reread your writing to check for accuracy and clarity. Show students that you cross out words or phrases that you don't like and insert new words or ideas. Encourage students to reread their own drafts as they write, revising as they go.

WRITING and COACHING

■ Coach writers as they begin to draft using the notes from their timelines and writer's notebooks. Guide them in choosing quotes to add to their writing, making sure to properly attribute them. Encourage students to experiment with language and add some interest to their narratives.

■ Be sure partners are aware that although they have researched together, they will each be creating their own drafts.

■ As writers begin to draft, some may realize that they need more information and need to return to the researching phase of the writing process.

■ Help writers remember that high-quality nonfiction pieces often include visual supports. This might be an ideal time for some students to consider where to include a hand-drawn illustration, map, or public-domain photograph.

SHARING and REFLECTING

TURN &TALK *Partners, talk about your writing so far. What were you working on today as a writer? How are you doing at converting your research notes and timelines into sentences and paragraphs? What was difficult? What can you do tomorrow to improve the process?*

■ Lead a class discussion to sum up what was learned. *Today you've had some time to begin drafting your informational narratives. You worked on writing leads that will draw your readers in, and you're crafting pieces of writing that will be a delight to read.* Explain that in the next session, students will focus on using temporal words and phrases to show the sequence of events in their narratives.

■ Collect the drafts and analyze students' attempts to write in complete sentences that communicate important information and capture readers' attention. Identify writers who may need additional modeling as well as those who are ready for higher levels of sophistication. Use the class writing development rubric or the individual student rubric on the *Resources* CD-ROM to track writing proficiencies.

It would eventually be known as "Custer's Last Stand," but on the hot, dry morning of June 25, 1875, Lieutenant Colonel George Armstrong Custer couldn't have known that he would not survive the fierce battle ahead.

Months previously, on December 3, 1875, the U.S. government had ordered Native Americans to return to their reservations or be considered hostile enemies. News of the government's orders spread through the Lakota and Cheyenne tribes like wildfire as General Custer and his troops began to round up the anguished native people.

Modeled Writing

TIP Show students how to skim and scan their research materials to locate important dates and facts to include in their timelines. You might model marking facts you've already used so that you don't use them multiple times in your draft.

SESSION 5
Using Temporal Words and Phrases

Writers focus on using temporal words to show the order of events in their narratives.

SESSION SNAPSHOT

Process Focus: Drafting, Revising

Trait(s): Organization, Word Choice

Mentor Text: "Battle at Hampton Roads," by Cynthia Nye

TIP Making a list of temporal words with students and displaying them in the classroom will assist students in selecting the ones they want to use when writing their own informational narratives. You might consider printing the list of Temporal Words and Phrases to Show Sequence from the Narrate section of the *Resources* CD-ROM for student reference or creating a list, inviting students to suggest words from various mentor texts they have examined.

FOCUSED MINILESSON

Review the learning goals from the previous session. If time allows, have students turn and talk about what they have learned so far.

Summarize the learning goals for today: *One of the ways writers help their readers understand the order of events is by infusing words that show time or sequence. Our focus today is making sure our informational narratives include some words that show when things happened.*

Using the Mentor Text

■ Revisit the mentor text.

> **TURN &TALK** *Partners, think together. Where has the author included words that show time? How does this help the reader understand what happened in the text?*

■ Invite partners to share their thinking with the class.

Modeling

■ *As I draft my informational narrative about the Battle of Little Bighorn, I am going to focus on including words that help my reader understand when things happened. Let's look at this sentence:* "They attacked Reno's soldiers. Then, the Lakota and Cheyenne saw hundreds of Custer's men coming toward them." *That's okay. The word* then *gives some time order, but I think I could revise the sentence so that it's even more specific. I want my readers to know that the Native Americans had just finished driving one group of soldiers out when another group of soldiers came toward them. I think I'll say,* "After they attacked Reno's soldiers, the Lakota and Cheyenne saw hundreds of Custer's men coming toward them." *I think that works much better.*

> **TURN &TALK** *Writers, think together. Do you see other places in my draft that would benefit from some words or phrases that show time?*

■ *I see another sentence here that could use a word that signals the order of events. Let's think together about a word that I could add to make the sequence of events really clear for my reader.*

■ Continue modeling the addition of temporal words.

Draft 1

They attacked Reno's soldiers. Then, the Lakota and Cheyenne saw hundreds of Custer's men coming toward them.

Draft 2

After they attacked Reno's soldiers, the Lakota and Cheyenne saw hundreds of Custer's men coming toward them.

Modeled Writing

WRITING and COACHING

■ As writers return to drafting, support them in adding words that provide a clear sequence of events.

■ Remind writers to pause and reread their writing from time to time, making sure it is clear and accurate.

■ Coach writers with questions such as *What words have you added to your piece to help your reader keep track of the order of events? Or Here's a place where I am not sure what happened first. Can you think of a word or phrase you can put here to make this less confusing?*

SHARING and REFLECTING

TURN &TALK *Identify a partner you haven't worked with yet. Share what you learned today about including words that show sequence and time order. Then, find a place in your own writing where you included a word or phrase that helps your reader understand the sequence of events.*

■ Return to the mentor text, an exemplary piece of student writing, or your own piece of modeled writing. Guide students to focus on temporal words by underlining or highlighting each temporal word that is used. Show students how these words strengthen the organization of the piece.

■ Gather the drafts and analyze your students' attempts to include temporal words and phrases. Identify writers who may need additional modeling as well as those who are ready for higher levels of sophistication. Use the class writing rubric or the individual student rubric on the *Resources* CD-ROM to track writing proficiencies.

TIP Some writers will still be researching at this point, while others will be almost finished with their drafts. Consider using a Workshop Organizer as shown in *A Guide to Teaching Nonfiction Writing*, page 49. This can provide a tool to use for monitoring the stages of the writing process for your students.

SESSION 6
Infusing Descriptions and Details

Writers integrate rich details and descriptive language into their informational narratives to rev up reader interest.

SESSION SNAPSHOT

Process Focus: Drafting, Revising

Trait(s): Ideas, Word Choice

Mentor Text: "Battle at Hampton Roads," by Cynthia Nye

FOCUSED MINILESSON

Review the learning goals from the previous session. If time allows, have students turn and talk about what they have learned so far.

Summarize the learning goals for today's session: *Informational narratives don't need to be dull and lifeless. Today I want to show you how writers infuse interesting details into their writing to make the writing a joy to read.*

Using the Mentor Text

■ Revisit the mentor text. *Let's begin by looking once again at the mentor text. Do you notice how the author included the detail that prior to the Civil War, all battleships were made of wood? She didn't have to include that detail, but as a reader, I'm glad she did! It makes me want to keep reading to see what else I might learn.*

TURN &TALK *Partners, look again at the mentor text. What other interesting facts did the author include? How do they boost the writing?*

Modeling

■ *As I write today, I am going to focus on adding some rich details that will make my writing more interesting to read. I am ready to tell about the Sundance Ceremony that was held on June 4 of 1876. As I look back at the facts I collected in my research notebook, I see that during that ceremony, Sitting Bull, the war chief of the Lakota tribe, received a vision of soldiers falling in his camp. He predicted that the Lakota would triumph over U.S. soldiers. I think that would be an interesting fact to include in my informational narrative, since that's exactly what happened in the Battle of Little Bighorn.*

TURN &TALK *Think together. What do you think of the detail that I'm considering including in my narrative? Do you think my reader will find it interesting and want to keep reading?*

> As Sitting Bull presided over the Sundance Ceremony of June 4, 1876, the familiar sounds of drumbeats and chants rose like smoke around him. According to eyewitness accounts, it was then that
> strange, glorious
> a vision formed before his eyes of soldiers falling into the camp before him. When the vision had passed, Sitting Bull
> fearless
> predicted that the Lakota would triumph
> over the U.S. soldiers.

Modeled Writing

■ *Watch as I write about the ceremony. As I write, I'm thinking about how I can craft a paragraph that would be so rich in detail that my readers would be able to visualize what I'm describing. I think I'll start my paragraph this way:* "As Sitting Bull presided over the Sundance Ceremony of June 4, 1876, the familiar sounds of drumbeats and chants rose like smoke around him. According to eyewitness accounts, it was then that a vision formed before his eyes of soldiers falling in the camp before him. When the vision had passed, Sitting Bull predicted that the Lakota would triumph over the U.S. soldiers."

■ *That's a pretty good paragraph, but I think a few details will make it more vivid for my readers. Watch as I add the adjectives* strange *and* glorious *to describe Sitting Bull's vision and* fearless *to describe the Lakota.* Show students how you play with language while drafting and sometimes experiment with crafting your sentences in several different ways before you select the one that suits you.

WRITING and COACHING

■ As writers return to drafting, remind them to experiment with adding interesting details to their pieces.

■ Remind students that it's okay to return to research materials to add interesting details.

■ Coach writers with questions such as *Tell me more about this part of your piece. Can you tell me exactly what happened? What details can you add here? How do you visualize the action?*

SHARING and REFLECTING

TURN &TALK *Writers, share a section of your draft with your partner. Is there a place where you added some interesting details to bring some pizzazz to the piece and help your readers visualize the action? What did you learn about yourself as a writer today?*

■ Sum up the learning, and lead a discussion of how rich details can improve a piece of descriptive writing. Explain that in the next session, they will see how descriptive language and strong details can enrich the conclusion of an informational narrative.

■ Gather the drafts and analyze your students' attempts to infuse interesting details. Identify writers who may need additional modeling as well as those who are ready for higher levels of sophistication. Use the class writing development rubric or the individual student rubric on the *Resources* CD-ROM to track writing proficiencies.

TIP At this point, some writers may feel that they are close to completing their drafts. For these writers, a modeled lesson on focused revision might be in order. Meeting with students according to their needs helps them grow as writers and make good use of their writing time.

SESSION 7
Crafting a Strong Ending

Writers identify features of a satisfying ending and ensure that those elements are present in their own informational narratives.

SESSION SNAPSHOT

Process Focus: Drafting, Revising

Trait(s): Organization, Voice

Mentor Text: "Battle at Hampton Roads," by Cynthia Nye

TIP Consider working with students to create a wall chart that lists the attributes of a strong ending. Encourage students to refer to the wall chart as they are writing and revising endings.

FOCUSED MINILESSON

Reflect on the learning goals from the last session. If time allows, have students turn and talk about what they have learned so far.

Summarize the learning goals for this session: *When we revise, we look at our piece of writing with a new set of eyes. We challenge ourselves to dig deep and look at our pieces as a reader might. One part of that process involves examining how our pieces end. That is our focus for today.*

Using the Mentor Text

■ Read the ending of the mentor text.

> **TURN &TALK** *Partners, think together. What does this author do to create an ending that brings closure and satisfaction to the reader?*

■ Invite writing partners to examine the endings of the samples of informational narratives from the *Resources* CD-ROM or from other mentor texts you've gathered. Ask, *Which ones bring about a sense of closure and satisfaction? Which ones are weak? What do you think are the attributes of a strong ending?*

Modeling

■ *Many of you discovered that when the writer ends with an abrupt "The End," it feels a bit like running into a brick wall! I heard some partners saying that they like endings that speak directly to the reader, make them think, or give an emotional connection to the piece. We like endings that wrap everything up in a neat bow. Let's look at draft 1 of my ending: "The Little Bighorn battleground. . . ." I think I need to revise! Draft 2: "The Battle of Little Bighorn is often. . . ."*

■ *Did you notice that I referenced the fact that this battle is often referred to as "Custer's Last Stand"? Now I want to add something that will make my reader think about this important event. Watch as I add something about the fact that the Lakota nation was defeated and broken within a year of the battle: "So, in a very real sense, it was their last stand, too."*

> **TURN &TALK** *Writers, analyze my second draft. What do you think? Is this a better ending? Could I improve it even more? What could you suggest to make the ending even more powerful?*

Draft 1

The Little Bighorn battleground became a national monument in 1943. The end.

Draft 2

The Battle of Little Bighorn is often remembered as "Custer's Last Stand." But, within a year following the battle, the Lakota nation was no more. So, in a very real sense, it was their last stand as well.

Modeled Writing

■ Lead students in a discussion about other ways to improve their endings. If you worked with them to create an anchor chart, encourage them to check as they write to be sure they've included each trait on the chart.

WRITING and COACHING

■ Coach writers as they return to their writing to craft their endings or to revise if they have already written their endings. Remind students to refer to the wall chart for attributes of strong endings. Students also might benefit from examining other nonfiction selections to determine how those authors end their pieces.

■ Coach students who are working on revising their narratives. Cue them with questions such as *What have you revised so far? How have the revisions improved your informational narrative? What have you learned about yourself as a writer as you revise?*

■ Remind students who are still in the drafting phase that they do not need to abandon their work. Encourage them to continue to write and work on their conclusions when they are ready to revise. You will need to provide additional time for these writers to finish their drafts.

■ For writers who have moved into the editing phase, remind them that they can still reread and experiment with different ways to end their pieces.

SHARING and REFLECTING

TURN &TALK *Partners, share your thinking about the endings you have crafted. If you haven't written your endings yet, share your thoughts about what you might say to wrap up your narrative.*

■ Bring the students back together to reflect on the attributes of a strong conclusion. *Today we focused on crafting endings that give our readers a sense of closure. We know that the ending gives us one more chance to make a good impression on our readers, so we want to choose our words carefully.*

■ Encourage writers to be on the lookout for powerful endings in the nonfiction books they read. Create space in the classroom to showcase powerful endings.

■ Gather the drafts and analyze your students' attempts to revise and craft enticing conclusions. Identify writers who may need additional modeling as well as those who are ready for higher levels of sophistication. Use the class writing development rubric or the individual student rubric on the *Resources* CD-ROM to track writing proficiencies.

TIP Revision is a process that takes practice. We can help writers gain control of revision by guiding them in "focused revisions," where we invite them to revise for **one** thing such as using powerful verbs or varying sentence length. When we ask students to revise with **everything** in mind, they often become overwhelmed.

Revising to Add Variety to Sentence Beginnings

Writers analyze their sentence beginnings and revise to add variety.

SESSION SNAPSHOT

Process Focus: Revising

Trait(s): Sentence Fluency, Voice

Mentor Text: "Battle at Hampton Roads," by Cynthia Nye

FOCUSED MINILESSON

Have students reflect on the learning goals from the last session. If time allows, have students turn and talk about what they have learned so far.

Summarize the learning goals: *Many of you have finished crafting powerful informational narratives about important events. Today I want to show you how to revise with one focus in mind: the way that you begin each sentence.*

Using the Mentor Text

■ Display a copy of the mentor text. Circle or point to the word or phrase that begins each sentence. Ask a student volunteer to read the words and phrases out loud. *Writers, what do you notice about the sentence beginnings this author has crafted?*

■ Guide students to realize that the author has worked hard to ensure that her sentences begin in a variety of ways.

■ *Writers, it would have been easy for this author to slip into a pattern of beginning many of her sentences with the words* the battle *or* the ships. *After all, that is the subject of this narrative, and the author could have used it to begin a lot of her sentences. After a while, though, that would have become repetitious and boring—just the things we want to avoid in our own writing.*

Modeling

■ *One challenge I have when I am writing is making sure my sentences don't all start the same way. One way to check to make sure you have used a variety of sentence beginnings is to use a sticky note to jot down the first word in each sentence and then decide if you need to revise. I've finished this paragraph describing what happened when Custer arrived at Little Bighorn. As I underline the first word of each sentence, I notice that I have used* he *or* Custer *to begin every sentence. I have some revising to do!*

> **TURN &TALK** *Partners, think together. How could I revise a few of my sentence beginnings so that I have some variety? How else could I begin these sentences?*

■ *I heard some great ideas. Let's take a look at how other writers begin their sentences. Display sections of quality nonfiction. I notice that this author used some prepositional phrases to begin these sentences about whales. He wrote, "Deep in the ocean, whales sing a distinctive song."*

In this book about Abraham Lincoln, the author began some sentences with phrases that focused on time. For example, "In the morning, a shocked nation began the process of grieving the beloved president." Finally, I noticed that this author chose to begin a few of his sentences with an adverb. For example, "Quietly, the crocodile creeps toward his prey."

- Continue focusing on varying sentence beginnings.

WRITING and COACHING

- As writers return to their narratives, encourage them to reread their work and focus on how they have begun their sentences. Coach students as they work to revise their sentences to provide variety.

- For writers who are still drafting, this may be an ideal time to show them how to think about sentence beginnings as they write each new sentence.

- Encourage students to experiment and start some sentences with prepositional phrases, adverbs, or phrases that focus on time. Remind them that rereading is the best way to check how their writing sounds.

- Some students may want to read their sentences out loud to a writing buddy. Encourage these students to read aloud twice—once after drafting and again after revising—to hear the difference.

SHARING and REFLECTING

TURN &TALK *Writers, share your revisions with your partner. Were there some sentences that you changed? What kinds of sentence beginnings did you try? What did you learn about yourself as a writer today?*

- Encourage your community of writers to come together and share their thinking about revising to add variety to sentence beginnings.

- Gather the drafts and analyze your students' attempts at revising to add variety to sentence beginnings. Identify writers who may need additional modeling as well as those who are ready for higher levels of sophistication. Use the rubrics on the *Resources* CD-ROM to track writing proficiencies.

TIP As you focus on varying beginnings, encourage students to write interesting sentences on sentence strips and add them to a class display. Students can use these ideas for inspiration for their own sentence writing.

TIP Some students might benefit from making a list of the beginning words of each sentence in their pieces. Repeated words can be denoted with a tally mark. Once students examine the words and tally marks, they become aware of their need to revise.

SESSION 9
Focused Edits

Writers reread their narratives for specific editing points.

SESSION SNAPSHOT

Process Focus: Editing

Trait(s): Conventions

TIP Regular and irregular past-tense verbs can be confusing for students. Consider crafting an anchor chart that outlines how to rewrite regular verbs in the past tense (add *–ed*). Create another anchor chart that showcases the irregular verbs that change when written in past tense (*blow, blew, blown*).

As Sitting Bull ~~preside~~ presided over the Sundance

Ceremony of June 4, 1876, the familiar

sounds of drumbeats and chants rose

like smoke around him. According to

eyewitness accounts, it was then that

a vision ~~form~~ formed before his eyes of

soldiers falling into the camp before him.

When the vision had passed, Sitting Bull

~~predicts~~ predicted that the Lakota would triumph

over the U.S. soldiers.

Modeled Writing

FOCUSED MINILESSON

Reflect on the learning goals from the last session. If time allows, have students turn and talk about what they have learned so far.

Summarize the learning goals for this session: *Now that we've crafted narratives that are informative and entertaining, it is time to focus our attention on editing. When we edit, we look at those items that a professional copy editor would attend to, such as spelling, punctuation, and the surface structures that help readers understand our writing. Today we are going to delve into a focused edit in which we reread for a specific editing point.*

Modeling

■ *In a focused edit, I want to focus on one editing point at a time while I ignore everything else. When I do that, I can spot errors that I might miss if I were thinking about all of the editing points at once. This first reading will focus on just the verbs that I used. Because I wrote about an important event in history, I know that my writing will contain past-tense verbs. I want to be sure that I have spelled them correctly. There may be other conventions in my piece that need editing, but for this reading, I am only going to think about the past-tense verbs I used.*

■ "It was then that a vision form"—*Oops,* form *is a present-tense verb, but this happened in the past. I need to add –ed to* form *so that it reads,* "It was then that a vision formed. . . ." *That works!*

■ *Did you notice that I didn't focus on capital letters or punctuation? I only looked at the verbs in my writing, checking to be sure I have used the correct tense throughout.*

TURN &TALK *Can you see any other verbs in my piece that need attention? Where do I need to focus next?*

■ Continue guiding students in focused edits with a single goal for each reading of the piece you have crafted. Consider sprinkling some errors throughout your piece so that students are able to identify mistakes that need attention.

WRITING and COACHING

- Have writers engage in focused edits with their work—focusing on only one convention at a time.

- For writers who are still drafting and revising, remind them that when they are ready to edit, you will expect them to focus their edits so they can notice more detail.

- Coach editors with questions such as *What is the editing focus of this reading? What is your single editing point? What will you read for on your next reading?*

SHARING and REFLECTING

TURN &TALK *Work with a partner, and share the work you have done in editing your informational narrative. Identify the editing points you used for each reading and the result of your editing work. What did you change?*

- Guide a discussion among writers about the power of focused editing and rereading for each editing point.

- Gather the drafts and analyze your students' attempts at focused edits. Identify writers who may need additional modeling as well as those who are ready for higher levels of sophistication. Use the rubrics on the *Resources* CD-ROM to track writing proficiencies.

TIP Editing checklists can guide students' thinking as they edit. See the *Resources* CD-ROM for an editing checklist you can use or adapt for your writers.

SESSION 10

Publishing and Adding Supportive Visuals

Writers publish their work, adding visuals that support the text.

SESSION SNAPSHOT

Process Focus: Presenting, Publishing

Trait(s): Ideas, Conventions

Mentor Text: "Battle at Hampton Roads," by Cynthia Nye

BEFORE THE LESSON

Consider the various options for publishing the modeled writing piece you have crafted. The options may include, but are not limited to, a traditional spiral-bound book, a class anthology, a PowerPoint presentation, or a video presentation. The lesson that follows outlines the process of using publishing paper to assemble a handwritten, spiral-bound book.

FOCUSED MINILESSON

Review the learning goals from the last session, and summarize the learning goals for today: *As part of our last session, we took the time to conduct focused edits of our informational narratives. Now we are ready to publish and present our work. Today we'll add visuals that will give our narratives a polished look.*

Using the Mentor Text

■ Display the mentor text, and direct students' attention to the publishing format (magazine article) and the text features and visuals the author used to support the narrative.

■ *This author didn't just use words to tell about the event. She included a map, photographs, captions, a timeline, and a list of sources. The photographs obviously make it easier to picture the action, the captions add or call out information we might have missed in the main article, and the timeline that runs across the bottom of the article really helps us keep track of what happened when. These are just the kinds of visuals and text features we will want to include in our own narratives.*

Modeling

■ *As I prepare to publish and share my writing with others, I want to think about the kinds of visuals I can include to make my event come to life. As I peruse other published narratives, I notice fascinating images, photographs, timelines, and maps. These visuals support the writing and add richness to the selection.*

■ *As I work to add the finishing touches to my piece on the Battle of Little Bighorn, I'm thinking a timeline would be helpful to include. I was careful to record dates while I was researching the battle, so it will be easy to construct a timeline from my notes.*

■ *Watch me as I reread my piece of writing to determine where to place the timeline. I want the placement to be intentional, so that it supports the narrative in a prominent way. I think I will place it across the bottom of my piece so readers can see it no matter which page they are on. Now I'll need to write a heading for the timeline.*

TURN &TALK *Think together. What would be a good title for this timeline? Notice how other authors use headings in their published work. What can I learn from them?*

- Continue modeling how you add photographs, illustrations, and maps that enhance the narrative. Demonstrate how you think about page layout and experiment with options for placement of text and visuals on the page.

Build up to Battle

December 3, 1875	June 4, 1876	June 26, 1876
Government orders Native Americans to return to reservation	Sitting Bull prophesized victory over US	Battle of Little Bighorn ends

May 16, 1876	June 25, 1876
Soldiers discover Lakota and Cheyenne camp on the Tongue River	Battle of Little Bighorn begins

Modeled Writing

WRITING and COACHING

- For writers who are ready to present and publish, provide access to publishing paper. If you have access to computers and the Internet, provide time for students to search for images, visuals, photographs, and maps to use in their published piece.

- Some students may still be drafting or revising their narratives. Assure these writers that they can think about the visuals they may want to include as they continue to craft the text.

- Remind students that they can include timelines in their writing. Encourage them to revisit the time line they created in Session 3 and add illustrations or photographs to enhance it.

SHARING and REFLECTING

- *It's time to celebrate our hard work! We've created some fantastic informational narratives, and I think others would benefit from reading our pieces. Let's engage in a "book walk." Please place your finished piece on your table along with a blank sheet of paper. For the next forty minutes, take some time to read the informational narratives we have created. When you've finished reading someone's piece, please use the blank paper to write a comment for the author. When time is up, you'll have a chance to return to your piece and read the comments your readers have left.*

  TURN &TALK *Partners, think together for a few minutes. What did you learn about writing an informational narrative? If you were going to teach someone how to write an informational narrative, what key points would you share? Work together to create a list of the key features that should be included in an informational narrative. At the bottom of your list, write a short paragraph detailing any advice you would give someone who wanted to write his or her own.*

- Gather the students' final pieces, and analyze their attempts at presentation. Identify writers who may need additional modeling as well as those who are ready for higher levels of sophistication. Use the rubrics on the *Resources* CD-ROM to track writing proficiencies and tailor future instruction.

TIP This might be an ideal time to address the issue of copyright. Consider inviting your school's media specialist to help you support students in deciding which visuals can be gathered from the Internet without infringing on copyright. You can also talk about how to credit visuals, quotations, and so on.

Personal Narrative with Suspense

Use a variety of words, phrases, or clauses to create suspense and highlight details.

The Front Door

It was a bright sunny day and I was feeling great as I sprinted home from soccer practice. Mom had warned me that I would be home before her and I was looking forward to having some time with the TV remote all for myself. Feeling very adult, I reached out to put the key into the lock and the door swung open by itself!

It wasn't locked. It wasn't even shut. A deafening silence poured through the open door and sent prickles running up and down my neck. My heart started pounding... something was terribly wrong.

FEATURES

- Enticing title
- Lead that establishes a tone or mood
- Setting and events that are tightly linked
- Sensory details
- Concrete words to make details stand out
- Variety of sentence types
- Variety of connectives
- Distinct ending

FOCUSED MINILESSON

When we write a personal narrative, it gives us an opportunity to relive a memorable event from our lives and then invite an audience to experience that event with us. I'm going to write about a time I went hiking on the Highline Trail. I am selecting that moment in time because I was absolutely terrified yet in awe of the scenery.

I'll begin by creating a lead that will not only let my reader know what my piece will be about but will also set the tone or the mood for the whole piece. I want to create some suspense. I remember that at one point, I was on a narrow trail that curved along a cliff. The trail was very narrow, and the ravine to my left seemed bottomless. I was really nervous, and it felt like I was holding my breath for a long time. I'll write, "As I inched . . . sea level."

TURN &TALK *Analyze the lead I have written. Is there a sense of suspense that has you wondering what will happen next?*

I know that in powerful personal narratives, the setting and the events are closely linked. I'll want to make sure that I create that tight link between the setting and the events, so I will use sensory details to be sure my reader can visualize the setting, the events, and tension. I want to tell about the safety cable next. That was important. I could say "I held it."

But the sensory images would be much stronger if I say "With trembling fingers, I clutched. . . ." Notice the difference it makes when I spend just a bit more time selecting words and phrases that emphasize detail and add to the suspense.

Continue demonstrating and thinking aloud as you finish your personal narrative.

I am ready for an enticing title that will draw my reader in. I could call my piece "Hiking the Highline Trail," or I could title this piece "Entranced and Terrified."

TURN &TALK *Partners, compare the two titles. My goal is to focus on emotion and suspense. Identify the title you think is stronger. Can you identify other titles that might work?*

Entranced and Terrified

As I inched along the edge of the cliff, my breath seemed to freeze in my lungs. The combination of exhilaration and fear had my heart racing as I was both entranced and terrified by the view from 6,800 feet above sea level. With trembling fingers, I clutched the safety cable and moved cautiously toward the summit.

Listen as I recap my goals. I wanted to focus on suspense by using sensory images that link the setting and the events. "Breath seemed to freeze in my lungs" and "with trembling fingers" are my favorites. I also wanted to have a great lead that set a tone or mood for the piece, and we agreed that that worked, too. Finally, I focused on an enticing title that would hint at the suspense in my piece.

TURN &TALK *Partners, think together. Consider the features I have included in my narrative, and identify specific words and phrases that helped create suspense and invite strong visualization.*

Summarize the features: Guide a discussion about the features of a personal narrative and specific steps writers can take to craft great leads, use sensory images, set the stage for suspense, and so on. Record these features on a chart that can serve as a visual support as writers create their drafts.

WRITING and COACHING

Now it's your turn! Think about a memorable event from your life and write about it. As you begin drafting, use your features chart to help you remember what to include in your narrative so it has suspense and sensory images.

As students begin their personal narratives, meet with individuals or small groups to support their attempts at creating an enticing title and lead and creating a tight link between the setting and the events. Some writers may benefit from using the Personal Narrative Planning Page on the *Resources* CD-ROM.

SHARING and REFLECTING

Sum it up! Writers, I noticed that many of you have created a personal narrative that includes many of the features we have listed. You drafted an enticing title and created a lead that established the tone of the piece for your reader. You also used sensory images that linked the setting and the events.

TURN &TALK *We will be reading our personal narratives to the students in the classroom across the hall. What features of a personal narrative do you want to be sure to mention as you share your writing? Think together and consider the most important narrative features that you will share.*

ASSESS THE LEARNING

Analyze the narratives to identify writers who need additional support in creating an enticing title and lead and those who need additional help with creating a tight link between the setting and events.

SELF-ASSESSMENT

SELF-ASSESSMENT
Personal Narrative

	YES	NO
1. **Enticing Title**	☐	☐
2. **Lead establishes a tone or mood**	☐	☐
3. **Setting and events are tightly linked**	☐	☐
4. **Sensory details**	☐	☐
5. **Concrete words make details stand out** ☉	☐	☐
6. **Variety of sentence types** ☉	☐	☐
7. **Variety of connectives** ☉	☐	☐
8. **Distinct ending** ☉	☐	☐

▷ TAKE IT FORWARD

▸ Encourage writers to utilize precise words and phrases that will make the details of their piece stand out. Explain that helping readers to see, hear, taste, touch, and smell will draw them more quickly into a setting.

▸ Identify a mentor text that utilizes a variety of sentence types such as Gary Paulsen's *Dogsong* or Debbie Allen's *Dancing in the Wings*. Identify ways in which the author used short, medium, and long sentences to create sentence fluency, how the sentence fluency impacted the mood or tone of the piece, and so on.

▸ Demonstrate how you include a variety of connectives to show cause and effect, sequence, or emphasis. For example, you might show emphasis by using connectives such as *above all, especially, indeed, most of all,* or *significantly*.

▸ Invite students to analyze the distinct endings in books that you share during read-aloud. Encourage writers to experiment with several endings before choosing one that provides a satisfying closure for the reader.

Personal Narrative of a Single Focused Moment in Time

White Out

Imagine yourself perched at the top of a steep ski run. The slope that had been packed with people on your last run is suddenly empty. There is no one in sight. The biting wind is pummeling you with ice crystals that feel like stinging nettles on your face and you have to plant your poles firmly in the snow to keep from being blown over. Fog has moved in creating a murky white landscape with limited light and no way to see moguls or irregularities in the terrain. You can't stay there shivering all day! So, you take a deep breath, soften your knees for the bumps you are sure to hit, and push off...

Use a strong lead and a variety of sentence patterns to establish a situation.

FEATURES

- Introduction
- Sensory details
- Variety of sentence patterns
- Speaks directly to the reader
- ◗ Relevant details that situate events in a time or place
- ◗ Connective words and phrases
- ◗ Significance or importance of situation is established
- ◗ Illustration or photo

Tea, Scones, and Hats

I'm not a hat-wearing person. I'm not. Don't get me wrong — I'll don a winter cap if the temperature dips below zero, but I don't care to wear the large, ornamental hats that some women enjoy on holidays or time in the sun. Still, one Saturday morning in May, I found myself sporting an enormous pink and green hat with soft feathers emerging from every direction — and I was enjoying it! Amazing! You see, I had wanted to take my sister somewhere special for her birthday.

Modeled Writing

FOCUSED MINILESSON

Personal narratives provide a vehicle for us to share and remember significant moments in our lives. I'm going to write a personal narrative about the time I took my sister to a tea cottage for lunch to celebrate her birthday. I'm not going to write about everything *that happened on our outing, but I'm going to hone in on one significant moment in time and how it affected me.*

It takes time, thought, and attention to begin a piece of writing in a way that draws the reader in. I want to create a lead, or introduction, that will make my reader want to read more. I could begin by writing "This is a story about when I took my sister to a tea cottage," or I could say "I'm not a hat-wearing person . . . birthday." There is no question; the second one speaks directly to my reader. The second lead is definitely the better choice.

TURN &TALK *Analyze my lead. How can you tell that I am speaking directly to a reader?*

Now I want to include some sensory details that will boost my writing and make my reader feel like he is right there with me. Since I began this piece by talking about hats, I think I'll describe the hat I wore at the tea cottage. It was quite a hat! I'll write "Still, one Saturday . . . enjoying it!" Notice the precise descriptive words and phrases I am including: "enormous, green, soft, feathers emerging from every direction." *These precise descriptors help a reader visualize and picture the scene.*

As I continue to describe my afternoon at the tea cottage, I'll want to make sure my sentences differ in length so that my piece reads smoothly. If all of my sentences were short, it would make my narrative sound choppy. I don't want my sentences to be long and rambling, either. I want to include some short sentences, some long sentences, and some that are medium length. As I examine the sentences I have written so far, I see that I have some medium-length sentences and a really long sentence. I have a two-word sentence: "I'm not." *Watch as I insert a single word for emphasis.* "Amazing!"

Continue modeling and thinking aloud as you finish the narrative. Draw attention to features of personal narrative such as enhancing the sensory images and varying sentence length.

TURN &TALK *Let's read my narrative again. Look closely and identify features I included such as speak directly to a reader, create sensory images, use a strong lead, and write sentences that are of varying lengths.*

Summarize the features: Invite students to help you construct a chart for the features of personal narrative, and then post it in a visible place to support them as they write independently.

WRITING and COACHING

Now you'll have a chance to craft a personal narrative of your own. Think back about a moment in time that you can remember well. Close your eyes and visualize the details. Think about how you can invite your reader in with a great lead. And consider language you can use to speak directly to your reader. As you begin to write, use the chart to help you remember the various features that will help your reader experience the moment with you.

As students develop their narratives, confer with individuals or small groups to scaffold their understanding. Consider pulling together a small group for explicit instruction on varying sentence length. Share the Sentence Fluency Tool from the *Resources* CD-ROM.

SHARING and REFLECTING

Sum it up! *Writers, you've included some sensory details that make your personal narratives rich! You spoke directly to your reader and used a wonderful variety of sentence patterns. And your clear and concise introductions draw readers into the situation!*

TURN &TALK *We will be meeting in teams of four to share the narratives you have created. Before we begin, take a moment to consider the features of personal narrative text you want to be sure to mention as you share your narrative. Give me a thumbs-up when you are ready to share in a team.*

ASSESS THE LEARNING

Examine the personal narratives to identify writers who need additional support in including sensory details and varying sentence length to convey a powerful personal narrative.

SELF-ASSESSMENT

SELF-ASSESSMENT

Personal Narrative of a Single, Focused Moment in Time

	YES	NO
1. **Introduction**	☐	☐
2. **Sensory details**	☐	☐
3. **Variety of sentence patterns**	☐	☐
4. **Speak directly to the reader**	☐	☐
5. **Relevant details situate events in a time or place** ○	☐	☐
6. **Connective words and phrases** ○	☐	☐
7. **Significance or importance of situation is established** ○	☐	☐
8. **Illustration or photo** ○	☐	☐

▷ T A K E   I T   F O R W A R D

▸ Encourage writers to include details that situate important events in a time or place. Together with the students, create and display an anchor chart of examples such as *the midnight sky was black and starless* or *crouched below the huge oak tree, we hid and tried not to make a sound.*

▸ Demonstrate how you utilize connective words and phrases to create a clear sequence of events. Display a list of phrases from which students might choose, for example, *later that day, after dinner, before sunrise, the next day, suddenly.*

▸ Show students how other authors communicate the significance or importance of a situation about which they write. Some mentor texts to consider are *Marshfield Dreams: When I Was a Kid* by Ralph Fletcher and *The Junkyard Wonders* by Patricia Polacco.

▸ Invite students to create an illustration or add a photograph to their personal narratives. Show students how to choose or create powerful visuals that will strengthen the message of their narrative.

Informational Narrative

Use simile and action to bring a reader close to a subject.

Dolphin

As the morning sun turns the sea into a medley of sparkling jewels, dolphin begins her dance. She slices through the current like a sleek torpedo, then bursts to the surface with water streaming from her shining skin. Graceful as a ballerina, her body arcs, dives, and then bursts entirely free in a leap that appears to be filled with joy. Moving to music of her own creation, the dance continues.

FEATURES

- Simile
- Onomatopoeia
- Action
- Accurate facts
- Focus on one
- Varied sentence structures
- Clear ending

FOCUSED MINILESSON

Writers, I think geckos are fascinating lizards. They are masters of camouflage and can free-fall from tall trees using their tails like rudders to navigate a safe landing. As I write about geckos, I am going to include similes because those provide readers with helpful comparisons. Watch as I write, "As still as . . . beams." Similes use as *or* like *to establish comparisons. Watch as I underline the similes in my two sentences. Notice also that you can position similes in different parts of a sentence. In the first sentence, I opened with a simile. In the second sentence, I used one as the ending for a sentence.*

TURN &TALK *Analyze the similes I selected, and consider additional similes that I might use to describe the adaptations of a gecko or the actions of a predator that is trying to capture the gecko.*

Another powerful tool we can use is onomatopoeia, words that represent sounds. Words like drip, splat, *and* swoosh *bring readers right into the setting. Watch as I write "Whoosh!" When we include onomatopoeia, it can be placed within a sentence or set apart by itself. In this case, I will add an exclamation point for emphasis and place the word by itself.*

TURN &TALK *Put your heads together, and identify additional onomatopoeia words that we might have considered here.*

Continue demonstrating and thinking aloud as you construct additional sentences with similes. As you model, guide writers in observing the power of action to support reader understanding. It is important to also help writers understand that you are using facts from a resource to ensure that your nonfiction writing is based on scientific evidence, not what you think you know about the topic.

TURN &TALK *Put your heads together, and analyze the nonfiction narrative I created. Notice the features that are included, and get ready to make a list. When you show me a thumbs-up, I will know that you are ready to move to teams of four and list the important features that you have seen in action today.*

Summarize the features: As teams of four work together to create lists of features that add power to informational narratives, guide and coach them to ensure that they include action, simile, onomatopoeia, and accurate facts.

<u>As still as a moss-covered tree branch,</u> the gecko flattens itself against a cluster of leaves. But, the seeking eyes of a hungry owl lock in <u>like bright laser beams.</u> Whoosh! Like a fighter jet, the fierce predator dives straight toward the tiny lizard. The gecko, sensing danger, free-falls into darkness and temporary safety—his tail like a rudder steering him to a safe landing on the ground.

Modeled Writing

WRITING and COACHING

Writers, to create powerful informational narratives, you need to begin by visualizing. Take time to create an action scene in your mind. See the details of the setting. Visualize the movements and behaviors of your subject or another element of the scene. But be careful. You aren't creating fiction. You are using research and real facts and then taking the extra step that places you and your reader right in the setting. As you visualize, you may want to create a sketch or jot action words and similes that might be helpful as you begin to write. I can hardly wait to read your work and become part of the action that your subject experience. Distribute copies of the Informational Narrative Planner from the *Resources* CD-ROM.

Encourage writers to meet with partners and describe the scenes and actions that will be the focus of their informational narratives. This oral rehearsal will strengthen the language and the level of detail that they include when they begin to draft. As writers develop their drafts, confer with individuals and focus their attention on action and simile as tools for improving narratives.

SHARING and REFLECTING

Sum it up! *Writers, it is very exciting to see how richly you have written these informational narratives. Your thoughtful planning and visualizations before writing really show in the action, the similes, the careful insertion of facts, and onomatopoeia!*

TURN &TALK *Please return to the four-person teams, and gather around the features lists you created. Think together about the features, and share with each other how you incorporated the features in your informational narratives. Consider additional features that you used that would be good additions to your chart.*

ASSESS THE LEARNING

Assess the charts created by each team for depth of understanding. Then, analyze the informational narratives to identify writers who need additional support or are ready to stretch to higher levels of proficiency.

SELF-ASSESSMENT

SELF-ASSESSMENT
Informational Narrative

	YES	NO
1. Simile	☐	☐
2. Onomatopoeia	☐	☐
3. Action	☐	☐
4. Accurate facts	☐	☐
5. Focus on one ○	☐	☐
6. Varied sentence structures ○	☐	☐
7. Clear ending ○	☐	☐

▷ TAKE IT FORWARD

▸ Guide a small group in rereading the modeled writing from this lesson and noticing the *focus on one*. Informational narratives can be strengthened when writers avoid using generic plural nouns and instead focus on a single gecko, a single owl, and so on. Help writers see that a focus on one will also affect articles and pronouns because they must be singular. Provide an opportunity for writers to practice creating a piece that focuses on one or reach for a high level of awareness if they have already used the technique.

▸ Return to the modeled writing from this lesson, and highlight the placement of the subject of each sentence. Help students notice that the subject is not always at the begin-ning of the sentence. Model additional sentences in which you open with an introductory element and save the subject for the middle of the sentence. Examples: *With ice-pick talons tucked under his chin, the owl. . . . Nestled in the oozing mud, the frog. . . .* Help writers understand that a key step is to ensure that their writing includes sentences of varying lengths and structures.

▸ Display an array of informational narratives such as *Bat Loves the Night* by Nicola Davies, *Tigress* by Nick Dowson, and *Think of an Eel* by Karen Wallace. Analyze the end-ings and compare them to nonfiction endings that are less satisfying.

Key Words and Summary

Use key words to support a summary.

FEATURES

- Key words on sticky notes
- Opens with a question
- Speaks to the reader
- Personal connections
- Boldface text
- ▷ Heading
- ▷ Using a dash

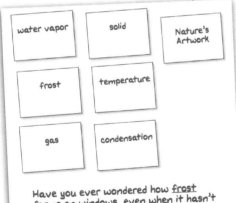

Have you ever wondered how <u>frost</u> forms on windows, even when it hasn't rained? When there is a sudden drop in temperature, <u>water vapor</u> will condense on cold surfaces—just like you see on a cold glass of soda on a warm summer day. If the <u>temperature</u> drops below freezing, the damp <u>condensation</u> that clings to a glass, a window, or even a spider web turns into <u>frost</u> because the <u>water vapor</u> has changed from a <u>gas</u> into a <u>solid</u>.

Modeled Writing

FOCUSED MINILESSON

As I read from A Drop of Water *by Walter Wick, I am going to collect key words and phrases that capture the most important ideas. Once I have collected key words, I can use them as I write a summary about how frost is formed.* Display the book, page 32. *The book says that water vapor condenses on cold surfaces, so I will write "water vapor" on a large sticky note. Next, I will take a second sticky note and write "condensation"—another important term that will help me when I summarize. Notice that I put the key words and phrases on separate sticky notes so I can move them around as I create my summary.*

Continue reading and collecting content-specific words and phrases, writing each on a separate sticky note. It may be helpful to identify a word that is of lesser importance and tell why you are not going to select it as a key word. Writers would also benefit from seeing you identify a few inferences such as "Nature's Artwork."

TURN &TALK *Evaluate my key words and phrases. Are there any other words and phrases that you think should be identified as highly important?*

Now that I have several key words and phrases, I can arrange them in an order that will help me create a summary. Show students how you can rearrange the sticky notes.

I want to use a writing technique that is often found in nonfiction narratives—beginning with a question. Starting with a question helps readers understand that you are speaking directly to them, so I will write, "Have you ever wondered. . . ?" In sentence two, I am going to continue speaking directly to my reader, so I will begin with "When there is . . . day." By including the example about a cold drink, I am deliberately trying to get my reader to connect to a personal experience. This helps comprehension!

Continue modeling and thinking aloud as you infuse key words and phrases into sentences, making them boldface as you write. *Writers, did you notice that I wrote my key words and phrases in bold print? That is a feature we often see in nonfiction resources and a tool that we can use as writers. Bold text helps readers notice important words.*

TURN &TALK *Compare my nonfiction narrative to a report or a description. Identify the features that make this informational narrative different.*

Summarize the features: Have partners use their writer's notebooks and create lists of the features of key words to support a summary.

WRITING and COACHING

Select a topic for students to investigate, collecting key words and phrases. *Writers, you are ready to use sticky notes and identify key words and phrases as you read. The idea is to collect words and phrases that will power up your summaries. But you also need to remember that this is an informational narrative, so you need to open with a question, speak directly to your reader, and help your reader make connections.*

Confer with individuals to provide coaching, or meet with a small group to coach and support as they select key words and phrases and then organize them into meaningful paragraphs with bold text.

SHARING and REFLECTING

Sum it up! *Writers, your writing is filled with key words that capture important ideas. Most of you remembered to open with a question and speak directly to your reader. I also noticed lots of examples that will help readers connect to your personal experiences.*

TURN &TALK *Your summaries were supported by key words and the use of specific writing techniques that helped you speak directly to your reader. Think together and then use your writer's notebooks to remind yourselves of the features and strategies that you used in this piece of writing.*

ASSESS THE LEARNING

While students are writing, circulate and tick off appropriately used features on a class record-keeping sheet. This will provide a formative assessment that you can use to identify students who need additional support and those who are ready to be stretched. See the *Resources* CD-ROM for a copy of the class record-keeping sheet.

SELF-ASSESSMENT

SELF-ASSESSMENT
Key Words and Summary

	YES	NO
1. Key words on sticky notes	☐	☐
2. Open with a question	☐	☐
3. Speak to the reader	☐	☐
4. Personal connections	☐	☐
5. Bold face text	☐	☐
6. Heading ○	☐	☐
7. Using a dash ○	☐	☐

▷TAKE IT FORWARD

▸ Model how to create headings using one of the key phrases or an inference that hits the big idea of the writing. If writers develop several headings before they begin to write, they will find that it is easy to produce well-organized paragraphs.

▸ Guide writers in reviewing the modeled writing from this lesson to analyze the use of the dash. Engage them in conversations about how a dash affects their oral reading and comprehension and when they might use dashes in their own writing. Model the creation of additional sentences to

show that dashes can be used in many ways. Examples: *Brianna gave me a terrible haircut—and she expected a tip! I was absolutely overwhelmed by the volume of work— housecleaning, grocery shopping, writing deadlines, and cooking—too much for me.*

▸ Demonstrate how to revise a first draft. Show writers how to use a caret mark, insert margin notes, or even cut a piece of writing up to paste in more room to write.

Narrative Poetry with a Partner

Craft a nonfiction narrative poem.

Owl Facts:

Detect tiny movements
Excellent vision and hearing
Hoots
Flies silently
Flat disks around eyes channel sound to ears
Eat mice and small birds
Nocturnal

Parter A	Partner B
I am owl	
	Partner B
Gliding, Blinking	Emperor of Night
Tiny movements catch my eye	Silent as the moon
Fallen leaves shiver with subtle movement	My eye disks channel sound to my ears
Dinner	Whooo! Whoo!
	Dinner

FEATURES

- Phrases and/or short sentences
- Descriptive detail
- Metaphor
- No punctuation
- Justified left or center
- Conclusion
- Title

FOCUSED MINILESSON

Narrative poetry is designed to tell a story with rich imagery and a minimum of words. To show you how it works, I am going to focus on the topic of night and what happens when night turns to sunrise. I will also use a metaphor, a literary device designed to offer comparisons. It is important to remember that a metaphor is different from a simile because it does not use the signal words like *and* as. *I will open my narrative poem with "A velvet pillow . . . darkness." Night isn't a real pillow, but comparing night to a big pillow that cushions the stars and caresses the earth helps me tell the story of night as a time of softness.*

TURN &TALK *Writers, reread the first three lines, and think about the metaphor of a pillow. Analyze the metaphor and share your thinking about the images that those three lines bring to you.*

In summertime, sometimes I sit outside and just listen to the noises of crickets, frogs, and other night creatures. A metaphor for animal sounds is orchestra—an animal orchestra! Watch as I write "Songs of . . . sleep." Did you notice that I slipped in another metaphor, "Songs of life?" Animal sounds aren't really songs. That is a metaphor!

Because narrative poems tell a story, they need to have an ending or a conclusion. Since I am writing about the change of night to day, a natural ending is something about sunrise. I could write about the colors of the sunrise, the shifting light through the shadows, or the activity of the birds, but that might detract from my focus on night. Instead, I will write, "The rising sun . . . aside."

TURN &TALK *Take a moment and look closely at the structure of the poem and the way it is arranged on the paper. What do you notice? Identify as many features of a narrative poem as you can.*

As students identify features, you may need to point out the left or center justification of the poem, the lack of punctuation, and the combination of phrases and complete sentences.

Night to Day

A velvet pillow
Cushioning the stars
Caressing the earth with soothing darkness
A chorus of small noises
Songs of life
Orchestra to our sleep
The rising sun lifts light from the shadows
Nudging night aside

Modeled Writing

Summarize the features: Have partners work together to analyze and list the features of a narrative poem that is informational. Once they have developed their lists, have them meet with another partner pair to share lists, and make sure that everyone has a complete list of features.

WRITING and COACHING

Today you will be working with a partner to select a topic and then write a nonfiction narrative poem that includes metaphor and descriptive detail. Be sure to use your list of features so the poems you create together are rich with descriptive detail, metaphors, and a clear conclusion. If you have difficulty identifying a topic, you may want to browse these great magazines on natural phenomena such as tornadoes, hurricanes, and volcanoes.

As partners research and draft, invite partner pairs to meet with you for support in planning, revising, or editing their nonfiction narrative poems.

SHARING and REFLECTING

Sum it up! *Writers, the narrative poems you wrote create wonderful imagery with descriptive details and metaphors. I see that you used phrases instead of sentences and that you justified either to the left or the center. I also notice that the conclusions make it very clear that this is the end of the "story."*

TURN &TALK *Partners, prepare to share your nonfiction narrative poems with a team of six. You will want to practice reading it aloud so it is performed with expression and plan which features you will point out in the poem so your listeners are sure to notice the ones that you remembered to use. When you are ready to share, please gather in teams of six.*

ASSESS THE LEARNING

Provide writers with the Self-Assessment Checklist on the *Resources* CD-ROM. Have them self-assess their work and then record their poems in their writers' notebooks so they can access them anytime they want to write additional narrative poems.

SELF-ASSESSMENT

SELF-ASSESSMENT Narrative Poetry with a Partner	YES	NO
1. Phrases and/or short sentences	☐	☐
2. Descriptive detail	☐	☐
3. Metaphor	☐	☐
4. No punctuation	☐	☐
5. Justify left or center	☐	☐
6. Conclusion	☐	☐
7. Title ○	☐	☐

▷TAKE IT FORWARD

▸ Titles are powerful tools for writers. Have students experiment with a variety of titles that offer additional imagery, a metaphor, or descriptive detail. They may want to consider alliteration for their titles as well.

▸ Guide students in experimenting with simile in narrative poetry as an additional literary device.

▸ Have students write nonfiction narrative poems about important people in history, specific events from history, or social studies units of study.

▸ Locate books by Robert Burleigh such as *Black Whiteness*, a narrative poem about Admiral Byrd, and analyze Burleigh's writing style and the features he has included. Diane Siebert (*I Am the Heartland*), Jonathan London (*Voices of the Wild*), Gary Paulson (*Dogsong*), and Jane Yolen (*Owl Moon*) also write richly constructed narrative poems that are available in picture book format.

▸ Invite students to write biographies of famous people in the format of nonfiction narrative poems.

Partner News Article

Write a news article using an inverted pyramid structure.

FEATURES

- Inverted pyramid structure
- Tells who, what, when, where, why
- Lead statement with main idea
- Opens with a question or surprising statement
- Most important facts in first paragraph
- Quotation
- Byline

BEFORE THE LESSON

Bring in real newspapers so students can examine the layout of news articles. Help them notice titles and boldface type, the lead statement that follows the title to provide the main idea of the piece, and so on.

FOCUSED MINILESSON

Writers, today I am going to create a news article focusing on the man who flew into the Grand Canyon with a wing and an engine on his back—no airplane! To do this, I need to write in the format of an inverted pyramid and write the most important ideas first and details last. Draw an inverted pyramid. *To get started, I will write a main idea statement that will serve as my lead. The lead statement should provide a reader with a quick overview of the article. Watch as I write: "Swiss Adventurer . . . ." Now I am ready for the first paragraph. The trick is to begin with a question or a statement that is surprising to a reader. Watch closely as I write, "Can people fly without an airplane?"*

TURN &TALK *Analyze my lead statement and the first sentence of the paragraph. Did I give a main idea that highlights the big ideas in the article, and did my first sentence make you want to keep reading? Do you have suggestions for improvement?*

Since I am writing in an inverted pyramid, I need to really pack the first paragraph with information. It needs to tell who, what, when, where, and why. Watch for those details as I write, "Swiss adventurer . . . floor."

TURN &TALK *What details do you think might be helpful as I move to the second paragraph?*

As I continue writing in the smaller portion of the pyramid, I can add quotations, details, and other interesting facts as long as I remember that the most important information must be at the top of the pyramid in paragraph one. Continue modeling and thinking aloud as you craft the second paragraph.

Summarize the features: Review the features of a news article and the importance of an inverted pyramid structure. Collaborate with students to create a Features of a News Article Checklist that you can post in a visible place so writers can reference it as they write their own articles.

Conquering the Canyon

Swiss Adventurer "Jetman" Rossy Wings Over Grand Canyon
By Linda Hoyt

Can people fly without an airplane? Swiss adventurer, Yves Rossy, proved that the answer is yes! On May 6, 2011, he strapped on jet-propelled wings and then soared from a helicopter over the Grand Canyon. Living the dream of many who believe that individual flight is possible, Rossy was airborne for about eight minutes, cruising at up to 190 miles per hour before deploying his parachute and landing safely on the canyon floor.

The custom-built jet suit that Rossy wears weighs 120 lbs. and has a 79" wing span. It averages speeds of 125 mph and has four engines—all carefully calibrated to keep Rossy in the air. The challenge has been that Rossy's suit does not have enough power for him to take off from the ground so he must gain elevation by hanging onto the side of a helicopter or airplane so he can initiate his flight from a high altitude. The adventurer said the flight was among "the most memorable experiences of his life."

http://www.dogonews.com/2011/5/15/yves-jetman-rossy-soars-over-the-grand-canyon

© 2012 Tony Stead and Linda Hoyt from *Explorations in Nonfiction Writing, Grade 5* (Portsmouth, NH: Heinemann). This page may be reproduced for classroom use only.

Modeled Writing

Science is Super

Inquiry and Science Lead the Way in Grade 5
On the scene reporting by Huan Ji and Bilal

Fifth grade inquiry teams explore life science topics of personal interest.

Team 1: Sharks
Alex, Julianna, Manuel, Habib, Morgan, Sam, Calvin, Bilal

Team 2: Metamorphosis
Alma, Tolmas, Aricelli, Victor, Delaney, Conner, Regi

Team 3: Bats
Rebecca, Caleb, Kara, Walter, Dominic, Huan Ji, Blake

Team 4: Life Cycles
Rich, Molly, Jennifer, Lexie, Tuana, Jac, Simon, Kiara

Inquiry is King

Wikipedia states that an inquiry is *"any process that has the aim of augmenting knowledge, resolving doubt, or solving a problem."* So fifth graders have worked in teams to develop lists of questions around a topic of personal interest. These central questions are being used to guide active research as students seek to find both answers and additional questions related to their topic. The pace is fast and furious as everyone wants to be ready for the science open house when the teams will present their findings to parents and interested community members. Team researchers are working with a variety of books, magazines, and online resources to find answers then create displays, visual texts, and published books on their topic.

Principal Corner

Mrs. De训

WRITING and COACHING

Writers, we are going to write and publish our own collection of news articles. The articles can be about current news events, a person you interview, or upcoming events in our community. As you have noticed, newspapers are more interesting when they include photographs, so you will want to plan for that as well. Find a partner and make a list of topics that you would like to write about. When you have reviewed your options and made a decision, you can use the News Article Planning Sheet (see the *Resources* CD-ROM) *and begin to plan your articles.*

Support individuals or small groups as necessary.

SHARING and REFLECTING

Sum it up! *Writers, you have created news articles on a wonderful array of topics. I see that you remembered to use the inverted pyramid and placed the most important information in the first paragraph. Your first paragraphs tell who, what, when, where, and why. I see lead statements that get right to the heart of your articles. I am also having fun noticing the questions and surprising statements that you used as your opening sentences.*

TURN &TALK *We are ready to publish our news articles, but first we need to review the features and be sure they are all in place. Find a new partner, and evaluate your articles. Use the Features of a News Article Checklist that we created, and assess your work. Think together and make sure all the features are in place.*

ASSESS THE LEARNING

Gather the news articles, and identify writers who have included all the features and are ready to be stretched as well as writers who need additional modeling and direct support to improve their news articles.

SELF-ASSESSMENT

SELF-ASSESSMENT

Partner News Article

	YES	NO
1. Inverted pyramid structure	☐	☐
2. Tells who, what, when, where, why	☐	☐
3. Lead statement with main idea	☐	☐
4. Opens with a question or surprising statement	☐	☐
5. Most important facts in first paragraph	☐	☐
6. Quotation ⊙	☐	☐
7. Byline ⊙	☐	☐

◁TAKE IT FORWARD

▸ Direct quotes are often found in news articles. Demonstrate how to gather a quote from a written source or from an interview. Display the correct punctuation for a quotation, and show writers how these additional features are often added in the lower portion of the inverted pyramid or used as a conclusion—as in the modeled writing for this lesson.

▸ Display published newspapers and show how the bylines are presented. Compare and contrast the presentation of a byline with the way an author is credited in a book or magazine.

▸ Captions are a feature regularly found in news articles. Provide an opportunity for writers to insert captions with their photographs.

▸ Guide students in examining a feature article, comparing and contrasting its features with those of a news article written in an inverted pyramid style.

▸ Compile articles into a newsletter/newspaper form, and publish them electronically.

VISUAL
LITERACY

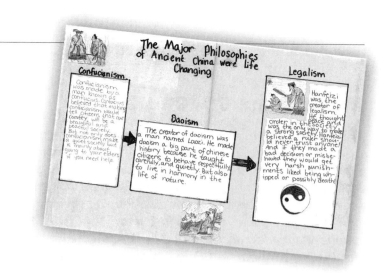

Flowchart

Sequence historical events with a flowchart.

FEATURES

- Text boxes
- Arrows to show order
- Explanatory narrative
- Introduction
- Sources are cited
- Title
- Linking words

FOCUSED MINILESSON

Flowcharts are a great way to put related events into a sequence and organize them for writing. I have been reading about the eruption of Mt. St. Helens in 1980, so I will use a flowchart to organize the events. Watch as I begin by creating a row of boxes and connect them with arrows. This shows the order in which things happen, but unlike a timeline, a flowchart gives me room to write some details and even add a sketch or a photograph.

I have printed some photographs that I think will help me tell the story of this eruption. Notice the picture of the mountain before the eruption as I place it in box 1. The shape is important because it changed after the eruption. In box 1, I will add notes about the beginning of seismic activity and the scientists who came to monitor it. Watch as I draw an arrow to the next box to show that the events are related and sequential.

TURN &TALK *Partners, think together. You know a bit about this eruption. Identify events that you think should appear in my flowchart. Consider where the events should be placed in our sequence.*

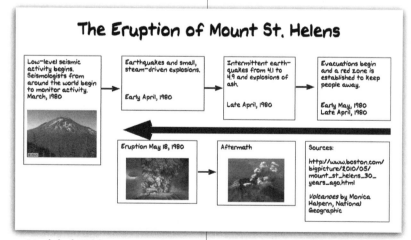

Modeled Writing

Continue thinking aloud, entering photographs, notes, and connecting arrows to the flowchart. Be sure to point out that you need to create a place on the page where you can cite your sources of information.

Now that the flowchart has key events and details, I am ready to write a narrative explaining how these events unfolded. I will begin with an introduction, "On a sunny morning in May, the spring air was shattered by the massive eruption of Mt. St. Helens. Earthquakes were felt hundreds of miles away as the sky turned black and ash began to drift in billowing black clouds that covered the sun. Here is how it happened. . . ." *Did you notice that I didn't start at the beginning of the flowchart? Instead, I tried to engage my reader by painting a picture of the eruption. Now I will go back and tell the story from the beginning.*

TURN &TALK *Analyze my introduction and talk about the benefits of hooking a reader before you begin to lay out a sequence of events. How might you use that technique in your own writing?*

Summarize the features: Invite students to work in teams and create features checklists for a flowchart with narrative text.

WRITING and COACHING

You will be working with a partner to create a flowchart to show the order in which related events occur. Remember that you need to create text boxes and link them with arrows to show order. You are welcome to add notes as well as visuals in the boxes. Once you have done your research and constructed your flowchart, you will be ready to write an informational narrative about your topic. Remember to start with a powerful introduction that hooks the reader and makes them want to know more!

As partners construct their flowcharts, guide them in confirming facts with available resources and in remembering that they don't need to deal with large units of time in history. The flowchart could be focused on the launch of a space shuttle, the repair of the Hubble telescope, Frederick Douglas' escape from slavery, Abraham Lincoln's bid for the presidency, the passage of a bill in Congress, and so on.

SHARING and REFLECTING

Sum it up! *Writers, I am impressed by the care with which you assembled your flowcharts. The visual nature of your charts makes the sequence of events very clear and establishes the fact that the events are related. I also see that you remembered to cite your sources! I can hardly wait to hear the introductions that you created to hook your readers.*

TURN &TALK *Partners, we will be meeting in teams to share flowcharts and narratives. Take a few minutes to review the features of a flowchart and informational narratives so you are prepared to show the other team members which features you used.*

ASSESS THE LEARNING

Review the flowcharts and informational narratives for use of the features, quality of factual information, and the clarity of the writing in the narratives.

SELF-ASSESSMENT

SELF-ASSESSMENT **Flowchart**	YES	NO
1. **Text boxes**	☐	☐
2. **Arrows to show order**	☐	☐
3. **Explanatory narrative**	☐	☐
4. **Introduction**	☐	☐
5. **Sources are cited**	☐	☐
6. **Title** ⊙	☐	☐
7. **Linking words** ⊙	☐	☐

▶TAKE IT FORWARD

▸ Engage students in a conversation about nonfiction titles that are especially engaging and the attributes that make those titles appealing to readers. Then, challenge them to create titles for their flowcharts and narratives that are powerful and engaging.

▸ Linking words provide internal support to writing that focuses on sequence or cause and effect. Work with students to create and post charts of linking words that support

these purposes in writing. See the *Resources* CD-ROM for lists of linking words for sequence, cause and effect, and conclusion.

▸ Create flowcharts for topics of historical significance to show the interrelatedness of events and outcomes.

▸ Use flowcharts to support scientific inquiry, recording ongoing observations and outcomes.

VISUAL LITERACY

Team Investigation

Craft a photo essay.

FEATURES

- Magazine-style layout
- Captions
- Photographs
- Quotations
- Impact statement
- Linking words
- Citations

BEFORE THE LESSON

Present photo essays such as those by Russell Freedman, and engage students in a conversation about the attributes of a photo essay or a photo biography. You may want to consider constructing the modeled writing on your computer as students observe through a projection system.

FOCUSED MINILESSON

When we examine informational magazines or photo essays such as those by Russell Freedman, it is clear that the photographs tell much of the story. They add detail and depth that are very hard to achieve with just words. I am going to construct a photo essay using photographs that were taken when Ruby Bridges, a courageous six-year-old, starting attending a school where only white children had been able to go. Since the photographs are large, I will arrange explanatory captions around them. Watch as I write the first and second captions: "On November . . . cafeteria." Notice how the captions add information that couldn't be identified from the picture alone. Notice also that I need to think about how the pictures and the captions are arranged. They should be visually appealing.

TURN &TALK *Writers, the next picture is of the crowd that gathered outside of the school. It tells quite a story as Ruby had to walk through that mob to get in and out of the building. Analyze the photograph and identify key points that you think I should make.*

Continue drafting captions and arranging photos.

Quotations from people who were actively involved in a situation add insights that can't be achieved with simple description. I selected two quotations from the book Through My Eyes *by Ruby Bridges that I thought would enrich this photo essay. The first one is from Ruby, who wrote "Don't follow . . . trail." That is so powerful, I want to be sure it is noticed. Watch closely as I position this at the top of my photo essay to ensure that it gets attention. Because it is a quotation, I am making it italic and adding Ruby Bridges' name. I also have a quote from John Steinbeck, a famous novelist. I will add that in the last caption.*

TURN &TALK *A photo essay is a visual text that has unique features. Review my photo essay, and consider how you might use these features in a photo essay of your own.*

"Don't follow the path. Go where there is no path and start a trail."
Ruby Bridges

On November 14, 1960, Ruby Bridges, a first grader, walked through what was described as a carnival atmosphere of jeering, fruit-throwing segregationists and entered a school that didn't want her. She had been selected to be the first black child to enter William Franz Elementary in New Orleans and her life would never be the same.

Ruby was the only child in the classroom because the white children stopped going to school when Ruby arrived. Federal Marshalls guarded the classroom to keep Ruby safe but she wasn't allowed to go on the playground or into the cafeteria.

The howling, hate-filled crowds grew larger and louder each day. Some carried signs while others screamed and chanted at Ruby. On one horrible day, someone even brought a black doll in a coffin to ensure that Ruby would be terrified.

Federal Marshalls escorted Ruby into the school each day, carefully keeping her behind the barricades and as far from the angry crowd as possible. John Steinbeck, observing the spectacle wrote: The little girl did not look at the howling crowd but from the side the whites of her eyes showed like those of a frightened fawn.

Modeled Writing

Summarize the features: Review the features of a photo essay, noting the importance of visual appeal and arrangement on a page, the balance of content communicated through pictures and through words, the use of quotations, and so on.

WRITING and COACHING

Writers, you will be working in teams of three to create photo essays that include visually appealing use of space, photographs, captions, and quotations. As you get ready to begin, be sure you have resources to provide real facts. With a photo essay, you can't tell about a person's entire life or about something huge like World War II. Your focus needs to be on important highlights of a specific time. So, select a person whose life you think is interesting or a historical event that you think would make a strong photo essay. Gather some really important facts, and select images that you will want to use.

Confer with teams as they research, gather facts, write their captions, and arrange space on the page. Be sure they focus on making the photographs the focal point and use captions to add information. Carefully selected and cited quotations are also important.

SHARING and REFLECTING

Sum it up! *The photo essays you have created present a visually powerful message. You have clearly checked your facts, listed your sources, and focused on visual layout. I see tempting titles, powerful photographs, captions, quotations, and so much more.*

TURN &TALK *I have made arrangements for each team to visit a classroom to present your photo essays. Put your heads together, and plan how you will share your work and also what you will teach your readers about creating a photo essay.*

ASSESS THE LEARNING

Have teams use the Self-Assessment Checklist on the *Resources* CD-ROM to assess their work. Then, invite them to meet with you and justify the ratings they gave to themselves. They should be prepared to rate the visual appeal and page arrangement, text quality of the captions, use of quotations, and photograph selection.

SELF-ASSESSMENT

SELF-ASSESSMENT
Team Investigation

	YES	NO
1. Magazine style layout	☐	☐
2. Captions	☐	☐
3. Photographs	☐	☐
4. Quotations	☐	☐
5. Impact statement	☐	☐
6. Linking words	☐	☐
7. Citations	☐	☐

▷ TAKE IT FORWARD

▸ Photo essays often conclude with an impact statement that reflects upon the impact of the events, situation, or behaviors profiled in the photo essay. An impact statement for Ruby Bridges might sound something like "Because of Ruby Bridges and the courage of children like her, all students in the United States now have the opportunity to go to their neighborhood school—regardless of the color of their skin."

▸ Draw the attention of your writers to powerful linking words to connect ideas such as *as soon as, finally, afterward,*

earlier, meanwhile, now, since, soon, then, while, when, because, even though. These are helpful in showing the passage of time and evidence of challenge in photo essays.

▸ Citations are vitally important in photo essays to show authenticity of photos and accuracy of information. Show writers how to record citations and post them in a visible place on their work.

Taking It Forward: Personal Writing Projects

· ·

After they have had the opportunity to work through the model unit and lessons in this section, cement your students' understandings about narrative writing by having them complete one or more *personal* writing projects on topics of their choice. This is an important follow-up to the model unit because it allows students to apply their new understandings to their own writing lives based on personal interests.

For example, the teaching processes outlined in the model units on personal narratives and informational narratives can easily be adapted to personal projects on a variety of topics and in a variety of forms. If students have trouble deciding what to write about, you might want to suggest topics and forms such as the ones that follow. Otherwise, give students the freedom to choose the topics they find most interesting—provided you deem them appropriate.

Possible Topics for Narrative Writing

Topics may correlate with content in your science and social studies standards, current events, or class interests.

Personal Narrative
My trip to the museum
A field trip experience
How I got to school today
A time when I was scared
A time when I was sad
A family tradition
A vacation experience
My first day at camp
A surprise
A visit with my relatives
Going to work with my parent
Playing a game
An achievement
A special experience
What I like to do best

Nonfiction Narrative
A favorite author
A favorite sports hero
A day in the life of a _____
A local event
Explanations Using the Narrative Form
How a spider catches a fly
How a snake sheds its skin
The life cycle of a frog
The water cycle
Where maple syrup comes from
How a road is made
How a thunderstorm forms
What causes a volcano
How a plant gets nutrients
Why leaves fall

Possible Forms for Narrative Writing

Retells
Recounts
Explanations
Personal stories
Biographies
Documentaries
Flowcharts

Autobiographies
Articles
Storyboards
Observation logs
Diagrams
Summaries
Photo essays

Illustrations
Postcards
Letters
Posters
Poems
Slide shows
Timelines

Planning and Implementing Personal Writing Projects

Your students will need preparation, coaching, prompting, and varying amounts of support as they move through their own personal explorations. The ten-session structure presented in the model unit may be too long for personal projects that assume less time spent on instruction and modeling. Give students the time they need to fully develop their topics and to move through the stages of the writing process, but don't be surprised if many students require fewer than ten sessions.

Use the following tips and strategies as needed to ensure each student's success.

Before the Personal Projects:

▸ Help students select topics that they are interested in, and provide research materials if needed.

▸ Continue to use information you gather from the Individual Assessment Record or your Ongoing Monitoring Sheet to provide specific instruction in whole-class, small-group, and individual settings as needed. Use the Daily Planner to lay out each day's lesson.

During the Personal Projects:

▸ Give students the personal checklists from the *Resources* CD-ROM to use as samples for creating their own checklists. A blank checklist can be found on the *Resources* CD-ROM and in the Resources section at the end of this book. Explain to the students that you will also be checking to see if they have included key features on the checklist.

▸ If needed, begin each session with a focused minilesson. Tailor the suggested minilesson to suit the needs of your students.

▸ Continue to provide high-quality mentor texts. Display mentor texts prominently, and allow students time to read them before they begin to write their own. Continue to call students' attention to the features list created during the model unit.

▸ You may want to write your own text along with the students as you did during the model unit to provide an additional model.

▸ Have writing partners conference with each other often to check one another's work for sense and clarity.

▸ As students work independently on their writing and illustrations, note those who are struggling and bring them together for small-group instruction. Use the Individual Assessment Record and/or the Ongoing Monitoring Sheet to assist in tailoring instruction to the needs of your students.

▸ Students who seem very confident and who have clearly grasped all of the concepts taught so far can be brought together in a small group to extend their understanding to more challenging work.

After the Personal Projects:

▶ Be sure to give students opportunities to share and celebrate their writing projects.

▶ Compare students' final writing products with their earlier attempts in order to evaluate their growth as writers.

▶ Distribute copies of the Student Self-Reflection Sheet (on the *Resources* CD-ROM). Students will benefit greatly from the chance to reflect on their progress and to hear their classmates' feedback.

▶ Reflect on the strengths and challenges of implementing the personal projects. How might the process be adjusted to maximize student learning?

▶ Look at common needs of the class, and address these when students are working on future projects.

Persuasive Writing Projects

Persuasive texts put forward a point of view to influence the reader to take action or to believe something. The purpose may be to convince someone to buy a particular product or to change someone's thinking about a specific issue. Students are most likely to encounter persuasive text in the form of advertisements, posters or articles meant to convince readers to do or think something, and book or movie reviews. Persuasive text may appear in many formats, including bumper stickers, flyers, posters, letters, speeches, debates, essays, editorials, reviews, and poems. Persuasive writing uses both facts and opinions. Persuasive texts are characterized by goals, statements of opinion, supporting facts (evidence), and direct appeal.

CONTENTS

The Big Picture

· ·

During the model unit that follows, students will write a persuasive letter taking a position on a school issue. The mentor text, "Martha's Letter," provides a model of the structure and features of a persuasive text. Students begin by observing features of the mentor text and then work in pairs or small groups to gather and organize information about a school issue of their choice, using their research notebooks and a persuasive text graphic organizer. (The mentor text is about homework; the modeled writing is about exercise. You'll probably want to remove those topics from the list of choices so students will not be tempted to copy from the models.) From their notes, students then write their persuasive letter. They revise, edit, and publish the letter, and may add supporting visuals. Finally, they share their letters with classmates and others and reflect on what they have learned about writing a persuasive text.

Session	Focused Minilesson	Writing and Coaching	Sharing and Reflecting
1	Identifying the purpose and features of a persuasive text	Draft an opinion statement in your research notebook.	Share opinion statements with a partner. What do you like about your partner's opinion statement?
2	Asking and answering questions	Ask questions to focus research; take notes to answer questions.	Share the questions you've asked and facts you've gathered. Which facts will be most persuasive?
3	Using a graphic organizer	Use a graphic organizer to organize your opinions, reasons, and facts.	Share organizers and evaluate reasons and facts. What further research is needed?
4	Drafting the introduction	Turn the opinion statement into a compelling introduction.	Share your lead. What do you like about your partner's lead? What might make it more compelling?
5	Drafting the body of the letter	Turn notes into sentences and paragraphs, using linking words to connect reasons and facts.	Share your draft. Can your partner identify the reason and supporting facts in each paragraph? Where were you able to connect ideas with linking words?
6	Drafting a strong conclusion	Draft an ending that includes powerful persuasive words and a call to action.	Share your ending. What powerful persuasive words do you see in your partner's conclusion? Is the call to action clear?
7	Revising for sentence variety	Read aloud and revise for varied sentence lengths and types.	Share your draft. Talk about places where you revised to vary sentence length. Where might you still want to revise?
8	Using a revision checklist	Use a revision checklist for persuasive text to reread and revise.	Share revisions with a partner. How did it help you to use a revision checklist?
9	Editing the letter	Edit for one point at a time, focusing on using apostrophes to form contractions.	Share your editing work with a partner. What did you change and why?
10	Publishing and sharing	Publish the letter and create supporting visuals with captions.	What advice would you give about writing a persuasive text? What features does it need to include?

Assessing Students' Needs

The model unit is designed to teach students about the structure and features of a specific type of persuasive writing as they apply basic writing strategies. Each of the focused minilessons provides you with suggested demonstrations, but you may want to tailor your instruction based on the common needs of your own students. You can assess students' strengths and needs during each unit, in an additional session beforehand, or by analyzing student work that you already have on hand.

Formal Pre-Assessment: After a basic introduction to each writing purpose and form as well as a review of various examples, have students write in the same form about a topic they already know a lot about. Encourage students to use as many of the features of the particular writing form as possible, but don't provide direct support. The goal here is to find out how much students already know about the writing purpose and form so you can tailor your teaching accordingly.

Experimentation in Research Notebooks: You might want to stop short of a formal pre-assessment and instead ask students to experiment with writing in their research notebooks at the end of the first session. This exercise may be less unnerving for some students and should yield enough information to form the basis of your pre-assessment.

Looking Back at Previous Work: Whether you choose to assess students' writing skills before beginning an Extended Writing Unit or during the first session, we recommend that you also consider unrelated writing projects that you've already collected from students. These may not reveal much about your students' ability to write a coherent persuasive letter, for example, but should tell you a great deal about their grasp of writing conventions and other traits such as focus, organization, voice, and sentence fluency. Depending on how much student work you already have on hand, you might not have to devote any class time to pre-assessment.

Focusing on Standards

Before introducing this model unit, carefully review the key skills and understandings below so you can keep the lesson objectives in mind as you teach, coach, and monitor students' growth as writers of persuasive texts.

KEY SKILLS AND UNDERSTANDINGS: PERSUASIVE WRITING GRADE 5
Purpose
Understands the purpose for writing a persuasive piece
Ideas/Research
Reflects research and planning to support an opinion or position
Bases writing on research and personal opinion or position
Includes facts from research to support opinions or positions
Gathers and uses information from multiple sources
Lists/cites sources
Organization/Text Features
Includes a title that reflects the topic and goal
Has a strong introduction that states an opinion or position
Includes reasons for the opinion or position that are supported by facts
Ends with a conclusion that summarizes and calls readers to action
Includes persuasive visuals
Language/Style
Shows a clear, consistent opinion throughout the piece
Puts information in his or her own words
Uses linking words and phrases to connect ideas (*because, therefore, for example,* etc.)
Uses powerful persuasive language
Demonstrates sentence variety and fluency
Conventions and Presentation
Begins sentences with capital letters
Uses correct end punctuation
Uses appropriate spelling
Uses apostrophes correctly to form contractions
Creates clear, persuasive page layouts with supporting visuals

This list is the basis for both the Individual Assessment Record and the Ongoing Monitoring Sheet shown in Figure 1.1. (Both forms can be found in the Resources section at the back of this book and also on the *Resources* CD-ROM.) Use the Individual Assessment Record if you want to keep separate records on individual students. The Ongoing Monitoring Sheet gives you a simple mechanism for recording information on all your students as you move around the class, evaluating their work in progress. Use this information to adapt instruction and session length as needed.

At the end of these and any additional units you may teach on persuasive writing, compare students' final publications with their initial attempts at writing in the text type. Use the Ongoing Monitoring Sheet and/or the Individual Assessment Record to record students' growth as writers.

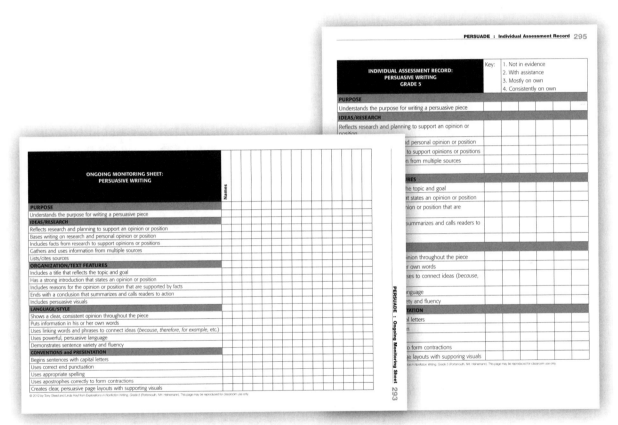

Figure 1.1 Individual Assessment Record and Ongoing Monitoring Sheet

Planning and Facilitating the Unit

Students will need preparation, coaching, prompting, and support as they move through this and other Extended Writing Units. Use the following tips and strategies as needed to ensure each student's success.

Before the Unit:

▸ When planning your teaching, bear in mind that each lesson in the model unit that follows is designed to be completed in one session. However, you will likely find that your students need more time for certain activities. Take the time you need to adequately respond to the unique needs of your students, and remember that they will likely progress through the writing process at their own pace.

▸ Begin building background knowledge about the text type and writing topics in advance. Shared reading, guided reading, and read-aloud experiences as well as group discussions will ensure that students are not dependent exclusively on their own research.

▸ For the research component, you may want to gather suitable books, magazine articles, encyclopedia entries, and websites in your classroom or work with the media center teacher to assemble a collection in advance. Make sure the research materials you gather are at a range of difficulty levels and include plenty of text features such as close-up photographs, captions, bold headings, and diagrams.

During the Unit:

▸ Begin each session with a focused minilesson to demonstrate the traits of writing the particular type of text you're exploring. Tailor the suggested minilesson to suit the needs of your students. The mentor texts on the *Resources* CD-ROM and in the *Book of Mentor Texts* are models you can use to show students the structure and features of each text type. You may want to use other mentor texts to assist you with your demonstrations.

▸ Be sure to model note-taking for students as you think aloud about information in reference materials. Use chart paper and sticky notes to capture your thinking, and display the models prominently as students work on their own research and note-taking.

▸ As students work independently on their writing and publishing, note those who are struggling and bring them together for small-group instruction. Use the Individual Assessment Record and/or the Ongoing Monitoring Sheet to assist in tailoring instruction to the needs of your students.

▸ Students who seem very confident and who have clearly grasped all of the concepts taught so far can be brought together in a small group to extend their understanding to more challenging work.

▸ Provide templates for students who need extra support when writing. You'll find a variety of graphic organizers on the *Resources* CD-ROM from which to choose.

After the Unit:

‣ Be sure to give students opportunities to share and celebrate their individual writing projects.

‣ Distribute copies of the Personal Checklist for Persuasive Writing (on the *Resources* CD-ROM and in the Resources section at the end of this book). Students will benefit greatly from the chance to reflect on their progress during the unit and to hear their classmates' feedback.

‣ Compare students' final writing products with pre-assessments and past work to evaluate their growth as writers of persuasive texts.

‣ Reflect on the strengths and challenges of implementing this series of lessons. How might it be adjusted to maximize student learning?

‣ Look at common needs of the class, and address these when planning future explorations or when using the Power Writes.

Personal Checklist for Persuasive Writing

Process Reflections:

Research:
I used the following resources in gathering facts:_____

Drafting:
I solved the following problems in my writing: _____

Revising:
When revising, I focused on improving my message by: _____

Editing:
To ensure that I edited effectively, I used an editing checklist and concentrated on: _____

Presentation:
I chose the following format to present my writing: _____

I am most proud of: _____

I have checked the following:
☐ My title reflects my topic and my opinion.
☐ I have a strong introduction that clearly states my opinion or position.
☐ I have given reasons and supported them with facts.
☐ I have used linking words and phrases such as *because, therefore,* and *for example* to connect ideas.
☐ I have used powerful, persuasive words.
☐ I have a conclusion that summarizes my position and calls readers to action.
☐ My writing has fluency and I have used a variety of sentence lengths and types.
☐ I have included persuasive visuals.
☐ I have listed my sources.

Figure 1.2 Personal Checklist for Persuasive Writing

SESSION 1

Identifying the Purpose and Features of a Persuasive Text

Students analyze the features of a persuasive text, choose a topic for their persuasive letter, and write an opinion statement.

SESSION SNAPSHOT

Genre Focus: Features of a Persuasive Text

Process Focus: Prewriting

Trait(s): Ideas

Mentor Text: "Martha's Letter"

BEFORE THE LESSON

Download the mentor text, and collect additional samples of persuasive writing for students to review.

> *Our students need more opportunities to be physically active during the school day.*

Modeled Writing

FOCUSED MINILESSON

Summarize the learning goals: *In this unit, we are going to focus on a kind of writing called persuasion. A persuasive text tries to convince readers to think or act in a certain way and can take many forms, such as a poster, letter, blog entry, essay, or PowerPoint presentation.*

Over the next few weeks, we will each write a persuasive letter to our principal or school board, asking for a change in a school program, policy, or activity that affects our learning. To ensure that our letters are as strong and convincing as they can be, we need to determine what features we should include and how our writing should be organized. The mentor text will help us do this.

Using the Mentor Text

- The mentor text for this unit is "Martha's Letter." You will find it on page 38 of the *Book of Mentor Texts* and in the Persuade section of the *Resources* CD-ROM. Make enough copies of the mentor text for each student to have one. You may also want to use an electronic projection device to display it for whole-class viewing.

- Read aloud the greeting and first two paragraphs. *Right away, I see one important feature of a persuasive text. Early in the writing, the writer introduces her topic and clearly states her opinion. In the rest of her letter, she is going to present the reasons why she thinks thirty minutes is the right amount of homework. As you continue to read, be on the lookout for more features of a persuasive text.*

- Guide students in examining the mentor text, perhaps by having them work in small groups to discover the features, including reasons, facts, and details that support the writer's opinion; words and phrases that connect reasons and details; sentence variety; persuasive language; and a convincing conclusion that sums up and restates the writer's opinion.

TURN &TALK *Writers, think together. What are the features of a great persuasive text?*

- Guide students as they share their observations, and record their thinking on a chart labeled "Features of a Great Persuasive Text."

Modeling

- *Writers, I am going to write a persuasive letter along with you. My goal will be to convince members of our school community that we need more physical activity in our school day. I'll have to do some research on my topic, but I need to first write my opinion statement. As we saw in the mentor text, each great persuasive piece has an introductory sentence or section that states the author's opinion about his or her topic. Watch as I write:* "Our students need more opportunities to be physically active during the school day."

- *Notice that my opinion statement is brief and tightly focused. Also, notice that an opinion statement doesn't have to include the reasons that support the opinion. Those can come later.*

- *Now it's your turn to choose a topic and write a strong opinion statement that will focus your research and writing.* You may want to provide students with a list of topics to choose from, such as more arts opportunities, an afterschool program, or healthier lunch choices. Make sure that students don't choose the same topic as the mentor text or the one you are modeling.

- Pair students who have selected the same topic so they can research together.

    TURN &TALK *Writers, when you write your persuasive letter, what features will you include?*

Features of a Great Persuasive Text

- Clear introduction that states an opinion or position
- Reasons logically ordered to support the opinion
- Facts and details that support reasons
- Linking words, phrases, and clauses that connect reasons and facts
- Persuasive language
- Strong conclusion that summarizes the opinion or position

WRITING and COACHING

- Coach students in drafting strong, clear opinion statements. Help students who struggle by asking leading questions: *Alex, you've told me before that you wish there were healthier snack choices in our vending machines. How can we write that as an opinion statement?*

- If it is hard to spot an opinion in your students' opening statements, it may be that they are unsure of the difference between a fact and an opinion. Remind them of this simple test: *Can it be checked and proven? Then, it's a fact. Does it tell what a person thinks or feels? Then, it's an opinion.*

- Other students may struggle because they don't know enough about their chosen topic. Steer these students to topics about which they already have sufficient background knowledge to get started. Inform students that they will have time after they research to go back and revise their opening statements if needed.

SHARING and REFLECTING

TURN &TALK *Writers, what do you like best about your partner's opinion statement? Is it easy to know how he or she feels about the topic?*

- Give students a chance to share their observations about their partners' work. Review the other features of a great persuasive text in preparation for subsequent sessions. Explain that during the next session, students will conduct research to back up their opinion statements with facts.

- Gather the drafts and analyze students' attempts to write clear opinion statements. Identify writers whose statements are unfocused. They may need additional coaching before moving on to research.

SESSION 2
Asking and Answering Questions

Students learn to ask open-ended questions that focus their research.

SESSION SNAPSHOT

Research Strategy: Asking and Answering Questions

Process Focus: Prewriting

Trait(s): Ideas

Mentor Text: "Martha's Letter"

BEFORE THE LESSON

Gather resources students can use to research their topics and get up-to-date facts. Resources might include books, articles, short videos, local publications, and reliable Internet websites.

TIP Students may find it difficult to find the facts they need to answer their questions. Showing them how to use Internet search engines effectively will help. Consider bookmarking websites and collecting appropriate print resources in advance to ensure students' success.

FOCUSED MINILESSON

Review the learning goals from the previous session. If time allows, have students turn and talk about what they have learned so far.

Summarize the learning goals for this session: *Today we're going to begin our research to locate facts that will help us make our letters as persuasive as possible. We will learn to use an important research strategy: asking questions about our topic to help us focus our research.*

Using the Mentor Text

■ Display the mentor text, and read the second paragraph aloud. *Writers, have you noticed that this writer doesn't just state her opinion and leave it at that? She provides a solution and reasons to support her opinion. And she supports her reasons with facts and details. Did you notice the question she asks?* "Why only 30 minutes?" *The rest of her letter answers that question. And it answers other questions as well. I think that like all good persuasive writers, this author asked herself what questions or concerns her readers might have. Then, she focused on answering those questions and concerns.*

■ *What other questions do you think this writer answers in her letter?* Guide students to identify unstated questions the author answers in her letter, for example, "What are the problems with working at home?

Modeling

■ *I need to gather details and facts that will help me persuade our school leaders that our students need more physical activity in the school day. I have collected some resources that I think might be helpful. They include a website, a magazine article, and a book about physical activity for children.*

■ *These resources contain more information than I need, so I'm going to think of some questions that will help me focus my research. First, I think my readers will want to know,* "Why do kids need to get more physical activity in school?" *Then, they might ask,* "Why don't we have more PE classes?" *I can ask the PE teacher to help me answer that question. And here is the big question I want to answer in my letter: How can we get more physical activity in the school day? Watch as I write each of these questions at the top of a page in my research notebook. As I research, I'll look for answers to these questions. If I think of new questions, I will write those in my notebook, too.*

■ *Watch as I use a website to gather facts to answer my research question about why kids need more physical activity in school. Here's an interesting fact: The U.S. Department of Health and Human Services recommends that young people age six to seventeen years participate in at least sixty minutes of physical activity daily. Now there's a fact that helps answer my question about why kids need more physical activity in school! Most kids I know don't get that much physical activity. Watch as I make a bullet and note this fact: "Kids need at least 1 hour every day." I'll note my observation, too: "Most kids don't get that much."*

TURN &TALK *Partners, think together. What other facts on this page would help me answer my question about why kids need more physical activity in school?*

■ Gather students' suggestions and model how you note the facts in your research notebook.

> Why do kids need to get more physical activity in school?
>
> • Kids need at least 1 hour every day
> • Most kids don't get that much.
> • P.E. in school helps

Modeled Writing

WRITING and COACHING

■ Coach research partners as they work together to develop open-ended questions that will focus their research. If they generate a lot of questions, encourage them to select a few to focus their research.

■ Support students who struggle by helping them use the questioning strategy. *Kate, you think that we should have a drama club at school. What information would make your opinion persuasive? Would it be helpful to know how kids benefit from drama education?*

■ Guide partners as they select facts that answer their questions and devise new questions that arise from their research. Keep students focused on their writing purpose—persuasion—by asking them questions such as *How will this fact help you explain your position?*

■ As you circulate, encourage students to jot down only the words and phrases that will best help them remember the most important information. Point out that this will make the research process move more quickly and also make it easier for them to write in their own words when it's time to begin drafting.

TIP If students find direct quotes that support their positions, this would be a good time to talk about avoiding plagiarism and quoting sources. Explain that direct quotations need to be recorded exactly and enclosed in quotation marks with the source cited. If time permits, show students how you record a quote for your topic.

SHARING and REFLECTING

TURN &TALK *Partners, meet with another partner pair or group. Share the questions you've asked and the facts you've gathered. What facts do you think will be most persuasive?*

■ Bring writers back together to review the day's session and the research strategy of asking and answering questions. Encourage students to identify questions or sources they might use to focus their next research session.

■ Gather the students' research notebooks, and analyze their questions and notes from research. Identify writers who seem to have copied full sentences from their sources, and plan to provide additional modeling if necessary.

SESSION 3
Using a Graphic Organizer

Students plan their letters and organize the reasons and facts they'll use to support their opinions.

SESSION SNAPSHOT

Research Strategy: Using a Graphic Organizer

Process Focus: Prewriting, Planning

Trait(s): Ideas, Organization

Mentor Text: "Martha's Letter"

FOCUSED MINILESSON

Review the learning goals from the previous session. If time allows, have students turn and talk about what they have learned so far.

Summarize the learning goals for today's session: *We need to get organized and plan our letters. Today we'll be using a graphic organizer that will help us organize our ideas and information logically and prepare to write.*

Using the Mentor Text

■ Return to the mentor text, and have students take turns reading it aloud for the class. As they read, underline or highlight the author's opinion statement, reasons, and conclusion. Point out and number the details and/or facts that support each reason. When you have finished, explain that the marked portions of the mentor text show the organizational structure, or "bones," of this persuasive text. Pass out copies of the Persuasive Text Graphic Organizer from the *Resources* CD-ROM.

TURN &TALK *Writers, how do you think this graphic organizer will help you prepare to write? Talk it over with your partner.*

Modeling

■ Use an electronic projection device to display the Persuasive Text Graphic Organizer from the *Resources* CD-ROM.

■ *Writers, I am going to use this graphic organizer to lay out the structure of my persuasive letter. I've already written my opinion statement, so I will copy it onto my organizer.*

Persuasive Text Graphic Organizer

Introductory Statement:
Our students need more opportunities to be physically active during the school day.

Reason: Physical activity is necessary for health.
Supporting Facts
• Helps reduce development of diabetes and heart disease.
•

Reason: We only have one PE class per week.
Supporting Facts
•

Reason:
Supporting Facts
•
•

Reason:
Supporting Facts
•
•

Conclusion/Call to Action:
Everyone needs to get their heart rate up for at least 20 minutes every day. Either extend recess or have a school-wide "get up and move" break for 20 minutes—or both!

Modeled Writing

■ *We've already discussed how the opinion or position expressed in a persuasive text needs to be supported by strong reasons and facts. I found some great facts while researching, and today I want to organize them to support the reasons for my opinion. Watch as I write one reason on my organizer:* "Physical activity is necessary for health." *Then, I'll note supporting facts from my research after the bullets. Watch as I write one fact:* "Helps reduce development of diabetes and heart disease."

■ *Another reason we need more physical activity is that we only have one PE class per week. I learned that children should have an hour of exercise every day, and most kids don't get enough. I also learned that our PE teacher has a full schedule, so we can't have more PE classes.* Continue listing reasons and supporting facts, adapting the organizer as needed. Include supporting details from your experience as well as facts from research. Then, move on to the conclusion box. *Writers, my conclusion is very important, and I will want to spend time on it when I draft and revise. For now, though, I'll just sketch out some ideas for what I might say, like this:* "Everyone needs to get their heart rate up for at least 20 minutes every day. Either extend recess or have a school-wide 'get up and move' break for 20 minutes—or both!"

TURN &TALK *Partners, how will you use the graphic organizer to plan your writing? What reasons and facts will you include?*

WRITING and COACHING

■ Guide partners as they formulate reasons for their opinions and gather supporting facts from their notes. Remind them that the goal of this session is to learn how an organizer can be a helpful tool, not necessarily to finish filling it in.

■ As you circulate, remind students that they do not need to write in complete sentences on the graphic organizer and will have plenty of time in subsequent sessions to turn their notes into running text.

■ Encourage students who have completed their research and filled in the organizer to begin drafting.

SHARING and REFLECTING

TURN &TALK *Partners, share your graphic organizers with another partner pair and evaluate each other's work. Are the reasons persuasive? Do the facts support them?*

■ Bring students back together to review the idea of using a graphic organizer to plan out their writing. Remind them that the overall goal of persuasion is to convince readers to think, feel, or act a certain way.

■ Gather the graphic organizers, and analyze your students' attempts to plan their persuasive writing. Identify writers who have included reasons or facts that don't clearly support their introductory statements. Provide additional modeling in small-group or one-on-one coaching for these students. Use the class writing development rubric or the individual student rubric on the *Resources* CD-ROM to track writing proficiencies.

TIP If students are ready for more sophistication, encourage them to think about organizing their reasons in an order that will draw in their readers and make the most sense. Do they want to start with their most powerful information first, or do they want to save their best information for last, so readers go away with that information fresh in their minds? Do some of their ideas lead up to or support other ideas in a logical way?

TIP If students have located lots of facts, help them highlight the strongest ones to use in their writing. Point out that writers of persuasive texts choose only the strongest reasons and most powerful facts to support their opinions.

SESSION 4
Drafting the Introduction

Students begin to draft their persuasive letters, focusing on a strong introductory paragraph.

SESSION SNAPSHOT

Process Focus: Drafting

Trait(s): Ideas, Organization, Voice

Mentor Text: "Martha's Letter"

FOCUSED MINILESSON

Review the learning goals from the previous session. If time allows, have students turn and talk about what they have learned so far.

Summarize the learning goals for this session: *Writers, today you'll begin to turn your notes into a persuasive letter by writing complete sentences in paragraph form. As you write, you'll focus on an important part of any persuasive text: the introduction.*

Using the Mentor Text

■ Display the mentor text, and read it aloud again. Draw students' attention to the introduction.

> **TURN &TALK** *Writers, evaluate the author's introductory paragraph. Does her writing grab your attention and make you want to read more? Why or why not? Does she state the topic of her letter and offer a clear opinion?*

Modeling

■ Use a document camera to project your graphic organizer from the last session. *I am going to use my graphic organizer to begin drafting my letter. Here is the introductory statement I wrote on the organizer:* "Our students need to get more physical activity in the school day."

> **TURN &TALK** *What do you think of my introductory statement? How could I make it stronger in my draft? Talk it over with your partner.*

■ *I agree that my introductory statement is a bit abrupt. It does a good job of stating my opinion, so it belongs in my introduction, but maybe it should be the last sentence instead of the first. I'll try giving my readers some background information about why I am writing to them:* "Dear Principal _____ and Vice Principal _____: In health class, my students have been learning about the importance of physical activity. They have discovered that many children don't get enough exercise, and they have come up with some excellent practical ideas for getting more physical activity into our school day. I am writing to share their research findings and suggestions with you."

■ *By providing background information that my readers can connect to, I improve the chances that they will want to read on. This is one way to craft a compelling beginning. Another way is to pose a question that will hook my readers. I'll try that technique next:* "What is one of the best things anyone can do for lifelong health? Get at least 20 minutes of heart rate raising exercise every day! We teach students about the importance of physical activity, but they don't get enough of it in school. My class has some suggestions for fixing this problem." *That would grab the attention of our school leaders. It could be a powerful lead for my letter. But I think my first introduction has a more appropriate tone for my audience.*

■ *The opinion statement from my graphic organizer got me started, but it took additional time and thought to craft a compelling introductory paragraph. Now you'll have the chance to experiment with techniques for writing your introductory paragraphs.*

> **TURN &TALK** *Think about your opening statement. Tell a partner how you might make it stronger. Offer suggestions to your partner on how to make his or her beginning more compelling.*

WRITING and COACHING

■ Support writers as they experiment with different ways to turn the opinion statements from their organizers into compelling introductory paragraphs. Make sure partners are aware that although they may have researched together, they will each be creating their own drafts.

■ As you circulate, ask questions to get students thinking: *Did you uncover an amazing fact from your research that might surprise your readers and entice them to read on? Is your opinion unexpected or outrageous? If so, you might want to lead with that. Can you think of a question that will get your readers wondering about your topic right from the start? Is there a situation your readers might experience that will get them thinking about your topic?*

■ Students who struggle to write compelling leads will benefit from examples. Be sure to have the mentor text available at all times as well as additional examples from local or national newspapers. Make sure the exemplars are brief and clearly written, with obvious opinion statements. It may be necessary to bring these students together for small-group instruction.

■ Extend more able students by getting them to raise questions they might use to begin their pieces. Begin a list of enticing questions that could be used to hook the reader, such as *Have you ever wondered what it would be like if. . . . Imagine our school if. . . .*

SHARING and REFLECTING

> **TURN &TALK** *Writers, find a partner and share your introductory paragraphs. What do you like best about your partner's work? What might make his or her lead more compelling?*

■ Give students time to share their reflections and talk about what they might do in the next session to improve their writing. Have one or two students share their introductory paragraphs with the class.

■ Gather the drafts and analyze your students' attempts to write compelling introductions that clearly state their opinions. Identify students who would benefit from additional modeling or a guided-writing session.

Draft 1

In health class, my students have been learning about the importance of physical activity. They have discovered that many children don't get enough exercise, and they have come up with some excellent, practical ideas for getting more physical activity into our school day. I am writing to share their research findings and suggestions with you.

Draft 2

What is one of the best things anyone can do for lifelong health? Get at least 20 minutes of heart rate raising exercise every day! We teach students about the importance of physical activity, but they don't get enough of it in school. My class has some suggestions for fixing this problem.

Modeled Writing

TIP Remind students that in a persuasive letter or other types of persuasive texts, the introductory paragraph must convey the author's opinion but does not have to include reasons for it. The reasons can come later in the body of the text.

SESSION 5
Drafting the Body of the Letter

Students continue to draft their persuasive letters, using linking words to connect their reasons and facts.

SESSION SNAPSHOT

Process Focus: Drafting

Trait(s): Organization, Word Choice

Mentor Text: "Martha's Letter"

TIP See the *Resources* CD-ROM for a list of linking words to display in the classroom. Encourage students to experiment with a variety of linking words to enhance the organization and impact of their writing.

FOCUSED MINILESSON

Review the learning goals from the previous session. If time allows, have students turn and talk about what they have learned so far.

Summarize the learning goals for this session: *Writers, today you'll begin to draft the body of your persuasive letters. You'll focus on providing reasons and facts that support your opinions, and you'll use linking words and phrases to connect the ideas.*

Using the Mentor Text

■ Show students the mentor text, and draw their attention to the body of the letter. *Writers, do you notice that in each paragraph in the body of this letter, the writer focuses on one reason why thirty minutes is the right amount of homework? First, she points out that many students have activities after school. In the next paragraph, she explains why it is hard to get help with homework. And in this paragraph, she tells us why kids need time to relax. The author has organized her arguments logically to support her position. She supports her reasons with helpful information, and she uses linking words and phrases to connect the ideas in her writing.*

TURN &TALK *Writing partners, look closely at this letter, and identify where the author has used linking words or phrases to connect information or ideas.*

Modeling

■ *I'm ready to write the body of my letter and to support my introductory paragraph with reasons and details that I hope will convince people to give us more opportunities for physical activity in our school day. Watch as I write:* "PE doesn't give students all the exercise they need. They only have one gym class a week. One day a week helps. It is not enough to promote a healthy lifestyle." *These facts support my point that students don't get enough exercise from PE, but I think I can make the connection between the ideas stronger by using linking words. I'll insert a caret mark between my first and second sentences and add the word* because. *Now my first sentence reads,* "PE doesn't give students all the exercise they need because they only have one gym class a week." *Do you see how the linking word connects my ideas and makes my writing smoother? I can use a comma and a linking word to connect the next two sentences and make them sound less choppy:* "One day a week helps, but it's not enough to promote a healthy lifestyle."

- Continue modeling how to turn the notes from your organizer into complete sentences and paragraphs that give your reasons for wanting to add physical activity to the school day. Emphasize that each reason is backed up with facts and that you use linking words or phrases to connect ideas.

- As you draft, ask students to identify the linking words or phrases you use. Some possibilities for this grade level include *because, therefore, since,* and *for instance.*

> **TURN &TALK** *Analyze my letter so far. Is my opinion clear? Have I drafted complete sentences that explain the reasons for my opinion and incorporate the facts from my graphic organizer? Have I used linking words to connect important ideas?*

> **Draft 1**
>
> PE doesn't give students all the exercise they need. They only have one gym class a week. One day a week helps. It is not enough to promote a healthy lifestyle.
>
> **Draft 2**
>
> PE doesn't give students all the exercise they need because they only have one gym class a week. One day a week helps, but it's not enough to promote a healthy lifestyle.

Modeled Writing

WRITING and COACHING

- Support writers as they begin to draft, turning their brief research notes into running text that supports their opinions. Encourage them to experiment with language as they write in complete sentences. Make sure partners are aware that although they have researched together, they will each be creating their own drafts.

- As you circulate, remind students to start a new paragraph for each new reason they give to support their opinion. Unlike other types of persuasive text, such as posters or slide presentations, a letter needs to be written in complete sentences and paragraph form.

- Some students may need additional coaching as they convert phrases to sentences and experiment with wording, linking words, and so on. These students would probably benefit from a small-group guided-writing experience.

TIP While drafting, it's important to consider which facts best support each of the reasons you provide for your main opinion. Show students how you start over, jot down ideas, cross things out and reconsider them, and so on.

SHARING and REFLECTING

> **TURN &TALK** *Find a partner and share what you wrote today. Can your partner identify the reason and supporting facts in each paragraph? Where were you able to connect your ideas with linking words? What could you do to improve your letter in our next session?*

- Give students time to share their thoughts and talk about what they might do in the next session to improve their writing.

- When the session is over, gather the drafts and analyze your students' attempts to write reasons that support their opinions and to connect ideas with linking words. Identify students who would benefit from additional modeling or a guided-writing session.

TIP If students lose control of the organizational structure for their writing, coach them to return to their organizers to review their introductory statement, supporting reasons and facts, and conclusion. Remind students that the graphic organizer is designed to provide the structure of a persuasive text and to make it easier to stay organized as they draft.

SESSION 6
Drafting a Strong Conclusion

Students draft conclusions that summarize their arguments and include strong persuasive language.

SESSION SNAPSHOT

Process Focus: Drafting

Trait(s): Voice, Word Choice

Mentor Text: "Martha's Letter"

I hope you will consider these suggestions carefully and implement a plan that will allow all of us to exercise more regularly. This will result in healthier students who will be more energized and prepared to focus on learning in the rest of the school day.

Modeled Writing

FOCUSED MINILESSON

Review the learning goals from the previous session. If time allows, have students turn and talk about what they have learned so far.

Summarize the learning goals for this session: *Writers, today you'll focus on another important part of a persuasive text: the conclusion. You're going to write strong conclusions that summarize your opinions and call your readers to action.*

Using the Mentor Text

■ Display the mentor text, and draw students' attention to the concluding paragraph. *This writer ended her letter with a strong conclusion:* "I know that I need to practice sometimes the things I've learned in school, so homework is a good thing. Just not too much!"

■ *In this conclusion, the writer acknowledges something her readers are likely to think: that homework is important. This shows that she understands their perspective. Then, she ends with a powerful phrase that summarizes her opinion:* "Just not too much!" *That phrase reminds her readers not to require too many minutes when they set the new homework policy. This is an effective conclusion for a persuasive letter.*

TURN &TALK *Tell your partner what idea you most want to communicate in your conclusion. What action do you want your readers to take?*

Modeling

■ *Watch as I draft a conclusion for my letter:* "So, in conclusion, please give us more opportunities for physical activity in our school day."

TURN &TALK *Writers, evaluate this ending. Is it strong enough? Does it summarize my opinion and reasons, use powerful persuasive words, and tell my readers what I want them to do? What advice would you give me for improving it?*

■ *My ending is polite, and it sounds appropriate for a letter to our school leaders, but I agree that it's not as strong as it could be. I haven't used persuasive language, and although I do include a call to action, I haven't included any specific requests.*

- *I can do better:* "I hope you will consider these suggestions carefully and implement a plan that will allow all of us to exercise more regularly. This will result in healthier students who will be more energized and prepared to focus on learning in the rest of the school day."

- *Now that's a great conclusion! I've summarized my opinion, and I've used powerful emotional words. I know our school leaders want students to be "healthier," "energized," and "prepared to focus on learning." That language will definitely encourage them to implement our suggestions.*

WRITING and COACHING

- Have writers draft their conclusions, making sure to include powerful, emotional words and phrases and a call to action that speaks directly to readers.

- Print out copies of the Powerful Persuasive Words List from the *Resources* CD-ROM, and encourage students to substitute some of these words for flat or dull words in their drafts. Encourage them to add to the list as well.

- If students struggle, consider providing additional mentor texts, such as editorials, advertisements, or other persuasive pieces. These mentor texts should include strong endings to which your writers can aspire.

- Coach writers as necessary with questions such as *If you read this ending, what would you feel compelled to do? What word could you add to tug at your readers' emotions and make them feel as strongly as you do about the topic?*

- Some writers may still be drafting, while others may have finished their writing and will be returning to their drafts to revise. Point out that writing is an ongoing process. Writers return to their drafts again and again to strengthen their messages and forge stronger connections with their readers.

SHARING and REFLECTING

TURN &TALK *Writing partners, share your endings with each other. What powerful persuasive words do you see in your partner's writing? Is the call to action clear? What do you like best about the conclusion?*

- Give students a chance to share their reflections, and then collect the drafts and analyze your students' attempts to summarize their positions, use persuasive language, and include a call to action. Identify students who might benefit from additional practice, guided-writing sessions, or further modeling.

TIP Remind students that a strong persuasive text relies on facts that support opinions. Caution writers to be careful not to lessen their arguments by letting their persuasive texts "slide" solely into opinions and emotional appeals. They should consistently check for facts that make persuasion strong.

TIP As you identify students who may be ready for greater levels of sophistication, consider introducing them to persuasive techniques such as *bandwagon* (convincing someone to do something because other people are already doing it) and *testimonial* (using real people to explain how a product or action has had a positive impact on them).

SESSION 7
Revising for Sentence Variety

Students revise their letters and add variety by experimenting with sentences of different lengths and types.

SESSION SNAPSHOT

Process Focus: Drafting, Revising

Trait(s): Sentence Fluency

Mentor Text: "Martha's Letter"

FOCUSED MINILESSON

Review the learning goals from the previous session. If time allows, have students turn and talk about what they have learned so far.

Summarize the learning goals for this session: *Writers, today you'll experiment with crafting sentences of different lengths as you start to revise your letters. This will make your writing smoother and more pleasing to the ear.*

Using the Mentor Text

■ Display the mentor text. Focus on the first two paragraphs, and ask students to help you classify each sentence as long, medium, or short. Guide writers to see that the text includes sentences of different lengths.

■ *The author of this letter has done a great job of using punctuation to craft a variety of sentences. In the first paragraph, she uses a comma to join ideas in the first sentence, which is long and conveys the reason why she is writing. She ends that paragraph with a short direct statement of her purpose. Did you notice that she includes a question in the second paragraph—and it is just a phrase? It's okay to use a phrase occasionally for impact. That quick, punchy question really gets the reader's attention.*

TURN &TALK *Writers, why does this author vary the length of her sentences? Why should we vary our sentence lengths when we are writing? Talk it over with your partner.*

Modeling

■ *Writers, I've heard some of you say that how a piece of writing sounds can be as important as what it says and that varying sentence lengths can make our writing sound better. It's also true that long sentences can convey a lot of related information, and short sentences can add impact by focusing on one clear idea. I am going to pay attention to sentence variety as I revise my letter.*

■ *Listen to this paragraph:* "Our students have recess every day. It is not long enough. It comes right after lunch. By the time students finish eating, they may have only 10 minutes left for recess. By the time they get outside, they may have just a few minutes to walk around outside."

Draft 1

Our students have recess every day. It is not long enough. It comes right after lunch. By the time students finish eating, they may have only 10 minutes left for recess. By the time they get outside, they may have just a few minutes to walk around outside.

Draft 2

Our students have recess every day, but it is not long enough, and it comes right after lunch. That gives them just a few minutes to walk around outside.

Modeled Writing

TURN &TALK *Writers, what do you think of my writing? Does it sound pleasing to the ear? Have I included a variety of sentence lengths? What could I do to improve this paragraph?*

- *I heard some of you say that my first three sentences are all short. Sometimes short sentences are punchy, but here they sound flat and repetitive. Watch as I use commas and caret marks to insert linking words and combine these related ideas:* "Our students have recess every day, but it is not long enough, and it comes right after lunch." *My next two sentences start with the same phrase. I'll cross out one and revise the sentence:* "That gives them just a few minutes to walk around outside."

- Read the revised paragraph aloud. *Now this paragraph has a variety of sentence lengths, and it sounds pleasing to the ear.*

- Continue modeling how you create sentences of varying lengths and types to give your writing fluency, clarity, and impact.

WRITING and COACHING

- Support writers as they attempt to revise for varied sentence length. Some will benefit from guided practice in combining related ideas. You might also provide a brief lesson on pronouns and encourage students to use them to identify the subjects of their sentences.

- Encourage students to reread their draft letters for sentence variety and to identify long, short, and medium-length sentences.

- Some students may be ready to look beyond repeated words and phrases to identify repetition in sentence structure. Help these students identify monotonous use of the typical subject-verb-object sentence pattern and begin to experiment with different patterns and sentence lengths.

SHARING and REFLECTING

TURN &TALK *Share your draft with a partner, and talk about places where you revised to vary sentence length. Ask for feedback on places where you might still want to revise.*

- Give students time to share their thoughts and talk about what they might do in the next session to improve their writing.

- Gather the drafts and analyze your students' attempts to use a variety of sentence lengths. Identify writers who would benefit from additional modeling as well as those who are ready for higher levels of sophistication. Use the class writing rubric or the individual student rubric on the *Resources* CD-ROM to track writing proficiencies.

TIP This session may be noisy! Encourage students to read their drafts aloud to writing partners as often as necessary for them to hear how their sentences sound. Emphasize that good writers write with their ears as much as with their minds and pencils.

SESSION 8
Using a Revision Checklist

Students continue to revise their letters, using a checklist that reminds them of what to look for in their draft.

SESSION SNAPSHOT

Process Focus: Revising

Trait(s): Ideas, Organization, Voice

Mentor Text: "Martha's Letter"

BEFORE THE LESSON

Print out copies of the Revision Checklist for Persuasive Text from the *Resources* CD-ROM, and ensure that each student has a copy before beginning to revise.

TIP Be sure your revision checklist includes only those features, traits, and craft elements that you have modeled through explicit instruction. The revision checklist on the *Resources* CD-ROM was developed specifically for use with this model unit, and you will want to adapt it to your own instruction.

FOCUSED MINILESSON

Review the learning goals from the last session. If time allows, have students turn and talk about what they have learned so far.

Summarize the learning goals for this session: *In our last session, you improved your letters by varying your sentences to make your writing flow smoothly. There are other things you'll want to pay attention to as you revise your letters, and a checklist will help you remember to check them all.*

Modeling

■ Explain how revision differs from editing: *When we edit, we are mostly concerned with making our writing correct. We look at grammar, punctuation, capitalization, spelling, and so on to ensure that our work does not contain errors. But when we revise, we are mostly concerned with the quality of our message and whether it is as strong and effective as it can possibly be. During revision, we look at how well we have incorporated the features of nonfiction writing, included facts and details, chosen our words, and crafted our sentences. Sometimes it's hard to keep all of these points in our heads, so a checklist can help us remember what to look for when we revise.*

■ *Watch as I use a revision checklist to remember what I need to look for as I revise my persuasive letter. The first point on my checklist says, "My introduction states my opinion." Listen as I read my introduction aloud:* "In health class, my students have been learning about the importance of physical activity. They have discovered that many children don't get enough exercise, and they have come up with some excellent practical ideas for getting more physical activity into our school day. I am writing to share their research findings and suggestions with you."

TURN &TALK *Writers, evaluate my introduction. Can I check off the first point on my revision checklist?*

■ Continue to work through the revision checklist, demonstrating how you check your work for each point and revise as needed. *The second point on my checklist is making sure my ideas are logically organized. Reading through my letter, I see that I have two paragraphs about the importance of physical activity, and they are separated by my paragraph about gym class. I will use an arrow to show that I want to put these paragraphs together in my final draft.*

WRITING and COACHING

- Coach students as they use the revision checklist to reread and revise their letters. Point out that although it is possible to read for more than one revision point at a time, the more times we reread our work, the more likely we will be to spot areas where our writing can be improved. Rereading for each revision point is a bit labor-intensive, but the payoff is usually worth the time.

- Writers who are still drafting will also benefit from examining the revision checklist. Show these students how to revise *as* they draft, pausing to reread what they have written so far.

SHARING and REFLECTING

TURN &TALK *Writers, you have read and reread your drafts several times today. When we do this, our writing becomes stronger and stronger. Take a moment to share your revisions with your partner. How did it help you to use a revision checklist?*

- Encourage your community of writers to come together and share their thinking about revising using a checklist. Gather the drafts and analyze your students' use of the revision checklist. Identify writers who may need additional modeling and practice in reading for one revision point at a time, as well as those who might be ready to add items to the checklist. Use the rubrics on the *Resources* CD-ROM to track writing proficiencies.

Revision Checklist
Persuasive Text

☐ My introduction states my opinion.

☐ My ideas are organized logically.

☐ I have included clear reasons for my opinion and supported them with facts.

☐ I have used linking words and phrases to connect ideas.

☐ I have used varied sentence lengths that make my writing flow smoothly.

☐ I have used powerful, persuasive language to convince my readers.

☐ My conclusion restates my position and includes a call to action.

Modeled Writing

TIP Less experienced writers may benefit from a shorter revision. Choose the revision points that will most benefit each student, customizing the checklist to meet individual needs.

SESSION 9
Editing the Letter

Writers reread for specific editing points, focusing especially on using apostrophes to form contractions.

SESSION SNAPSHOT

Process Focus: Editing

Trait(s): Conventions

Mentor Text: "Martha's Letter"

FOCUSED MINILESSON

Review the learning goals from the last session. If time allows, have students turn and talk about what they have learned so far.

Summarize the learning goals for this session: *Now that you've revised our letters to make them as persuasive as possible, it's time to shift our attention to editing. Because others will be reading our letters, we want to make sure we catch and fix any errors in spelling, grammar, and punctuation.*

Using the Mentor Text

■ Display the mentor text using an overhead projection device or electronic whiteboard. *The author of this letter has used many different types of punctuation. Let's focus on apostrophes. Look at this sentence: "Another point to consider is that when students work at home, it's hard to get help with homework." This mark, called an apostrophe, shows that two words—*it *and* is—*were joined to make one word,* it's. *A word formed this way is called a contraction.*

TURN &TALK *What other contractions do you see in this letter? Talk them over with your partner.*

■ Ask for student volunteers to circle the other contractions in the text, and guide students to name them and talk about what words are joined to form each contraction.

Modeling

■ Read a section of your modeled writing that includes contractions. "We've thought about all the classes and activities that already have to fit into a school day—and it's a lot! Wouldnt it be fantastic if kids got enough exercise outside of school? Some kids do, but most dont. Not all kids can be on a sports team. Many cant take classes like karate or ballet. Its hard to get motivated to exercise on your own at home."

■ *I used an apostrophe in* we've, *which is a contraction of* we *and* have. *I used an apostrophe in* it's, *because here it is a contraction of* it *and* is. *But I need to add an apostrophe in* wouldn't *because it is a contraction of* would *and* not. *Watch as I use a caret mark to show where to put the apostrophe in my final draft.*

We've thought about all the classes and activities that already have to fit into a school day—and it's a lot! Wouldn't it be fantastic if kids got enough exercise outside of school? Some kids do, but most don't. Not all kids can be on a sports team. Many can't take classes like karate or ballet. It's hard to get motivated to exercise on your own at home.

Modeled Writing

TURN &TALK *Writers, what other contractions have I used in my letter? Do you see other places where I need to add an apostrophe?*

■ After you have edited the contractions in your letter, move on to other conventions such as capital letters, end punctuation, spelling, and subject-verb agreement. Show students how you read for each editing point.

WRITING and COACHING

■ Have writers edit their letters, focusing on one editing point at a time. Distribute copies of the editing checklist from the *Resources* CD-ROM, or see the teaching tip at right.

■ After students have edited their letters, encourage them to pair up and edit each other's work. Point out that a second set of eyes may find mistakes that have gone unnoticed before.

■ Assure writers who are still revising that they will have a chance to carefully edit their letters as well.

SHARING and REFLECTING

TURN &TALK *Work with a partner, and share the work you have done in editing your letter. What did you change and why?*

■ Guide a discussion of changes students made as they edited their letters. You might want to make a list of contractions students used in their letters to display in the classroom.

■ Gather the drafts and analyze your students' attempts to edit. Identify writers who do not seem to understand how to use contractions, and pull these students aside for reteaching and additional modeling.

■ Consider tailoring editing checklists to specific points of grammar and mechanics instruction that you have already introduced in your class.

■ Use the rubrics on the *Resources* CD-ROM to track writing proficiencies and tailor future instruction.

TIP Make a chart to help students edit for commonly confused words such as *its* and *it's*, *were* and *we're*, *your* and *you're*. Collect example sentences from students' work, or work with students to write example sentences to post in the classroom.

TIP Editing checklists can guide students' thinking as they edit, and the process of creating an individualized checklist helps hone students' thinking about the edits they need to make to their own writing. Be sure to point out the value of editing—to make messages accessible to readers. Don't focus on editing as an extra task but as an integral part of creating writing that readers understand and appreciate.

SESSION 10
Publishing and Sharing

Students type or rewrite their letters and create visuals that enhance the persuasion in their writing.

SESSION SNAPSHOT

Process Focus: Presenting, Publishing

Trait(s): Conventions, Organization, Ideas

Mentor Text: "Martha's Letter"

FOCUSED MINILESSON

Review the learning goals from the last session. If time allows, have students turn and talk about what they have learned so far.

Summarize the learning goals for this session: *Your drafts are polished, edited, and ready to be published. Today you will type or neatly print your letters on publishing paper and create visuals to support your writing.*

Using the Mentor Text

■ Display the mentor text electronically if possible. Ask students to look it over once more, paying special attention to its format and supporting features.

> **TURN &TALK** *Writers, what special features has the author included to make her letter more persuasive?*

■ Give students a chance to share their observations, and then summarize what you heard. *Because this is a letter, the author begins with a friendly greeting, "Dear Mr. Woods," and ends with a polite closing phrase, "Sincerely," and her name. She also provides visuals that support her persuasive message. These visuals support the author's message that kids should have only thirty minutes of homework so they have time for other activities and won't have to stay up too late at night.*

Modeling

■ Display your modeled writing, and point out the features of a letter. *Because I am writing a letter, I am starting with a greeting, "Dear Principal ___ and Superintendent _____," and ending with a closing phrase, "Sincerely." I'll sign my letter when I print it out.*

■ *Now I want to add some persuasive visuals. Help me make a line graph to show how many hours of physical activity kids in our class get in a week. I'll put the number of hours along the x axis and number of students up the y axis. You all get two hours—gym class and recess time. But then the line goes down, depending on how many other activities you participate in. Fifteen of you get three hours, twelve of you get four hours, ten get five hours, nine get six hours, and only eight of you get seven or more hours of exercise in a week. This is a powerful visual image. I am adding this graph to my letter, and I will write a caption to make my point: "According to the U.S. Department of Health and Human Services, fifth graders should get at least 7 hours of physical activity a week. Fewer than half the students in our class get enough exercise."*

TURN &TALK *Partners, analyze what I've done so far. What do you think of the way I've presented my letter? What other features might I add?*

- If possible, display your modeled writing using an electronic projection device, and show students how you add more visuals, such as photographs, drawings, graphs, or bulleted lists of helpful facts. Emphasize that your goal is not to add window dressing. It's to add elements that support your message and persuade your readers.

WRITING and COACHING

- Provide time for students to search for images, visuals, photographs, and so on that would support their letters. Add sessions as needed so students have enough time to locate appropriate visuals and craft captions.
- Remind writers that visuals can be enhanced with captions. Help them create captions that are both descriptive and concise to add to the overall effect of the letter.
- Some students may still be editing their letters. Remind them that they can be thinking about the visuals they may want to include as they continue to edit.

SHARING and REFLECTING

- When all students have finished publishing their letters, bring the class together and review the features of a great persuasive text.

TURN &TALK *Writers, if you were to tell the students in another class how to write a great persuasive text, what would you tell them? What features would they need to include?*

- If possible, provide an authentic audience for your students' published work. Consider sending their letters to the principal, or invite members of the school board to visit your class to listen as students read their letters out loud or present their opinions orally.
- After the unit, gather the students' final pieces, and analyze their attempts at writing persuasive texts. Use the rubrics on the *Resources* CD-ROM to track writing proficiencies and tailor future instruction.

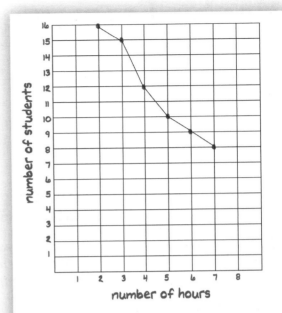

According to the U.S. Department of Health and Human Services, fifth graders should get at least 7 hours of physical activity a week. Fewer than half the students in our class get enough exercise.

Modeled Writing

TIP Persuasive writing is suitable for a wide range of formats, and you may prefer to have students present their arguments as video presentations, posters, flyers, or oral presentations. See the *Book of Mentor Texts* and *Resources* CD-ROM for additional presentation ideas.

TIP Be sure to keep the mentor text on display during this publishing session and to provide additional examples of well-designed persuasive letters that make good use of visuals and captions.

Maybe Framework

Use a framework to compare and contrast arguments to draw a conclusion.

FEATURES

- Controversial statement
- Two perspectives on the same topic
- ▷ Conclusion that includes linking words of summation such as *because, since, in conclusion, based on the evidence*
- ▷ Linking statements that acknowledge an opposing view such as *it could be said that, some people suggest, the opposing view might argue that*

BEFORE THE LESSON

Familiarize students with the Maybe Framework from the *Resources* CD-ROM. Discuss how to draw a conclusion: Use what you know and what you've read to make a new statement.

Maybe

Controversial Statement

Fast food restaurants should eliminate unhealthy choices from their menus.

Agree	Disagree
Many people eat at restaurants and need healthy choices. It is easy to make the choices at a restaurant healthy, such as including more salads or reducing the special sauce on hamburgers.	Restaurants should be free to serve what they want. People should make the choices for themselves, not a corporation

Conclusion

Healthy choices should be provided. People should be able to make their own choices, but they need options.

Modeled Writing

FOCUSED MINILESSON

If someone said, "It's important to get a good night's sleep," would you argue with that statement? Probably not! But some arguments are more difficult to figure out, because they have two sides to them. If we want to explore a question without a clear answer, we can use a Maybe Framework.

Use chart paper or a document camera to display the framework. *I want to explore a controversial statement: "Fast-food restaurants should eliminate unhealthy choices from their menus." Watch as I write the statement in the top box.*

TURN &TALK *We'll use the Maybe Framework to explore both sides of the statement. Think together with your partner, and identify reasons you'd disagree with this statement. Be ready to share!*

Watch as I use the framework to record reasons to disagree with the statement. One reason I disagree is that I think restaurants should be free to serve whatever they want. If people don't want to eat the food there, they could go somewhere else with healthier options! Record the reason in the organizer. *Watch as I record another reason that I disagree with this statement: "People should make. . . ."*

I have listed some strong reasons for disagreeing with the statement, so now I am ready to move to the Agree column on the planner. Think aloud as you model jotting down ideas for the Agree column. Elicit ideas from students, being sure that each idea supports the argument that fast-food restaurants should eliminate unhealthy choices from their menus.

I am taking a look over the planner, and I think our reasons point to a conclusion that makes sense. Restaurants probably don't need to eliminate all the unhealthy choices, because people deserve to have a choice. But restaurants should provide healthy choices to give people more options. A conclusion should sum up your thinking. Watch as I capture these ideas: "Healthy choices should be. . . ."

TURN &TALK *Partners, evaluate the arguments and the conclusion on the planner. Are there reasons that would be more convincing to agree, to disagree, or both? What conclusion would you draw? Be ready to share!*

Summarize the features: Display your modeled writing. Have partners work together to identify the features of the Maybe Framework and consider what they need to remember when they create one of their own. Display the model for students' reference as they write.

WRITING and COACHING

Choose a controversial statement, and work with a partner on completing the framework. Remember to include reasons to both agree and disagree with the statement. Then, use the ideas you gather to draw a conclusion. Use the planner to capture your ideas. Then, write about them!

As partners work together, meet with them as necessary to scaffold understanding. Be sure they classify supporting arguments into categories and use a range of considerations to draw conclusions.

SHARING and REFLECTING

Sum it up! Writers, your controversial statement allowed for deep thinking. You came up with reasons to both agree and disagree, and you drew a conclusion that took those reasons into account. When we engage in persuasive thinking and writing, it is important to consider multiple points of view.

TURN & TALK *We're going to teach another class how to analyze a controversial statement using a Maybe Framework. What features of the framework do you want to be sure to mention? What guidelines about writing arguments and drawing conclusions would be good for the class to know? Think together about what you would tell them.*

ASSESS THE LEARNING

Analyze the arguments to identify writers who need additional support in presenting ideas that support each side of a controversial statement and drawing a conclusion that is supported by the arguments. Note those who are ready to add additional features to their planners and to their conclusions.

SELF-ASSESSMENT

SELF-ASSESSMENT

Maybe Framework

	YES	NO
1. **Controversial statement**	☐	☐
2. **Two perspectives on the same topic**	☐	☐
3. **Conclusion that includes linking words of summation such as:** *because, since, in conclusion, based on the evidence* ○	☐	☐
4. **Linking statements that acknowledge an opposing view such as:** *it could be said that, some people suggest, the opposing view might argue that...* ○	☐	☐

▷TAKE IT FORWARD

▸ Students might want to revise their persuasive writing to include linking words and phrases, such as *because, since, in conclusion,* and *based on the evidence.* Model inserting a linking word into your conclusion, such as *Based on the evidence, fast-food restaurants should provide additional healthy items on their menus.*

▸ Help writers understand that presenting an opposing view lends strength to their own arguments. To assist them in presenting opposing views clearly, help writers identify linking statements such as *it could be said that, some people suggest,* and *the opposing view might argue that.*

▸ Have partners present their arguments and explain how they came to their conclusions. Students may want to present their arguments as debates, with each partner advocating for the agree or the disagree point of view.

▸ When writers transform their planner into a draft, they may want to strengthen their piece with a call to action as part of the opener and a restatement of the call to action at the end.

▸ Help students apply the Maybe Framework to an analysis of a historical event, considering the pros and cons of the actions of people in history.

Public Service Announcement

Use persuasive techniques to focus the public on health, safety, environment, or national spirit.

Public Service Announcement

Animal lovers of the world, it's time to take action against animal abuse.

You see, some animals have loving homes but in the United States last year, 1300 cases of abused animals were reported and probably countless more weren't reported.

Animals are DYING!

It's time to take action and donate to organizations that rescue and care for abused animals.

Go to www.humanesociety.org to find out how to donate today!

If we all work together, we can end animal abuse.

FEATURES

- Call to action (a question, a statement, or emotionally engaging image)
- Directly addresses the reader
- Details support call to action
- Connecting phrases: *it should be noted, in addition, based on the evidence, for example, to illustrate, you see, research has shown, as a result*
- Conclusion restates the call to action

  Opposing view integrated into announcement

FOCUSED MINILESSON

As you saw when we watched public service announcements, these announcements provide the public with important information about health, safety, and even national pride. For my public service announcement, I want to raise awareness that children need to get flu vaccines. Watch as I open with a call to make parents want to take action: "Parents, it is time. . . ." Public service announcements speak directly to a listener or viewer, so my next sentence will begin with "You see. . . ." That should make it clear that I am speaking directly to my reader or listener.

It is important to add details that support your position, so I am going to explain that children are vulnerable to complications from the flu. Look closely as I give credibility to my argument by stating, "Recent research has documented. . . ." This makes it clear that I am not making up these facts.

TURN &TALK *Writers, I need a powerful closing with a restatement of the call to action. I want this public service announcement to make people feel like they need to take action. Think together and share ideas about a powerful closing.*

I want to be sure that the closing shows that all parents need to take action, so I am trying to decide between "Let's all take action and get kids vaccinated" and "Together, we can all fight the flu. It's time for action— Vaccinate your kids today!" Let's vote and select the more powerful conclusion.

TURN &TALK *Writers, analyze my public service announcement. Is my argument convincing? Do you think it would make parents want to get their kids vaccinated? Consider ways I could make this announcement even more powerful.*

Summarize the features: Have partners generate a list of the features of an explanation to place in their writers' notebooks. This will serve as a visual support as they create their own public service announcements.

Parents, it is time to vaccinate your children to protect them against the flu.

You see, children are especially vulnerable to serious complications from the flu, which could lead to hospitalization – and even death.

As a result, I am urging parents everywhere to get their children vaccinated.

Recent research has documented that vaccination is safe and is the most effective way to prevent the flu.

Get the facts at flu.gov.

Together, we can all fight the flu!

Modeled Writing

WRITING and COACHING

It is your turn to create a public service announcement. You will be working with a partner to identify a problem and then create an announcement that has all the features you listed on your list.

As writers research and develop their drafts, meet with individuals to confer or small groups to support and scaffold understanding. Some students may benefit from using the Persuasive Framework from the *Resources* CD-ROM.

SHARING and REFLECTING

Sum it up! *Writers, your public service announcements offer powerful arguments. They engage emotions and direct attention to important issues related to health, safety, and the environment. Best of all, they present a clear call to action that is supported by details, connecting phrases, and strong conclusions.*

TURN &TALK *You will be sharing your public service announcements with partners from the classroom next door and then coaching them on how to construct a public service announcement. Work together to identify the points you want to be sure to teach about public service announcements and their features.*

Analyze the public service announcements to identify writers who need additional support in creating a call to action, infusing supportive details, adding connecting phrases, and creating powerful conclusions. Identify writers who may be ready for additional levels of sophistication in their writing.

ASSESS THE LEARNING

Analyze the public service announcements to identify writers who need additional support in creating a call to action, infusing supportive details, adding connecting phrases, and creating powerful conclusions. Identify writers who may be ready for additional levels of sophistication in their writing.

SELF-ASSESSMENT

SELF-ASSESSMENT

Public Service Announcement

	YES	NO
1. Call to action (a question, a statement, or emotionally engaging image)	☐	☐
2. Directly address the reader	☐	☐
3. Details support call to action	☐	☐
4. Connecting phrases: *It should be noted, in addition, based on the evidence, for example, to illustrate, you see, research has shown, as a result*	☐	☐
5. Conclusion restates the call to action	☐	☐
6. Integrate the opposing view	☐	☐

▷ TAKE IT FORWARD

- Integrate the opposing view with linking statements such as *it could be said that, some people suggest, the opposing view might argue that.*

- Videotape the public service announcements, and present them to parents, other classrooms, or the local newspaper.

- Create videotaped public service announcements for school-based issues. Possible examples: washing hands before lunch, safely exiting the school bus when being dropped off at the bus stop, wearing weather-appropriate clothing, taking care to clean up food spills in the cafeteria to prevent slip and fall injuries.

- Introduce additional features for students who are ready, such as using repetition to solidify the message, varying the lead (with a question, statement, slogan, or powerful picture), and focusing on strong word choice. Add these elements to your own modeled writing to lead students in focusing on their own work.

Electronic Slide Show

Create a slide show to show support for an argument.

FEATURES

- Statement of opinion
- Build supporting evidence with visuals and text
- Bullet points
- Anticipate and respond to the opposing view
- ▷ Conclusion

FOCUSED MINILESSON

Today I want to make a case for an idea that I think is important. I believe that students should wear uniforms in school. An electronic slide show is a great way to deliver a message to many people at once.

I am going to start by stating my opinion as the title of a slide: "Uniforms Build a Strong School!" Notice that this statement is concise and powerful. Of course, others might disagree with this statement, so I want to offer proof for the statement. I think that uniforms build a sense of community and belonging because all students are wearing the same thing to school. Watch as I state that idea concisely on the slide: "Uniforms create. . . ." Did you notice that I started the statement with a bullet point? Bullet points keep statements organized and help viewers focus on the statements on the slides.

TURN &TALK *What are some other reasons that uniforms might build a stronger school? Remember, I want to build a strong case and justify my opinion. Think together about what I might add to this slide.*

Finish the slide, adding concise bullet-pointed statements that support the opinion. *Slides are very visual, so I want to add a strong image to support my opinion. I found this photograph of a student in a uniform. The uniform looks comfortable, and the student looks happy. Watch as I copy and then paste it onto the slide.*

Now I am ready to start another slide. I think uniforms are great for students because as adults, many will have to wear uniforms or nice clothes for their jobs. I know, however, that some people believe workplaces are much more casual now. I want to argue against that idea in my slide. Watch as I write: "It could be said that. . . ." I anticipated an argument against my position, and that makes my argument even stronger! I found a great photograph for this slide, showing a man in a suit at his job. It supports the idea that wearing a uniform prepares students for jobs later in life.

TURN &TALK *Take a close look at my slides. Evaluate them together. How do they support my argument about school uniforms? Are there arguments that might be even more powerful?*

Uniforms Build a Strong School!

- Uniforms create a sense of community.
- Discipline is stronger.
- Academics are driven up.

Uniforms Prepare Students for Jobs

It could be said that many businesses allow workers to dress more casually for work than they used to, but uniforms in school prepare students to wear uniforms or suits when they go to work as adults.

Modeled Writing

Summarize the features: Ask students to mention features of a persuasive slide show as you capture ideas in a list. Students can create memo checklists for their desks based on the class checklist.

WRITING and COACHING

Work with a partner to make a few slides either in favor of or against school uniforms. You can also pick another topic such as year-round schooling and develop slides that either support or contest the value of year-round schools. Remember that visuals and text work together in a slide show. Think, too, about how you might anticipate and respond to the opposing point of view.

As writers develop their drafts, confer with individuals or small groups as needed. You might show students professionally done slide shows and ask them what features they include. They can be inspiration for students' work. Help students keep text on their slides brief. Remind them that slide shows need to be easily viewed from across a room.

SHARING and REFLECTING

Sum it up! *Writers, your slide shows are engaging and informative! You crafted concise statements that support your opinions and fused visuals and text together for powerful presentations. You also thought about the arguments against your point of view and masterfully responded to those arguments.*

TURN &TALK *We're going to share our slide shows at our parents' night. We need to share how we created them. What features should we highlight for parents? Think with your partner as you list them.*

ASSESS THE LEARNING

Analyze the slide shows to identify writers who need additional support in supporting opinions and using visuals and text together. Note those who are ready to add more features to their slide shows.

SELF-ASSESSMENT

SELF-ASSESSMENT
Electronic Slide Show

	YES	NO
1. Statement of opinion	☐	☐
2. Build supporting evidence with visuals and text	☐	☐
3. Anticipate and respond to the opposing view	☐	☐
4. Conclusion	☐	☐

▶ TAKE IT FORWARD

▸ Discuss how to create a slide to conclude the show. The concluding slide might be a powerful statement, a call to action, a riveting statistic, a quotation from an expert—anything that leaves viewers with a last impression that will prompt them to agree with the point of view in the slide show.

▸ Have students return to previous persuasive pieces they have crafted and focus on anticipating and responding to the opposing point of view. Point out how this technique strengthens arguments by softening opposition to them.

▸ Students may want to incorporate what they have learned about visuals and concise text to create posters. Posters have the same features as slides. Students will enjoy creating persuasive texts in this format.

Video Commercial

Create a plan for an engaging video commercial.

Sonnys

Question: Are you tired of eating at fast food places?
Visual: a family eating at McDonalds looking bored.
Question: Would you rather eat at a healthier place for once?
Visual: A whole family coming out of their seats nodding their heads.
Voice Over: Well don't just sit there, come to Sonny's! Have some real food for once.
Visual: A family riding in a car
Voice Over: They have the best barecue ribs in the world!
Visual: People licking their lips
Conclusion: Make healthier choices and come to sonny's with friends and family members.

FEATURES

- Enticing title
- Convincing argument
- Exaggeration
- Speak directly to the viewer
- Action and visuals
- Conclusion with linking words of summation such as *because, as you can see, since, based on the evidence, in conclusion*
- Comparisons: metaphor, simile, analogy

BEFORE THE LESSON

Present the Commercial Planning Tool from the *Resources* CD-ROM and explain how to use it. Discuss the features of commercials, and identify students who know how to operate video equipment for filming the team presentations.

FOCUSED MINILESSON

Today teams are going to write a plan for a video commercial for our spring play, Alice in Wonderland. *Watch as I begin by writing the title for the commercial on its own line at the top of the planning page. Remember that one important element to any kind of commercial is an intriguing title that convinces viewers to keep watching!*

After the title, the planner provides space to consider questions or premises that I can include to convince my viewers to come to the play. Watch as I write, "Are you going to spend. . . ?" *Did you notice that this was a question that was also designed to add a bit of humor? There's some humor in there and a bit of exaggeration. The popcorn that people eat on movie night is probably not stale. But this exaggeration serves to show that the choice of sitting on your couch will not be as exciting as going to a play.*

TURN & TALK *Analyze my opening question. Would this make you want to know more? Does it make you smile? Share your ideas for other questions that might add humor and interest—or exaggeration.*

Now I want to add a convincing argument to my commercial. Many times, we are swayed by critics' opinions about shows and books. I am going to add information about critics—100% of those who saw the play

---

Title: Join Us—in an Amazing Wonderland!

Question: Are you going to spend another Saturday evening alone with nothing exciting to do except watching reruns and eating stale popcorn?

Visual: Person on couch spilling popcorn.

Question: Would you like to do something exciting for a change?

Visual: Person looking up and nodding.

Voice-over: Not only do people wait in long lines to see this play, but also 100% of critics have something to say about it. Based on the evidence, this is truly the play to see!

Visual: people waiting in line at a box office

Voice-over: Take my word for it! This was the best Saturday night! I was on the edge of my seat. I didn't know whether to laugh uproariously or cry great tears of sadness. I couldn't recommend this play more. It's the best play I've ever seen at this school!

Visual: 10-year-old boy with a microphone.

Conclusion: You've heard it here! Be the first on your block, grab your friends, ask your mom... But whatever you do, don't miss this year's spring play!

Modeled Writing

recommended it. Now that's convincing! I am indicating that this is a voice-over. Viewers will hear this part: "Not only do people . . . this is truly the play to see!" Did you notice the phrase "based on the evidence?" I chose a linking phrase to make my argument even more powerful.

TURN &TALK *This is going to be a video, so I need to include action. What action do you recommend that would have viewers wanting to leap off the couch and come to the play?*

Finish the model by adding a visual and then a powerful conclusion that will convince others to see the play.

Summarize the features: Have writers work with a partner to list features of a great commercial, and then create a class chart of features that incorporates their shared thinking.

WRITING and COACHING

Gather into teams and get ready. It's your turn! Choose a real restaurant, business, or event that you want people to experience for themselves. Use the planning tool to plan your commercial before you begin writing, and rehearse thoroughly before you begin filming.

As writers develop their drafts, confer with individuals or small groups to support and scaffold understanding. You might pull together a small group for direct instruction on using persuasive techniques, such as exaggeration.

SHARING and REFLECTING

Sum it up! Writers, you thought carefully about how to use persuasive techniques to present a commercial for a real business, restaurant, or event. You did a great job using the framework to make a compelling argument with exaggeration, an enticing title, and great action. In addition, you spoke directly to your viewer and had a powerful conclusion.

TURN &TALK *I have invited members of the Chamber of Commerce to come and view your video commercials with you. When you meet with them, you will want to point out the features that you consciously included in your commercials. Think together. What do you want to be especially sure that they notice?*

ASSESS THE LEARNING

Analyze the commercials to identify writers who need additional support in designing an enticing title, using exaggeration, speaking directly to the reader, or developing a strong conclusion. Note those who are ready for more sophisticated features.

SELF-ASSESSMENT

SELF-ASSESSMENT
Video Commercial

	YES	NO
1. **Enticing title**	☐	☐
2. **Convincing argument**	☐	☐
3. **Exaggeration**	☐	☐
4. **Speak directly to the reader**	☐	☐
5. **Action and visuals**	☐	☐
6. **Conclusion with linking words of summation such as:** *as you can see, because, since, based on the evidence, in conclusion*	☐	☐
7. **Comparisons: metaphor, simile, analogy** ⊚	☐	☐

▷ TAKE IT FORWARD

▸ Model how to add comparisons to the commercial to connect ideas. Discuss similes, metaphors, and analogies. Help students understand how these are related and can be used in their paragraphs.

▸ Adding linking words of summation can ensure that the conclusion is memorable. Have students experiment with different kinds of calls to action, such as questions, slogans, or emotional images.

▸ Introduce testimonials for students who are ready. Model how to slip in a quotation from a satisfied customer, and discuss how a testimonial strengthens a commercial.

▸ Model how to change the planning tool into a script. Choose the best question or premise, and lead with it. Use humor, exaggeration, or other persuasive devices to build a relationship with the viewer. As you continue creating a script, make sure that all the ideas are connected. Help students understand how to keep the commercial on task, even if they think of many different and interesting tidbits they want their viewers to know about the topic.

Debate Plan

Work with a partner to plan for a persuasive debate.

FEATURES

- Statement of opinion or call to action
- Detailed evidence supports call to action
- Strong emotional appeal
- Acknowledgement of the opposing view
- Summary and restatement of call to action
- ▷ May use a hypothetical situation
- ▷ Linking words of comparison: *however, but, although, on the other hand, similarly, likewise, in contrast to*

FOCUSED MINILESSON

A debate is a discussion of two different points of view. Our school cafeteria is considering adding one of two items—chicken nuggets or corn dogs. I want to craft an argument for a debate today. I would argue for chicken nuggets! But I know others might argue for corn dogs. How could I make my argument more powerful than the other one? That's an important part of a debate— to convince my listeners that my point of view is the better one.

Watch as I begin with a title that shows the topic: "Corn Dogs or Chicken Nuggets? Choose Chicken!" *Now I am writing my own answer to state how I feel in this debate:* "It is imperative that chicken nuggets are the new item on our school lunch menu. As the cafeteria staff fine-tunes our menu, chicken nuggets need to be on the list!"

Notice that I used the words imperative *and* need. *Those words mean that something is very important. It shows strong feelings toward chicken nuggets.*

TURN & TALK *Writers, now I need to prove my point. Think together about how you might prove that chicken nuggets are a better choice than corn dogs.*

I was thinking about writing that chicken nuggets taste great with barbecue sauce. But that's not a very strong reason to support chicken nuggets. Some people might not like barbecue sauce. I need to think of a reason that others would believe in. I know that chicken nuggets are packed with protein and might be a healthier choice, especially if they are baked in the oven rather than fried in oil. Watch as I write: "Chicken nuggets contain mostly protein. . . ."

I already know that my debate partner might argue that corn dogs are easier to eat. After all, they are on a stick, easy to carry, and convenient for lunchers! I want to argue strongly in favor of chicken nuggets, so I am going to soften the opposition by saying that chicken nuggets are convenient to eat, too. Watch as I write: "It could be said that. . . ."

Corn Dogs or Chicken Nuggets? Choose Chicken!

It is imperative that chicken nuggets are the new item on our school lunch menu. As the cafeteria staff fine-tunes our menu, chicken nuggets need to be on the list!

Chicken nuggets contain mostly protein. Especially if the nuggets are baked rather than fried, they are a healthier choice than carbohydrate-wrapped hot dogs.

It could be said that corn dogs are more convenient to eat because kids can just pick up a stick to eat them. But chicken nuggets are convenient, too. Most kids aren't afraid to pick them up and dip them!

Chicken nuggets are protein packed, tasty, and convenient. Let's add them to the menu today!

Debate Organizer

Debate Question
What is the best sport Volleyball Or Basketball?

Opinion: I strongly believe that vollyball is the best sport!

Points that support opinion:
- You don't need lot of equipment to play vollyball.
- It gives more mosols to your arms.
- Vollyball ruls are not that hard to learn.
- Volleyball Game

Statement acknowledging other point of view: It could be said that basketball rules are complicated, but Vollyball is important to know that it gives more mosols than basket ball does

Conclusion: Restatement of position and call for action Vollyball is a great extensie for your arms, does not need lot of equipment and not alot ruls to know. Grub a ball and your best friend and go to a park and play volley ball.

I want to leave my readers with a strong impression. I am choosing ideas about chicken nuggets that are convincing and am encouraging my listeners to take action. Watch as I write: "Chicken nuggets are protein packed, tasty, and convenient. Let's add them to the menu today!"

TURN &TALK *Partners, evaluate my arguments. How does acknowledging the other point of view make the argument stronger? What might you suggest for making this even more powerfully in favor of chicken nuggets?*

Summarize the features: Have students work in groups to generate checklists for a debate plan. Compile groups' ideas into a class checklist to display as students work.

WRITING and COACHING

It's your turn! With a partner, plan a persuasive debate. Choose a topic such as "What is the best sport?" *or* "What does our city need—more bike paths or a new water park?" *Each of you will use the debate planner together to identify points for your answers. Once you're prepared with points to defend your points of view—and arguments to soften your partner's arguments—you'll be set to present to another partner pair!*

As writers develop their drafts, confer with individuals or small groups to support and scaffold understanding. Assist students in using the framework to support their opinions.

SHARING and REFLECTING

Sum it up! *Writers, you wrote a clear statement of opinion and included two points of support for each one. Your arguments are so strong because you've carefully considered how to support them. I'm sure your listeners were convinced!*

TURN &TALK *You are going to present your debates to a new set of partners. Be prepared to talk about how you developed your debate plans. What features of persuasive debates do you want to be sure to mention? Think together about the most important features.*

ASSESS THE LEARNING

Analyze the drafts to identify writers who need assistance to prove an opinion in a debate. Identify students who may be ready for additional levels of sophistication in their writing, such as adding linking words to compare.

SELF-ASSESSMENT

SELF-ASSESSMENT
Debate Plan

	YES	NO
1. Statement of opinion or call to action	☐	☐
2. Detailed evidence supports call to action	☐	☐
3. Strong emotional appeal	☐	☐
4. Acknowledge the opposing view	☐	☐
5. Summary and restatement of call to action	☐	☐
6. May use a hypothetical situation ☺	☐	☐
7. Linking words of comparison: *however, but, although, on the other hand, similarly, likewise, in contrast to* ☺	☐	☐

▶ TAKE IT FORWARD

▸ Model how to use linking words of comparison in developing a debate. Linking words to consider include *however, but, although, on the other hand, similarly, likewise,* and *in contrast to*. Model how to weave these words into a debate to consider the point of view, such as *Although students need to spend a lot of time reading, data suggest that students need more exercise for healthier bodies, too*. Use the Debate Sentence Frames form from the *Resources* CD-ROM.

▸ Encourage students to use a hypothetical situation as an opener to the debate, such as *Have you ever wanted. . . ?* Prompt students to consider how openings such as these

draw readers and listeners in by having them imagine situations and feel connected to the speaker and situation.

▸ A debate is a fantastic tool for developing students' confidence as speakers. Discuss topics that will lead to success in presentation, such as making eye contact and using a strong steady voice.

▸ Have students return to persuasive writing they have already written with an eye toward adding emotional appeal. Have them think about how they used the debate format to convince others of a point of view. How can they infuse features of debates into other types of persuasive writing?

Formal Letter

Write a persuasive letter to the editor.

Dear Editor,

I believe that the Old Leatherman's body should not be exhumed. I believe this for two reasons: the cost of the process and respect.

The cost would be a huge factor costing the government thousands of dollars getting DNA samples and running scientific experiments on his body to determine the cause of death and attempt to determine his actual identity.

While some may see the desire to exhume his body as a respectful attempt to place the grave further from the highway, there is really no reason to disturb his final resting place. The Leatherman survived in harsh conditions with only a cave for shelter. He lived off the land and treated others with respect. The Leatherman's legend is a powerful one. Let him rest in peace.

Respectfully,

Andrea

FEATURES

- Greeting, body, closing
- Position statement
- Facts to support position
- Linking words to support specific examples: *for example, in fact, of course, consequently, specifically, to illustrate, for instance*
- Formal and respectful voice
- Restatement of position in conclusion
- Call for action
- Emotive words to make the reader feel an emotional connection
- Reader questions are anticipated

FOCUSED MINILESSON

Today I want to write a persuasive letter about a policy we've had at school about leaving the lights on at night. I think this policy wastes energy, so I want to write a letter about it and appeal for change. This letter will be to the editor of our local newspaper, so it will have a different tone than a note to a friend. It will sound a bit more formal. Notice that I start with a greeting: "To the editor." In a friendly letter, we end our greetings with commas. For this letter, because it's more formal, I'll use a colon.

Now I am ready to begin my writing. I want to start right away with the purpose for writing and with my position. This organizes my writing and gets the letter off to a strong start! Watch as I begin: "If you go by the school late at night, you'll notice that many of the lights are still on! That's because current policy is to leave the lights on for safety. This policy wastes energy and needs to be changed." *Notice that I stated the purpose of the letter: I believe that the policy wastes energy and needs to be changed.*

I need to support my position with facts. I want to focus on building security in the first paragraph. I could just say something like "We don't need lights on to keep the building safe," *but that's not very convincing.*

TURN &TALK *Writers, what facts about turning off lights will convince our readers that it's the right thing to do?*

I am starting by describing the reason for the policy that has kept lights on for so many years and want to add an example that proves why this policy isn't necessarily correct. I am thinking about using a linking word to link this statement with strong support for it. Watch as I begin: "For example, outdoor LED lights. . . ." *Notice that the phrase "for example" cues my readers. I am giving an example that shows why the lights in the building can be turned off.*

Continue modeling, adding a paragraph with another idea that supports turning off interior lights with evidence or proof. *Writers, it's important to end my letter on a strong note. I want to sum up my arguments and then end*

To the editor:

If you go by the school late at night, you'll notice that many of the lights are still on! That's because current policy is to leave the lights on for safety. This policy wastes energy and needs to be changed.

For many years, the lights have been left on to cast a glow around the school that would discourage intruders from entering the building. But there are other security measures that would keep our building safe at night, such as outdoor LED lights, which do not use as much energy as the lights inside the building.

Turning off the indoor lights will save a huge amount of energy. Not only will this measure reduce our carbon footprint and make the world cleaner, it will also allow the school to use the energy savings to pay for something we really need, like more books or gym equipment.

I urge our administration to make a decision that is safe for the school and for the environment. Turn off the lights!

Sincerely yours,

Robert Thomas

Modeled Writing

with a call to action. I am going to use the words "I urge" to frame my call to action while still keeping a respectful tone. I would never say, "This rule is a stupid idea!" Finish the letter, ending with a strong call to action and concluding with a closing and signature.

TURN &TALK *Writers, evaluate this letter. What makes it particularly persuasive? What might you add to make the arguments more powerful?*

Summarize the features: Students can work in groups to generate features checklists for letters that support arguments. Have them use the checklists as they work on their own letters and save them in their writing folders for future writing assignments.

WRITING and COACHING

Write a letter to a newspaper or magazine arguing for a change. Remember that your letter should be polite and formal. This may be the only communication you have with the editor, and you want your letter printed! You'll want to think about how to start your letter and what facts you can use to support your position.

Consider having students first list issues that can be the basis for persuasive letters. Share with students a list of linking words that will help them connect ideas in their writing, such as *because, therefore, since,* and *for example.* Remind students that opinions and reasons should be linked.

SHARING and REFLECTING

Sum it up! *Writers, your letters start with strong position statements, include facts that support the position, and include all the parts of a letter. No doubt your readers will be swayed by the arguments you've presented in your letters.*

TURN &TALK *Take your letters home, and talk with your family members about how you crafted them. What features will you mention? Put your heads together, and think about what you should tell your families. Ask your families to help you mail your letters.*

ASSESS THE LEARNING

Analyze the letters to identify writers who need additional support in opening with a position and using facts to support it. Look for opportunities to help writers add more sophisticated features to their work.

SELF-ASSESSMENT

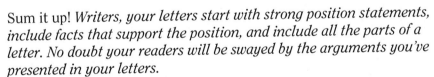

SELF-ASSESSMENT **Formal Letter**	YES	NO
1. **Greeting, body, closing**	☐	☐
2. **Position statement**	☐	☐
3. **Facts to support position**	☐	☐
4. **Linking words to support specific examples:** *for example, in fact, of course, consequently, specifically to illustrate, for instance*	☐	☐
5. **Voice is formal and respectful**	☐	☐
6. **Restatement of position in conclusion**	☐	☐
7. **Call for action**		
8. **Emotive words make the reader feel an emotional connection** ⊙		
9. **Anticipate reader questions** ⊙		

▶TAKE IT FORWARD

▸ Focus on emotive words and sentences that make readers feel strongly about topics. You might add words of urgency to your model, such as *What would happen if a student had to stay after school, stuck without a ride? A dangerous situation could happen if students are stranded without cell phones.* Prompt students to do the same in their writing.

▸ Sometimes the best letters are those that anticipate the concerns of others. Have students think about the other side of the argument they are presenting. What might someone argue against? How can they include a rebuttal

in their letter? Place a sentence in your own model to illustrate. *(While some may say that electronics are distracting, we know that sometimes listening to soft music can help us focus on tasks we are doing.)*

▸ Discuss audience for writing. How is a persuasive letter to a parent, for example, different from a persuasive letter to a principal or a friend? How would a letter of invitation differ in voice from a persuasive letter? Students can consider voice as they write letters for different purposes and audiences.

Multi-Paragraph Essay

Write a multi-paragraph essay supporting a position.

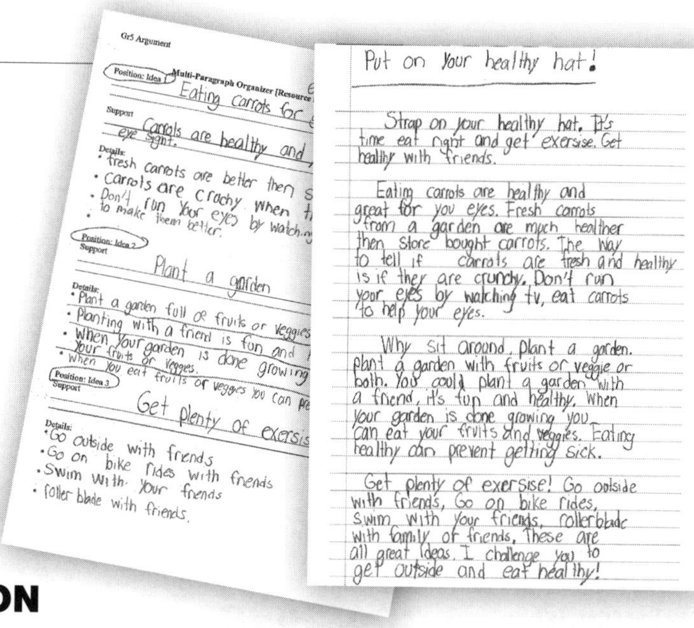

FEATURES

- Enticing title
- Clear organizational structure
- Facts and details support each paragraph
- Writing appeals to emotions
- Repetition solidifies message
- Strong, emotional ending that repeats premise
- ▶ Comparisons: metaphor, simile, analogy
- ▶ Potential objections are addressed
- ▶ Prognosticates—offer a glimpse into the future

BEFORE THE LESSON

Use the Multi-Paragraph Essay Planner from the *Resources* CD-ROM to organize points for the essay. Show the points on chart paper or display them so that students can see the link between the organizer and the writing.

FOCUSED MINILESSON

Today we're going to write a multi-paragraph essay convincing our readers to agree with us about an issue that we care about: turning off the television. I want to persuade people to turn off the television and do something different with their time.

Watch as I begin by writing the title on its own line at the top of the page. Now I can move to the next line to begin the first paragraph.

TURN & TALK *Writers, I want to start by writing "Watching television is not the best way to spend your evening." Evaluate this beginning. What might you suggest to make it stronger?*

I want to draw my readers into the topic right away. I love the idea of using humor to convince people to understand my argument. Watch as I begin with a snappy, crackling sentence: "Turn off. . . ." Now I think I have my readers' attention!

In my next paragraph, I want to focus on health. Watch as I write a statement to get my readers thinking: "Think about all . . . television?" This is powerful! You could sleep and get more exercise than if you watched television! I was thinking in this paragraph about writing how to use the free time you'd get if you turned off the television. But when I think about that, I realize it makes more sense to start a new paragraph with that idea. It's not exactly the same as health. So, I am going to wrap up this paragraph about health and then start a new paragraph about exercise.

Model creating a paragraph focused on exercise, thinking aloud as you consider which facts belong in the paragraph. *I am going to craft another paragraph that really will tug at my readers' emotions! If you turn off the television, you can spend more time with your family. That's an argument with strong emotional appeal, especially for people who want to spend more time with their family members. I am going to create a strong image of a family enjoying time together. This will help my readers connect to the idea of turning off the television. It will make their relationships with family members even stronger!*

Turn Off the Television This Week!

Turn off the talking box! We all know that television does not foster healthy activity or conversation. This week turn off the television and rediscover your family and friends.

Think about all the time that you spend in front of the television watching your favorite shows. Did you know that some scientists have shown that you expend more calories sleeping than in front of the television? Taken together, those facts point to one reason why kids are less healthy than they used to be.

What will you do with all this free time? Exercise! Take a ball to the playground and start a pick up-game with a few friends. Lace up some roller blades and roll to your local park. Exercise is a great thing to do with the television off.

Turning off the television may encourage you to turn to your family for companionship. Eat dinner with your family and talk about your day. After dinner, pitch in and help with the dishes to spend some quality time with your dad. If there's no homework, play a game with your family or solve a puzzle.

It's easy to fill your time with other things than television. You'll find yourself more rested, healthier, and connected to your family.

Modeled Writing

[handwritten organizer]

Gr5 Argument

Multi-Paragraph Organizer (Resource

Position: Idea 1
Eating carrots for

Support
Carrots are healthy and
eye sight.

Details:
- fresh carrots are better then s
- carrots are crochy when th
- Don't run your eyes by watch
  to make them better.

Position: Idea 2
Support
Plant a garden

Details:
- Plant a garden full of fruits or veggies
- Planting with a friend is fun and
- When your garden is done growing
  your fruits or veggies
- When you eat fruits or veggies you can pa

Position: Idea 3
Support
Get plenty of exercis

Details:
- Go outside with friends
- Go on bike rides with friends
- Swim with your friends
- roller blade with friends.

[handwritten essay]

Put on your healthy hat!

Strap on your healthy hat. It's time eat right and get exercise. Get healthy with friends.

Eating carrots are healthy and great for you eyes. Fresh carrots from a garden are much healther then store bought carrots. The way to tell if carrots are fresh and healthy is if they are crunchy. Don't run your eyes by watching tv, eat carrots to help your eyes.

Why sit around, plant a garden. Plant a garden with fruits or veggie or both. You could plant a garden with a friend, it's fun and healthy. When your garden is done growing you can eat your fruits and veggies. Eating healthy can prevent getting sick.

Get plenty of exercise! Go outside with friends, Go on bike rides, swim with your friends, rollerblade with family or friends, these are all great ideas. I challenge you to get outside and eat healthy!

Finish a paragraph with strong emotional appeal, and then add a conclusion. Highlight your thinking as you sum up the main points of the writing for a final statement that leaves a strong impression on readers.

TURN &TALK *Writers, think together as you evaluate this writing. What do you notice about the paragraphs? What arguments here have strong emotional appeal for readers? Can you think of ways to make this essay even stronger?*

Summarize the features: Work with students to create a features chart for multi-paragraph essays that persuade. Post the chart for students' reference as they work.

WRITING and COACHING

It's your turn! Choose a topic that you feel strongly about, such as instituting a recycling plan in your community or serving healthier choices in the school cafeteria. Use the organizer to plan your paragraphs before you begin writing.

As writers develop their drafts, confer with individuals or small groups to support and scaffold understanding. You might pull together a small group for direct instruction on constructing and organizing a cohesive paragraph.

SHARING and REFLECTING

Sum it up! *Writers, you seamlessly moved your ideas from the organizer to your paragraphs, weaving strong persuasive language with solid facts. Each paragraph develops a new point, so your readers can follow your arguments. I know I'm convinced!*

TURN &TALK *Your essays are so well crafted that I want to include them on a class website. What could we tell visitors to our website about how we crafted these essays? Think together about the features you want to be sure to mention.*

ASSESS THE LEARNING

Analyze the essays to identify writers who need additional support in organizing an argument, using clear language to call readers to action, and writing a conclusion. Note those who are ready for more sophisticated features.

SELF-ASSESSMENT

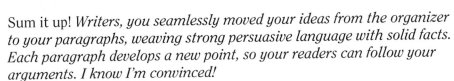

SELF-ASSESSMENT **Multi-Paragraph Essay**	YES	NO
1. Enticing title	☐	☐
2. Clear organizational structure	☐	☐
3. Facts and details support each paragraph	☐	☐
4. Writing appeals to emotions	☐	☐
5. Repetition solidifies message	☐	☐
6. Strong, emotional ending that repeats premise	☐	☐
7. Comparisons are used: metaphor, simile, analogy ○	☐	☐
8. Potential objections are addressed ○	☐	☐
9. Prognosticate--offers a glimpse into the future ○	☐	☐

▷TAKE IT FORWARD

▸ Model how to add comparisons to the essay to connect ideas and to form strong images in readers' minds. Discuss similes, metaphors, and analogies. Help students understand how these are related and can be used in their paragraphs.

▸ Have students experiment with different kinds of calls to action, such as questions, slogans, or emotional images. Help students understand that using a glimpse into the future might help convince their readers to agree with them. For example, *Doing ____ will make you wealthier, healthier, and wiser.*

▸ Remind students that persuasive pieces often include sentences that address potential objections. They can revise their essays to include responses to these objections. For example, *You may wonder if you will miss television, but there are too many other things to do.*

▸ Students may want to add visuals to their essays. You might add a photograph of a family doing an activity together to your model. You could add a graph that gives information about calories expended in different types of exercise as opposed to calories expended watching television.

Persuasive Framework

Create a persuasive framework to show how reasons support a position.

Position—Call to Action

Cigarettes to the Trash!

Support:
•Poison sticks hurt your body, heart and other people.
•Lung cancer, gum cancer, heart disease
•Teeth yellow and weak.
•Nicotene is addictive.

Support:
•Second hand smoke hurts others.
•People who have never smoked can get lung cancer when they are exposed to second hand smoke.

Support:
•Save money
•Less need for medical care
•Smell better
•Be healthy!

Conclusion
Take my advise and put your cigarettes in the TRASH!

FEATURES

- Visual layout
- Facts and reasons arranged in a logical sequence
- Arrows connect sections and show order of thinking
- Concise phrases present facts
- Linking words: *so, therefore, if, then, as a result, because, since, as, in conclusion*
- Conclusion restates problem and key points
- Call to action uses imperative language

FOCUSED MINILESSON

Writers, I think that community gardens are a great idea for so many reasons. But some people aren't sure that they should devote that much space to a garden. So, I want to convince others that cities need to set aside space for community gardens. I am going to use this special framework to organize my ideas. Display the framework on chart paper or with a document camera.

Watch as I begin by writing my position in the top box: "Cities need to set aside spaces for community gardens." Now I want to jot down in one of the support boxes why this is such a great idea. I think that if people grow their own food, they will eat healthier. After all, food from a garden isn't processed from a factory—it's fresh! Notice as I write this reason in the box, I am keeping the writing brief. A graphic organizer is an at-a-glance view. I can use these ideas later to write a persuasive summary or even a letter to the editor. But for now, I am just thinking of great reasons to support my position and noting them in the organizer.

TURN &TALK *Partners, think together. The next thing I want to do is write that gardens make neighborhoods better. What advice would you give me as I move into the next frame on the organizer?*

I heard a great idea to include a linking word. That linking word will make the support even stronger: "Gardens can revitalize neighborhoods because. . . ." That's a great support for my statement! Now I want to add a third reason. Remember, I am adding a reason to support my claim that cities need to set aside space. I wouldn't want to add an argument like "Flower gardens are better than vegetable gardens" because that doesn't support my position. I'll add another reason: "Community gardens help reduce the fossil fuels that. . . ."

Now I want to end with a conclusion. The conclusion will sum up the ideas in the organizer and include a call to action. Model completing the organizer by taking the supporting statements into account as you craft a conclusion. Add a strong call to action based on the arguments in your framework.

Persuasive Framework

Position

Cities need to set aside spaces for community gardens.

Support

Growing their own food means that people will eat healthier.

Support

Gardens can revitalize neighborhoods because they make people want to live there.

Support

Community gardens help reduce the fossil fuels that trucks use to transport food across the country.

Conclusion

Community gardens in cities create healthier populations, beautiful spaces, and reduce greenhouse gases. Urge your community officials to support this movement.

Modeled Writing

Summarize the features: Have students work with you to create a features list for a persuasive framework. Display the features list with your model as a reference while students write.

WRITING and COACHING

It's your turn! Think about how we used a framework to defend a position. Use the framework to support another statement. Think about topics you are particularly concerned about to create your framework.

As writers develop their drafts, confer with individuals or small groups to support and scaffold understanding. You might pull together a small group to provide instruction on how to support an argument.

SHARING and REFLECTING

Sum it up! *Writers, you arranged your facts using the framework and used your framework to write a conclusion that includes powerful arguments and includes a call to action. What a terrific organizing tool for persuasion!*

TURN &TALK *We're going to teach another class how to create persuasive frameworks. What features of the framework do you want to be sure to mention? Think together as you list the most important features.*

ASSESS THE LEARNING

Analyze the frameworks to identify writers who need additional help in organizing support for an argument and using supports in a conclusion that makes sense. Note those who may be ready for more sophistication in the frameworks they create.

SELF-ASSESSMENT

SELF-ASSESSMENT **Persuasive Framework**	YES	NO
1. Visual layout	☐	☐
2. Facts and reasons arranged in a logical sequence	☐	☐
3. Arrows connect sections and show order of thinking	☐	☐
4. Concise phrases present facts	☐	☐
5. Linking words: *so, therefore, if, then, as a result, because, since, as, in conclusion*	☐	☐
6. Conclusion restates problem and key points ⊙	☐	☐
7. Call to action uses imperative language ⊙	☐	☐

▶ TAKE IT FORWARD

▸ Model how to sum up the points in a framework in a clear and concise conclusion. Have students add a call to action to their frameworks. These should use imperative language but engage the readers and give them a reason for agreeing.

▸ Invite pairs to evaluate their frameworks. Are there suggestions or changes students would make? Have them discuss why they would make these particular changes.

▸ Students may want to present their frameworks. Encourage students to ask each other questions. Remind students that

arguments can benefit when the presenter thinks about both sides of the argument. Students can add visuals and post their frameworks in the classroom.

▸ Students can turn their frameworks into essays. Remind them to use good organization as they decide where to put their sentences. They can use linking words to help their readers understand which points are most important.

Investigation

Convince readers of an argument using a magazine-style layout.

FEATURES

- Magazine-style layout with text boxes and visuals
- Title states a position
- Text boxes with headings include points of support for position, including specific examples from author
- Linking words to connect ideas

BEFORE THE LESSON

Show students several magazine articles. They should be familiar with the different layouts a magazine can have, such as text boxes, titles, quotations, and captions.

FOCUSED MINILESSON

I want to make a case today for why the beginning of the American colonies is an important time in history. Instead of just writing sentences about the time period, I am going to create an investigation. Just like the pages in a magazine, I hope the words and images will jump off the page so that readers agree with me that this was an important time!

I could just begin with the time period at the top of the page, but that title doesn't make my case or capture readers' attention. I think that this is an important time period. Watch as I capture that idea in a title: "The beginning of the . . . history!" Notice that I center the title so that if this were two pages in a magazine, the title would spill across the center part of the pages, called the gutter. I end it with an exclamation point to show my strong feelings toward it!

Now it's time to plan the investigation. I am not going to write until I know what I want to include. This part of the planning is fun! I am going to play around with possible layouts until I'm sure I've created a visually pleasing layout that convinces my readers.

TURN & TALK *Writers, we've learned a lot about this time period. What features would convince others that this is an important time period? Identify a few ideas as you consider the colonies.*

The American colonies included many important people who had many excellent ideas. They came to this country to build something better than what they left. Watch as I sketch out space to capture each of these ideas. Right now, I am placing the text boxes on the page so that I can support each of these ideas when I write.

I am also going to plan for visuals. I found this clip art of Thomas Jefferson crafting the Declaration of Independence. What an important moment from that time period! I am going to include this visual on the pages. A map would help this investigation, too, just to jog readers' memories of which states were the original thirteen. I am going to leave room for a map that shows the colonies.

The beginning of the American colonies is an important moment in history!

Important people!

ORIGINAL 13 COLONIES

Building a Better Country

Excellent ideas!

The colonists faced many challenges. Instead of shrinking, they used these challenges to their advantage and worked to build a better country. It is one we are still proud of today.

Modeled Writing

These are both persuasive! The clip art shows how important this era was in forming our country. The map shows how our country began. This was an important part of forming the country that we know today!

TURN &TALK *Partners, work together to analyze the plan for the investigation. Is there anything that you would add or change? What might make this investigation even more convincing?*

Summarize the features: Have partners work in groups to generate features checklists for an investigation. They can use the checklists as a reference as they write and then save their checklists for future writing.

WRITING and COACHING

It's your turn! What is another important time period in history? Choose the one you think is most important, and design an investigation that supports your position. Remember to start with an interesting title and include text boxes with ideas that support your point of view. Visuals will spice up your investigations, too!

Confer with individuals and small groups as necessary. Talk about features that students might want to include as they plan out their space. Encourage them to use sticky notes in place of text boxes so they can pick them up and move them around until they have their placement determined.

SHARING and REFLECTING

Sum it up! *Writers, you created enticing layouts in which every part works together to support your nomination for the most important moment in history. Your compelling reasons are organized in a way that will both inform and entice your readers!*

TURN &TALK *We're going to share our investigations with our families and see what they think about our opinions. We will want to explain how we created these visual texts. What guidelines about writing persuasive investigations would you want to mention? Think together about the most important features.*

ASSESS THE LEARNING

Analyze the investigations to identify writers who need additional support in creating attractive layouts that support a position. Note those who are ready to add other features, such as linking words, bulleted lists, or strong conclusions.

SELF-ASSESSMENT

SELF-ASSESSMENT

Investigation

		YES	NO
1.	Magazine-style layout with text boxes and visuals	☐	☐
2.	Title states a position	☐	☐
3.	Text boxes with headings include points of support for position, including specific examples from author	☐	☐
4.	Linking words to connect ideas	☐	☐

▶ TAKE IT FORWARD

▸ Encourage students to use linking words to connect ideas in their text boxes. List words for students to consider, such as *because, so, when, since, also, and, besides, in addition, further,* and *therefore.* Model: *This time period is a good example of the equality present in early America, since some of the people who fought in the war or worked as spies were women.*

▸ Model adding a strong conclusion to the investigation. The conclusion should call readers to action. *Learn more about this important era in our history!* Some of the best conclusions use imperative language.

▸ Students can add quotes to their layouts, such as quotations from important people during the time period. You may want to show students how quotes are used in other magazines, pulled out or displayed in different colors and fonts.

▸ Students might use the investigation format to show other arguments, such as for the best fiction book, the best pet, or the best destination for a field trip.

▸ Put together the investigations, and create a class magazine. Share the magazine with families.

Taking It Forward: Personal Writing Projects

· ·

After they have had the opportunity to work through the model unit and lessons in this section, cement your students' understandings about persuasive writing by having them complete one or more *personal* writing projects on topics of their choice. This is an important follow-up to the model unit because it allows students to apply their new understandings to their own writing lives based on personal interests.

For example, the teaching processes outlined in the model unit on environmental issues can easily be adapted to personal projects on a variety of topics and in a variety of forms. If students have trouble deciding what to write about, you might want to suggest topics and forms such as the ones that follow. Otherwise, give students the freedom to choose the topics they find most interesting—provided you deem them appropriate.

Possible Topics for Persuasive Writing

Topics may correlate with content in your science and social studies standards, current events, or class interests.

- Do aliens exist?

- Should we be afraid of snakes?

- Which planet is the best?

- What was the most interesting time in history?

- What is the best game?

- Writing a letter to a friend, family member, or person in the school to ask or advocate for something

- What is the best invention of the past twenty years?

- Which was the best display in the museum?

- Should we have to clean up our rooms?

- What animal makes the best pet?

- Does school go for too long?

- Should we help our parents with housework?

- Why should we get exercise/brush our teeth/eat vegetables?

- What would be some good rules to have in our classroom?

- What is the best drink?

Possible Forms for Persuasive Writing

Letters	Debates	Ratings
Posters	Reviews	Charts
Bumper stickers	Advertisements	Essays
Signs	Diagrams	Articles
Notes	Illustrations	Speeches
Poems	Photo essays	Commercials
Slide shows	Comparisons	Announcements

Planning and Implementing Personal Writing Projects

Your students will need preparation, coaching, prompting, and varying amounts of support as they move through their own personal explorations. The ten-session structure presented in the model unit may be too long for personal projects that assume less time spent on instruction and modeling. Give students the time they need to fully develop their topics and to move through the stages of the writing process, but don't be surprised if many students require fewer than ten sessions.

Use the following tips and strategies as needed to ensure each student's success.

Before the Personal Projects:

▸ Help students select topics that they are interested in, and provide research materials if needed.

▸ Continue to use information you gather from the Individual Assessment Record or your Ongoing Monitoring Sheet to provide specific instruction in whole-class, small-group, and individual settings as needed. Use the Daily Planner to lay out each day's lesson.

During the Personal Projects:

▸ Give students the personal checklists from the *Resources* CD-ROM to use as samples for creating their own checklists. A blank checklist can be found on the *Resources* CD-ROM and in the Resources section at the end of this book. Explain to the students that you will also be checking to see if they have included key features on the checklist.

▸ If needed, begin each session with a focused minilesson. Tailor the suggested minilesson to suit the needs of your students.

▸ Continue to provide high-quality mentor texts. Display mentor texts prominently, and allow students time to read them before they begin to write their own. Continue to call students' attention to the features list created during the model unit.

▸ You may want to write your own text along with the students as you did during the model unit to provide an additional model.

▸ Have writing partners conference with each other often to check one another's work for sense and clarity.

▸ As students work independently on their writing and illustrations, note those who are struggling and bring them together for small-group instruction. Use the Individual Assessment Record and/or the Ongoing Monitoring Sheet to assist in tailoring instruction to the needs of your students.

▸ Students who seem very confident and who have clearly grasped all of the concepts taught so far can be brought together in a small group to extend their understanding to more challenging work.

After the Personal Projects:

▸ Be sure to give students opportunities to share and celebrate their writing projects.

▸ Compare students' final writing products with their earlier attempts in order to evaluate their growth as writers.

▸ Distribute copies of the Student Self-Reflection Sheet (on the *Resources* CD-ROM). Students will benefit greatly from the chance to reflect on their progress and to hear their classmates' feedback.

▸ Reflect on the strengths and challenges of implementing the personal projects. How might the process be adjusted to maximize student learning?

▸ Look at common needs of the class, and address these when students are working on future projects.

Response Writing Projects

Responses express a factual, critical, or personal response to a prompt or text. Students might be asked to respond to a piece of literature by writing what they liked or disliked about it, what they want to ask the author, what they think about a character, or what they learned from a piece of nonfiction. Academic prompts might ask students to answer questions or write about what they did or observed during a class activity. Responses can take many forms such as learning logs, sketches, summaries, diagrams, descriptions, written reflections, quick writes, book reviews, and reaction pieces. The writer responds to the piece of literature or prompt by expressing opinions backed up with examples from the text or facts.

CONTENTS

EXTENDED WRITING UNIT

POWER WRITES

The Big Picture

. . . .

During the model unit that follows, students will write analytical responses to a novel. The mentor text, *"Esperanza Rising* Will Raise Your Hopes, Too,"* provides a model of the structure and features of a great analytical response. Students begin by observing features of the mentor text and then work in pairs or small groups to discuss and organize their response to a novel of their choice, using their research notebooks and a graphic organizer. (The modeled writing is a response to Esther Forbes' novel, *Johnny Tremain*. You will probably want to have students choose a novel other than *Esperanza Rising* or *Johnny Tremain* so they are not tempted to copy from the models.) From their notes, students then write their analytical response. They revise, edit, and publish the response in a booklet format, adding pull quotes, headings, and illustrations. Finally, they share their publications with classmates and others and reflect on what they have learned about writing an analytical response.

Session	Focused Minilesson	Writing and Coaching	Sharing and Reflecting
1	Identifying the purpose and features of an analytical response	Draft an opening statement in your research notebook.	Evaluate your partner's opening statement. Can you suggest ways to improve it?
2	Supporting opinions with evidence	Record opinions and collect textual evidence in your research notebook.	Which opinions do you plan to write about in your response?
3	Planning with a graphic organizer	Use a graphic organizer to chart opinions and supporting evidence to include in the response.	Share your organizer with a partner. Do you have strong opinions? Do you have supporting evidence? Have you included references to the text?
4	Writing a strong introduction	Experiment with a few leads and develop one.	Share your introduction. Give feedback on your partner's lead.
5	Drafting from notes	Continue drafting, writing sentences in paragraph form from your notes.	Talk about your draft with a partner. How have your organizer and research notebook helped you create a successful draft?
6	Using linking words and phrases	Experiment with using linking words to connect opinions and examples.	Share what you wrote. Point out where you used a linking word or phrase to connect ideas.
7	Writing a strong conclusion	Write a conclusion that sums up your opinions and feelings.	Share with a partner. What would you say to teach someone to write a conclusion to an analytical response?
8	Revising for effective punctuation	Reread and revise, focusing on punctuation for clarity and impact.	Choose a well-punctuated paragraph, and read aloud to your partner with expression.
9	Using an editing checklist	Edit for one point at a time, and use editing symbols.	Share your edited draft. What did you change? How did the checklist help you?
10	Publishing and sharing	Plan pull quotes, headings, and visuals; lay out pages; and publish.	What are the features of a great analytical response? What advice would you give about writing one?

Assessing Students' Needs

The model unit is designed to teach students about the structure and features of a specific type of response writing as they apply basic writing strategies. Each of the focused minilessons provides you with suggested demonstrations, but you may want to tailor your instruction based on the common needs of your own students. You can assess students' strengths and needs during each unit, in an additional session beforehand, or by analyzing student work that you already have on hand.

Formal Pre-Assessment: After a basic introduction to each writing purpose and form as well as a review of various examples, have students write in the same form about a topic they already know a lot about. Encourage students to use as many of the features of the particular writing form as possible, but don't provide direct support. The goal here is to find out how much students already know about the writing purpose and form so you can tailor your teaching accordingly.

Experimentation in Research Notebooks: You might want to stop short of a formal pre-assessment and instead ask students to experiment with writing in their research notebooks at the end of the first session. This exercise may be less unnerving for some students and should yield enough information to form the basis of your pre-assessment.

Looking Back at Previous Work: Whether you choose to assess students' writing skills before beginning an Extended Writing Unit or during the first session, we recommend that you also consider unrelated writing projects that you've already collected from students. These may not reveal much about your students' ability to write a coherent analytical response, for example, but should tell you a great deal about their grasp of writing conventions and other traits such as focus, organization, voice, and sentence fluency. Depending on how much student work you already have on hand, you might not have to devote any class time to pre-assessment.

Focusing on Standards

Before introducing this model unit, carefully review the key skills and understandings below so you can keep the lesson objectives in mind as you teach, coach, and monitor students' growth as writers of responses.

KEY SKILLS AND UNDERSTANDINGS: RESPONSE WRITING GRADE 5
Purpose
Understands the purpose for writing a response piece
Ideas/Research
Responds directly to a piece of literature or prompt
Expresses opinions
Supports opinions with examples from text or facts
Includes references for examples from text
Organization/Text Features
Includes a title that reflects the purpose or task
Has a strong opening statement
Is organized in paragraphs that express central ideas or opinions
Supports central ideas and opinions with details and evidence from text
Has a conclusion that summarizes and expresses feelings
Includes illustrations that support the response
Includes text features that support the response
Language/Style
Shows a clear point of view
Expresses personal opinions and feelings
Uses linking words and phrases (*for example, specifically, in fact*, etc.) to connect opinions to examples
Demonstrates sentence variety and fluency
Uses specific vocabulary related to topic and genre
Conventions and Presentation
Begins sentences with capital letters
Capitalizes proper nouns
Uses end punctuation correctly
Uses a variety of punctuation marks (commas, dashes, colons, etc.)
Uses appropriate spelling
Creates clear, effective page layouts with supporting visuals and text features

This list is the basis for both the Individual Assessment Record and the Ongoing Monitoring Sheet shown in Figure 1.1. (Both forms can be found in the Resources section at the back of this book and also on the *Resources* CD-ROM.) Use the Individual Assessment Record if you want to keep separate records on individual students. The Ongoing Monitoring Sheet gives you a simple mechanism for recording information on all your students as you move around the class, evaluating their work in progress. Use this information to adapt instruction and session length as needed.

At the end of these and any additional units you may teach on response writing, compare students' final publications with their initial attempts at writing in the text type. Use the Ongoing Monitoring Sheet and/or the Individual Assessment Record to record students' growth as writers.

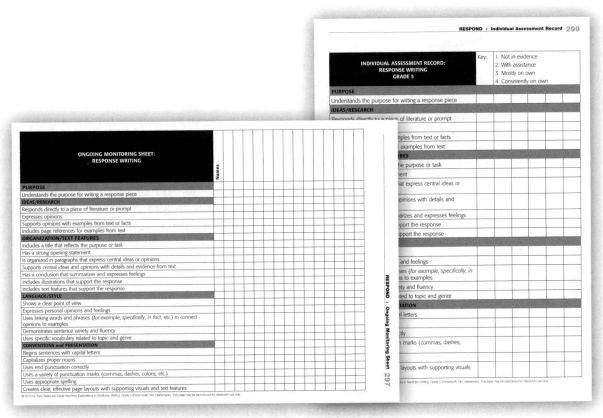

Figure 1.1 Individual Assessment Record and Ongoing Monitoring Sheet

Planning and Facilitating the Unit

Students will need preparation, coaching, prompting, and support as they move through this and other Extended Writing Units. Use the following tips and strategies as needed to ensure each student's success.

Before the Unit:

‣ When planning your teaching, bear in mind that each lesson in the model unit that follows is designed to be completed in one session. However, you will likely find that your students need more time for certain activities. Take the time you need to adequately respond to the unique needs of your students, and remember that they will likely progress through the writing process at their own pace.

‣ Begin building background knowledge about the text type and writing topics in advance. Shared reading, guided reading, and read-aloud experiences as well as group discussions will ensure that students are not dependent exclusively on their own research.

‣ For the research component, you may want to gather suitable books, magazine articles, encyclopedia entries, and websites in your classroom or work with the media center teacher to assemble a collection in advance. Make sure the research materials you gather are at a range of difficulty levels and include plenty of text features such as close-up photographs, captions, bold headings, and diagrams.

During the Unit:

‣ Begin each session with a focused minilesson to demonstrate the traits of writing the particular type of text you're exploring. Tailor the suggested minilesson to suit the needs of your students. The mentor texts on the *Resources* CD-ROM and in the *Book of Mentor Texts* are models you can use to show students the structure and features of each text type. You may want to use other mentor texts to assist you with your demonstrations.

‣ Be sure to model note-taking for students as you think aloud about information in reference materials. Use chart paper and sticky notes to capture your thinking, and display the models prominently as students work on their own research and note-taking.

‣ As students work independently on their writing and publishing, note those who are struggling and bring them together for small-group instruction. Use the Individual Assessment Record and/or the Ongoing Monitoring Sheet to assist in tailoring instruction to the needs of your students.

‣ Students who seem very confident and who have clearly grasped all of the concepts taught so far can be brought together in a small group to extend their understanding to more challenging work.

‣ Provide templates for students who need extra support when writing. You'll find a variety of graphic organizers on the *Resources* CD-ROM from which to choose.

After the Unit:

▸ Be sure to give students opportunities to share and celebrate their individual writing projects.

▸ Distribute copies of the Personal Checklist for Response Writing as shown in Figure 1.2. (Both forms can be found on the *Resources* CD-ROM and in the Resources section at the end of this book). Students will benefit greatly from the chance to reflect on their progress during the unit and to hear their classmates' feedback.

▸ Compare students' final writing products with pre-assessments and past work to evaluate their growth as writers of responses.

▸ Reflect on the strengths and challenges of implementing this series of lessons. How might it be adjusted to maximize student learning?

▸ Look at common needs of the class, and address these when planning future explorations or when using the Power Writes.

Personal Checklist for Response Writing

Process Reflections:

Research:
I read the following text and/or used the following resources: _____

Drafting:
I solved the following problems in my writing: _____

Revising:
When revising, I focused on improving my message by: _____

Editing:
To ensure that I edited effectively, I used an editing checklist and concentrated on: _____

Presentation:
I chose the following format to present my writing: _____

I am most proud of: _____

I have checked the following:

☐ My title reflects my topic and my opinion.
☐ I have a strong opening statement that expresses my opinion.
☐ I have paragraphs that express my central ideas.
☐ I have used details and examples from the text to support my opinions.
☐ I have included references for my examples from the text.
☐ I have used linking words such as *for example, specifically,* and *in fact* to connect my opinions to examples.
☐ I have used specific vocabulary related to my topic.
☐ I have a memorable ending that summarizes my opinions and point of view.
☐ My writing has fluency and I have used a variety of sentence lengths.
☐ I have included illustrations that support my response.
☐ I have included text features that support my response.

© 2012 by Tony Stead and Linda Hoyt from *Explorations in Nonfiction Writing, Grade 5* (Portsmouth, NH: Heinemann). This page may be reproduced for classroom use only.

Figure 1.2 Personal Checklist for Response Writing

SESSION 1
Identifying the Purpose and Features of an Analytical Response

Students identify the features of an analytical response and then write an opening statement for their own responses.

SESSION SNAPSHOT

Genre Focus: Features of an Analytical Response

Process Focus: Prewriting

Trait(s): Ideas, Organization

Mentor Text: *"Esperanza Rising* Will Raise Your Hopes, Too," by Mandy McDonald

TIP This unit has a focus on historical novels, but you can adapt the lessons to fit any fiction or nonfiction text. You may want to have students respond to a book from a literature circle or to a text that has been read to the class. It is important that students have read the text recently so that their ideas and reactions are fresh in their memories.

> I really enjoyed reading <u>Johnny Tremain</u> by Esther Forbes. This novel looks at history through the eyes of a young boy, which is a unique approach. It's also different from other books about the Revolutionary War because it considers the feelings and emotions of different people in the time that led up to the war.

Modeled Writing

FOCUSED MINILESSON

Before the unit: This unit assumes that students have read the books they will write about in their responses and have copies available for reference. You may want to provide a list of novels for students to choose from. You will also want to select a book to be the basis of your modeled writing. The modeled writing in this unit is based on *Johnny Tremain*, by Esther Forbes.

Summarize the learning goals: *In this unit, we are going to explore a type of nonfiction writing called* response writing. *Responses can take many forms, such as a book review, a friendly or formal letter, a written answer to a prompt or test question, even a sketch or diagram. We're each going to write an analytical response to a novel we've read. When we write analytical responses to literature, we tell what we think and feel about what we have read, and we give good reasons for our opinions, supported by examples from the text.*

For us to write a great analytical response, we first need to learn about the features and structure of this type of writing. Let's see how one writer wrote a response to Esperanza Rising, *by Pam Muñoz Ryan which you'll find on page 45 of the* Book of Mentor Texts.

Using the Mentor Text

■ Distribute copies of the mentor text, and read the opening sentences aloud. *I have already noticed one feature of an analytical response: This is a strong introduction that pulls us into the response. Did you notice that the writer tells us in the first few sentences which novel she is responding to? And she clearly states her opinion:* "This novel has a nonstop plot, strong characters, historical details, and vivid writing." *I feel breathless just reading her list of what she thinks is great in this novel! I definitely want to read on and find out more about what this writer thinks about this book.*

■ Guide students in examining the mentor text, perhaps by having them work in small groups to discover the features. As needed, help them to notice the key features and to understand that the response is organized around central ideas or opinions that are supported by details and examples from the novel.

> **TURN &TALK** *Turn to your partner. When you write your response, what features do you want to be sure you include? Identify the features that you think are most important for a great analytical response.*

- Guide students as they share their observations, and record their thinking on a chart labeled "Features of a Great Analytical Response."

Modeling

- To help students follow your modeling, have a copy of the book you are responding to on hand. *I'm going to write an analytical response along with you. I'll start by writing an opening statement that introduces the book and gives my general opinion and thoughts about it:* "I really enjoyed reading <u>Johnny Tremain</u> by Esther Forbes. This novel looks at history through the eyes of a young boy, which is a unique approach. It's also different from other books about the Revolutionary War because it considers the feelings and emotions of different people in the time that led up to the war."

> **TURN &TALK** *Writers, think together. What do you notice about my opening statement? How do you know that I am writing an analytical response?*

- Give students a chance to share their impressions before summing up and moving on to independent writing. *Did you notice that I didn't just say, "I like this book"? Instead, I gave my opinion and told **why I** think it's a good book. I will explore these ideas further as I continue my analysis. An analytical response goes beyond just telling your opinion; it also tells your thoughts, feelings, and reactions about what you read.*

WRITING and COACHING

- Guide students as they think about their books and write their opening statements. What is it about the text that supports their general opinions? Encourage them to list opinions, thoughts, and feelings they have about the text that they might like to explore in their responses.

- Coach students by asking questions that will spark analytical thinking: *How did it make you feel to read this book? Why? What elements or features of the book stood out to you? What did you notice about the author's craft or style?*

- If time allows, have students meet in pairs or small groups to share their impressions of the books they have selected. Be sure they have their research notebooks on hand so they have ideas to share and can jot down new ideas that come up during discussion. This will help get their ideas flowing.

SHARING and REFLECTING

> **TURN &TALK** *Evaluate your partner's opening statement. Can you identify his or her opinion and reasons for the opinion? Can you suggest ways to improve the opening statement?*

- Provide time for students to share their observations, and then review the list of features developed earlier in the session. Revisit the mentor text to help students consolidate their understandings about the writing purpose.

- Gather the research notebooks, and analyze students' attempts to write opening statements. Identify writers who may need additional coaching to form opinions, and support them with ideas from the text, as well writers who are ready for higher levels of sophistication.

Features of a Great Analytical Response

- Introduction that clearly states an opinion
- An organization with logically grouped ideas
- Reasons supported by facts and details from the text
- Words, phrases, and clauses that link opinions to examples (for example, consequently, specifically, such as)
- Specific vocabulary
- Conclusion that summarizes and reinforces the opinion

TIP You may need to explain more thoroughly to students how an analytical/evaluative response is different from the type of simple responses they may have written in the lower grades. In an analytical/evaluative response, we not only tell what we like about the text but also think carefully about why we feel the way we do and pay close attention to the author's craft. Helping students focus on the "why" behind their opinions is the first step toward the more sophisticated analytical/ evaluative writing that will be expected of them in the upper grades.

TIP If students struggle to move beyond flat opening statements like "I really liked this book" or "This was the worst book I ever read," encourage them to talk it over with a writing partner, or ask leading questions such as *How did it make you feel to read this very boring book?* or *What was it like for you to learn so much information about one of your favorite subjects?* Encouraging students to really think about their feelings this way may lead to more substantial opening statements.

SESSION 2
Supporting Opinions with Evidence

Students develop opinions supported by evidence gathered from the text and possibly from research.

SESSION SNAPSHOT

Organization Strategy: Supporting Opinions with Facts and Details

Process Focus: Prewriting

Trait(s): Ideas, Organization

Mentor Text: *"Esperanza Rising* Will Raise Your Hopes, Too," by Mandy McDonald

Esther Forbes richly portrays characters by exploring their thoughts and feelings.

—Johnny feels loved and accepted when Isannah kisses his injured hand.

—Johnny shows his loyalty to his country as he is preparing to go to battle.

Modeled Writing

FOCUSED MINILESSON

Review the learning goals from the previous session. If time allows, have students turn and talk about what they have learned so far.

Summarize the learning goals for this session: *Remember, the purpose of an analytical response is to give our opinions and support them with details and facts. Today we will focus on forming opinions and finding and noting evidence from our books to support our opinions.*

Using the Mentor Text

■ Display the mentor text, and read the introduction aloud. *Right away, I know that the writer likes the book and has strong reasons why she likes it. I notice that as the response continues, she focuses on the things that she thinks are done well.* Draw students' attention to the section "Historical Details," and read it aloud. *In this paragraph, she states that the book accurately portrays the experience of moving to the United States from Mexico in 1930. To support her opinion, she cites historical events and facts that are woven into the story. To know that the events are accurately portrayed, she may have done some research. She gathered evidence to support her opinion that the novel is historically accurate.*

Modeling

■ *When I am planning an analytical response, I do the same thing. I start out with an opinion about the text or about one of its features, such as its characters, dialogue, or descriptions. The opinion explains my thoughts, feelings, or reactions to the book. Remember—not all opinions are positive! I might think, for example, that the dialogue in* Johnny Tremain *doesn't sound the way that people really talk and that makes it difficult to understand the book. Once I've written an opinion, I need to find evidence to support it.*

■ *In my opinion, the author of* Johnny Tremain *did a great job of describing the thoughts and feelings of the characters. Watch as I write this opinion at the top of a page in my research notebook:* "Esther Forbes richly portrays characters by exploring their thoughts and feelings." *Now I need evidence from the text to support my opinion. Watch as I write a few notes:* "Johnny feels loved and accepted when Isannah kisses his injured hand; Johnny shows his loyalty to his country as he is preparing to go to battle."

TURN &TALK *Partners, think about the examples I listed from the text. How do they support my opinion? What other support might I include for this opinion?*

- *I am going to write my other opinions about the book in my research notebook, one opinion at the top of each page. Then, as I look back through the book, I will cite evidence for each opinion. It's important to put quotation marks around phrases or sentences that come directly from the book. I am also including page numbers from the book in my notebook. That way, I can return to the book to double-check my support as I write.*

- *I will need to do some research to prove one of my opinions. I've written, "*Johnny Tremain *has a fascinating blend of accurate historical facts mixed with fictional characters." To prove that, I need to mention specific historical facts from the book. I want to be sure those facts are accurate, so I am going to use reference sources to check their validity.*

WRITING and COACHING

- Guide students as they record their opinions and collect textual evidence in their research notebooks.

- Encourage students to meet in small groups with other students who are analyzing the same text. Have them talk about their opinions and share examples from the text to support these ideas. Prompt them to move beyond saying what they liked or disliked to evaluating the text and recording specific opinions and reasons.

- Coach students to focus on opinions they can support with examples and evidence from the book and to discard opinions that they cannot support.

SHARING and REFLECTING

TURN &TALK *Writers, you have noted quite a few opinions! Tell your partner which opinions you plan to write about in your response.*

- After students have shared the opinions they plan to write about, bring writers back together to review the process of forming and supporting opinions. Refer back to the features chart developed in the first session.

- Gather the research notebooks, and analyze students' attempts to form opinions and support them with details and facts. Identify writers who may need additional modeling as well as those who are ready for higher levels of sophistication.

TIP As you talk about the mentor text, your writing, and students' responses, use specific vocabulary and encourage students to use it, too. You might work with students to make a chart of vocabulary specific both to fiction, such as *setting, plot, character, dialogue,* and *theme,* and to author's craft, such as *creativity, imagery, clarity,* and *voice.*

TIP As students record evidence from the text, remind them about the importance of giving the author credit for his or her work. As they write their notes, they should put ideas into their own words. If they want to use a direct quote, remind them to enclose the author's words in quotation marks and to include the page number.

TIP Be sure students use reliable sources to research information on the Internet. A student's page about the Revolutionary War, for example, is not a reliable source. A website sponsored by the Smithsonian Museum is trustworthy. Have students look for the extensions .edu and .gov as a first check of reliability.

Planning with a Graphic Organizer

Students organize their opinions and evidence on a graphic organizer in preparation for writing.

SESSION SNAPSHOT

Process Focus: Prewriting, Planning

Trait(s): Organization

TIP Be flexible with the number of opinions and details that students will include in their responses. Some students may be able to share only an opinion or two, while others will be able to flesh out richer responses.

FOCUSED MINILESSON

Review the learning goals from the previous session. If time allows, have students turn and talk about what they have learned so far.

Summarize the learning goals for this session: *Now that you've identified your opinions about the book and noted supporting evidence in your research notebooks, it's time to plan your response. In this session, you'll learn how a graphic organizer can help you organize your opinions and link them to strong textual evidence.*

Modeling

- Use a piece of chart paper to draw a spider map like the one on the *Resources* CD-ROM. *Writers, I have decided to write about four opinions I identified in our last session.* Think aloud as you write the title of the book in the center and your selected opinions on the lines coming out of the center.

- *Writers, notice that I haven't written complete sentences. Instead, I've written phrases:* "unique main character, different perspectives on war, richly developed characters," *and* "historical accuracy." *Phrases work well when I'm getting organized. These are the opinions I will focus on in my response.*

- Model how you select evidence to support one of your opinions. *Now I am going to think about how the novel shows different perspectives on the war. I have written ideas in my notes already, and I am going to choose the best examples to put in my organizer. Lavinia's character is a great example of how some people wanted to keep things the same because the colonists had benefited from British rule. Watch as I note this example on the first short line:* "Lavinia—views of a British supporter." *In my notebook, I've recorded details from the story that show her allegiance: she entertains British soldiers and returns to England when war begins. I'll use those details when I write my response. Next, I want to discuss someone who was against British rule. I could use Johnny as an example, but I've noted that Johnny isn't very aware of the war until he meets Rab. Rab is a better example, so I'll put him on the second line:* "Rab—supported revolution from beginning." *I have noted that Rab risked his life by being part of the meetings and that he volunteered to fight in the first skirmish. When I write, I'll use those details to show Rab is a good example of a person who supported the war.*

■ Continue modeling how you use the chart to link your opinions with supporting evidence from the book. Point out that there is limited room on the organizer, so you can't list everything. Instead, you need to choose the strongest support for the opinions you've written on the chart.

TURN &TALK *Writers, what do you think of this organizer? How will it help you to fill out a chart like this before writing your response?*

■ Give students a chance to share their reflections; then, pass out copies of the organizer from the *Resources* CD-ROM, and have students begin their independent writing.

WRITING and COACHING

■ Guide students as they select opinions and supporting evidence to include in their responses.

■ Encourage students to experiment with drawing arrows and numbering ideas in their research notebooks to help them order their notes and think about related ideas.

■ If some students find it difficult to locate evidence in the text, have them work with another student for support.

SHARING and REFLECTING

TURN &TALK *Partners, share your organizers with each other. Do you have strong opinions to discuss? Do you have evidence to support your opinions? Have you included references to the text?*

■ Guide a conversation that returns students' attention to the overall goal of writing a response. How do they think these organizers will help them as they write?

■ Gather the graphic organizers, and analyze your students' attempts to organize their opinions and supporting details. Identify writers who may need additional modeling to form and support opinions, as well as those who are ready for higher levels of sophistication. Use the class writing development rubric or the individual student rubric on the *Resources* CD-ROM to track writing proficiencies.

Name: _____   Date: _____

Spider Map

Write main ideas on the slanted lines that connect to the oval.
Write details on the branching lines.

Lavinia—views of a British supporter

Rab—supported revolution from beginning

unique main character

different perspectives on war

historical accuracy

richly developed characters

Topic

Johnny Tremain

Modeled Writing

TIP Throughout the year, introduce students to various uses of this organizer. Students can use this chart to organize key facts, character traits, points in a persuasive text, and so on.

TIP Encourage students to skim the text for examples to support their opinions. When they find an example, they can mark it with a sticky note to review later or note it in their research notebooks with a page number. Emphasize that writers may return to the text at any point in the writing process.

SESSION 4
Writing a Strong Introduction

Students focus on writing strong introductions for their responses.

SESSION SNAPSHOT

Process Focus: Drafting, Revising

Trait(s): Organization, Ideas, Voice

Mentor Text: *"Esperanza Rising* Will Raise Your Hopes, Too," by Mandy McDonald

FOCUSED MINILESSON

Review the learning goals from the previous session. If time allows, have students turn and talk about what they have learned so far.

Summarize the learning goals for this session: *Writers, today we're going to focus on creating an inviting lead or revising the leads we've already crafted to grab our readers' attention while we introduce the novel and preview our opinions. Those are the qualities of a great response introduction.*

Using the Mentor Text

■ Read aloud the first paragraph of the mentor text. *This writer could have just written, "Esperanza Rising, by Pam Muñoz Ryan, is a great novel." If I read that sentence, it wouldn't get me very excited about the book or the response. Instead, the writer captures my attention with a powerful quote from the novel and an image of Esperanza learning to crochet from her grandmother. Then, she identifies the book and the author and previews the opinions she will develop in her response.*

> **TURN &TALK** *Turn to your partner. When you write or revise your introduction, what features will you be sure to include?*

■ Work with students to chart the features of a strong introduction.

Modeling

■ *Now I'm going to look at my opening sentences from the first session:* "I really enjoyed reading <u>Johnny Tremain</u> by Esther Forbes. This novel looks at history through the eyes of a young boy, which is a unique approach. It's also different from other books about the Revolutionary War because it considers the feelings and emotions of different people during the time that led up to the war."

■ *These sentences introduce the novel and my opinions, but I think I can write a more compelling introduction. I'm going to use a separate piece of paper to try some different approaches. One way to grab a reader's attention is with a description. Watch as I write:* "It's 1775 in colonial America. Some people are going about their regular work—making silver, selling barrels, sailing ships. Others are gathered in secret meetings, about to start a rebellion." *I like the way this creates a picture in the reader's mind. Let me try another one. I'll describe an incident:* "It's 1775, and you live in colonial America. British soldiers are all over your town and refusing to allow needed supplies in. What do you do?

Do you support their right to govern the colonies, or do you grab a gun and get ready for battle?" *I like this lead, too, because the incident and questions will make readers wonder and help them connect to the story.*

TURN &TALK *Writers, analyze my two leads. Which do you prefer and why? Discuss your ideas with your partner.*

■ *I'm going to use my second idea. Now I'll add the book information and opinions from my opening sentences, but I'm going to revise those ideas to flow smoothly from my new sentences. Watch as I continue writing:* "Johnny Tremain *by Esther Forbes not only is a captivating story about a boy growing up but also gives readers an interesting perspective into the thoughts and feelings of different people during the Revolutionary War.*"

■ Reread your lead paragraph aloud, revise to your liking, and confirm with students that you have included the features of a strong introduction.

WRITING and COACHING

■ Support writers as they experiment with a few different leads and develop the one they feel is most engaging. Assure them that they can revise or replace their lead at any point in the writing process.

■ Encourage students to share their ideas for leads with a partner to help them decide which is their most engaging or compelling approach.

■ When students finish crafting their introductions, remind them to reread and make sure they have included all the features of a strong introduction: an engaging lead, the book title and author's name, and clearly stated opinions that tell readers what to expect in the upcoming paragraphs.

SHARING and REFLECTING

TURN &TALK *Writers, share your introduction with a partner. What do you like best about your partner's lead? Do you have any suggestions for improving it?*

■ Gather the drafts and analyze your students' attempts to write strong introductions. Identify writers who may need additional modeling as well as those who are ready for higher levels of sophistication. Use the rubrics found on the *Resources* CD-ROM to track writing proficiencies.

Lead #1

It's 1775 in colonial America. Some people are going about their regular work—making silver, selling barrels, sailing ships. Others are gathered in secret meetings, about to start a rebellion.

Lead #2

It's 1775, and you live in colonial America. British soldiers are all over your town and refusing to allow needed supplies in. What do you do? Do you support their right to govern the colonies, or do you grab a gun and get ready for battle?

Modeled Writing

Johnny Tremain by Esther Forbes is not only a captivating story about a boy growing up, but it also gives readers an interesting perspective into thoughts and feelings of different people during the Revolutionary War.

Modeled Writing

TIP Provide a variety of responses for students to review, and help them notice how writers craft openings. Create a chart of strong openings to post in the writing center as examples, and identify different strategies such as asking questions, starting with a description, leading with a quotation, and describing an incident.

SESSION 5
Drafting from Notes

Students turn the notes from their graphic organizers and research notebooks into a draft.

SESSION SNAPSHOT

Process Focus: Drafting

Trait(s): Organization, Voice

Mentor Text: *"Esperanza Rising* Will Raise Your Hopes, Too," by Mandy McDonald

FOCUSED MINILESSON

Review the learning goals from the previous session. If time allows, have students turn and talk about what they have learned so far.

Summarize the learning goals for today's session: *Now that we've collected opinions and evidence in our notebooks and used our organizers to lay out our responses, it's time to start drafting in paragraph form. In this session, you'll learn how to turn notes into running text.*

Using the Mentor Text

- If possible, display the mentor text on an electronic whiteboard or projection screen. Read the entire selection aloud, highlighting the opinion and evidence discussed in each paragraph.

- *Writers, did you notice how this writer started with an engaging lead and organized the rest of her response around what she thinks are the novel's strengths? Each paragraph has a main idea, supporting details or reasons for the writer's opinion, and evidence from the text.*

Modeling

- Display your organizer and have your research notebook on hand. *Writers, I've drafted my introduction. Now watch as I begin to write the body of my response in paragraph form, using my organizer and research notebook as I go.*

- Model how you order opinions on your organizer. *My first step is to look at my organizer and decide on an order for my main ideas. I think it makes sense to begin with Johnny's character and show how he grows up through the story. I'll number that section 1. (Model how you order your other main ideas.) Numbering the main ideas on my organizer will keep my response focused.*

- Think aloud as you draft the first paragraph. *I'll begin by stating my opinion:* "This novel looks at history through the eyes of a young boy, Johnny, which is a unique approach." *Now I will support my statement with evidence from the book. Notice that I am not summarizing. I am selecting details that support my opinion. Watch as I write:* "When we meet Johnny, he is an apprentice to a silversmith, learning a skilled trade. Then, his hand is ruined by molten silver. Unable to work at the job he loves, he spends a lot of time on the streets of Boston. Gradually, he meets people like Rab and Dr. Warren, learns about the brewing revolution, and eventually joins the fight. In deciding what to do about the war and his life, he grows up." *Now I want to include a detail from the author's writing to prove my point. Watch as I write:* "The last section of the book is titled 'A Man Can Stand Up.' When Forbes writes, 'This was his land and these his people' (page 292), you know that Johnny will stand up for his country. He has become a man."

■ Continue modeling how to turn notes from the organizer and your notebook into sentences and paragraphs. As you model, show that each main section on the graphic organizer can become a paragraph, or you can split a section into two or more paragraphs if you have enough evidence.

■ Emphasize that you are drafting. Show students that drafting is a process by crossing out words, inserting ideas, and thinking aloud as you model.

WRITING and COACHING

■ Support writers as they begin to draft complete sentences in paragraph form. Encourage a community of writers by giving students time to discuss their work in progress with writing buddies.

■ As writers begin to draft, some may realize that some of their main ideas can be combined or that they need more or different examples from the text. Explain that drafting often exposes weaknesses in planning, and allow time for students to revise their charts and return to the text as often as needed.

■ Help writers remember that nonfiction writing has special structures that make messages easier for readers to understand. Even though this is a draft, students can begin thinking about text structures, such as boldface words that emphasize important ideas or headings that organize the text.

SHARING and REFLECTING

TURN &TALK *Find a partner and talk about your drafts. What went well? What challenges did you face today? How have your graphic organizers and research notebooks helped you create a successful draft?*

■ Give students time to reflect and share their thoughts, and then gather the drafts and analyze your students' attempts to turn notes into running text. Identify writers who may need additional modeling as well as those who are ready for higher levels of sophistication.

This novel looks at history through the eyes of a young boy, Johnny, which is a unique approach. When we meet Johnny, he is an apprentice to a silversmith, learning a skilled trade. Then his hand is ruined by molten silver. Unable to work at the job he loves, he spends a lot of time on the streets of Boston. Gradually, he meets people like Rab and Dr. Warren, learns about the brewing revolution, and eventually joins the fight. In deciding what to do about the war and his life, he grows up. The last section of the book is titled, "A Man Can Stand Up." When Forbes writes, "This was his land and these his people" (page 292), you know that Johnny will stand up for his country. He has become a man.

Modeled Writing

TIP Small-group writing experiences are the perfect opportunity to help coach students who need support in fleshing out their ideas. These writers will benefit from guiding questions: *What examples from the book support your idea that the author writes great descriptions? You wrote that the pictures are awesome. Can you think of a word that gives more information than* awesome?

SESSION 6
Using Linking Words and Phrases

Students continue to draft, focusing on using linking words to connect opinions to evidence and organize their writing.

SESSION SNAPSHOT

Process Focus: Drafting, Revising

Trait(s): Word Choice, Organization

Mentor Text: *"Esperanza Rising* Will Raise Your Hopes, Too,"* by Mandy McDonald

FOCUSED MINILESSON

Review the learning goals from the previous session. If time allows, have students turn and talk about what they have learned so far.

Summarize the learning goals for this session: *We've all been working hard on drafting responses that tell our opinions about the novel and support them with evidence and examples from the text. Today we'll explore how certain words, called* linking words, *can help our readers know that an example is coming and can make our writing more organized and easier to understand.*

Using the Mentor Text

- Revisit the mentor text. Read aloud the section "Wonderful Writing" and emphasize the linking words: *Pam Muñoz Ryan's writing style sweeps you along in her story. She often conveys events and characters' emotions through small clever details, such as when Tío Luis "hands Mama Papa's silver belt buckle, the only one of its kind, engraved with the brand of the ranch" (page 20). You know, without actually knowing yet, that Esperanza's beloved Papa is dead.*

  TURN &TALK *Partners, think together. What linking words introduce the example?*

  - Invite students to search other sections for linking words and phrases that introduce evidence and connect ideas in the mentor text.

Modeling

- Begin a chart of linking words and phrases. *As I continue drafting my response, I am going to think about using evidence to support my opinions. To get ready to write, I will start a list of linking words that I can use:* for example, in fact, such as, also, specifically, consequently, however, later in the story.

- *Watch as I begin my paragraph:* "As I read the novel, I realized there were many different perspectives about the war. Many authors show the perspective of the freedom fighters, but Esther Forbes also shows you the perspective of other people."

  TURN &TALK *Now I want to tell about Lavinia. Partners, think together. What words could I use to link my example to my main idea?*

As I read the novel, I realized there were many different perspectives about the war. Many authors show the perspective of the freedom fighters, but Esther Forbes also shows you the perspective of other people. Specifically, the character of Lavinia shows the views of a British supporter. For example, she entertains the British soldiers when they are garrisoned in Boston. She calls the first skirmish a "little insurrection," which means a rebellion, instead of a fight. As the war begins, Lavinia returns to England...

Modeled Writing

■ *Watch as I continue writing:* "Specifically, the character of Lavinia shows the views of a British supporter." *Next, I'll use linking words and phrases to help me organize my evidence:* "For example, she entertains the British soldiers when they are garrisoned in Boston. She calls the first skirmish a 'little insurrection,' which means a rebellion, instead of a fight. As the war begins, Lavinia returns to England."

■ *I put a lot of evidence into that paragraph, so I am going to start a new paragraph for my next example:* "Rab supported the revolution from the beginning. He risked his life by being part of the meetings, and he volunteered to fight in the first skirmish. Rab is a good example of a person who supported the war."

■ Reread the sentences. *Okay, I think this section is almost done. I just need to link this paragraph to the one before, since they both show perspectives on the war. Watch as I insert a sentence or two to make my connection:* "Of course, the author also needs to show the perspective of a colonist fighting for freedom. Consequently, the character of Rab is important. Rab supported. . . ." *Wow, my writing is messier, but I think this sounds much better!*

■ Continue thinking aloud and inviting students to offer suggestions on where to use linking words and phrases in your response. Show students how you play with language while drafting, experimenting with several options before you select the one you like the best.

TIP For students who may need direct instruction on linking words, explain that linking words are used to connect or link one sentence to another or one part of a sentence to another. Challenge them to find examples of linking words in their nonfiction texts and add them to the list you started. You might also print the resource Linking Words That Add Information from the *Resources* CD-ROM.

WRITING and COACHING

■ As writers return to drafting, remind them to experiment with using different linking words to connect their ideas and examples.

■ Remind students to use a variety of linking words, and suggest they use the class list as a reference.

■ Coach writers with questions such as *Where have you included an example? What words can you use to link that idea to the main idea? How could you connect these ideas to make them flow more smoothly?*

TIP At this point, some students may feel that they are close to finishing their drafts. For these students, a craft lesson focused on the other purposes of linking words such as summarizing (*in all, in summary, finally*), contrasting (*instead, rather, however*), and emphasizing (*especially, particularly*) may be beneficial.

SHARING and REFLECTING

TURN &TALK *Partners, share what you wrote today. Point out where you used a linking word or phrase to connect an example to your opinion.*

■ Give partners ample opportunity to share their reflections, and then gather the drafts and analyze your students' attempts to use linking words to cue readers to examples. Identify writers who may need reteaching or additional modeling as well as those who are ready for higher levels of sophistication. Use the rubrics on the *Resources* CD-ROM to track writing proficiencies.

SESSION 7
Writing a Strong Conclusion

Students end their responses by summarizing their feelings and opinions about the text.

SESSION SNAPSHOT

Process Focus: Drafting, Revising

Trait(s): Organization, Voice

Mentor Text: *"Esperanza Rising* Will Raise Your Hopes, Too," by Mandy McDonald

TIP Provide a variety of responses for students to review, and help them notice how other writers craft conclusions. Identify strong conclusions and post them in the writing center as examples.

Esther Forbes' famous novel is long and challenging to read, but it is definitely worth the effort. Johnny Tremain weaves the fictional life of young Johnny with the factual historical events that led up to the Revolutionary War. This story of pride, adventure, tragedy, and hope will live on in your mind long after you've read the last page.

Modeled Writing

FOCUSED MINILESSON

Reflect on the learning goals from the last session. If time allows, have students turn and talk about what they have learned so far.

Summarize the learning goals for this session: *In our very first session, we identified an important feature of a great analytical response: a conclusion that summarizes. In this session, you'll learn how to bring your response to a satisfying close by summing up your thoughts and feelings about your selected book.*

Using the Mentor Text

■ Return to the mentor text, and read the conclusion aloud.

> **TURN &TALK** *Writers, what do you notice about how this writer ended her response? Why do you think it's important to include a strong ending? Talk about the ending with your partner.*

■ Guide students to realize that the conclusion of this response is a summary of the author's main opinions about the text. Be sure to point out that although this final section summarizes ideas that have been expressed before, it does so in different ways, with writing that is clear in its message and compelling in its craft.

Modeling

■ *Writers, I think I've done a good job of listing my opinions about Esther Forbes' book and backing them up with examples in the body of my response, but I want to be sure that my readers really get the message that I liked the book even though it was long and dense with historical details. I need a strong statement to begin my conclusion:* "Esther Forbes' famous novel is long and challenging to read, but it is definitely worth the effort."

■ *Watch as I summarize my reasons for saying this:* "Johnny Tremain weaves the fictional life of young Johnny with the factual historical events that led up to the Revolutionary War. This story of pride, adventure, tragedy, and hope will live on in your mind long after you've read the last page."

> **TURN &TALK** *Writers, did you notice how I summarized the same main ideas I discussed in the body of my response but in different ways? Did the conclusion of my response leave you with any doubts about my feelings and opinions? Did it make you want to read the book? Talk it over with your partner.*

WRITING and COACHING

■ Many students will struggle to write a conclusion that summarizes without simply repeating what they have already written. Help students who are stuck by explaining that the conclusion of an analytical response is a place to expose their emotions about the work. *I see that in the body of your response, you've said that the author's writing style is clever and humorous. Did parts of the book make you laugh out loud or fall off your chair? The conclusion is the place to say so!*

■ Encourage students to share their conclusions in progress with writing partners to solicit feedback. Students can then revise to clarify their main message or add more emotion to their writing.

■ Ask leading questions to help students expand their conclusions beyond one or two sentences: *Is there any weakness in the author's work? What makes up for it? What words in your response sum up your feelings? Did you read a fact or a critic's opinion (e.g., on a book cover) that you could include here? Is there an idea in your research notebook that you haven't used yet? Did you try a few introductions before you chose one? Could you use your alternate idea here?*

SHARING and REFLECTING

TURN &TALK *Find a partner you haven't worked with yet, and talk about what makes a strong conclusion to an analytical response. Imagine you are asked to teach someone else how to write a great conclusion. Tell your partner what you would say.*

■ Give students a chance to share their ideas, and then explain that once their drafts are complete, they will move on to revision, editing, and publishing in the sessions that follow.

■ Gather the drafts and analyze your students' attempts to write conclusions that summarize. Identify writers who may need additional modeling as well as those who are ready for higher levels of sophistication. Use the rubrics on the *Resources* CD-ROM to track writing proficiencies.

TIP Have students help you create a list of feeling or opinion words to use in their conclusions. Positive words might include *fantastic, exciting, lovely, compelling,* and so on, while negative words might be *boring, horrible, dull, stale,* and so on. Encourage students to try out new words when summarizing in their conclusions.

TIP Writers are likely to be in different places in the writing process by this point—some are still drafting while others are ready to revise or edit. A Workshop Organizer as shown in *A Guide to Teaching Nonfiction Writing,* page 49, is a great tool to help you monitor the stages of the process for your students.

SESSION 8
Revising for Effective Punctuation

Students carefully review their drafts and revise to include effective punctuation, focusing especially on direct quotes.

SESSION SNAPSHOT

Process Focus: Revising

Trait(s): Conventions

Mentor Text: *"Esperanza Rising* Will Raise Your Hopes, Too," by Mandy McDonald

TIP Less experienced writers may struggle with the idea of using punctuation for impact. Have these students focus first on revising for correct use of punctuation marks; then, work with them one-on-one or in small groups to review examples of impactful punctuation. Read aloud each example once without the punctuation and then with punctuation in place. Use your voice to demonstrate how the punctuation affects the writing's flow, sound, and impact.

FOCUSED MINILESSON

Reflect on the learning goals from the last session. If time allows, have students turn and talk about what they have learned so far.

Summarize the learning goals for this session: *In this session, you'll revise your drafts, focusing on using punctuation to help control the flow of your writing, to enhance its meaning, and to make sure your text evidence is credited properly.*

Using the Mentor Text

■ Read aloud the first paragraph in the section "Wonderful Writing," and focus on the second sentence: "She often conveys events and characters' emotions through small, clever details, such as when Tío Luis 'hands Mama Papa's silver belt buckle, the only one of its kind, engraved with the brand of the ranch'" (page 20).

> **TURN &TALK** *Writers, ignoring the commas for a moment, identify the punctuation marks in this sentence. What do these marks tell you?*

■ Lead a discussion to review the importance of using quotation marks to enclose a direct quote and parentheses to note the page reference. Have students identify other examples of quotes in the mentor text.

■ Invite students to find other punctuation marks in the mentor text and identify the purpose of each mark. Guide students to understand that punctuation marks help the writer clarify ideas, combine or separate thoughts, and add interest and impact to the response.

Modeling

■ *Today I am going to reread my entire response, focusing only on punctuation. I want to make sure that I have punctuated my text references correctly. I also want to be sure that I haven't missed opportunities to use punctuation in ways that make my message clearer or more interesting.*

■ Display your modeled writing, and have the class follow along as you read and think aloud. "It's 1775, and you live in colonial America. British soldiers are all over your town and refusing to allow needed supplies in. What do you do? Do you support their right to govern the colonies, or do you grab a gun and get ready for battle?" *I love how I started my response! Those questions will really grab my readers' attention and put them in the situation.* Continue reading to where you can use a comma to introduce an example. "Many authors just show you the perspective of the freedom fighters, but Esther Forbes also shows you the perspective of other people. Specifically she introduces the character of Lavinia, who is satisfied with the current situation in the colonies." *I need to put a comma after the linking word* specifically, *to set it off from the rest of the sentence. A comma tells the reader to pause, so it slows down the flow of words. This way, the part of the sentence that comes after the comma will have more impact. Reading my writing aloud helps me decide where to use a comma.*

- Continue reading through your response and thinking aloud about missing or ineffective punctuation. Emphasize that punctuation is both a necessity and a tool for writers. Demonstrate the importance of using a variety of punctuation marks to make your writing clear, lively, and interesting.

> Many authors just show you the perspective of the freedom fighters, but Esther Forbes also shows you the perspective of other people. Specifically⌄she introduces the character of Lavinia, who is satisfied with the current situation in the colonies.

Modeled Writing

WRITING and COACHING

- As writers begin to revise their work, encourage them to use a variety of punctuation marks for clarity and impact. Consider posting stellar examples of mentor sentences that use a variety of punctuation marks for students to use as reference and inspiration.

- Coach writers by asking leading questions such as *Where does this sentence end? Are there any phrases that need to be separated from the rest of the sentence?*

- Encourage writers to read their writing aloud slowly and listen for where they could use punctuation to improve the flow or impact of their ideas. Point out that they may also find places to change or delete punctuation that does not support their meaning.

- Remind writers to check their text references to make sure they have used quotation marks correctly and included page references.

- If writers are still drafting, encourage them to "revise as they go" by thinking carefully about their punctuation and including a variety of sentence types. Point out that revising is not an afterthought but an integral part of the writing process. Revising during writing makes the draft stronger and keeps the writer's mind on how to make the text engaging and easy to understand.

TIP Revision is a multifaceted process, and it can take a long time for writers to feel confident of their skills. It may be helpful to post a list of revision strategies or to offer revision checklists such as the ones on the *Resources CD-ROM.*

SHARING and REFLECTING

TURN &TALK *Writers, today we focused on revising to include a variety of punctuation marks to improve the flow, sound, and impact of our writing. Find a particularly well-punctuated paragraph in your writing, and read it aloud with expression to your partner.*

- Give partners a chance to share some of their paragraphs with the class, and then gather the drafts and analyze your students' attempts to revise for correct, varied, and impactful use of punctuation. Identify writers who have not moved beyond proper use of beginning and end punctuation, as well as those who are ready to use more sophisticated marks such as semicolons or dashes. Use the rubrics on the *Resources CD-ROM* to track writing proficiencies.

Using an Editing Checklist

Students use editing checklists and learn to use editing symbols to help them edit their final drafts.

SESSION SNAPSHOT

Process Focus: Editing

Trait(s): Conventions

FOCUSED MINILESSON

Reflect on the learning goals from the last session. If time allows, have students turn and talk about what they have learned so far.

Summarize the learning goals for this session: *Writers, today each of you will use an editing checklist to be sure that your writing is ready to share with others. We will also learn to use editing symbols to mark the changes we want to make when we publish our writing.*

Modeling

- Note: Make sure to leave some spelling and capitalization mistakes in your modeled writing so students will have some real editing to do.

- *An editing checklist is a great tool because it reminds us of important things to look for as we edit our writing. The best way to use an editing checklist is to start with the first item on the list and read your draft with only that editing point in mind. The first thing on our editing checklist is to make sure that we end each sentence with correct punctuation. I did a lot of work on punctuation in our last session, but I want to give my draft one more look. Watch as I read through my introduction. Notice that I am only checking the end punctuation. I am not thinking about spelling or capital letters right now—only about end punctuation. That makes it easier to catch mistakes! If I find a place where I need to add an end mark, I can just add it, or I can use a caret mark to show where I want to insert the mark.*

- *The next point on our checklist is to capitalize words at the beginning of a sentence. Watch as I read through my introduction again. I will run my finger under each sentence and make sure the first word is capitalized. If I find a letter I need to capitalize, I will draw three small lines under the letter. That will remind me to capitalize it in my final text.*

- *The next point on our checklist is to capitalize proper nouns. Watch as I skim my introduction and look for proper nouns, which include the book's title, author's name, characters' names, place-names, and historical events. Oops. I forgot to capitalize the W in "Revolutionary war." I'll draw three lines underneath the w.*

TURN &TALK *The next item on our checklist is spelling. Partners, read this part of my response, focusing only on spelling. How should I edit this section?*

■ As students point out the misspelled words in your model, remind them of any tools or resources that are available in your classroom for help with spelling, such as high-frequency word lists and word walls. Demonstrate how you cross out the misspelled word and use a caret mark to insert the correctly spelled word.

WRITING and COACHING

■ Have writers systematically use their checklists to review their drafts for each editing point. If they appear overwhelmed by the checklist, remind them that the items on the list are things they already know how to do.

■ Coach editors with questions such as *What are you editing for? Have you read through the entire piece for that point before moving on to the next?*

■ Remind writers who are still drafting and revising that they will be expected to use an editing checklist when they are ready to review their final drafts.

SHARING and REFLECTING

TURN &TALK *Share your edited draft with your partner. What did you change? How did the checklist help you? What might you do differently next time?*

■ Give students a chance to share their reflections on the editing checklist, and then gather the drafts and analyze your students' attempts to use editing symbols. Identify writers who may need additional modeling as well as those who are ready for higher levels of sophistication. Use the rubrics on the *Resources* CD-ROM to track writing proficiencies and tailor future instruction.

TIP The editing checklist should be carefully matched to the developmental level and previous editing experiences of your writers. As students learn more editing skills, the checklist can be updated. You can post the checklist in the classroom or place individual copies in students' writer's notebooks.

TIP Examples of editing checklists can be found on the *Resources* CD-ROM. If struggling writers are overwhelmed, cross out some of the items so they can focus on just a few points. Always tailor editing checklists to students' individual needs.

SESSION 10
Publishing and Sharing

Students publish their polished responses, focusing on visuals that support their opinions about the book.

SESSION SNAPSHOT

Process Focus: Presenting, Publishing

Trait(s): Organization, Conventions, Voice

Mentor Text: "*Esperanza Rising* Will Raise Your Hopes, Too," by Mandy McDonald

BEFORE THE LESSON

Decide in advance what format you will use to publish your analytical response. This lesson centers on a straightforward booklet with hand-drawn illustrations, but other options include a poster (see the *Resources* CD-ROM for sample), video presentation, electronic slide show, or bulletin board display for the school library or media center.

FOCUSED MINILESSON

Review the learning goals from the last session, and summarize the learning goals for today: *In our last session, we used an editing checklist to look over our writing one more time. Now it's time for us to publish and present our analytical responses. It's an exciting time because we get to take our drafts and embellish them with visuals, type choices, and interesting page layouts.*

Using the Mentor Text

■ Revisit the mentor text, this time focusing on its layout, design, and visual elements.

> **TURN &TALK** *Writers, what do you notice about how this analytical response is presented? How do the layout, type choices, and other visual elements enhance the writer's response about* Esperanza Rising? *Talk it over with your partner.*

■ Give students a chance to share their thoughts and opinions, making sure they notice the writer's use of drawings, pull quotes, and typography to support her message.

Modeling

■ *Writers, I particularly like the way the writer of our mentor text used quotes from her response to highlight important points. These are called "pull quotes" because the writer literally pulls them from what has already been written. I think pull quotes will call attention to the important points I want to make in my response.*

■ Display a copy of your final draft, using an overhead projector, electronic whiteboard, or some other projection device. *Writers, I would like my readers to know that this novel blends historical facts with fiction. As I skim my response, I find a sentence that perfectly expresses this point: "*Johnny Tremain *has a fascinating blend of accurate historical facts mixed with fictional characters." This will make a great pull quote! Watch as I circle it on my draft so I will remember it when I'm ready to publish.*

> **TURN &TALK** *Writers, scan my response and look for other sentences that might make good pull quotes. Share your ideas with your partners.*

■ Give students a chance to share their ideas, circling their suggestions on your draft.

■ *I've identified a few pull quotes to use when I publish my response, and now I need to figure out where I'll put them. It's time to plan a page layout that will incorporate the title and body of my response, my pull quotes, and drawings of some of the interesting elements in the novel. I'm going to start with my title page. I've come up with a title that captures my topic and my point of view in a few words:* "Johnny Tremain: A Novel That Takes You Back to the American Revolution." *Next, I'll write my byline. Now I'm ready to insert my introductory paragraph. I will put a picture of a Minute Man here with a caption to capture the reader's attention and give a visual clue to the time I am describing.*

■ *As I lay out the sections of my response, I want to incorporate text features that will help make my writing understandable and interesting to a reader. I wrote each section with a main idea, and I can use that main idea as a heading. For example, my first section is about the main character. I will write* "Johnny—A Fictional Character Who Lives History" *as my heading and make the letters larger and darker so they stand out. I have circled a pull quote for this section, so I'll include it on this page.*

■ Continue modeling options for page layouts and visuals, highlighting the way you can enhance text sections with headings, pull quotes, pictures, and captions to create a clear and visually pleasing arrangement.

WRITING and COACHING

■ For writers who are ready to present and publish, provide access to crayons, markers, and colored pencils for the writers to create illustrations or frame their texts.

■ For writers who may still be drafting or revising, assure them that they can think about their layouts and presentations while they move forward with their writing.

■ Note that students will likely need more than one session for publishing, so you will want to plan additional time.

SHARING and REFLECTING

TURN &TALK *Writers, think together. What are the features of a great analytical response? What advice would you give to students in another class who wanted to write their own analytical responses?*

■ Consider arranging a time when students can share their responses with another class. Be sure to have your students point out the features of an analytical response and describe the process they used to publish their final work. You might want to have the librarian display the responses next to the books.

■ Gather the students' final pieces, and analyze their attempts at presentation. Identify writers who may need additional modeling as well as those who are ready for higher levels of sophistication. Use the rubrics on the *Resources* CD-ROM to track writing proficiencies and tailor future instruction.

TIP Students who need additional support in choosing titles and headings would benefit from a small-group writing session in which you guide them in examining several nonfiction resources for ideas on how to create titles and headings that are informative and interesting.

Quote It!

Draw inferences from quotations.

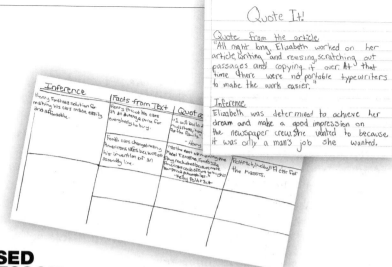

FEATURES

- Quotation
- Inferences derived from the quotation
- Support for inferences
- Citation
- Summarizing paragraph

BEFORE THE LESSON

Print "A Car for the Masses" from the *Resources* CD-ROM for students' reference. Read the article with students before the lesson.

FOCUSED MINILESSON

Today I want to extend my thinking as I respond to an article and draw inferences. An inference is an idea that is not directly stated in an article. Instead, it is supported by facts and background knowledge. Sometimes a quotation can be a fact. After all, a quotation is a person's actual words. What better way to get insight into someone? I am going to use this Quote It! Planner to capture a quotation and then make inferences based on it. Display the planner on chart paper, or project it with a document camera.

One of the things that struck me when I read this article was that Henry Ford had some compelling reasons for wanting to create the Model T. One reason that he wanted to create a car was to make sure that many people could own a car. Here is a quotation from the article—a quotation from Henry Ford himself. Watch as I record it in the planner: " 'But it will be low in price that no man making a good salary will be unable to own one.'—Henry Ford." *Notice that I put the quotation in quotation marks to show that it is the exact words of the speaker. I also write a dash and put the speaker's name to be sure that he is credited for what he says. Now I want to draw an inference about the quotation. An inference is an idea that is based on facts and what I know, too. It's what I think based on the quotation. I think it was important to Ford that people be able to buy cars, even if they weren't the richest people. Watch as I record my inference in the box:* "Before . . . sell."

TURN &TALK *Writers, what do you think about this inference? Is it supported by the quotation? Why do you think so?*

I want to write why I chose this particular quotation. I think it shows Henry Ford's dream to make an affordable car. It's important to remember that. Without his desire to do that, who knows how long it would have taken for more than just the wealthiest drivers to own cars? Without Ford's dream, it may have taken many more years before people could buy their own cars.

Repeat the process with another quotation from the article. Show how you choose a quotation, draw an inference, and explain why that quotation is important. As time allows, elicit students' assistance in drawing inferences.

Quote It! Planner

Quotation from Article	Inference Based on Quotation	Why I Selected This Quote
"But it will be low in price that no man making a good salary will be unable to own one."—Henry Ford	Before Ford's Model T, cars were expensive—too expensive for most people to buy. Ford wanted anyone with a job to be able to afford a car. He cared about people, and he also knew he could sell something he could sell.	Ford invented an assembly line to make his cars affordable. The assembly line was successful!
"As the cost of making the Model T dropped, Ford's sales skyrocketed because more Americans could afford to buy his low-priced automobiles."—Kelly Poltrack	Ford invented an assembly line to make his cars affordable. The assembly line was successful!	To show that Ford not only had the desire to make cars more affordable he also had the know-how to get the job done.

Source: Poltrack, Kelly. "A Car for the Masses"

Modeled Writing

It's important for my readers to know from where I extracted these quotations. They might want to read the article themselves, and it gives some oomph to my writing to show that I have used a real source! Watch as I list the author of the article, last name first. I use the last name as an organizational tool. If I consulted other works about the automobile, I'd put all my references in alphabetical order. Now I am finishing with the name of the article in quotation marks. If this were a book, I'd underline the title instead.

TURN &TALK *Writers, take a close look at the work I've done so far. What other inferences might you be able to draw from the quotations we chose?*

Summarize the features: Have students take a close look at their Quote It! Planners to note the features and to create a list of tips for using the strategy. Have students share their ideas as you note them on a wall chart for reference.

WRITING and COACHING

Writers, use the Quote It! Planner to record another quotation from the article. Explain what inference you can draw from the quotation, and tell why you chose it.

Support individuals or small groups as necessary. Guide writers to identify inferences that can be fully supported by the text. If students need help getting started, provide a quotation and several inferences, asking students which inference is best supported by the quotation. With this kind of scaffolding, students will soon be able to draw inferences on their own and support them with both evidence and background knowledge.

SHARING and REFLECTING

Sum it up! *Writers, I noticed you chose quotations that were rich with opportunity for inferences. Your citations show your readers that you've pulled the quotation directly from a source, so you are giving authors and speakers credit.*

TURN &TALK *You'll be meeting a partner to share your Quote It! responses. Before you meet, check your work against the features list. Are all the features in place? Take the time to add anything that's missing from your responses.*

ASSESS THE LEARNING

Analyze the Quote It! Planners to determine which students need assistance to draw inferences based on quotations.

SELF-ASSESSMENT

SELF-ASSESSMENT **Quote It!**	YES	NO
1. Quotation	☐	☐
2. Inferences derived from the quotation	☐	☐
3. Support for inferences	☐	☐
4. Citation	☐	☐
5. Summarizing paragraph ☺	☐	☐

▶TAKE IT FORWARD

▸ Once students have used their planners to show support for inferences with textual evidence, encourage them to craft paragraphs with the information on their planners. Model how to write the inference in the topic sentence and craft sentences that support that topic sentence with facts and quotations from the text.

▸ Students may want to create posters that feature provocative and intriguing quotations about various topics. Have them use various sources to collect a variety of quotations all focused on one topic. Encourage them to compare and contrast points of view.

▸ Work with students to create more sophisticated citation lists—bibliographies. Post examples showing how to quote various types of sources, such as websites, magazine articles, and nonfiction books. Be sure to emphasize how to use quotation marks to enclose the exact words of a speaker or the exact words from a source.

▸ Encourage students to return to responses they have previously crafted to insert a quotation from a text. The quotation should support inferences about the text. Be sure students accurately cite the source of the quotation.

Summary: Main Ideas

Determine two or more main ideas, and support them with details from the text.

FEATURES

- Opening statement: gist
- Paragraph headings represent main ideas
- Evidence from text under headings
- Linking words to add information: *because, so, when, since, also, and, besides, in addition, for example, it is important to note, to illustrate*
- Concluding statement that recaps main idea(s)

BEFORE THE LESSON

Read the article "Antarctica: Frozen Desert" with students to prepare for writing. (See the *Resources* CD-ROM.) Print the article for students' reference.

FOCUSED MINILESSON

Antarctica is such a mysterious place! I found this article fascinating. I want to share ideas in the article with readers, so I am going to reread it with a closer eye toward main ideas. After I identify some main ideas, I am going to write a few sentences to support each one more fully.

To begin, I am writing a gist statement. The gist statement is a preview of the content, but it doesn't tell everything in the writing. It just piques readers' interest so they'll want to find out more. Watch as I begin: "When you picture a desert, you probably think of scorching temperatures and blowing sand. But believe it or not, the icy expanse of Antarctica is a desert!"

TURN &TALK *Take a closer look at the gist statement. How does it capture main ideas from the article? What suggestions might you have for making it even more powerful?*

Now it's time to think about the main ideas. One main idea is that Antarctica is a desert. I am going to write that heading as a question, because I think that surprises a lot of people. They wonder how such a cold place can be a desert. Another main idea is that plants and animals need to be adapted to survive in such a place. Not all plants and animals can thrive in that environment. So, I'll make that a heading, too.

Now I'll turn to the first heading: "Why is Antarctica a desert?" *I was thinking about starting with the sentence* "It's dry there." *That sentence certainly answers the question, but I want to develop this main idea with more details from the text. Watch as I begin:* "A desert is . . . you can see." *I want to emphasize that not only is Antarctica cold, but it's also dry, and that's what makes it a desert. So, I am inserting a group of linking words to show that I am adding information. I am beginning with* "But it's important to note. . . ."

TURN &TALK *Partners, I need your advice. I want to write about the next heading,* "How do plants and animals survive?" *What should I do as I continue?*

Think aloud as you write a paragraph focused on the main idea of plants' and animals' adaptations and how they allow organisms to survive. Point out that the details come in your response to the text and not from your own background knowledge. Showcase your thinking as you use the linking word *because* to add information.

Polar bears are Endaingered
They need many things to survive but some of these things are becoming less and less, let me tell you what these things are.

Getting Fat is Important
The polar bear eats four to five days. Bears also need to build up layers of blubber by eating lots of food. They travel way up to 660 pounds even more. Getting fat creates layers of blubber that helps them keep warm.

It's harder for bears to survive
When Ice melts earlier. When Ice melts early It's harder for bears to survive because they go to land wich is closer to humans and they eat trash. They get more tierd when on land than snow.

Polar bears are Endaingered. Finding food is harder. Pack Ice is breaking faster and thats why the have to go on land were humans are and eat garbage and don't have enough fat and can staive to death.

Summarize the features: Display your modeled writing, and ask students to reflect on the features of a response focused on main ideas and details. As they name features, list them on a wall chart. Post the wall chart for students' reference as they write.

WRITING and COACHING

Writers, think carefully about the features I modeled as you create a summary of another nonfiction text. Begin with a gist statement to frame the rest of your work. Then, organize your summary with headings, noting important details in fully developed sentences under each heading. Use linking words and phrases to add information.

Check in with writers, and offer support for those who need it. Provide the Main Idea Response Organizer from the *Resources* CD-ROM. You might pull together a small group of students who need additional instruction in using linking words that add information.

SHARING and REFLECTING

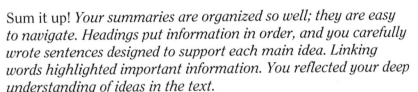

Sum it up! *Your summaries are organized so well; they are easy to navigate. Headings put information in order, and you carefully wrote sentences designed to support each main idea. Linking words highlighted important information. You reflected your deep understanding of ideas in the text.*

TURN &TALK *Get ready to take home both the text and your summary to share with your families. What features of the summary do you want to point out to your families? With your partner, discuss ideas. Then, jot them down on the back of the summary to help you remember.*

ASSESS THE LEARNING

Have students use the self-assessment checklist to determine with which features they may need your support. Some students may be ready for additional features. Pull them together in a group to take it forward!

When you picture a desert, you probably think of scorching temperatures and blowing sand. But believe it or not, the icy expanse of Antarctica is a desert!

Why is Antarctica a desert?

A desert is a region that receives very little precipitation. Unlike most deserts, Antarctica is frigid, with ice and snow as far as the eye can see. It's important to note that the continent is also very dry—so it's classified as a desert.

How do plants and animals survive?

Plants and animals in Antarctica are hardy! Some plants, mostly mosses, thrive only in a very small ice-free region while others grow only in the summer. Because of the climate, many animals live on the continent only during the breeding season. The year-round inhabitants are tiny ground-huggers.

Modeled Writing

SELF-ASSESSMENT

SELF-ASSESSMENT		
Summary: Main Ideas		
	YES	NO
1. Opening statement: gist	☐	☐
2. Paragraph headings represent main ideas	☐	☐
3. Evidence from text under headings	☐	☐
4. Linking words to add information: *because, so, when, since, also, and, besides, in addition, for example, it is important to note, to illustrate*	☐	☐
5. Concluding statement that recaps main idea(s) ⊙	☐	☐

▷TAKE IT FORWARD

▸ Provide opportunities for students to add concluding statements to their work. Offer a variety of powerful endings from mentor texts for students to consider. Students can work in teams to write endings for the modeled writing before moving to drafting conclusions of their own summaries.

▸ Students may want to revisit other summaries they have written to look for opportunities to insert headings for added organization. As they consider where to place headings, they may also notice that they have some details that need to be moved to other sections. Reinforce the idea that headings reflect gist statements. If students' previous gist statements are not strong, they may want to revise them as well.

Compare and Contrast

Compare and contrast two or more subjects, settings, or events.

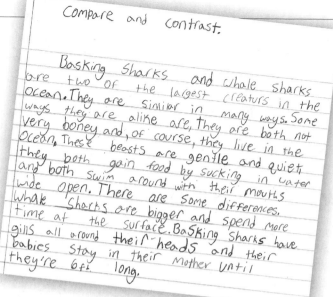

Compare and contrast.

Basking Sharks and whale sharks are two of the largest creatures in the ocean. They are similar in many ways. Some ways they are alike are, they are both not very boney and, of course, they live in the ocean. These beasts are gentle and quiet, they both gain food by sucking in water and both swim around with their mouths wide open. There are some differences. Whale sharks are bigger and spend more time at the surface. Basking Sharks have gills all around their heads and their babies stay in their mother until they're 6ft long.

FEATURES

- Opening: gist statement
- Linking words of comparison: *however, but, although, on the other hand, similarly, likewise, in contrast to, both*
- Specific details
- Conclusion
- Supporting graphic or visual

BEFORE THE LESSON

Share a resource, such as Seymour Simon's *Volcanoes* or a nonfiction magazine article about volcanoes with students. Consider using a topic from an area of study in your class.

FOCUSED MINILESSON

Writers, today I want to showcase information about two types of volcanoes in a paragraph that compares and contrasts, or tells how two or more subjects are alike and different. I have two resources to help me with this. One is a list of linking words that compare and contrast to help me. The other is the book we read, Seymour Simon's Volcanoes. *With all the great information, it's going to be easy to respond to the text by drawing out facts about two types of volcanoes—shield volcanoes and composite volcanoes.*

I am going to begin with a gist statement. A gist statement pulls the readers in with a preview of the information but doesn't give away all the details. Watch as I begin: "Volcanoes may cause massive amounts of destruction in a flash or just emit wispy puffs of smoke—it all depends on the type of volcano!" *Notice in my gist statement that I included specific details about two types of volcanoes. Now my readers will want to know—how does the type of volcano affect the amount of destruction it can cause? I have my readers' attention. Now it's time to tell how two types of volcanoes—shield volcanoes and composite volcanoes—are alike and different.*

TURN & TALK *Partners, think together. Identify some ways in which shield and composite volcanoes are alike and different. Be ready to share.*

I think it's important to note that each volcano expels magma from under the ground. I am going to use a linking word of comparison to highlight this similarity: both. *Watch as I begin:* "Both shield and composite volcanoes. . . ." *The magma in a shield volcano is thin and runny. That's a specific detail I want to capture in a sentence. Composite volcanoes have a different type of magma. To highlight the difference between them, I am using a linking phrase to showcase the difference:* in contrast. *Watch as I write about the magma, inserting the phrase* in contrast *as an opening element:* "The magma in a shield volcano is thin and runny. In contrast, the magma in a composite volcano is thick and sticky."

Continue writing, thinking aloud as you consider specific details about the volcanoes that underscore how they are alike and different. Be sure to show that you are responding to a text by culling facts directly from the resource. Carefully

---

Volcanoes may cause massive amounts of destruction in a flash or just emit wispy puffs of smoke—it all depends on the type of volcano! Both shield and composite volcanoes expel magma from deep under the ground. The magma in a shield volcano is thin and runny. In contrast, the magma in a composite volcano is thick and sticky. A shield volcano builds slowly as lava peacefully flows down the sides. Composite volcanoes, on the other hand, explode as pressure builds, sending huge clouds of gas and chunks of burning rock into the sky. Which volcano would you be more willing to explore up close?

Modeled Writing

choose linking words to show similarities and differences. *Now I want to add a conclusion to the paragraph. I could just restate the beginning or say something like* "Now you know how these two volcanoes are alike and different." *But I'd rather end with a question that leaves my readers thinking. One of these volcanoes is very explosive, but the other is safer to be around. Watch as I wrap up with an intriguing question as a conclusion:* "Which volcano would you be more willing to explore up close?"

TURN &TALK *Partners, think together as you evaluate the writing. What words point out similarities and differences? How can I make this stronger?*

Summarize the features: Have students turn to their writer's notebooks and list features of writing that compares and contrasts. They can compare their lists with partners to be sure they aren't missing any important features.

WRITING and COACHING

Choose at least two other subjects or events to compare and contrast based on reading that you have done. You might, for example, compare and contrast body systems, rock classifications, types of volcanoes, or Revolutionary War battles. As you compare and contrast, remember to include specific details that you cull directly from the text. Think carefully about how you will link ideas in your writing and wrap up the paragraph.

Confer with partner teams or small groups to support and scaffold understanding. Provide the Linking Words That Signal Comparisons from the *Resources* CD-ROM for students who need additional support.

SHARING and REFLECTING

Sum it up! *Your writing to compare and contrast reflects deep thinking about facts in a text. You not only included important details but also masterfully chose linking words to underscore similarities and striking differences in the topics you chose. Your gist statements got your writing off to a strong start—I know I was hanging on every word right from the first one! You wrapped up the writing nicely, too.*

TURN &TALK *Get together with a new partner to share your writing. What features of writing that compares and contrasts did you both use? List them together.*

▷TAKE IT FORWARD

▸ Students may want to create Venn diagrams either to organize their thoughts or to support their writing. Share the features of this visual text for those who are ready. Labeled diagrams or other graphics may support students' writing. Model adding labeled diagrams to your model to illustrate the shapes of different volcanoes.

▸ Encourage students to infuse a variety of openings into their writing. Powerful writing may begin, for example, with a quotation or statistic, a thought-provoking question, or a strong sensory image. Share mentor texts with particularly strong beginnings, and challenge students to analyze what about these beginnings makes them especially noteworthy.

▸ Encourage students to return to comparisons and contrasts they have previously written with an eye toward revising for linking words. Model how to use linking words in a variety of positions in sentences, such as opening elements that are followed by commas or conjunctions that join phrases and clauses together.

Summarizing from Multiple Sources

Determine main ideas in multiple texts, and support them with details from the text.

Sea Turtles

Sea turtles, the gentle giants of the ocean, are making a come back with the help of humans. After years of being endangered, it is exciting to see that turtle populations around the world are growing and people are the reason!

People are doing a better job of controlling waste so there are few pollutants in the ocean. In addition, shrimp fishermen have devised new kinds of nets that allow the turtles to escape shrimp nets so they don't drown by staying under water too long. It is also helpful that scientists sometimes collect sea turtle eggs and protect them in a lab until they hatch. Then they return the babies to the beach where their mother laid the eggs and make sure that they safely cross the beach and slide into the sea.

Sources:

Allen, Saving the Turtles. New York, 2008.

http://en.wikipedia.org/wiki/Sea_turtle

FEATURES

- Opens with a gist statement
- Headings
- Details using justification from multiple sources
- Linking words to connect ideas: *because, so, when, since, also, and, besides, in addition, for example*
- ▶ Conclusion
- ▶ Visuals
- ▶ List of sources

BEFORE THE LESSON

Read the articles "Let There Be Light" and "Out of Darkness" with students to prepare for writing. (See the *Resources* CD-ROM.) Print the articles for students' reference.

FOCUSED MINILESSON

When we write nonfiction, we often use multiple sources to gather ideas. That way, we can be assured we have a complete picture of a subject. I have two articles about the invention of the lightbulb. My goal is to read both of them for main ideas and details. I want to be able to justify my main ideas with details from more than one source if I can. First, I want to focus on this article—"Let There Be Light." For right now, I want to gather information about who invented the lightbulb. Watch as I take notes. I am jotting down some important details about what inspired Thomas Edison and his team and who worked on bringing electric light into businesses and homes. Notice that I am writing phrases from the articles. I don't need to write complete sentences, because I am only taking notes.

Think aloud as you take notes from both sources. Move into another main idea as you take notes—how a lightbulb works. Showcase your thinking as you categorize ideas to make them easier to infuse into your writing later.

I have gathered details by taking notes about both sources. Now I am ready to write. To begin, I am going to use a gist statement. A gist statement gets readers interested without giving away all the details. I want to pull my readers right into the topic, so I am beginning with a scenario. Before there were lightbulbs, people had to use candles or dangerous gas lamps for light. I am going to write a gist statement with a "you are there" scenario to get my readers interested. Watch as I begin: "Can you imagine. . . ."

TURN &TALK *Partners, evaluate my gist statement. What information does it preview? How does it capture interest?*

With my gist statement written, it's time to start my writing. One main idea focuses on who invented the lightbulb. I am crafting a heading that I'll make stand out by using a bold marker and by having it set aside on its own line: "Who invented. . . ?" *As I write about this heading, I'll include details from both texts and focus only on this heading. There is a lot of exciting information about lightbulbs, but that will have to wait! Watch as I begin:* "Inspired by the work of . . . New York City!" *I realize that this makes it sound like Edison invented the lightbulb all by himself. Others worked on it with him. I am going to add more information about inventors. Watch as I use a linking word to show that I am connecting ideas:* "In addition, a team of scientists. . . ."

TURN &TALK *What advice would you give me as I continue? Turn to your partner as you talk about what you would do next.*

Think aloud as you create a paragraph to describe how a lightbulb works. Be sure that you are using details from your notes as you craft the paragraph, showing students how to turn notes from sources into writing. Use at least one linking word to connect ideas.

Summarize the features: Display your model and ask students to reflect on the features of a response focused on main ideas and details from multiple sources. Have them note features in lists in their writer's notebooks for reference.

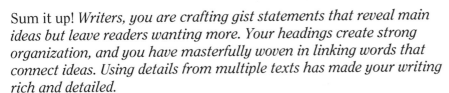

The Light Bulb—A Brilliant Invention!

Can you imagine doing your homework by candlelight or risking burning your house down by lighting a gas lamp? Before the invention of the light bulb, light could be dim—or dangerous!

Who invented the light bulb?

Inspired by the work of Edward Weston's invention of the arc lamp, Thomas Alva Edison explored the idea of creating an electrical lighting system to light up all of lower New York City! In addition, a team of scientists tirelessly tested ideas that made electric light bulbs long lasting and safe.

How does a light bulb work?

A light bulb is made of glass and sealed to keep air out with a filament bulging up into the bulb. Electricity is passed through the filament. Edison faced an obstacle, though. What material was best for the filament? He tried many materials, for example, platinum, wood, and even coconut hair. The best material turned out to be carbonized cotton sewing thread. Eventually, the team used a metal called tungsten.

Modeled Writing

WRITING and COACHING

Writers, you'll be following the steps I modeled to respond to multiple texts. Start with a powerful gist statement that will capture readers' attention, and then use headings to organize your work. Be sure the headings reflect information from both the resources you used. Support each heading with details from the texts, and use linking words.

As students work, take note of those who need additional scaffolding. Provide the Main Idea Response Organizer from the *Resources* CD-ROM for students who need assistance to get started. Note those who are ready to add more sophisticated features to their writing.

SHARING and REFLECTING

Sum it up! *Writers, you are crafting gist statements that reveal main ideas but leave readers wanting more. Your headings create strong organization, and you have masterfully woven in linking words that connect ideas. Using details from multiple texts has made your writing rich and detailed.*

TURN &TALK *Get ready to share your summaries with partners. Take a look at your writing to be sure that all the features are in place. Use the self-assessment checklist. Once you are sure all the features are in place, meet with your partner to share your work.*

ASSESS THE LEARNING

Analyze students' work to identify those writers who need additional support to determine main ideas and to support them with details from the text. Be sure students understand how to craft gist statements. Look for use of linking words to connect ideas from multiple sources.

SELF-ASSESSMENT

SELF-ASSESSMENT

Summarizing from Multiple Sources

	YES	NO
1. Open with a gist statement	☐	☐
2. Headings	☐	☐
3. Details using justification from multiple sources	☐	☐
4. Linking words to connect ideas: *because, so, when, since, also, and, besides, in addition, for example*	☐	☐
5. Conclusion ⊙	☐	☐
6. Visuals ⊙	☐	☐
7. List sources ⊙	☐	☐

▶TAKE IT FORWARD

▸ Model how to craft a strong conclusion so that students who are ready can follow your lead. Consider several possibilities, such as restating the gist statement or closing with a quotation from Thomas Edison.

▸ Encourage students to add visuals to their main idea responses. Have them consider which visuals would most support their text—photographs with captions? Charts or tables? Maps? Timelines? Share examples of

visuals from mentor texts for reference and inspiration.

▸ Students can create bibliographies or works cited lists to note which sources they used to create their summaries. Work with them to list authors' names and names of texts or articles. Provide a reference for students to use to list electronic sources as well. (See the *Resources* CD-ROM for Citation Formats.)

▸ Have students return to responses they have already written to infuse linking words that connect ideas. Show them a variety of ways to use linking words. Some can be used to combine short sentences and phrases, while others are perfect for opening elements followed by commas. Model how to revise with a caret mark.

Partner Book Review

Compare text structures and information.

FEATURES

- Linking words of comparison: *however, but, although, on the other hand, similarly, even though, still, though, yet, also, likewise, similarly*

- Signal words are identified for target text types

- Specific examples from texts

- Rating for each book

- Justification for rating

▷ Introduction

FOCUSED MINILESSON

Writers, today I want to review some books we've read. Instead of just focusing on whether I liked the books and what made them my favorites—or not—I want to dig deeper. I am going to take a look at the structures of these texts. I am going to be thinking, What clues to the structure did I find? Is this the right structure to use for this kind of information? To help me with this, I am going to use a special form where I can capture the information before I write. Display the form on chart paper or with a document camera. *Notice that this form is divided into parts to note the text structure and the clues that helped me figure it out as well as to rate the book. I also have a text structure chart to remind me of the various structures.*

I am starting with Walter Wick's book A Drop of Water. *Flipping through the book, I notice that this book is focused on description. I am noting that in the structure section.*

TURN & TALK *Partners, think together. What clues in the book verify that this book is a descriptive text? Identify a few clues together.*

This book lists features and attributes of water. I also noted words like for example *that point to an overall descriptive text structure. I am noting these in the chart, too. Now it's time to rate the book. I am giving the book a 3.5 out of 5 for text structure. Why this rating? I think the structure is perfect for telling more about water. But many of the descriptions are short. The photographs carry the descriptions. So that's why it doesn't get a higher ranking from me. The content, on the other hand, is near perfect for me. The photographs are compelling, and that makes this content stand out. Notice that I am capturing all these justifications for my ranking right on the planner. It's important not just to assign a ranking but to explain where my ranking comes from.*

Lead students to fill in the chart for another nonfiction text. Focus on text structure, eliciting clues from students that point them to the structure of the book. Have them work with you to rate the book and to justify the rankings.

Now that I have gathered information about both books, I am going to compare and contrast them. I am focusing on how each author used text structure and on my rankings. As I

Book Review

A Drop of Water	Passage to Freedom
Walter Wick	Ken Mochizuki
Walter Wick	Dom Lee
Two nonfiction books open readers' eyes to different worlds—the fascinating world of water and the world of people literally fighting for their lives.	
Description Clues that helped you identify it ▪ lists features ▪ lists attributes ▪ for example ▪ like	**Chronology** Clues that helped you identify it ▪ describes events in order ▪ when ▪ I was five years old. ▪ For about a month ▪ Every day
Rating: Use of Text Structure: 3.5 Content: 3.5 Overall: 4	**Rating:** Use of Text Structure: 4.5 Content: 3.5 Overall: 4
▪ text structure great for telling about water ▪ descriptions are short—more information is carried in the photographs than the text ▪ Fascinating content brought to life in new ways	▪ chronological order—good way to tell a true story ▪ limited by point of view ▪ a lot of unanswered questions—what happened to the family? to the refugees?
While A Drop of Water is a descriptive text that offers amazing glimpses into the science of water, Passage to Freedom is the true story of one man's sacrifice to save refugees from the Nazis. While both books earn a ranking of 4, they have different strengths. A Drop of Water showcases water science with striking photographs and compelling captions. Passage to Freedom tells a gripping story but leaves the reader with many unanswered questions.	

Modeled Writing

compare and contrast, I am going to use linking words of comparison to showcase both similarities and differences. Write the comparison as you showcase your thinking, drawing ideas directly from your planning sheet.

TURN &TALK *Writers, think together. How does honing in on text structure really help you do deep thinking about texts? What else might you add to this review?*

Summarize the features: Have students work in small groups to list the steps in comparing and contrasting text structures and using information to rate books. Compile groups' lists to create a master chart to display along with the model review.

WRITING and COACHING

Choose two more books to evaluate with your partner. Use the text structure chart to help you determine the structure. Think carefully about the information in each text and why you would give each text a particular rating. Then, consider ways to infuse linking words into your comparison of the texts.

Pull together small groups of students who need assistance with identifying text structures. Some students may also benefit from small-group instruction on using linking words to compare. Be sure students are justifying their rankings.

SHARING and REFLECTING

Sum it up! *Your responses show a deep level of thinking about the structure of the writing and the information in resources. As you compared and contrasted resources, you carefully rated them and justified your rankings. Your work shows evidence of careful analysis!*

TURN &TALK *We are going to share books with our third-grade reading buddies based on which ranked the highest! How will you explain your choice of books to share? Be ready to share your reviews. List a few important features you want to talk about.*

ASSESS THE LEARNING

Analyze reviews to determine which students are able to justify their rankings, use specific examples, identify text structures, and use linking words of comparison.

SELF-ASSESSMENT

SELF-ASSESSMENT

Partner Book Review

	YES	NO
1. **Linking words of comparison:** *however, but, although, on the other hand, similarly, even though, still, though, yet, also, likewise, similarly*	☐	☐
2. **Signal words are identified for target text types**	☐	☐
3. **Specific examples from texts**	☐	☐
4. **Rating for each book**	☐	☐
5. **Justification for rating**	☐	☐
6. **Introduction**	☐	☐

▶TAKE IT FORWARD

▸ Model adding an introduction to your review. An introduction should mention both resources, preparing the readers for the rest of the review. Model several options, such as a statement about the two texts or a question that ties the two together.

▸ Challenge students to move beyond the planning sheet and write powerful reviews. Rather than including numerical ratings, students can craft sentences that explain both justifications and the reasoning behind them.

▸ Students can create reviews of products, movies, musical selections, and so on. Remind them to justify their ratings and to compare two or more using linking words of comparison.

▸ Have students evaluate sources to determine if authors made the best use of text structure. Guide their thinking. *Is this structure the best way to tell about the events of the Civil War? Why do you think so?* or *Would you have chosen this structure for a description of sedimentary rocks? What structure might work better?*

Two-Word Strategy: Lewis and Clark

Choose two words that describe the traits of significant historical figures.

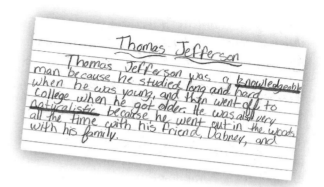

FEATURES

- Two words that offer inferences based on details in a text
- Justification with real events or factual content
- Bold words
- Supporting visuals

BEFORE THE LESSON

Present a text or nonfiction resource about Lewis and Clark. Share the book as a read-aloud, or do a book talk, sharing the essence of the content. Have sticky notes on hand to note Two-Word Strategy words about Lewis and Clark. You might consider adapting the think-aloud to a current unit of study in your classroom.

FOCUSED MINILESSON

Writers, today I want to select two words—only two—that reflect my thinking about Lewis and Clark and their expedition. I am thinking about what I learned in the book we read. I learned that Lewis and Clark went to an area that was largely unexplored. Even Thomas Jefferson thought that they would find creatures like woolly mammoths, which could definitely be scary. They weren't even sure what the terrain would be like as they traveled or what they might encounter. That made these men courageous. Watch as I write the word courageous *on a sticky note and place it on the chart paper. The book doesn't use the word* courageous *to describe Lewis and Clark. But when I think about the facts, that word definitely comes to mind.*

I am using a second sticky note to add the word diplomatic *to the chart paper. I know that Lewis and Clark met people with whom they had to be diplomatic. They needed to establish relationships with people they met along the way. This helped ensure the safety of the men and their team and allowed them to survive, so this was an important quality to have! The book didn't use this word to describe Lewis and Clark, but it makes sense given the facts in the book.*

TURN &TALK *Partners, take a close look at the words I've selected. Do they reflect the most important information we have gained about Lewis and Clark? If not, what other words might you select to hone in on the key ideas in this book?*

Now that I have identified the words, I am going to justify my choices in writing sentences that respond to the book. I am starting with courageous. *Watch as I begin with a question and then use the word in response to that question: "Can you imagine journeying into a land full of unknowns? Lewis and Clark were courageous as they ventured into uncharted territory." I am going to continue adding some specific details to show just how courageous the journey was. I want to emphasize the word* courageous, *so I am using a marker to make it bolder than the rest of the text.*

TURN &TALK *Writers, now I want to incorporate the word* diplomatic *in my response. Think together. What details support that inference about Lewis and Clark? Construct a sentence or two using the word* diplomatic.

Lewis and Clark

Courageous   **Diplomatic**

Can you imagine journeying into a land full of unknowns? Lewis and Clark were **courageous** as they ventured into uncharted territory. When Thomas Jefferson suggested the trip to the West to discover a travel route to Asia, he expected the travelers would find woolly mammoths and volcanoes! It took courage to explore an area that could be so dangerous. Lewis and Clark's success on the journey came in part because they were **diplomatic**. As they met various Native American tribes, they established relationships with people that allowed them to survive some brutal conditions along the trail.

Modeled Writing

As you continue to write, explain that the goal is to use two powerful words to generate a response to the book.

Summarize the features: Invite students to name features they need to use in the Two-Word Strategy as you list them on a chart. Post the chart for students' reference as they write.

WRITING and COACHING

You may want to have your writers use the Two-Word Strategy to respond to a new section of the book or identify a different topic. *Choose another resource, such as one on a different historical figure or event. You could choose a science resource, too. Then, think deeply about the text as you choose two words that reflect your thinking. Justify the words you chose by writing about them. Once you have checked your writing against the features list and know it is complete, use a marker to bold your two words.*

Support individuals or small groups as necessary. Guide writers to choose the best words that summarize their response to the important ideas in the text. They might brainstorm words first to have a bank from which to choose the two most important words.

SHARING and REFLECTING

Sum it up! *Writers, your two words reflected your deep thinking about the text. You crafted responses that showed why those two words were so important and made those words bold so that they would stand out in your responses, too!*

TURN &TALK *Get ready to share your Two-Word Strategy responses with partners. First, use the self-assessment checklist to be sure that all features are there. Then, meet with your partner to talk about your work. What advice can you give each other on how to make your responses even stronger?*

ASSESS THE LEARNING

Analyze the Two-Word Strategy responses to determine which students need assistance in choosing two inferential words based on the text and then including them in a response.

SELF-ASSESSMENT

SELF-ASSESSMENT
Two-Word Strategy

	YES	NO
1. Two words that offer inference based on factual details	☐	☐
2. Justification with real events or factual content	☐	☐
3. Bold words	☐	☐
4. Supporting visuals	☐	☐

▷TAKE IT FORWARD

▸ Have students consider powerful visuals they can add to their responses. A science response, for example, might include a labeled diagram of rock layers, causes of volcanoes, and so on. A response about a historical figure or event could include a map or photographs. Students should be sure that their visuals support their writing. They should also write explanatory captions.

▸ Have students select one word that they think is the most helpful in reflecting on the text and write it on an index card. On the back of the card, they can tell why they chose this word and how it relates to the reading. Students can meet in groups to share and compare their words.

▸ Encourage students to select powerful descriptive words that can be used to talk about historical figures. Capture selections on a word wall that students can use as a reference for writing responses, character trait analyses, and so on. They can add to the word wall as an ongoing project.

VISUAL LITERACY

Sketch to Stretch

Respond to a poem with a Sketch to Stretch.

The Flag Goes By

From hearing the poem I imagine a celebration that cannot be described as happieness, it is much more. People would feel so safe that they would dance in the street without a care in the world. The strength the Flag gives a soldier is huge because so many people died to have it stand proudly.

FEATURES

- Series of sketches to reflect images brought forward by different sections of the poem
- Caption for each sketch
- Summative paragraph

FOCUSED MINILESSON

Writers, I know that sometimes when I read, I visualize to get a better understanding of the content. When I am reading about earthquakes, for example, I picture the plates scraping against each other when all of a sudden—Bam!—a jolting of the plates triggers a quake. Poems are ripe with images, too. Today I want to use a special strategy called Sketch to Stretch to stretch my thinking about the images in a poem and to think deeply about the mood the poet is trying to create as I respond to this work.

Listen as I read the first two stanzas aloud. Close your eyes and visualize. What images come to mind? When I read that, I pictured the snorkel allowing the swimmer to breathe. I could see the line that separates water from air, bobbing up and down because of the movement of waves. It's a unique feeling, to be in bobbing water! I am sketching a swimmer with a snorkel, drawing a wavy line above her to show the water line. Notice that my sketch isn't perfect! My goal is to capture what I visualize and focus on the most important details. Under my sketch, I am writing a caption about what I visualize: "It's darker underwater than on top of the surface. I hear the whoosh of air going in and out of the snorkel."

Read the next stanza to students: "A few rays penetrate . . . behind them."

TURN &TALK *Writers, as you listened, what did you visualize? What could you see and hear? Identify some details you'd include in a sketch.*

I am sketching what the water might look like from behind a pair of swim goggles. The colorful shapes are fish. The word dart *shows me that the fish are moving quickly while the diver is still in the water, watching them go by. It's a peaceful feeling, but it's also like being an intruder in the fish's space. I also am drawing lines to show the rays of the sun coming through the water. They hit the water at one angle and then move through the water at another.*

Continue your modeling, writing a caption for the second sketch and then creating a third sketch showing the seaweed swaying in the water. Emphasize that your sketches draw on details in the poem and capture images. Captions include what you hear or feel as you read the poem.

It's darker underwater than on top of the surface. I hear the whoosh of air going in and out of the snorkel.

Modeled Writing

TURN &TALK *Partners, think together as you evaluate this strategy. What makes sketching useful for capturing images? How might you use this strategy in a subject like science?*

Summarize the features: Have students work with partners as they list features of Sketch to Stretch in their writer's notebooks. Have them get together with another partner pair to be sure that all features are included.

WRITING and COACHING

You watched as I sketched images and explained my thinking in response to a poem. Now it's your turn. Choose a poem and read it through several times. You might have a partner read it aloud as you close your eyes and visualize in response to the words. Then, use a Sketch to Stretch to reflect your thinking. Sketch images that come to mind, and write captions to go with them. Think beyond the words on the page to the images and feelings the poem evokes.

Students may need to work with you in a small group to identify images evoked by a poem before they begin to sketch. Remind them that sketches are not meant to be works of art. The key is to use the sketches for holding on to content and images.

SHARING and REFLECTING

Sum it up! *Writers, today you used a different way to respond to content—sketching to stretch. What a powerful way to focus on the images in a poem! Your sketches reflect those images. It is important that you also wrote captions to capture your thinking.*

TURN &TALK *Your families will be interested in seeing your sketches. Get ready to take home both your poems and your sketches. What features of your sketches do you want to be sure to share with your families? Get together with a partner to list them. Write them on sticky notes, and place them on your responses.*

ASSESS THE LEARNING

Analyze the sketches to note which students need assistance in visualizing and drawing in response to a poem. Students should include explanatory captions with their sketches.

SELF-ASSESSMENT

SELF-ASSESSMENT
Sketch to Stretch

	YES	NO
1. Series of sketches to reflect images brought forward by different sections of the poem	☐	☐
2. Caption for each sketch	☐	☐
3. Summative paragraph ⊙	☐	☐

▷TAKE IT FORWARD

▸ Have students use their captions to write summative paragraphs about their responses to the images in the poem. Model a summary of your own about the mentor text, focusing on the feelings evoked about the underwater world.

▸ Students can use the Sketch to Stretch strategy as a way to summarize academic content. Encourage them to add labels to their sketches to set off important elements and use academic vocabulary.

▸ Have students prepare dramatic readings of their poems and use their sketches to support their presentations.

Venn Diagram (Three-Circle)

Use a Venn diagram to analyze multiple accounts of the same event or topic.

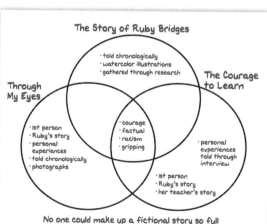

FEATURES

- Overlapping circles
- Key words and phrases
- Summative paragraph
- Linking words of comparison: *however, but, although, similarly, even though, still, yet, also, in contrast to*
- Description of similarities and differences
- ▶ Precise language

BEFORE THE LESSON

This lesson focuses on three different texts about Ruby Bridges, but you could base the instruction on any three texts on the same topic that feature different points of view. Whatever texts you choose, read them aloud with students before the lesson, and keep them on hand for reference.

FOCUSED MINILESSON

I notice some big differences in these three texts about Ruby Bridges. They are told from various points of view and give us different glimpses into the events that surrounded Ruby's days as the only African American student at a previously all-white school. I want to capture some of these ideas in a Venn diagram. Because I have three sources, my Venn diagram will have three circles. Watch as I draw three circles that overlap in the middle. In this part, I am going to write key words and phrases that reflect similarities among all three sources.

TURN &TALK *Writers, think together. What key words capture ideas from all three texts? Identify a few and be ready to share.*

Although these texts focus on different points of view, they do have similar ideas. Watch as I note these ideas where the circles overlap. Notice that I am just writing the words "courage; factual; racism; and gripping."

Now I am ready to write some ideas that pertain to each separate text. I'll place them in the circles that correspond. For example, "Through My Eyes" is Ruby's own story. It uses a first-person point of view and includes her personal insight in a chronological account. I'll capture these ideas in the diagram. *Continue the diagram, highlighting your thinking as you note important words and phrases about each resource. Be sure you have included some similarities and some differences.*

Now I am set to write. In my first sentence, I am going to show how all three of the resources are the same. I'm going to pull some key words and phrases from the center of the Venn diagram to be sure that I've reflected

Modeled Writing

ideas that are true about all three resources: "No one could make up . . . from an outsider's point of view." Did you notice that I wrote about the point of view of "The Story of Ruby Bridges"? The point of view of the other texts is different. I am going to point out that difference by including a linking phrase that contrasts, on the other hand.

Continue modeling. Show that you use words from the Venn diagram, making it a true tool for planning your writing.

TURN &TALK *What words in this writing compare and contrast? How is a Venn diagram a helpful tool for writing a response?*

Summarize the features: Have students open their writer's notebooks and work with partners to create labeled models of three-circle Venn diagrams and to list words they could use to compare and contrast in their summaries.

WRITING and COACHING

Comparing three different viewpoints can be tricky, but it certainly gave us insight from multiple perspectives as we respond to texts! Choose another episode from history about which you can gather multiple perspectives. Or you could find editorials about a local issue and compare and contrast their viewpoints with your own. Create a three-circle Venn diagram to organize your thoughts before you write a paragraph to sum up your thinking.

Confer with writers who need more support to list ideas in Venn diagrams and to use those organizers as the basis for writing. Provide the Linking Words That Signal Comparisons reference from the *Resources* CD-ROM for students who need extra support.

SHARING and REFLECTING

Sum it up! *Writers, you used Venn diagrams to capture key words and phrases and similarities and differences about three texts. Then, you used linking words in a summative paragraph to respond to these ideas. Your responses are thorough, fact-grounded, and easy to navigate.*

TURN &TALK *Check your work against the model in your writer's notebook, then meet up with your partner. What important features did you both consider as you checked over your work?*

▶TAKE IT FORWARD

▸ Have students focus on precision in their writing by including academic words that come out of the content.

▸ Have students use a three-circle Venn diagram to compare and contrast three subjects, such as three types of volcanoes, three types of rock, or three battles in the American Revolution.

▸ Have students compare and contrast the treatment of a topic in three different media, such as a textbook, a magazine article, and an interview. Students might interview three classmates about a topic and compare and contrast responses.

▸ Have students return to previous responses they have completed in

which they compare and contrast subjects or points of view with an eye toward infusing linking words. Model inserting them into a piece you have previously written, using a caret mark to show the insertion.

Taking It Forward: Personal Writing Projects

After they have had the opportunity to work through the model unit and lessons in this section, cement your students' understandings about response writing by having them complete one or more *personal* writing projects on topics of their choice. This is an important follow-up to the model unit because it allows students to apply their new understandings to their own writing lives based on personal interests.

For example, the teaching processes outlined in the model unit on author responses can easily be adapted to personal projects on a variety of topics and in a variety of forms. If students have trouble deciding what to write about, you might want to suggest topics and forms such as the ones that follow. Otherwise, give students the freedom to choose the topics they find most interesting—provided you deem them appropriate.

Possible Topics for Response Writing

Topics may correlate with content in your science and social studies standards, current events, or class interests.

- What do you think about this book, author, or subject?
- What did you like and dislike about the book?
- What connections can you make to the poem?
- What did you learn from that part of the book?
- What are you wondering about what you just read?
- What would you like to ask the author?
- What is the big idea in this book?
- How do the illustrations support the text?
- Would you recommend this book/movie/restaurant/TV show? Why?
- What was the best part of the field trip?
- How did you solve that problem?
- What did you learn from the experiment/activity?
- What is your opinion of this book/picture/piece of music? Why?
- How are these two things similar? How are they different?
- Who does this character remind you of?
- What do you think the main character should do?
- What is the problem in this story, and how is it solved?
- Why is this book worth reading?
- Do you agree with the author? Why or why not?

Possible Forms for Response Writing

Reading journals	Illustrations	Ratings
Interactive journals	Descriptions	Letters
Two-column journals	Summaries	Posters
Learning logs	Venn diagrams	Poems
Observation logs	Labeled diagrams	Quick writes
Reaction pieces	Writer's notebooks	Book reviews
Explanations	Written reflections	Essays

Planning and Implementing Personal Writing Projects

Your students will need preparation, coaching, prompting, and varying amounts of support as they move through their own personal explorations. The ten-session structure presented in the model unit may be too long for personal projects that assume less time spent on instruction and modeling. Give students the time they need to fully develop their topics and to move through the stages of the writing process, but don't be surprised if many students require fewer than ten sessions.

Use the following tips and strategies as needed to ensure each student's success.

Before the Personal Projects:

▸ Help students select topics that they are interested in, and provide research materials if needed.

▸ Continue to use information you gather from the Individual Assessment Record or your Ongoing Monitoring Sheet to provide specific instruction in whole-class, small-group, and individual settings as needed. Use the Daily Planner to lay out each day's lesson.

During the Personal Projects:

▸ Give students the personal checklists from the *Resources* CD-ROM to use as samples for creating their own checklists. A blank checklist can be found on the *Resources* CD-ROM and in the Resources section at the end of this book. Explain to the students that you will also be checking to see if they have included key features on the checklist.

▸ If needed, begin each session with a focused minilesson. Tailor the suggested minilesson to suit the needs of your students.

▸ Continue to provide high-quality mentor texts. Display mentor texts prominently, and allow students time to read them before they begin to write their own. Continue to call students' attention to the features list created during the model unit.

▸ You may want to write your own text along with the students as you did during the model unit to provide an additional model.

▸ Have writing partners conference with each other often to check one another's work for sense and clarity.

▸ As students work independently on their writing and illustrations, note those who are struggling and bring them together for small-group instruction. Use the Individual Assessment Record and/or the Ongoing Monitoring Sheet to assist in tailoring instruction to the needs of your students.

▸ Students who seem very confident and who have clearly grasped all of the concepts taught so far can be brought together in a small group to extend their understanding to more challenging work.

After the Personal Projects:

▸ Be sure to give students opportunities to share and celebrate their writing projects.

▸ Compare students' final writing products with their earlier attempts in order to evaluate their growth as writers.

▸ Distribute copies of the Student Self-Reflection Sheet (on the *Resources* CD-ROM). Students will benefit greatly from the chance to reflect on their progress and to hear their classmates' feedback.

▸ Reflect on the strengths and challenges of implementing the personal projects. How might the process be adjusted to maximize student learning?

▸ Look at common needs of the class, and address these when students are working on future projects.

Resources for Teaching Nonfiction Writing

CONTENTS

GENERAL RESOURCES

Research Opportunities

▸ Classroom Resources and Organization

▸ Research Strategies

Index of Model Lessons by Subject Area

Index of Lessons by Writing Form

Index of Lessons by Mentor Text

Tools Researchers Use

CHECKLISTS AND FORMS

Inform

▸ Ongoing Monitoring Sheet

▸ Daily Planner

▸ Individual Assessment Record

▸ Personal Checklist for Informational Writing

Instruct

▸ Ongoing Monitoring Sheet

▸ Daily Planner

▸ Individual Assessment Record

▸ Personal Checklist for Procedural Writing

Narrate

▸ Ongoing Monitoring Sheet

▸ Daily Planner

▸ Individual Assessment Record

▸ Personal Checklist for Narrative Writing

Persuade

▸ Ongoing Monitoring Sheet

▸ Daily Planner

▸ Individual Assessment Record

▸ Personal Checklist for Persuasive Writing

Respond

▸ Ongoing Monitoring Sheet

▸ Daily Planner

▸ Individual Assessment Record

▸ Personal Checklist for Response Writing

Research Opportunities

Research is a unique requirement of writing nonfiction. All nonfiction texts, from personal narratives to informational reports, are based on information, and research is the process of gathering that information. Research can involve searching one's own memory for personal narrative; trying out a procedure in preparation for writing instructions; or observing, reading, viewing, or listening in order to write an informational text. All of these inquiries yield the facts that are the basis of nonfiction writing.

Specifically, research opportunities can:

▸ Explicitly support your curriculum and content standards

▸ Provide students with a variety of age-appropriate resources

▸ Actively engage students in discovering information for themselves, thus developing their sense of inquiry

▸ Make it easy for students to access information related to their topic

▸ Provide a forum for student collaboration and enhance learning

As the Common Core standards and most state academic standards make clear, students in grades 3–5 should be expected to search for, locate, and use information from multiple sources on their own. It is critical that writers develop an arsenal of research strategies that they can readily implement as they interact with live observations, online sources, and informational sources. Armed with a variety of research strategies, intermediate-age writers quickly learn how to extract information from print and visuals and then to organize it for later use in their drafts.

To help writers transfer understandings from research to writing, it is essential to explicitly show them how to gather data, make notes, create labeled diagrams, and record facts from their research. With a focus on research, writers in grades 3, 4, and 5 quickly learn that facts must be verified so writing is supported by critical thinking, high-quality resources, and a conscious focus on determining importance. See pages 260–268 for a full list of the research strategies you'll find in this lesson book.

GATHERING RESOURCES

Before beginning a curriculum unit or a project, you need to assemble curriculum and standards-based resources—magazines, textbooks, reference books, DVDs, appropriate websites, and the like. At the same time, you'll want to alert your school and community librarians. They will be able to identify available resources—print as well as other media—for you to borrow or catalog in a reference list. In addition, they may be able to set aside a cart containing these topic-specific sources for your class to use.

Ensure that the material you gather is not too challenging for students to read or understand. They need to be able to access facts easily and gain the information to record in their research notebooks, on sticky notes, or on individual R.A.N. folders or R.A.N. organizers (see page 262). For students who find some of the written material too challenging, encourage them to use pictures or video to gather information.

Articles, Books, and Magazines

Ensure that articles, books, and magazines are readily accessible so your writers can quickly access information while working independently. Include texts with detailed, enticing photographs and diagrams. Offer brief, interesting articles from magazines and newspapers or adapted from the Internet. Paste them onto the front and back of poster board, heavy card stock, or even cereal boxes. Laminate these, and place them into baskets with books on the topic being explored. (Lamination will ensure that they last for many years.) It is also a good idea to include leveled nonfiction books at reading levels that are comfortable for your students.

If students from previous years have published their own books, posters, or articles on the topic, save some of these to add to your resources. In addition, make available big books, articles, and mentor texts that you have introduced in whole-class settings for students to review to gather relevant facts.

Encourage students to share with their fellow researchers the information they have learned before recording it. This will help them put the information into their own words and not simply copy the new facts they are learning. Strategies such as the Key Word strategy (pages 00 and 00), and the R.A.N. strategy (pages 260–269), can be particularly helpful in this regard.

Realia or Observations

If a topic lends itself to students being able to make direct observations, gather the necessary items for research. For example, if students are studying a specific plant, you could bring in the plant for them to observe. If students are studying a specific country, provide artifacts with brief descriptions that students can observe, discuss, and record information about. Provide magnifying glasses to help students observe live animals, plants, and other artifacts brought in for observation.

Students' up-close observations of their class gecko spur further questions for research.

Sometimes observations outside the classroom are helpful. These can be as simple as looking out the window to study weather conditions or opening the door to take an observational nature walk or as involved as taking field trips to community services, museums, or other cultural research-related locations.

As always with research opportunities, encourage students to discuss with each other what they are observing before recording the information.

Encourage students to cite their sources as they gather relevant information, and demonstrate how these can be listed at the back of their projects

Computer and Internet

Internet research needs to be streamlined, both to protect students and to ensure that relevant information is easy to locate. You may want to begin by organizing texts, visuals, and Internet links in topic-labeled folders on your classroom computers to make it easy for writers to access appropriate materials. To provide online content, look for sites that are kid-friendly and easy to navigate. Narrow down the field of available websites on the topic being explored. Adding the words "for children" or "for kids" when you type in the topic will help narrow the field considerably. Then, bookmark appropriate sites, including any relevant video clips you find, so that students are not overwhelmed with too many sites to select from.

As students move up the grade levels, computers become their main sources of information.

You may also want to provide access to teacher-created wikis—safe and controlled websites in which students can research and deposit their own writing for real audiences to review and comment on. For more able students, provide focused lessons on how to locate relevant websites for themselves. Below are some suggestions.

How to Locate Websites

▸ Think about what it is you really want to find out.

▸ Make a list of key words.

▸ Try to use key nouns and verbs.

▸ Look at the first page of the websites listed to see if they are about what you are looking for. If they are not, look for key words on the websites listed and the sponsored links to help you become more specific in your search.

▸ Once you have located websites, open them to see that the information is relevant and can be easily read and understood.

▸ Look for reliable websites. Websites that have ".org" are usually reliable sources of information.

If you have access to only a limited number of computers, pair students so that two can use the computer at the same time. Pairing students to work on one computer is a great way to get them to talk to each other about what they are learning. This makes it easier for them to record their information.

Visual Literacy: Pictures, Photographs, Maps, Diagrams, Graphs, and Models

Collect and laminate a variety of visuals from magazines, books, and websites for students to observe for information. Studying graphic information is a great way for students to hone their inferencing skills—drawing conclusions and figuring out information without being directly told. Make sure you highlight different types of graphs and maps in mathematic sessions so students understand how to gain relevant information for research.

Encourage students to discuss what they are seeing with their peers, to raise questions about what they are seeing, and to record what they see—in sketches or in note form—in their research notebooks or on a R.A.N. folder. Be sure to check in with each group from time to time to make sure their thinking has not gone astray.

Enhance students' visual comprehension by using a masking tool (such as a piece of cardboard or paper with a circular cutout) to focus in on smaller sections of a picture. Then, zoom out to reexamine the whole in view of the details they've studied.

DVDs and Videos

Bookmark video clips on the Web, or locate commercially produced DVD documentaries on the topics of your students' research.

For inspiration, consider recording videos of students presenting their individual explorations and making them available for students in future years—or savoring them again in the current year. These not only boost the morale of your current students but also give subsequent classes something to aim for.

As with audio resources, have students view small portions of the DVD, stop and talk, and then record what they have learned. They can then go back and view more information. Breaking up the viewing makes information less overwhelming and ensures that students will gather far more information.

Audiotapes/CDs: Scaffolds for Striving Learners

Although most intermediate-age students will be ready for independent research with print and online materials, some of your students may still benefit from audio recordings of information on nonfiction topics that you can make yourself. During read-alouds and shared readings of nonfiction texts or mentor texts, flip on the recorder as you read to create a lasting audio resource. Alternatively, encourage your students to practice enough to create expressive read-aloud recordings. Keep the read-aloud and shared-reading books and articles with the audiotapes so students can both read and hear the information.

You also might want to make topic-specific audiotapes or CDs for students to listen to. Narrate a collection of photographs, for example, or read aloud a tabbed section of an article or book that might be too difficult for students to read. This is a good way to ensure that students "discover" important information required by your curriculum or standards.

Have students listen to only a small portion of the audio, stop and talk, and then record what they have learned. They can then go back and listen to the next small portion of information. By breaking up the listening, students will gather far more information and not become overwhelmed with large volumes of facts in one hearing.

Demonstrate How to Collect and Record Information

While engaging with research, nonfiction writers record their learning in sketches, words, phrases, and sentences, ending up with a research notebook or R.A.N. folder filled with facts on their topic. But it is essential to scaffold success by showing students how to locate information and how to transfer their facts and learning onto paper. Show students the materials available to them for research, and use think-aloud language to demonstrate how you would gather information. Both the Extended Writing Units and the Power Writes in this resource explicitly model how to help students collect and record information. You will find support for:

Recording Methods

▸ Note-taking

▸ Using sketches to record ideas

▸ Transferring notes into running text

▸ Recording information without copying

▸ Using a graphic organizer

▸ Researching using multiple sources

▸ Locating relevant information for research

▸ Gaining information from visual sources

▸ Selecting the most important facts and details

▸ Citing information gathered from specific resources

▸ Using research notebooks and personal R.A.N. folders

MANAGING RESEARCH OPPORTUNITIES

Strategies for managing research opportunities for students will help your learners research successfully.

Set Up a Task Management Board

If you have a multitude of different research opportunities, a task management board will assist students in knowing what materials are available for their use each day. Assigning a particular set of students to each set of materials allows you to keep the research groups to a reasonable number, to group students across genders and abilities, and to make sure students progress to different research opportunities in an orderly manner.

Research Materials	Assigned Teams
Books	Team A
Magazines	Team D
Computer	Team B
DVD	Team E
Listening	Team C
Observations	Team F

Chart or Poster with Names

One way to set up a task management board is to write the name of each research opportunity on a card, display the cards in a pocket chart, and slip a photograph of each research team next to the appropriate card. Change the cards as needed to rotate groups through the full range of available resources. (Alternatively, use sticky notes for research opportunities and students, and display these on a large piece of poster board.)

A task management board or chart keeps researchers moving through the available resources.

Recording Information from Research

To keep each student's research information in one place, consider beginning a new research notebook for each topic students are studying or making research folders or individual R.A.N. folders for each student.

While research is always a good idea, it will be particularly crucial in the Extended Writing Units focused on informational reports and explanations. For these research-based writing projects, writers will need to have a system for collecting and organizing facts. While there are many ways to do this, we find that research notebooks, research folders, concept webs, and R.A.N. folders and organizers are all powerful tools for writers.

Research Notebooks

A research notebook is made from half-size sheets of plain paper that are stapled together into a small journal. Like a content web, the research notebook serves as an organizer where facts can be inserted with other related information. You may want to include headings in the research notebook to help students keep their information organized. For example, an exploration about a famous explorer might have headings such as "Birth and Early Years," "Early Journeys," "Later Journeys," "The Final Years," and "Interesting Facts."

With a research notebook in hand, writers interact with research materials by collecting specific facts from books, magazines, videos, audiobooks, and so on. Because facts related to a concept such as "Birth and Early Years" all go on the same page, facts are gathered in an organized manner that is highly supportive of the writing that will follow.

Research Folders

Research folders are an alternative to research notebooks. Simple to create, they are file folders with envelopes glued inside. Each envelope carries a category related to the topic being explored. As researchers gather facts—in the form of sketches, single words, or phrases—they jot their information on small pieces of paper. The notes are then slipped into the appropriate envelopes. When the writer is ready to construct a text, it is easy to arrange the notes in an order that supports sentence and paragraph development.

Concept Maps and Graphic Organizers

Concept maps and other types of graphic organizers are helpful tools for organizing facts and information. They can be part of either a research folder or a research notebook. The organizer shown here was designed to assist students as they collect and organize facts to use when writing an informational article.

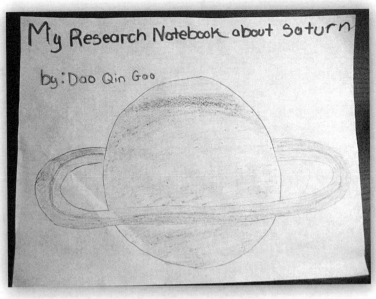

My Research Notebook about Saturn
by: Dao Qin Goo

Writers can use research notebooks to collect and organize facts from multiple sources.

Name: _____ Date: _____

Article Planning Organizer

Question	Essential Information
Who?	
What?	
When?	
Where?	
Why?	

The organizer shown here was designed to assist students as they collect and organize facts to use when writing an informational article.

THE R.A.N. STRATEGY: READING AND ANALYZING NONFICTION

The strategy for reading and analyzing nonfiction, or the R.A.N. strategy, is an excellent tool for students to use as writers when researching a specific topic for either class or personal projects. With this strategy, researchers collect information and organize their ideas in folders or on graphic organizers to make their thinking visible. The R.A.N. chart or folder is used throughout a research project to record and categorize information on the go. This strategy helps writers in two critical ways: first, it helps them be aware of and critically examine their thinking, and second, it aids them in organizing research information in preparation for writing.

The R.A.N. strategy is a modification of the KWL strategy—What We Know, What We Want to Know, What We Learned (Ogle, 1986)—and expands KWL into a critical research process. The comparison between the two strategies can be seen below.

KWL STRATEGY		
What We Know	**What We Want to Know**	**What We Learned**
Students state information they know or think they know about the topic.	Students come up with questions they want answered.	Students research to answer specific questions raised.

R.A.N. STRATEGY				
What we think we know	**Yes, we were right, or Confirmed information**	**We don't think this anymore, or Misconceptions**	**New learning, or New facts**	**Wonderings**
Students state information they believe to be correct about the topic (prior knowledge).	Students read to confirm prior knowledge.	Students read to discard incorrect prior knowledge.	Students read to locate additional information not part of prior knowledge.	Students raise questions based on the new information gathered.

Comparison of the KWL and R.A.N. strategies.

OVERVIEW OF THE R.A.N. HEADINGS

1. "What we think we know" is similar to the KWL first step. This heading acknowledges that students come to school with background knowledge and that this background knowledge may not be correct.

2. "Yes, we were right" or "Confirmed information" gives students an opportunity to confirm prior knowledge as they research a given topic. It gives them a sense of success as they confirm facts that they already know.

3. "We don't think this anymore" or "Misconceptions" helps students understand that when researching, the information they locate may be different from or even contradict their prior knowledge. It encourages students to rethink what they previously thought to be correct.

4. "New learning" or "New facts" encourages students to think about information that is new learning and to gather new literal understandings. This helps deepen their content understandings about a topic.

5. "Wonderings" is the same as the KWL heading "What we want to know." In the R.A.N. strategy, this heading is applied after students have researched and not before. This is because researchers raise questions during and after they explore a topic, not just before. It is difficult for students to raise questions about a topic they have little prior knowledge about.

Individual R.A.N. Folders

Individual R.A.N. (Reading and Analyzing Nonfiction) folders may be used for writing projects. We recommend that you guide students several times through the R.A.N. strategy's thinking analysis in a whole-class setting before expecting them to use it on their own.

Individual R.A.N. folders can be constructed in many ways. One option is to create a sturdy folder that can store and organize sticky notes and can be reused again and again. It is advisable to laminate the file folders before you put them together. This will ensure that the R.A.N. folder will last for the entire school year. If you do not have access to file folders, you can use paper or card stock as an alternative.

Step 1: Start with two file folders. Place the left half of folder 2 on top of the right half of folder 1.

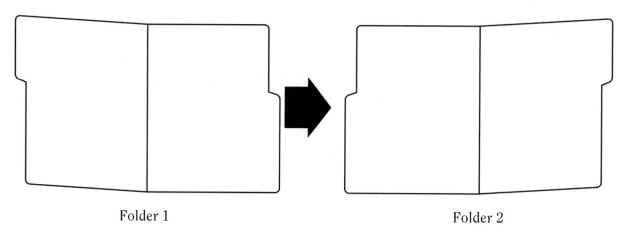

Folder 1   Folder 2

Step 2: Staple, glue, or tape the overlapped sections together.

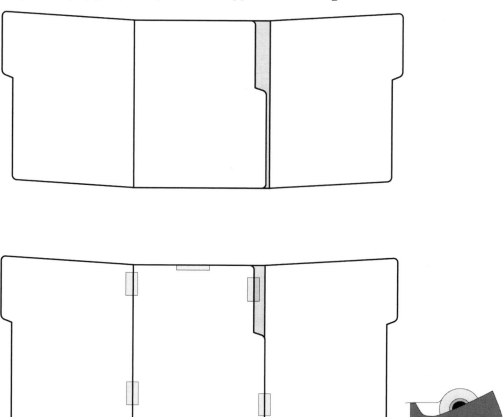

Step 3: Label the three sections at the top: "What I think I know," "Confirmed information," and "New learning."

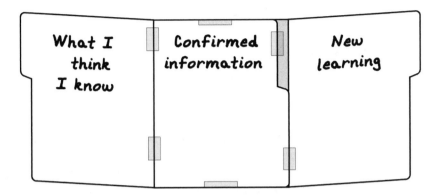

Step 4: Turn the joined folders over and label the three sections. Make the left-hand panel a cover page, "My R.A.N. Chart," with a space for the student's name. Write the headings "Wonderings" and "Misconceptions" on the middle and right-hand panels.

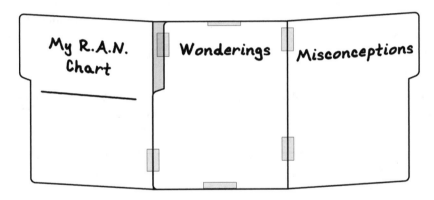

Step 5: Turn to the first side again. Fold "What I think I know" over "Confirmed information." Then, fold the cover panel to the front.

INTRODUCING THE R.A.N. FOLDER

Provide an overview of the R.A.N. folder by explaining its purpose and how each of the thinking-analysis headings supports research.

What We Think We Know

Begin research by asking students to think about and then record their prior knowledge about the topic they are exploring. Model the thinking you expect students to engage in.

The first thing we're going to do is record all the important information we already think we know about our habitats. Point to the "What we think we know" column in the folder. *Well, one thing I think I know about the rainforest is there are lots of trees, but that seems like information that everyone will know. I only want to record interesting or amazing facts. I also know that there are many different species of animals and plants that can only be found in this habitat. That's better information. I'm going to write* "unique species" *on my sticky note and put it in the* "What we think we know" *column in my folder.*

Then, ask writers to record what they think they know about their selected topics. Accept all students' background knowledge, whether it is accurate or not. This is their prior thinking. Having them share is a wonderful way to assess their content knowledge on a particular topic and will help you extend their content understandings.

Have students record their responses using sticky notes. Remind students to limit their information to what they consider to be their best or "Wow!" facts. This will help them understand that nonfiction writers only include important information.

If you find that your students possess little background knowledge on a topic, introduce the topic ahead of time by using a read-aloud or a shared reading or by making available books and magazines for independent reading before asking again for "What we think we know." This will give all students some accurate prior knowledge to contribute and will give them a sense of success when they confirm their prior thinking through research.

Yes, We Were Right, or Confirmed Information

As students research, encourage them to look for facts to confirm the prior knowledge that has been posted in their folders. Use think-aloud language to demonstrate this process: *I wrote under* "What I think I know" *that* "The largest rainforest is the Amazon." *Well, I did some research and found I was correct. So, I am moving this sticky note across to the* "Confirmed information" *column in my folder.*

When moving facts from "What I think I know" to "Confirmed information," encourage students to provide evidence for their information by citing their sources. Have them write the source from which they were able to confirm the information on the back of the sticky note. This is a valuable way to begin teaching students how to cite sources as they research.

For example: *I am going to write the name of the book where I found this information on the back of my sticky note. It's important to always cite my sources. Good researchers and writers always make sure their information is accurate.*

If students are unable to confirm their prior thinking after research and still have a lot of information in the "What we think we know" column, you may need to guide them toward specific sources or look for additional resources that will help them achieve this goal.

We Don't Think This Anymore, or Misconceptions

In addition to finding information to confirm their prior knowledge, encourage students to look for information that contradicts any facts they thought they knew: *I was looking at a website trying to confirm my information that rainforests cover about 10 percent of the world, and I found out that they only cover 6 percent of our earth. I'm going to move my sticky note to the* "I don't think this anymore" *heading in my R.A.N. folder. I'm also going to write* "Covers 6% of Earth" *on a new sticky note and add this to my* "New Facts" *heading in my folder.*

Be alert to any misconceptions you see in the "What I think I know" column, and try to provide students with adequate resources to correct these misconceptions. If important sources are not easily accessible, use your read-aloud or shared reading time to highlight specific information.

New Learning, or New Facts

Although confirming and refuting prior knowledge is an important research skill, locating new information is at the heart of research. New information builds new learning and broadens students' knowledge base. Give students ample opportunities to research together to locate and record new facts. Refer to the section on research opportunities (pages 253–259) to assist students with this task.

Fan the flames of students' excitement at discovering and learning new information. Encourage researchers' amazement, curiosity, and engagement. *Wow! I just found out that more than two-thirds of known plant species live in rainforests. That's amazing! What interesting facts have you found?*

When the class comes together to share new information from their R.A.N. folders, continue to encourage them to limit their contributions to what they consider to be their best or "Wow!" facts to keep the volume of information manageable.

Continue to encourage your students to record the sources for their information. At the conclusion of the unit, you can demonstrate how to use this information to create a bibliography or reference page.

Wonderings

One way to ensure learners' engagement with information and ideas is to teach them to wonder. Learning doesn't stop with gathering, recording, and evaluating facts. We don't want students to just collect facts; we want them to connect with, and infer from, the information they are discovering. This is fueled by taking the next step toward further research: raising questions, or "wonderings," about the facts students researched.

Demonstrate how to raise wonderings by posing questions that use the standard "wh" question words—*who, what, when, where, why,* and *how*—and prompting students to do the same. Select a fact, confirmed or new, from your R.A.N. folder, and use a think-aloud to model wondering or questioning with the question words. For example: *I found out that the Amazon is the world's largest river. I want to know how long it is and how much water it holds. I am going to write this wondering on a sticky note and place it under the heading "Wonderings" in my R.A.N. folder. When I locate the answer to this wondering, I'm going to write the information under the heading "New Facts." I can then discard or throw away this wondering because I found the answer. Good researchers don't just look for facts. They ask themselves questions about the information they are discovering.*

Use students' wonderings to stimulate further research. Have researchers find answers to their wonderings and chart these answers under the heading "New learning." Also, encourage students to share their R.A.N. folders with each other and look at the wonderings raised by other students to see if they can find the answers.

Once the research is finished, any information remaining under the heading "What I think I know" that has not been confirmed or deemed a misconception can be moved across to the "Wonderings" column. This helps students understand that not all of their prior knowledge can be verified and that unverified facts become unanswered wonderings.

Using a R.A.N. Organizer

After regular use of the R.A.N. folders, many students will become familiar enough with the thinking to use a graphic organizer of the R.A.N. instead of their folders. In addition to the thinking-analysis headings, a R.A.N. organizer specifies content categories of information. Content categories are derived from the specific content you want to cover as well as your research sources—you may want to identify subtopics for which you have the most information available. These categories help writers sift through and organize their research notes in preparation for writing. In this sample, a R.A.N. chart for a report about the rainforest, the content categories are "Location," "Climate," "Flora," "Fauna," "People," and "Other Great Facts." You'll find a blank R.A.N. organizer that you can customize for any topic on the *Resources* CD-ROM.

Before giving students a R.A.N. organizer, model how you would use one. Model the first category, and then have students research and draft the first category on their organizers. This will ensure you don't overload them with too lengthy a demonstration. It will also allow you to monitor how successful students are in researching and drafting the first category on the organizer and provide more focused future demonstrations based on your observations.

Researchers, I have a R.A.N. organizer about rainforests. You can see that I have looked at the first category, "Location." I have listed what I think I know about where rainforests are located around the world. Watch how I write "The United States, Australia, Africa, and Europe." That's because I think that's where rainforests are located in the world.

After researching, I found that there are no rainforests in the United States and Europe, so I have put a check mark under the heading "M," which stands for "Misconceptions." I found that there are rainforests in Australia and Africa, so I have put a check mark under the heading "C," which stands for "Confirmed information."

I also found new information when I researched. I found out that the biggest rainforest is in South America and is called the Amazon and that the rainforest in Australia is in the state of Queensland. I also found out that rainforests are located in Central America and Southeast Asia. I have recorded this information in note form under the heading "New Facts." I found this information from a book about rainforests and a website, so I am writing these sources on the back of my R.A.N. organizer. This will help me later when I write up where I got my information. Good researchers always cite their sources.

When I found out that the Amazon was the biggest rainforest in the world, I had a wondering. I wanted to know how long the Amazon River is. Can you see how I have written my wondering under the heading "Wonderings"? I researched further and found out the Amazon River is about 250 miles long. Can you see how I have written the answer to this wondering underneath my question? I again wrote where I found this information on the back of my organizer. I couldn't find the answer to my next wondering, "How much water does the Amazon hold"? so I put a question mark next to it. I will have to come back to that wondering to see if I can find an answer. Sometimes our wonderings are not always answered. I was able to answer my last wondering, "How much of the world is covered with rainforests?" So, I put the answer underneath and again cited my source on the back of my organizer.

Now I am ready to begin drafting the first section of my report about rainforests. This will be the first paragraph in my report. Once I have finished drafting this section, I can go back to my R.A.N. organizer and work on the second category on my chart, which is about the climate of rainforests.

Refer to the *Nonfiction Writing: Intentional, Connected, and Engaging* DVD (3–5) for a visual example on how to model the use of a R.A.N. organizer.

Headings → Categories ↓	**1** What we think we know	**2** Confirmed ✔	**3** We Don't Think This Anymore ✘	**4** New Learning 💡	**5** Wonderings ?
Location					
Climate					
Flora					
Fauna					
People					
Other Great Facts ★					

Individual R.A.N. chart for informational report on rainforests.

Modification for Striving Writers

When first introducing the R.A.N. strategy to striving writers, it may be advisable to create your R.A.N. chart using only headings 1, 2, and 4 ("What we think we know," "Yes, we were right," and "New learning"). This way, students won't become overwhelmed on their first attempt at working with this new research strategy. As students become more comfortable working with the R.A.N. strategy, you can introduce headings 3 and 5.

More R.A.N. Resources

For further information on using the R.A.N. strategy, see the following resources.

Hoyt, L. and T. Stead. 2012. *Nonfiction Writing: Intentional, Connected, and Engaging,* DVD, 3–5. Portsmouth, NH: Heinemann.

Hoyt, L. and T. Stead. 2011. *Nonfiction Writing: Intentional, Connected, and Engaging,* DVD, K–2. Portsmouth, NH: Heinemann.

Stead, T. 2009. *Good Choice! Supporting Independent Reading and Response.* Portland, ME: Stenhouse.

Stead, T. 2006. *Reality Checks: Teaching Reading Comprehension with Nonfiction,* Chapter 2. Portland, ME: Stenhouse.

Grade 5
Index of Model Lessons by Subject Area

Math

Topic	Writing Form	Lesson or Unit
Fractions	Pass-Around Explanation	Inform Power Write, page 28
Math Problems	Problem-Solving Guide	Instruct Power Write, page 82
Shapes	Pass-Around Explanation	Inform Power Write, page 28

Reading

Topic	Writing Form	Lesson or Unit
Biography	Quote It!	Respond Power Write, page 234
	Summarizing from Multiple Sources	Respond Power Write, page 240
	Team Investigation: Photo Essay ⓥ	Narrate Power Write, page 154
	Two-Word Strategy	Respond Power Write, page 244
	Venn Diagram (Three-Circle) ⓥ	Respond Power Write, page 248
Book Review	Analytical Response	Respond Extended Writing Unit, page 214
Historical Fiction	Analytical Response	Respond Extended Writing Unit, page 214
Nonfiction Text Structure	Partner Book Review	Respond Power Write, page 242
Poems	Narrative Poetry with a Partner	Narrate Power Write, page 148
	Partner Description: List Poem	Inform Power Write, page 32
	Sketch to Stretch ⓥ	Respond Power Write, page 246
Point of View	Venn Diagram (Three-Circle) ⓥ	Respond Power Write, page 248
Response	Analytical Response	Respond Extended Writing Unit, page 214
	Compare and Contrast	Respond Power Write, page 238
	Partner Book Review	Respond Power Write, page 242
	Quote It!	Respond Power Write, page 234
	Sketch to Stretch ⓥ	Respond Power Write, page 246
	Summarizing from Multiple Sources	Respond Power Write, page 240
	Summary: Main Ideas	Respond Power Write, page 236
	Two-Word Strategy	Respond Power Write, page 244
	Venn Diagram (Three-Circle) ⓥ	Respond Power Write, page 248
Summary	Key Words and Summary	Narrate Power Write, page 146
	Pass-Around Explanation	Inform Power Write, page 28
	Summarizing from Multiple Sources	Respond Power Write, page 240
	Summary: Main Ideas	Respond Power Write, page 236

	Summary with Headings	Inform Power Write, page 36
	Two-Word Strategy	Respond Power Write, page 244
Text Structure	Partner Book Review	Respond Power Write, page 242

Science

Topic	Writing Form	Lesson or Unit
Animals	Informational Narrative	Narrate Power Write, page 144
	Partner Description: List Poem	Inform Power Write, page 32
Antarctica	Summary: Main Ideas	Respond Power Write, page 236
Beach Clean-Up	Personal Narrative	Narrative Extended Writing Unit, page 100
Environmental Issues	Formal Letter	Persuade Power Write, page 196
	Multi-Paragraph Essay	Persuade Power Write, page 198
	Persuasive Framework **VL**	Persuade Power Write, page 200
Forces and Motion	Dictionary of Terms	Inform Power Write, page 30
	Explanation Focused on Why	Inform Power Write, page 38
Flight	Partner News Article	Narrate Power Write, page 150
Health	Debate Plan	Persuade Power Write, page 194
	Explanation Focused on Why and How	Inform Power Write, page 40
	Instructions	Instruct Power Write, page 78
	Maybe Framework	Persuade Power Write, page 186
	Multi-Paragraph Essay	Persuade Power Write, page 198
	Persuasive Framework **VL**	Persuade Power Write, page 200
	Public Service Announcement	Persuade Power Write, page 188
Human Body	Diagram with Key **VL**	Inform Power Write, page 42
	Explanation	Inform Extended Writing Unit, page 8
	Flowchart **VL**	Inform Power Write, page 44
	Scientific Description	Inform Power Write, page 34
Inventors/Inventions	Partner News Article	Narrate Power Write, page 150
	Summarizing from Multiple Sources	Respond Power Write, page 240
	Summary: Main Ideas	Respond Power Write, page 236
Lab Equipment and Procedures	Procedural Text	Instruct Extended Writing Unit, page 58
Science Books	Partner Book Review	Respond Power Write, page 242
Seeds, Planting	Oral Presentation **VL**	Instruct Power Write, page 84
Stargazing	Personal Narrative	Narrative Extended Writing Unit, page 100
Volcanoes	Compare and Contrast	Respond Power Write, page 238
	Flowchart **VL**	Narrate Power Write, page 152
Water	Key Words and Summary	Narrate Power Write, page 146

	Partner Book Review	Respond Power Write, page 242
Weather	Partner Explanation	Instruct Power Write, page 80
	Partner Line Graph (vl)	Instruct Power Write, page 86

Social Studies

Topic	Writing Form	Lesson or Unit
Bridges, Ruby	Team Investigation: Photo Essay (vl)	Narrate Power Write, page 154
	Venn Diagram (Three-Circle) (vl)	Respond Power Write, page 248
Civil Rights Movement	Summary with Headings	Inform Power Write, page 36
	Team Investigation: Photo Essay (vl)	Narrate Power Write, page 154
	Venn Diagram (Three-Circle) (vl)	Respond Power Write, page 248
Civil War	Informational Narrative	Narrative Extended Writing Unit, page 120
	Summary with Headings	Inform Power Write, page 36
Colonial America	Investigation: Colonial America (vl)	Inform Power Write, page 46
	Investigation: Important Time in History (vl)	Persuade Power Write, page 202
Communication	Debate Plan	Persuade Power Write, page 194
	Electronic Slide Show	Persuade Power Write, page 190
	Formal Letter	Persuade Power Write, page 196
	Maybe Framework	Persuade Power Write, page 186
	Multi-Paragraph Essay	Persuade Power Write, page 198
	Oral Presentation (vl)	Instruct Power Write, page 84
	Partner News Article	Narrate Power Write, page 150
	Persuasive Framework (vl)	Persuade Power Write, page 200
	Public Service Announcement	Persuade Power Write, page 188
	Team Investigation: Photo Essay (vl)	Narrate Power Write, page 154
	Video Commercial	Persuade Power Write, page 192
Community Action	Formal Letter	Persuade Power Write, page 196
	Maybe Framework	Persuade Power Write, page 186
	Multi-Paragraph Essay	Persuade Power Write, page 198
	Persuasive Framework (vl)	Persuade Power Write, page 200
	Public Service Announcement	Persuade Power Write, page 188
Geography	Partner Line Graph (vl)	Instruct Power Write, page 86
	Summary: Main Ideas	Respond Power Write, page 236
Health	Debate Plan	Persuade Power Write, page 194
	Explanation Focused on Why and How	Inform Power Write, page 40
	Instructions	Instruct Power Write, page 78
	Formal Letter	Persuade Power Write, page 196

	Multi-Paragraph Essay	Persuade Power Write, page 198
	Persuasive Framework **VL**	Persuade Power Write, page 200
	Public Service Announcement	Persuade Power Write, page 188
Historical Events	Flowchart **VL**	Narrate Power Write, page 152
	Informational Narrative	Narrative Extended Writing Unit, page 120
	Team Investigation: Photo Essay **VL**	Narrate Power Write, page 154
Historical Fiction	Analytical Response	Respond Extended Writing Unit, page 214
Inventors/Inventions	Partner News Article	Narrate Power Write, page 150
	Quote It!	Respond Power Write, page 234
	Summarizing from Multiple Sources	Respond Power Write, page 240
Lewis and Clark	Two-Word Strategy	Respond Power Write, page 244
Personal Story	Personal Narrative	Narrative Extended Writing Unit, page 100
	Personal Narrative of a Single Focused Moment in Time	Narrate Power Write, page 142
	Personal Narrative with Suspense	Narrate Power Write, page 140
	Sketch to Stretch **VL**	Respond Power Write, page 246
School Issues	Electronic Slide Show	Persuade Power Write, page 190
	Persuasive Text (Letter)	Persuade Extended Writing Unit, page 166
Underground Railroad	Summary with Headings	Inform Power Write, page 36

Grade 5
Index of Lessons by Writing Form

	Explanation	Inform Extended Writing Unit, page 8
	Explanation Focused on Why	Inform Power Write, page 38
	Explanation Focused on Why and How	Inform Power Write, page 40
	Flowchart (VL)	Inform Power Write, page 44
	Investigation: Colonial America (VL)	Inform Power Write, page 46
	Oral Presentation (VL)	Instruct Power Write, page 84
	Partner Explanation	Instruct Power Write, page 80
	Pass-Around Explanation	Inform Power Write, page 28
	Problem-Solving Guide	Instruct Power Write, page 82
	Summary with Headings	Inform Power Write, page 36
Flowchart	Explanation	Inform Extended Writing Unit, page 8
	Flowchart (VL)	Inform Power Write, page 44
	Flowchart (VL)	Narrate Power Write, page 152
	Oral Presentation (VL)	Instruct Power Write, page 84
Graph	Partner Line Graph (VL)	Instruct Power Write, page 86
Guide	Problem Solving Guide	Instruct Power Write, page 82
Instructions	Instructions	Instruct Power Write, page 78
	Procedural Text	Instruct Extended Writing Unit, page 58
Investigation	Investigation: Colonial America (VL)	Inform Power Write, page 46
	Investigation: Important Time in History (VL)	Persuade Power Write, page 202
	Team Investigation: Photo Essay (VL)	Narrate Power Write, page 154
Letter	Formal Letter	Persuade Power Write, page 196
	Persuasive Text (Letter)	Persuade Extended Writing Unit, page 166
List	Dictionary of Terms	Inform Power Write, page 30
	Partner Description: List Poem	Inform Power Write, page 32
Narrative, Informational	Flowchart (VL)	Narrate Power Write, page 152
	Informational Narrative	Narrate Extended Writing Unit, page 120
	Informational Narrative	Narrate Power Write, page 144
	Key Words and Summary	Narrate Power Write, page 146
	Partner News Article	Narrate Power Write, page 150
	Team Investigation: Photo Essay (VL)	Narrate Power Write, page 154
Narrative, Personal	Narrative Poetry with a Partner	Narrate Power Write, page 148
	Personal Narrative	Narrate Extended Writing Unit, page 100
	Personal Narrative of a Single Focused Moment in Time	Narrate Power Write, page 142
	Personal Narrative with Suspense	Narrate Power Write, page 140
Oral Presentation	Oral Presentation (VL)	Instruct Power Write, page 84

Organizer	Analytical Response	Respond Extended Writing Unit, page 214
	Debate Plan	Persuade Power Write, page 194
	Explanation	Inform Extended Writing Unit, page 8
	Flowchart **VL**	Narrate Power Write, page 152
	Informational Narrative	Narrate Extended Writing Unit, page 120
	Informational Narrative	Narrate Power Write, page 144
	Maybe Framework	Persuade Power Write, page 186
	Multi-Paragraph Essay	Persuade Power Write, page 198
	Partner Book Review	Respond Power Write, page 242
	Partner News Article	Narrate Power Write, page 150
	Personal Narrative	Narrate Extended Writing Unit, page 100
	Personal Narrative of a Single Focused Moment in Time	Narrate Power Write, page 142
	Personal Narrative with Suspense	Narrate Power Write, page 140
	Persuasive Framework **VL**	Persuade Power Write, page 200
	Persuasive Text	Persuade Extended Writing Unit, page 166
	Problem-Solving Guide	Instruct Power Write, page 82
	Public Service Announcement	Persuade Power Write, page 188
	Quote It!	Respond Power Write, page 234
	Summarizing from Multiple Sources	Respond Power Write, page 240
	Summary: Main Ideas	Respond Power Write, page 236
	Venn Diagram (Three-Circle) **VL**	Respond Power Write, page 248
	Video Commercial	Persuade Power Write, page 192
Photo Essay	Team Investigation: Photo Essay **VL**	Narrate Power Write, page 154
Poem	Narrative Poetry with a Partner	Narrate Power Write, page 148
	Partner Description: List Poem	Inform Power Write, page 32
Procedure	Instructions	Instruct Power Write, page 78
	Oral Presentation **VL**	Instruct Power Write, page 84
	Partner Explanation	Instruct Power Write, page 80
	Partner Line Graph **VL**	Instruct Power Write, page 86
	Problem-Solving Guide	Instruct Power Write, page 82
	Procedural Text	Instruct Extended Writing Unit, page 58
Ratings	Partner Book Review	Respond Power Write, page 242
Response	Analytical Response	Respond Extended Writing Unit, page 214
	Compare and Contrast	Respond Power Write, page 238
	Partner Book Review	Respond Power Write, page 242
	Quote It!	Respond Power Write, page 234
	Sketch to Stretch **VL**	Respond Power Write, page 246

	Summarizing from Multiple Sources	Respond Power Write, page 240
	Summary: Main Ideas	Respond Power Write, page 236
	Two-Word Strategy: Lewis and Clark	Respond Power Write, page 244
	Venn Diagram (Three-Circle) **VL**	Respond Power Write, page 248
Review	Analytical Response	Respond Extended Writing Unit, page 214
	Partner Book Review	Respond Power Write, page 242
Sketch to Stretch	Sketch to Stretch	Respond Power Write, page 246
Slide Show	Electronic Slide Show	Persuade Power Write, page 190
Speech	Oral Presentation **VL**	Instruct Power Write, page 84
Storyboard	Oral Presentation **VL**	Instruct Power Write, page 84
Summary	Key Words and Summary	Narrate Power Write, page 146
	Pass-Around Explanation	Inform Power Write, page 28
	Summarizing from Multiple Sources	Respond Power Write, page 240
	Summary: Main Ideas	Respond Power Write, page 236
	Summary with Headings	Inform Power Write, page 36
	Two-Word Strategy: Lewis and Clark	Respond Power Write, page 244
Timeline	Informational Narrative	Narrate Extended Writing Unit, page 120
Two-Word Strategy	Two-Word Strategy: Lewis and Clark	Respond Power Write, page 244

Grade 5
Index of Lessons by Mentor Text

Tools Researchers Use

- **Create a list of questions for inquiry**

- **Search for answers in a variety of resources (print and electronic)**

- **Look closely at photographs and visuals**

- **Label and sketch**

- **Jot notes**

- **Record ideas in a research notebook**

- **Record ideas in a research folder**

- **Talk to a thinking partner**

	Names																								

ONGOING MONITORING SHEET: INFORMATIONAL WRITING

PURPOSE

Understands the purpose for writing an informational piece

IDEAS/RESEARCH

Reflects research and planning

Includes facts and details from research

Gathers and uses information from multiple sources

Consolidates information using the Very Important Points (VIP) strategy

Lists/cites sources

ORGANIZATION/TEXT FEATURES

Includes a title that tells what the piece is about

Includes a strong lead that draws readers into the text

Presents well-organized factual information

Supports main ideas with strong details

Includes a strong conclusion that sums up the piece

Includes labeled illustrations and supporting visuals

LANGUAGE/STYLE

Puts information in his or her own words

Uses sequence and/or linking words and phrases

Uses specific vocabulary

Uses precise, powerful verbs

Demonstrates sentence variety and fluency

CONVENTIONS and PRESENTATION

Begins sentences with capital letters

Ends sentences with appropriate punctuation

Uses appropriate spelling

Edits using an editing checklist

Creates interesting, effective page layouts with headings and sections

DAILY PLANNER

Daily Planner for Extended Writing Units   Day_____ Date_____

Focused Minilesson: Topic _____

Unit and Lesson Number _____

Students I need to confer with individually:

Student's Name	Focus of Instruction

Small group I need to gather for instruction:

Student's Name	Focus of Instruction

Sharing/Reflections

TURN &TALK   Focus for Partner Sharing:

Focus for Class Reflection:

INDIVIDUAL ASSESSMENT RECORD: INFORMATIONAL WRITING GRADE 5	Key:	1. Not in evidence 2. With assistance 3. Mostly on own 4. Consistently on own					
PURPOSE							
Understands the purpose for writing an informational piece							
IDEAS/RESEARCH							
Reflects research and planning							
Includes facts and details from research							
Gathers and uses information from multiple sources							
Consolidates information using the Very Important Points (VIP) strategy							
Lists/cites sources							
ORGANIZATION/TEXT FEATURES							
Includes a title that tells what the piece is about							
Includes a strong lead that draws readers into the text							
Presents well-organized factual information							
Supports main ideas with strong details							
Includes a strong conclusion that sums up the piece							
Includes labeled illustrations and supporting visuals							
LANGUAGE/STYLE							
Puts information in his or her own words							
Uses sequence and/or linking words and phrases							
Uses specific vocabulary							
Uses precise, powerful verbs							
Demonstrates sentence variety and fluency							
CONVENTIONS and PRESENTATION							
Begins sentences with capital letters							
Ends sentences with appropriate punctuation							
Uses appropriate spelling							
Edits using an editing checklist							
Creates interesting, effective page layouts with headings and sections							

Personal Checklist for Informational Writing

Process Reflections:

Research:
I used the following resources in gathering facts: _____
_____.

Drafting:
I solved the following problems in my writing: _____
_____.

Revising:
When revising, I focused on improving my message by: _____
_____

Editing:
To ensure that I edited effectively, I used an editing checklist and concentrated on: _____
_____

Presentation:
I chose the following format to present my writing: _____
_____

I am most proud of: _____
_____.

I have checked the following:

- ☐ My title tells what will be explained or described.
- ☐ There is a strong lead that draws the reader in.
- ☐ The information is clearly organized in paragraphs and sections.
- ☐ My paragraphs have main ideas and supporting details.
- ☐ Depending on my topic, I have included cause-effect words or words that show passage of time.
- ☐ I have used linking words such as *for example, specifically,* and *in addition* to connect ideas.
- ☐ I have included facts and details throughout my writing.
- ☐ I have used precise vocabulary to describe or explain.
- ☐ A conclusion emphasizes the main ideas and provides a satisfying ending.
- ☐ My writing has sentence fluency and I have used a variety of sentence lengths.
- ☐ The published presentation includes thoughtful page layout and interesting visuals.
- ☐ I have listed my sources.

Names																		

ONGOING MONITORING SHEET: PROCEDURAL WRITING

PURPOSE

Understands the purpose for writing a procedural piece

IDEAS/RESEARCH

Reflects research and planning

Includes facts and details from research

Gathers information from multiple sources

Lists/cites sources

ORGANIZATION/TEXT FEATURES

Includes a title that tells what the procedure is

Includes a clear introduction

Presents steps or tips in sequence

Includes labeled diagrams that support the text

May include a conclusion

LANGUAGE/STYLE

Puts information in his or her own words

Uses strong present-tense verbs

Uses academic vocabulary and precise details

Uses words and phrases that signal the passage of time

Demonstrates sentence variety and fluency

CONVENTIONS and PRESENTATION

Begins sentences with capital letters

Uses correct end punctuation

Uses appropriate spelling

Edits using an editing checklist

Creates clear and interesting page layouts, depending on form

DAILY PLANNER

Daily Planner for Extended Writing Units   Day_____ Date_____

Focused Minilesson: Topic _____

Unit and Lesson Number _____

Students I need to confer with individually:

Student's Name	Focus of Instruction

Small group I need to gather for instruction:

Student's Name	Focus of Instruction

Sharing/Reflections

TURN &TALK   Focus for Partner Sharing:

Focus for Class Reflection:

INDIVIDUAL ASSESSMENT RECORD: PROCEDURAL WRITING GRADE 5	Key:	1. Not in evidence 2. With assistance 3. Mostly on own 4. Consistently on own					
PURPOSE							
Understands the purpose for writing a procedural piece							
IDEAS/RESEARCH							
Reflects research and planning							
Includes facts and details from research							
Gathers information from multiple sources							
Lists/cites sources							
ORGANIZATION/TEXT FEATURES							
Includes a title that tells what the procedure is							
Includes a clear introduction							
Presents steps or tips in sequence							
Includes labeled diagrams that support the text							
May include a conclusion							
LANGUAGE/STYLE							
Puts information in his or her own words							
Uses powerful present-tense verbs							
Uses specific vocabulary and precise details							
Uses words and phrases that signal the passage of time							
Demonstrates sentence variety and fluency							
CONVENTIONS and PRESENTATION							
Begins sentences with capital letters							
Uses correct end punctuation							
Uses appropriate spelling							
Edits using an editing checklist							
Creates clear and interesting page layouts, depending on form							

Personal Checklist for Procedural Writing

Process Reflections:
Research:
I used the following resources in gathering facts: _____

_____.

Drafting:
I solved the following problems in my writing: _____

_____.

Revising:
When revising, I focused on improving my message by: _____

_____

Editing:
To ensure that I edited effectively, I used an editing checklist and concentrated on: _____

_____.

Presentation:
I chose the following format to present my writing: _____

_____

I am most proud of: _____

_____.

I have checked the following:

- ☐ My title tells what the procedure is.
- ☐ I have included a clear introduction.
- ☐ The information is organized in sequence.
- ☐ The steps are complete and accurate.
- ☐ I have used words and phrases that show sequence or passage of time.
- ☐ I have used strong present-tense verbs.
- ☐ I have included precise vocabulary and details.
- ☐ My writing has sentence fluency, and I have used a variety of sentence lengths.
- ☐ I have included labeled visuals that help readers understand the procedure.
- ☐ The published procedure has a clear, organized layout.
- ☐ I have listed my sources.

ONGOING MONITORING SHEET: NARRATIVE WRITING

Names																

PURPOSE

Understands the purpose for writing a narrative piece

IDEAS/RESEARCH

Generates ideas

Focuses on an event or series of events

Organizes ideas and plans writing

Provides factual information

Includes engaging related details

Lists/cites sources

ORGANIZATION/TEXT FEATURES

Includes a title that relates closely to the narrative

Includes an engaging lead

Relates an event or sequence of events in time order

Presents information in paragraphs with main ideas and supporting details

Has a conclusion that includes thoughts and feelings and wraps up the piece

Includes illustrations and/or visuals that support the narrative

LANGUAGE/STYLE

Uses first person for personal narratives

Uses third person for informational narratives

Uses a consistent verb tense

Includes precise, powerful words

Includes vivid descriptions and images

Uses temporal words and phrases (*at first, finally,* etc.)

Demonstrates sentence variety and fluency

CONVENTIONS and PRESENTATION

Uses complete sentences

Begins sentences with capital letters

Ends sentences with correct punctuation

Uses appropriate spelling

Creates interesting, effective page layouts

DAILY PLANNER

Daily Planner for Extended Writing Units   Day_____   Date_____

Focused Minilesson: Topic _____

Unit and Lesson Number _____

Students I need to confer with individually:

Student's Name	Focus of Instruction

Small group I need to gather for instruction:

Student's Name	Focus of Instruction

Sharing/Reflections

TURN &TALK   Focus for Partner Sharing:

Focus for Class Reflection:

INDIVIDUAL ASSESSMENT RECORD: NARRATIVE WRITING GRADE 5	Key:	1. Not in evidence 2. With assistance 3. Mostly on own 4. Consistently on own				
PURPOSE						
Understands the purpose for writing a narrative piece						
IDEAS/RESEARCH						
Generates ideas						
Focuses on an event or series of events						
Organizes ideas and plans writing						
Provides factual information						
Includes engaging related details						
Lists/cites sources						
ORGANIZATION/TEXT FEATURES						
Includes a title that relates closely to the narrative						
Includes an engaging lead						
Relates an event or sequence of events in time order						
Presents information in paragraphs with main ideas and supporting details						
Has a conclusion that includes thoughts and feelings and wraps up the piece						
Includes illustrations and/or visuals that support the narrative						
LANGUAGE/STYLE						
Uses first person for personal narratives						
Uses third person for informational narratives						
Uses a consistent verb tense						
Includes precise and powerful vocabulary						
Includes vivid descriptions and images						
Uses temporal words and phrases (*at first, finally,* etc.)						
Demonstrates sentence variety and fluency						
CONVENTIONS and PRESENTATION						
Uses complete sentences						
Begins sentences with capital letters						
Ends sentences with correct punctuation						
Uses appropriate spelling						
Creates interesting, effective page layouts						

Personal Checklist for Narrative Writing

Process Reflections:
Research:
I used the following resources in gathering facts: _____
_____.

Drafting:
I solved the following problems in my writing: _____
_____.

Revising:
When revising, I focused on improving my message by: _____
_____

Editing:
To ensure that I edited effectively, I used an editing checklist and concentrated on: _____
_____.

Presentation:
I chose the following format to present my writing: _____
_____

I am most proud of: _____
_____.

I have checked the following:

- [ ] My title tells who or what the narrative is about.
- [ ] There is an inviting lead that draws the reader in.
- [ ] The information is organized and separated into paragraphs with main ideas and supporting details.
- [ ] I have included factual information throughout.
- [ ] I have included words and phrases such as *at first* and *finally* that show the passage of time.
- [ ] I have included descriptive details and vivid images.
- [ ] I have used precise, powerful words.
- [ ] I have used the first-person or third-person point of view consistently.
- [ ] The closing includes my thoughts and feelings and wraps up the narrative.
- [ ] My writing has sentence fluency, and I have used a variety of sentence beginnings.
- [ ] I have included visuals that support the narrative.
- [ ] The published narrative has an organized and engaging layout.
- [ ] I have listed my sources.

Names																					

ONGOING MONITORING SHEET: PERSUASIVE WRITING

PURPOSE

Understands the purpose for writing a persuasive piece

IDEAS/RESEARCH

Reflects research and planning to support an opinion or position

Bases writing on research and personal opinion or position

Includes facts from research to support opinions or positions

Gathers and uses information from multiple sources

Lists/cites sources

ORGANIZATION/TEXT FEATURES

Includes a title that reflects the topic and goal

Has a strong introduction that states an opinion or position

Includes reasons for the opinion or position that are supported by facts

Ends with a conclusion that summarizes and calls readers to action

Includes persuasive visuals

LANGUAGE/STYLE

Shows a clear, consistent opinion throughout the piece

Puts information in his or her own words

Uses linking words and phrases to connect ideas (*because, therefore, for example, etc.*)

Uses powerful, persuasive language

Demonstrates sentence variety and fluency

CONVENTIONS and PRESENTATION

Begins sentences with capital letters

Uses correct end punctuation

Uses appropriate spelling

Uses apostrophes correctly to form contractions

Creates clear, persuasive page layouts with supporting visuals

DAILY PLANNER

Daily Planner for Extended Writing Units   Day_____   Date_____

Focused Minilesson: Topic _____

Unit and Lesson Number _____

Students I need to confer with individually:

Student's Name	Focus of Instruction

Small group I need to gather for instruction:

Student's Name	Focus of Instruction

Sharing/Reflections

TURN &TALK   Focus for Partner Sharing:

Focus for Class Reflection:

INDIVIDUAL ASSESSMENT RECORD: PERSUASIVE WRITING GRADE 5	Key:	1. Not in evidence 2. With assistance 3. Mostly on own 4. Consistently on own					
PURPOSE							
Understands the purpose for writing a persuasive piece							
IDEAS/RESEARCH							
Reflects research and planning to support an opinion or position							
Bases writing on research and personal opinion or position							
Includes facts from research to support opinions or positions							
Gathers and uses information from multiple sources							
Lists/cites sources							
ORGANIZATION/TEXT FEATURES							
Includes a title that reflects the topic and goal							
Has a strong introduction that states an opinion or position							
Includes reasons for the opinion or position that are supported by facts							
Ends with a conclusion that summarizes and calls readers to action							
Includes persuasive visuals							
LANGUAGE/STYLE							
Shows a clear, consistent opinion throughout the piece							
Puts information in his or her own words							
Uses linking words and phrases to connect ideas (*because, therefore, for example*, etc.)							
Uses powerful, persuasive language							
Demonstrates sentence variety and fluency							
CONVENTIONS and PRESENTATION							
Begins sentences with capital letters							
Uses correct end punctuation							
Uses appropriate spelling							
Uses apostrophes correctly to form contractions							
Creates clear, persuasive page layouts with supporing visuals							

Personal Checklist for Persuasive Writing

Process Reflections:

Research:
I used the following resources in gathering facts:_____
_____.

Drafting:
I solved the following problems in my writing: _____
_____.

Revising:
When revising, I focused on improving my message by: _____
_____

Editing:
To ensure that I edited effectively, I used an editing checklist and concentrated on: _____
_____

Presentation:
I chose the following format to present my writing: _____
_____

I am most proud of: _____

I have checked the following:

- ☐ My title reflects my topic and my opinion.
- ☐ I have a strong introduction that clearly states my opinion or position.
- ☐ I have given reasons and supported them with facts.
- ☐ I have used linking words and phrases such as *because, therefore,* and *for example* to connect ideas.
- ☐ I have used powerful, persuasive words.
- ☐ I have a conclusion that summarizes my position and calls readers to action.
- ☐ My writing has fluency and I have used a variety of sentence lengths and types.
- ☐ I have included persuasive visuals.
- ☐ I have listed my sources.

Names

**ONGOING MONITORING SHEET:
RESPONSE WRITING**

PURPOSE

Understands the purpose for writing a response piece

IDEAS/RESEARCH

Responds directly to a piece of literature or prompt

Expresses opinions

Supports opinions with examples from text or facts

Includes page references for examples from text

ORGANIZATION/TEXT FEATURES

Includes a title that reflects the purpose or task

Has a strong opening statement

Is organized in paragraphs that express central ideas or opinions

Supports central ideas and opinions with details and evidence from text

Has a conclusion that summarizes and expresses feelings

Includes illustrations that support the response

Includes text features that support the response

LANGUAGE/STYLE

Shows a clear point of view

Expresses personal opinions and feelings

Uses linking words and phrases (*for example, specifically, in fact,* etc.) to connect opinions to examples

Demonstrates sentence variety and fluency

Uses specific vocabulary related to topic and genre

CONVENTIONS and PRESENTATION

Begins sentences with capital letters

Capitalizes proper nouns

Uses end punctuation correctly

Uses a variety of punctuation marks (commas, dashes, colons, etc.)

Uses appropriate spelling

Creates clear, effective page layouts with supporting visuals and text features

DAILY PLANNER

Daily Planner for Extended Writing Units   Day_____   Date_____

Focused Minilesson: Topic _____

Unit and Lesson Number _____

Students I need to confer with individually:

Student's Name	Focus of Instruction

Small group I need to gather for instruction:

Student's Name	Focus of Instruction

Sharing/Reflections

TURN &TALK   Focus for Partner Sharing:

Focus for Class Reflection:

INDIVIDUAL ASSESSMENT RECORD: RESPONSE WRITING GRADE 5	Key:	1. Not in evidence 2. With assistance 3. Mostly on own 4. Consistently on own					
PURPOSE							
Understands the purpose for writing a response piece							
IDEAS/RESEARCH							
Responds directly to a piece of literature or prompt							
Expresses opinions							
Supports opinions with examples from text or facts							
Includes page references for examples from text							
ORGANIZATION/TEXT FEATURES							
Includes a title that reflects the purpose or task							
Has a strong opening statement							
Is organized in paragraphs that express central ideas or opinions							
Supports central ideas and opinions with details and evidence from text							
Has a conclusion that summarizes and expresses feelings							
Includes illustrations that support the response							
Includes text features that support the response							
LANGUAGE/STYLE							
Shows a clear point of view							
Expresses personal opinions and feelings							
Uses linking words and phrases (*for example, specifically, in fact*, etc.) to connect opinions to examples							
Demonstrates sentence variety and fluency							
Uses specific vocabulary related to topic and genre							
CONVENTIONS and PRESENTATION							
Begins sentences with capital letters							
Capitalizes proper nouns							
Uses end punctuation correctly							
Uses a variety of punctuation marks (commas, dashes, colons, etc.)							
Uses appropriate spelling							
Creates clear, effective page layouts with supporting visuals and text features							

Personal Checklist for Response Writing

Process Reflections:

Research:
I read the following text and/or used the following resources: _____
_____.

Drafting:
I solved the following problems in my writing: _____
_____.

Revising:
When revising, I focused on improving my message by: _____
_____.

Editing:
To ensure that I edited effectively, I used an editing checklist and concentrated on: _____
_____.

Presentation:
I chose the following format to present my writing: _____
_____.

I am most proud of: _____
_____.

I have checked the following:

- ☐ My title reflects my topic and my opinion.
- ☐ I have a strong opening statement that expresses my opinion.
- ☐ I have paragraphs that express my central ideas.
- ☐ I have used details and examples from the text to support my opinions.
- ☐ I have included references for my examples from the text.
- ☐ I have used linking words such as *for example, specifically,* and *in fact* to connect my opinions to examples.
- ☐ I have used specific vocabulary related to my topic.
- ☐ I have a memorable ending that summarizes my opinions and point of view.
- ☐ My writing has fluency and I have used a variety of sentence lengths.
- ☐ I have included illustrations that support my response.
- ☐ I have included text features that support my response.